PUBLIC RELATIONS:
PRINCIPLES AND PRACTICE

Philip J. Kitchen

Senior Lectures Marketing
Strathclyde University

THOMSON
™
LEARNING

Australia • Canada • Mexico • Singapore • Spain • United Kingdom • United States

THOMSON LEARNING

Public Relations: Principies and Practice

Copyright © 1997 Philip J. Kitchen

First published by International Thomson Business Press

The Thomson Learning logo is a registered trademark used herein under license.

British Library Cataloguing-in-Publication Data
A catalogue record for this book is available from the British Library

First Edition 1997
Reprinted 2000 by Thomson Learning

Printed in Croatia by ZRINSKI d.d.

ISBN 186 152 0913

Thomson Learning
Berkshire House
168-173 High Holborn
London WC1V 7AA
UK

http://www.thomsonlearning.co.uk

PUBLIC RELATIONS:
PRINCIPLES AND PRACTICE

Philip J. Kitchen, the Editor of *Public Relations: Principles and Practice*, has published many articles in UK, European and United States journals on subjects pertaining to marketing communications, promotional management, public relations and corporate communications. Subsequent to his university degree in English and History, he attended the University of Manchester, Institute of Science and Technology (UMIST) completing an MSc in Marketing. This was followed by an MBSc at Manchester Business School (1987) and a PhD from the University of Keele (1993). The final degree explored the development of public relations in corporate and marketing communications with large UK fast moving consumer goods firms.

Dr Kitchen was founder and first director of the Keele-based Research Centre for Corporate and Marketing Communications. He is Editor of the *Journal of Marketing Communications*. In 1996, he organised and chaired the First International Conference on Corporate and Marketing Communications at Keele; this has now become an annual event, scheduled for Belgium in 1997.

Since February 1996, Dr Kitchen has been based at the Department of Marketing, Strathclyde University, Scotland, where he is Senior Lecturer in Marketing, specialising in teaching marketing communications and promotional management mainly to postgraduate and post-experience students.

Dedicated to my Father and Mother

PJK

CONTENTS

PREFACE

The rationale behind the emergence of *Public Relations: Principles and Practice* was a sense of annoyance that so many UK PR texts had so little to do with theory and seemed to adopt the stance that 'how it is done' or 'how it may be done' is the sum total of required knowledge in this area. Not only is this wrong, it is also an intellectually lazy way of approaching the subject. This text attempts to redress the balance in favour of theory, admittedly, but is supported by case vignettes, longer case studies and discussion topics which tackle many of the issues involved in both the principles and practice of public relations as we approach a new millennium.

Many of the authors who have contributed chapters are ardent exponents of the subject; they either teach or practice public relations. To each of these authors I owe and acknowledge a significant debt of gratitude for taking the time, and for sharing their knowledge, in what was to become a highly structured editorial format. The authors are listed below in alphabetical order rather than the order in which they appear in the text.

- *Geraldine Hanrahan* (de Montfort University) *Chapter 9*
- *Shirley Harrison* (Leeds Metropolitan University) *Chapter 8*
- *Judy Larkin* (Regester-Larkin Limited) *Chapter 12*
- *Jacquie L'Etang* (Stirling University) *Chapter 5*
- *Kevin Moloney* (Bournemouth University) *Chapter 10*
- *Danny Moss* (Manchester Metropolitan University) *Chapters 2 and 4*
- *Ioanna Papasolomou* (Keele University) *Chapter 14*
- *Magda Pieczka* (Stirling University) *Chapter 5*
- *Heike Puchan* (Stirling University) *Chapter 5*
- *Michael Regester* (Regester-Larkin Limited) *Chapter 12*
- *Ralph Tench* (Leeds Metropolitan University) *Chapter 11*
- *Richard Varey* (Salford University) *Chapters 6 and 7*
- *Gary Warnaby* (Manchester Metropolitan University) *Chapters 2 and 4*
- *Tom Watson* (Hallmark Public Relations) *Chapter 16*

The text is intended for students and practitioners who wish to develop knowledge, skills and ability in public relations. Unlike other texts, however, this one is based on sound theoretical foundations while drawing upon the opinions, views, expertise and understanding of the subject of practitioners and theorists as listed above. The text, however, has been edited and so, of course, any problems of interpretation and expression are the Editor's alone.

The book is needed. At a time when courses and modules in public relations, corporate communications and public affairs are multiplying – i.e. not only for the CAM diploma but also the excellent programmes being offered at undergraduate and postgraduate levels by UK universities – it is time for what is perceived to be a good quality UK-generated textbook to be made available to help satisfy student demand. The new approach, adopted in this text has been indicated above. There has been a determination to use the very latest research findings from the public relations journals and magazines and to present these in an attractive and readable style to students required to read and ultimately master the principles involved.

The book is designed for the following groups:

- CAM (Communications, Advertising, Marketing (and Education) Foundation) Diploma Students (CAM Diploma in Public Relations)
- undergraduate students studying for a BA/BSc in Public Relations or courses where PR plays a prominent role, either as a stream of study, or as a specialist option
- postgraduate students studying for a direct qualification in Public Relations (MA, MPhil, MSc) or for a course offering public relations as an elective (i.e. MBA or other functional management course)
- as additional reading for students registered for a PhD in the PR field
- also suitable for practitioner reading.

Dr Philip J. Kitchen
Strathclyde University

1

INTRODUCTION AND OVERVIEW OF PUBLIC RELATIONS

Philip J. Kitchen

CHAPTER AIMS

- to provide readers with an outline and overview of the text

ILLUSTRATION: 'IDENTITY CRISIS'

In light of the solid (year-on-year) performance delivered by agencies in the top 150 (as delivered annually by *PR Week* (1996)), now would seem a perverse time to question the future of public relations. Yet that is precisely what many senior practitioners are doing.

In general the figures are good, but they mask a paradox. For although the services offered by the leading agencies clearly find favour with clients – the league tables speak clearly enough in this regard – at the same time the term 'public relations', or 'PR', has acquired many negative associations. Controversialists might even go so far as to suggest it has been discredited.

For many clients and publics, PR is confused with the activities of publicity agents and celebrity party organisers. To others, it is nothing more than a by-word for media relations, an execution service rather than strategic consultancy. 'Frankly, most of us find the words public relations unhelpful,' says Countrywide Communications chairman Peter Hehir. 'One can debate it endlessly but it no longer means what it should mean. When we talk to people about crisis management we are taken far more seriously than when we talk about PR. There is an example of language creating very differing first impressions.'

Who can fail to spot the irony in PR, the business of managing reputations, having image problems of its own? But few in the industry find this awkward state of affairs amusing. Clients are quite rightly entitled to ask why they believe PR can do a good job for them if it is incapable of engineering a positive perception of itself.

Discomfiting reactions of this kind have made some consultancies downplay the term 'PR' or even drop it altogether as an appendage to their company name. Among the top 10, Burson-Marsteller, as widely reported, has chosen to re-style itself as a perception management consultancy. However, concern with identity is by no means the preserve of the major league players. For example, Mike Evans, chairman of regional group Mistral, prefers to use the term 'communicator' rather than PR, while pharmaceutical specialist Greenlines recently sloughed off the PR tag because it was felt it no longer described the level and breadth of service it offered.

'PR is poorly understood and the term pre-conditions people's understanding of what an agency does,' says Greenlines senior account director Andrew Day. 'Many clients think of a PR agency as someone just writing press releases and talking to journalists. There is also more of a demand from some clients for the agencies they work with to provide more of an integrated communications service.'

(*Source*: *PR Week*, 26 April 1996: 5, used with permission.)

* * *

INTRODUCTION

Public relations which, at this stage, could be defined as communications with various publics is the subject of this text. As indicated in the illustration, PR is undergoing a degree of change as questions are raised as to what PR is, how it works, and its relevance and meaning to modern business organisations. *Public Relations: Principles and Practice* is intended for students and practitioners who wish to develop a knowledge base, a skills base, and overall ability in the public relations domain. Admittedly questions arise, and the questions are important. This is why this text is firmly based on sound theoretical foundations, unlike many other texts, and draws on the opinions, views, and expertise of practitioners and theorists. The text draws various chapters from recognised experts in the many different areas that public relations exemplifies. Each chapter, excepting this, comes complete with mini case studies, and questions for seminar discussion.

Public relations has undergone over a century of evolution and it is still evolving. This does not mean, however, that there are recognisable answers to PR-type issues, which is why students and practitioners are urged to adopt a critical perspective towards both the principles and practice of public relations. They should do so because public relations is a contemporary, dynamic, and interesting managerial and theoretical discipline, and because readers should become (if they are not already) contemporary, dynamic and knowledgeable about the domain of public relations.

The book is needed. At at time when courses in public relations and corporate communications are multiplying – that is not only the typical CAM (Communication, Advertising, Marketing (and Education) Foundation) Diploma, but also many other undergraduate and postgraduate courses offered at UK institutions – it is high time for a textbook such as this to satisfy student demand. As noted above, the text includes many case vignettes and questions for discussion. There is a determination to use the very latest scientific research from the public relations journals and magazines, but it is presented in such a way as to be comprehensible to students who are required to read and master the issues involved.

ORGANISATION OF THE TEXT

Chapter 1 – provides an introduction and overview of the entire text.

Chapter 2 – indicates the role and function of public relations in modern organisations as an important managerial discipline which, if allowed to do so, can play an important strategic role in managing organisational relationships with external and internal stakeholder groups whose support may be crucial to organisational success.

Chapter 3 – describes the evolution of public relations in terms of principles and practice. This evolution is underpinned by sound theoretical foundations dating back to at least the early 1900s and, some argue, much earlier. From a somewhat shady pursuit of 'press agentry', public relations, in the late 1990s, is now a multifaceted managerial discipline offering tried and tested techniques, principles and practices of relevance to both corporate and marketing communications.

Chapter 4 – further developing the argument from Chapters 2 and 3, investigates how the concepts of strategy and strategic management can be applied in a public relations context. It further examines the extent to which major UK organisations treat public relations as a strategically important function; and illustrates how PR can, in practice, contribute importantly to the development of effective corporate strategies.

Chapter 5 – considers internal communications media by first evaluating the complex matrix of unifying and centrifugal forces that serve as checks and balances in modern business organisations. Management, by and large, consists of managing these two forces in the context of public relations and development of an internal communications strategy in a flexible, multidimensional and co-ordinated fashion which is clearly synchronised with the overarching business strategy.

Chapter 6 – is the first of two chapters considering PR from an external communications context. This chapter considers the context of external public relations, while Chapter 7 considers the context of activities. Such external 'publics' are those groups or individuals who a) hold expectations; and b) whose behaviour, judgement and opinions can influence and impact upon organisational operations and performance. The role of the public relations manager in this context is to harmonise organisational interests with external public interests. In turn, this may impact strongly upon organisational strategy and plans (see Chapters 2 and 4).

Chapter 7 – evaluates the external publics context by identifying and discussing the major external activities of public relations managers and their functions and provides insight into the breadth of these functions or activities. The chapter also provides a research emphasis for public relations activity planning and gives detailed illustration of how external public relations activities are co-ordinated with wider business aims and objectives.

Chapter 8 – considers corporate social responsibility and the objectives of many businesses to link corporate behaviour with reputation and image. How companies act, and, more importantly, how they are perceived to act by their publics is possibly the greatest factor in the management of their reputation. The chapter underlines the view that the role of business extends well beyond sales, profits, market share and return on investment. Firms need to consider the wider context or society in which they operate.

Chapter 9 – considers financial and investor public relations by outlining significant developments which make financial and investor relations so important. It also serves to illustrate the complex web of publics that financial corporations interact with in retail, wholesale, investment, capital and money markets. Financial PR strategies for financial markets are given, as is an indication of the types of research applicable to this contextual circumstance.

Chapter 10 – evaluates government and lobbying activities in terms of their role as a highly specialist subdivision of public relations. A definition of lobbying in a practical and theoretical sense is provided and differential competitive perspectives are given. The need for lobbying is vital in the context of pluralistic Western capitalist democracies. Tasks, skills and functions of lobbyists are provided and the issue or question of effectiveness answered affirmatively, albeit tentatively.

Chapter 11 – considers the mechanisms by which corporate advertising is deployed. A start is made by defining and evaluating what is meant by corporate advertising from a public relations context. Much of the textual material is drawn admittedly from a North American context and an attempt is made to develop understanding away from this context. Various facets of corporate advertising are then considered including psychological success factors, brand value(s) analysis, who is involved in the UK, new technology implications, and in-depth provision of case materials.

Chapter 12 – outlines the necessary fail-safe procedures associated with issue and crisis management.

Chapter 13 – evaluates the thorny and tangled interactions between PR and marketing. Together, these two areas form the major avenues of organisational communication. The question is tackled as to where the boundary lies between these two communication functions. The placing of both into separate and discrete functions adds little to communication dynamics or communication effectiveness. The emergence of integrated marketing communications (IMC) as discussed in Chapter 14 heralds a new, substantive and enriching interrelationship between PR and marketing.

Chapter 14 – considers the emergence of marketing PR, as typified by Harris (1993). As indicated in the previous chapter there is a need for greater analysis of the issues underpinning the debate between PR and marketing. This is done by considering both the marketing and public relations view of PR, and asking whether PR can be seen as a corrective or as a complement to marketing. The argument suggests that both communication disciplines be seen as corporate allies rather than adversaries. The chapter concludes by ascertaining whether 'MPR' can be taken as a distinctive new discipline and considering how it might be used in practice.

Chapter 15 – explores the differences between inductive and deductive research frameworks, and suggests a need for the former, given the contextual and theoretical basis of public relations as developed in this text. PR appears to be at an early stage in terms of its theoretical and empirical development and there is a great need for theory generation juxtaposed to the testing of theory. A specific model of how to operationalise research in the PR domain is suggested.

Chapter 16 – indicates how the success rate of PR programmes and processes can be measured by reviewing the nature of evaluation in the context of the practitioner culture of public relations. Barriers to and models of evaluation are developed by analysing existing models and/or proposing new ones. Each model is considered in the context of effects-based planning of both PR campaigns and PR programmes.

Chapter 17 – summarises and concludes the text.

SUMMARY AND CONCLUSIONS

This chapter has sought to provide an outline of what readers might expect to find in the text. While precise definition of public relations is open to flux and change, its ability and power to influence key publics is universally acknowledged. Understanding public relations principles underpins successful practice or management of public relations practice. Change and variability of tasks makes the practice of PR one of the most interesting and dynamic fields of management activity, but also one of the most complex in business. It is hoped that by earnest study of the text and other readings, students will develop skills in public relations.

REFERENCES

'Identity crisis', *PR Week*, 26 April 1996: 5, used with permission. (Readers are strongly encouraged to read the entire article, pp. 5–6.)

2

THE ROLE OF PUBLIC RELATIONS IN ORGANISATIONS

Gary Warnaby and Danny Moss

CHAPTER AIMS

- to provide a definition of public relations as a management discipline
- to identify the characteristics of various conceptual models of public relations practice in organisations
- to identify the strategic potential of the public relations function through its boundary-spanning capability
- to illustrate various roles that can be played by public relations practitioners in organisations

ILLUSTRATION: 'BARCLAYS NEW FUTURES'

One of the biggest commercial educational sponsorships to date in the UK is the Barclays New Futures initiative, sponsored by Barclays Bank. The New Futures scheme is designed to help young people in secondary education participate in community work and to encourage the training of socially useful skills among the young. The initiative is of five years duration and makes available a total of £1m a year to successful applications received from schools to address issues such as truancy, care in the community, anorexia, bullying, vandalism, and alcohol and drug abuse. The main emphasis of the scheme is to provide professional support to teachers in implementing these schemes in order to avoid any potential controversy arising from a commercial sponsor being perceived as impelling teachers to carry out additional unpaid work.

The involvement of Barclays Bank as sponsors of the scheme (with a sponsorship team from the sponsorship consultant Kellaway) arose from a review of Barclays' sponsorship activity and the inclusion of an explicit clause on social responsibility in the corporate mission statement. The Barclays New Futures initiative aims to emphasise Barclays' role as a supporter of community-based social action projects and enhance the bank's image as a socially responsible company. Initial results for Barclays appear to be encouraging with numerous favourable stories in national and regional print and broadcast media, with the Barclays involvement normally made clear in any editorial coverage.

(*Source*: Based on Kavanagh, 'Barclays looks into the future', *PR Week*, 27 October 1995.)

INTRODUCTION

This chapter considers the key dimensions of the public relations function within organisations, emphasising the fact that public relations should be regarded as a *management* discipline. The characteristics of Grunig's models of public relations practice – press agentry, public information, two-way asymmetrical and two-way symmetrical – are described and placed into the context of the reality of public relations practice. Grunig and Grunig's later conceptualisation of craft and professional public relations is also discussed. The chapter argues that the main potential for public relations to take a *strategic* role in organisation is through its boundary-spanning capability, and the implications of this are discussed. However, despite the potential role for public relations in organisations, questions have to be asked as to whether public relations practitioners are allowed by management to fulfil this potential. The various roles that public relations practitioners can potentially play in organisations (using Cutlip et al.'s 1994 classification) are considered, along with implications for the profession.

PUBLIC RELATIONS: A MANAGEMENT DISCIPLINE

There is an increasing need for public relations to be treated as an important *management* discipline and one which, if allowed to do so, can play an important strategic role in managing organisational relationships with those external and internal stakeholder groups whose support may be crucial to the achievement of the organisation's goals. The notion of public relations as a *managerial* function is explicit in many of the definitions put forward to explain the nature of the discipline. For example, one definition which emphasises the strong managerial dimension of public relations practice is that agreed by representatives of over thirty national and regional public relations associations at a meeting in Mexico City in 1978 (the so-called Mexican Statement):

> Public relations practice is the art and social science of analysing trends, predicting their consequences, counselling organisation's leadership, and implementing planned programmes of action which will serve both the organisation's and the public interest.

Definitions of public relations have also been developed by the professional bodies in those countries where public relations has become well established. These definitions are normally intended to capture and convey the essence of the practice for interested parties. In the UK, for example, the Institute of Public Relations has adopted the following definition:

> Public relations practice is the deliberate, planned, and sustained effort to establish and maintain mutual understanding between an organisation and its publics.

Indeed, definitions of public relations abound. A study undertaken by Harlow (1976) commissioned by the Foundation for Public Relations Research and Education to search for a universal definition of public relations identified nearly

500 different definitions of the discipline. This reflects perhaps the broad scope of the function, and, equally, may reflect the fact that public relations is a constantly evolving profession. However, a number of common themes can be distilled from a review of the various definitions of public relations that have been offered. In brief these can be summarised as:

- Public relations is essentially a communications function, but with the emphasis on the two-way nature of the communications process.
- Public relations is concerned with establishing and maintaining mutual understanding (and goodwill) between organisations and particular groups of people (publics).
- Public relations serves as an intelligence function, analysing and interpreting trends and issues in the environment that may have potential consequences for an organisation and its stakeholders.
- Public relations is concerned with assisting organisations to both formulate and achieve socially acceptable goals, thus achieving a balance between commercial imperatives and socially responsible behaviour.

It must be stressed, however, that these themes relate to the way public relations has been defined by various scholars and professional bodies, and may not necessarily reflect the way in which it is always practised.

MODELS OF PUBLIC RELATIONS PRACTICE

It has been argued that the reason for the existence of so many definitions of public relations lies in the diverse and continually evolving nature of the profession. In addition, the diverse range of activities that fall within the remit of public relations practice have militated against attempts to classify the behaviour of practitioners in any meaningful way. However, J. Grunig (1976; 1984; Grunig and Hunt, 1984) has attempted to identify an effective approach for classifying the different forms of public relations practice, conceptualising four models of public relations practice: the press agentry model; the public information model; the two-way asymmetrical model; and the two-way symmetrical model of public relations (Grunig and Hunt, 1984). The characteristics of the various models are given in Figure 2.1.

Each of these models describes a set of values and a pattern of behaviour that characterise the approach taken by a public relations department or individual practitioner to all programmes, or, in some cases, to specific programmes or campaigns. In attempting to construct a model to describe the various forms of public relations practice, Grunig and Hunt (1984) acknowledged that models are inevitably abstractions of reality. Thus, no one (or even all) of their four models would be capable of capturing fully the diversity found within public relations practice. However, they maintained that the way most practitioners or public relations departments operate could be fitted within one or other of their models.

The models differ from one another in terms of two key variables, the *direction* and *purpose* of the form of public relations practice they describe. 'Direction' describes the extent to which the communications between an organisation and its publics are either one-way (a monologue) or two-way (a dialogue). In the case of the

Characteristic	Models			
	Press agentry/ publicity	Public information	Two-way asymmetric	Two-way symmetric
Purpose	propaganda	dissemination of information	scientific persuasion	mutual understanding
Nature of communication	one-way complete, truth not essential	one-way truth important	two-way imbalanced effects	two-way balanced effects
Communications model	source ⟶ rec	source ⟶ rec	source ⟶ rec ← feedback	group ⟶ group ← feedback
Nature of research	little if any	little, readership readability	formative attitude evaluation	formative evaluation of understanding
Examples of current practice	product promotion, sponsorship theatre	government, non-profit-making associations, businesses	competitive business agencies	regulated business agencies

Figure 2.1 Characteristics of the four models of public relations.

Source: Adapted from Grunig and Hunt (1984).

press agentry and public information models, the communications are character-istically one-way, whereas in the case of the two-way asymmetrical and two-way symmetrical models they are characteristically two-way. 'Purpose' describes the function which public relations performs for an organisation, defined, as Grunig (1992) suggests, in terms of whether the model is essentially asymmetrical or symmetrical. Asymmetrical communications are imbalanced, leave the organisation unchanged and attempt to change the public(s), whereas symmetrical communica-tions are balanced and attempt to adjust the relationship between the organisation and its publics.

Although Grunig (1992) maintains that subsequent studies have shown that examples of all four models can be found being practised today, he admits that most organisations do not appear to practice public relations as a two-way symmetrical function – the model which he argued defines the most 'excellent' way of practising public relations – at least not on a regular basis. Thus, he concluded that the two-way symmetrical model should be seen as offering a 'normative' theory of excellent public relations practice (describing an idealised view of how public relations should be practised to be most effective), rather than providing a 'positive' theory of public relations (describing how practitioners actually practise public relations).

The fact that Grunig and his fellow researchers found the 'press agentry' model to be the most widely practised form of public relations reflects the emphasis which is placed, particularly by clients, on media relations and the achievement of media publicity. The public information model, which Grunig predicted would be the most common model practised, was in fact revealed to be the least common model practised within business organisations, but was found to be the most common model practised among the public sector organisations. Although neither the two-way asymmetrical nor two-way symmetrical models emerged as dominant models in any of the organisations examined, both these models were found to be practised by a variety of organisations. The two-way asymmetrical model showed up most often in commercial organisations, whereas the two-way symmetrical model was more commonly found to be practised in governmental organisations.

In discussing the implications of the models of public relations practice, it may be more realistic to accept that organisations will tend to alternate between different forms of practice (between different models) according to the type of problem situations that they are facing, rather than seeking to identify a single dominant model to describe the way public relations is practised in any particular organisation. This pattern of organisations alternating between different models of public relations is, in fact, what Grunig and his fellow researchers tended to find in the studies they conducted.

Reflection on the criticisms of the original four models as a means of explaining the reality of modern public relations practice led Grunig and Grunig (1992) to re-conceptualise the models, positioning them along two continua which they designated 'craft public relations' and 'professional public relations' (see Figure 2.2).

The 'craft public relations' continuum represents a techniques-orientation in which practitioners view the effective application of communications techniques as an end in itself. The 'professional public relations' continuum represents a strategic-orientation in which practitioners view their role more broadly as one of using communication to resolve conflict and manage organisational relationships with strategic publics that may limit the autonomy of the organisation. Professional public relations practice was identified as ranging between asymmetrical compliance-gaining tactics and symmetrical problem-solving tactics. Although their

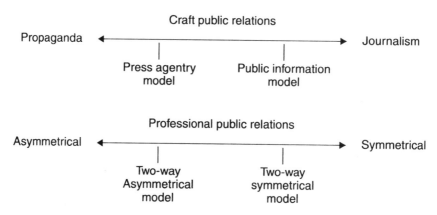

Figure 2.2 The re-conceptualisation of Grunig and Hunt's four models of public relations along two continua.

Source: Adapted from Grunig (1992).

re-conceptualisation of the models was intended to provide a sounder basis for the further development of their theory of 'excellence' in public relations, Grunig and Grunig also recognised that it reflected more accurately the differences in the way public relations is practised in organisations today.

The fact that the press agentry model appears to describe the most common form of public relations practised by organisations today has important implications for whether public relations can be considered to be a *strategic* function. Clearly, if, by implication, most public relations practitioners operate largely along what Grunig and Grunig (1992) term the 'craft public relations' continuum, working largely to generate publicity on behalf of organisations, they can hardly claim to play a significant strategic role on behalf of their organisations.

It may be misleading, however, to assume that this 'craft orientation' is as dominant as it might appear. Clearly, dealing with press or media relations occupies a disproportionate amount of time spent by most practitioners or public relations departments. But, not all media relations work is simply to do with generating publicity, or certainly not generating publicity for its own sake. Publicity can have a more strategic role, particularly when it is intended to help bring about important changes in either the attitudes or behaviour of key stakeholder publics. What seems more important is to look at the overall balance of the work which practitioners carry out, to identify how their role fits into the wider 'scheme of things' within the organisation, and, perhaps most importantly, how their role is perceived by senior management.

While many practitioners may well be preoccupied with the task of generating publicity – if only to justify their existence – for a good many others publicity may be seen as simply one of a number of means to achieving a more strategic end. As Grunig's research revealed, practitioners do vary the mode in which they work; at times carrying out largely tactical communications programmes designed to generate publicity for their organisations; at other times developing symmetrical communications programmes to handle organisational relationships with activist groups, government agencies, or to deal with a crisis situation. Therefore, while accepting that press agentry or publicity work probably remains the dominant activity performed by practitioners (particularly in commercial organisations), it should also be recognised that many practitioners and public relations departments also use public relations to support the achievement of longer term strategic goals. Thus, using Grunig and Grunig's (1992) craft and professional public relations continua, a possible interpretation of how many practitioners operate is to see them as alternating between the two continua – at times serving as publicity agents, and at other times performing a more strategic relationship-building role with an organisation's key stakeholders.

However, the strategic potential for the public relations function inherent in the conceptualisation of 'professional' public relations is often denied to practitioners in many organisations. From a management perspective, public relations is viewed largely as a functionary activity. This largely ignores the fact that the public relations function has, potentially, a direct role to play in the strategy-making process of the organisation by virtue of the fact that it is a boundary-spanning function.

11

BOUNDARY SPANNING AND SYSTEMS THEORY

The concept of public relations as a boundary-spanning function has its origins in systems theory, which has been used by organisational theorists to explain the structure and working of organisations as well as their interaction with their social environment. Basically, a system is defined as sets of interacting parts or subsystems which affect one another as well as the functioning of the organisation as a whole. Cutlip et al. (1985:184) offer the following more detailed definition:

> A system is a set of interacting units which endures through time within an established boundary by responding and adjusting to change pressures from the environment in order to achieve and maintain goal states.

Using a systems perspective, the role of public relations can be seen as one of helping to develop and maintain mutually dependent relationships between an organisation and its environment, or more specifically, between an organisation and various groups of individuals (publics) within its social environment. From this systems perspective, public relations personnel are usually seen as performing a 'boundary-spanning' function. White and Dozier define boundary spanners as 'individuals within the organisation who frequently interact with the organisation's environment and who gather, select and relay information from the environment to decision makers in the dominant coalition [of the organisation]' (1992:93). Similarly, Leifer and Delbecq describe boundary spanners as functioning 'as exchange agents between the organisation and its environment' (1978:41).

The fact that public relations works at the interface between the organisational system and its environment and acts in a liaison capacity between the organisation and various external groups or individuals ensures that practitioners help support the other subsystems of an organisation by helping them to communicate across the boundaries within the organisation with both external publics as well as with other subsystems within the organisation.

Grunig and Hunt (1984) suggest that typically an organisational system might consist of five major subsystems: the production subsystem; the disposal subsystem (responsible for the marketing and distribution functions); the maintenance subsystem (responsible for co-ordinating the work of employees – e.g. the personnel and training functions); the adaptive subsystem (responsible for helping the organisation adapt to change – e.g. the R&D function or planning departments); and the management subsystem (responsible for the control and integration of the other subsystems). In this systems model, public relations is seen as part of the management subsystem of an organisation, although it may also support other subsystems, such as the production subsystem or disposal subsystem. This theoretical organisational systems model is illustrated in Figure 2.3.

The systems model shown in Figure 2.3, like all theoretical models, is, of course, an abstraction of what in reality may be a highly complex organisational system involving many different subsystems or functions. This is likely to be particularly so when one attempts to apply the systems concept to some of today's large multinational organisations. However, the basic principle of dividing an organisation into a number of interacting subsystems, illustrated by this model, can be

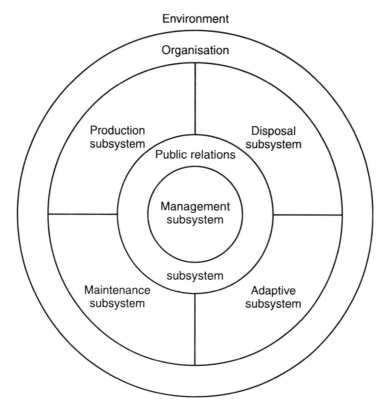

Figure 2.3 A generic view of organisational subsystems and of the location of the public relations subsystem.

Source: Adapted from Grunig and Hunt (1984).

applied to virtually any organisation irrespective of its size and complexity. Applying the systems concept helps focus attention on the important linkages between organisational departments and functions as well as between the organisation as a whole and key external groups. Public relations in its boundary-spanning role helps keep an organisation aware of change taking place in its environment and thus helps it to adapt or adjust to the changing conditions it may face. This boundary-spanning role is clearly implicit in many of the definitions of public relations discussed earlier.

Another important aspect of systems theory is the idea that all systems can be classified according to the type and extent of the 'exchange' they have with their environments. Here organisational systems can be seen to exist along a continuum ranging from, at one extreme, entirely closed systems to, at the other extreme, open systems. A closed system is one that has no exchange with its environment – it neither adapts nor adjusts to external change – and so eventually disintegrates. In practice, no social system can be entirely closed nor completely open, and they therefore tend to be either *relatively* open or closed. The extent to which an organisational system is seen to be open or closed reflects the degree to which it is sensitive to and ultimately adapts to change in the external environment.

A complementary conceptualisation of boundary spanning is advanced by Leifer and Delbecq (1978:41) who define a boundary as 'the demarcation line or region between one system and another, that protects the members of the system from extrasystem influences and that regulates the flow of information, material and people into or out of the system'.

They go on to introduce the concept of 'boundary permeability', in terms of the degree to which boundaries are open or receptive to inputs. Boundary permeability can apply to both the organisation as a whole and to subunits within the organisation, each of which may have its own boundary. Clearly, if an organisation is to be sensitive and responsive to external influences when developing strategy, then information from the environment must be able to pass through both the organisation's boundary as well as those of its subunits in order to reach the decision-makers within.

It is here that 'boundary spanners' can play an important role in facilitating the transference of information from outside the organisation across organisational boundaries to decision-makers – what in the strategy literature is often referred to as environmental scanning. Environmental scanning has been defined as 'the varied information gathering, analysis and dissemination activities that firms pursue in order to keep up to date with changes in the business environment' (Brownlie, 1991:103). Thus, public relations practitioners in their role as boundary spanners can be seen to act as what Liefer and Delbecq (1978) have termed 'exchange agents' between organisation and environment. In this role of 'exchange agents' Aldrich and Herker (1977) regard boundary spanners as performing two main functions: *information processing* and *external representation*.

Aldrich and Herker see boundary spanners as the main line of organisational defence against information overload, by virtue of the fact that boundary spanners act as both *filters* and *facilitators* of information transmittal, selectively acting on relevant information and filtering it prior to communication to relevant decision-makers. Thus, the importance of this function to organisational decision-making can be seen to be crucial.

In terms of their external representation function, boundary spanners are seen to be concerned with maintaining or improving the legitimacy of the organisation with 'actors' in the environment, and they can also help in mediating between the organisation and important outside organisations and groups in ways that will affect the power of the focal organisation *vis-à-vis* these other groups.

Extending this argument, Aldrich and Herker suggest that all organisations have some boundary-spanning roles, and suggest that boundary-spanning behaviour within an organisation may be quite widespread in that many positions outside the 'technical core' of the organisation involve some extra-organisational interaction. However, they maintain that only a few positions within the organisation involve intensive interaction with the environment – positions such as communications managers and public relations practitioners. As a result, such boundary spanners may have a disproportionate influence within the organisation because of the strategically important nature of the information which they have access to (Jemison, 1981). Indeed, Brownlie (1994:148) suggests that boundary-spanning functions 'compete for the right to absorb environmental uncertainty and to control what is and is not put on the agenda for decision-making priorities', thus creating a potential for influence and power within the organisation. Here it can be argued that the potential influence of the boundary-spanning function is likely to be greatest when the nature of the decisions to be made require the construction of new meanings about the organisation in relation to its environment – in other words, in situations which involve modifying what can be termed the 'enacted' environment.

The term 'enactment' refers to the process whereby organisations select what they perceive to be salient parts of the total information flow from the environment for further scrutiny and analysis (Weick, 1969; 1979). Weick argues that most organisations are unable to attend and respond to all the information that may emanate from the environment, and thus must exercise a deliberate choice as to what information they will process. This will be influenced by the individual and collective 'cognitive maps' (Axelrod, 1976) of managers within the organisation. Such cognitive structures consist of interconnected sets of understandings comprised of implicit views of one's own interests, concerns and tasks (Lenz and Engledow, 1986), through which events in the environment will be filtered and interpreted. Thus, as Weick argues, the environment (as well as the organisation itself) can be seen as a psychological creation of the members of an organisation by virtue of the fact that only some of the information from outside the organisation is heeded, and only this information is used to form the perceptions of the external world upon which all subsequent decisions are based.

Starbuck (1976:1078) also emphasises the subjective nature of the process by which members of an organisation perceive and define the environment and their own organisation, suggesting that 'an organisation's environment is an arbitrary invention of the organisation itself'. From this perspective, the boundaries between organisation and environment may become increasingly blurred and defined perhaps by the extent of shared perceptions, which, as far as the members of the organisation are concerned, represent reality.

In recognising the potentially subjective nature of the way in which organisational-environmental boundaries are defined, Lenz and Engledow (1986) suggest that environmental scanning comprises more than a mere information collection and dissemination function, but encompasses an *influencing* role, which is, arguably, more important by virtue of the fact that information gained can be used 'to justify, or persuade, others within and without the organisation, to make choices and decisions that may have already been made in the minds of managers – i.e. to influence, to manage impressions, and thus to participate in the negotiation of what environmental trends and events mean in a given context' (Brownlie, 1994:147).

From this perspective, the importance of organisational boundary spanners becomes apparent, particularly in terms of helping to define the organisational-environmental boundaries as well as managing exchanges across boundaries. It is here that public relations, through its boundary-spanning capability, can be seen to make the most significant contribution to the formulation of organisational strategies. In this capacity, public relations can potentially perform a strategic role, acting in both an intelligence capacity, gathering feedback from the environment and counselling management on its implications, and assisting organisations to explain their policies to external publics, thus winning acceptance and support for them.

PUBLIC RELATIONS PRACTITIONERS' ROLES

It might be expected that public relations practitioners (through their boundary-spanning role) should have considerable potential to influence the process of strategic decision-making through the insights that they can offer to management about the organisation's environment and in particular about the organisation's relationships with key stakeholders within its environment. However, as has been suggested, practitioners may often fail to realise this potential because of how their role is perceived by others within the organisation. As Cutlip et al. (1994:42) suggest, public relations practitioners 'adopt roles in organisations by taking on patterns of behaviours to deal with recurring types of situations and to accommodate others' expectations'. Drawing on the earlier work of Broom and Smith (1979) and Broom (1982), Cutlip et al. go on to describe four types of public relations roles that practitioners may fulfil: communication technician; expert prescriber; communication facilitator; and problem-solving facilitator. While Cutlip et al. acknowledge that practitioners may fulfil all these roles to varying degrees, they argue that a dominant role will tend to emerge over time. The four types of practitioner roles which they identified comprise:

- *Expert prescriber:* in this role practitioners are regarded as experts on public relations and consequently they are seen as best qualified to handle public relations problems and identify solutions to them.
- *Communication facilitator:* in this role practitioners are cast as sensitive listeners and information brokers who act in a 'go-between' role, facilitating communications.
- *Problem-solving facilitator:* in this role practitioners collaborate with other managers to help define and solve organisational communications problems. Whereas the expert prescriber role implies a passive role for other managers in the problem-solving process, in this role practitioners work with other managers to arrive at solutions to the problems facing an organisation.
- *Communication technician:* in this role practitioners merely provide technical communications services such as writing releases and features for the media, preparing and editing newsletters, and handling contacts with the media. All decisions regarding strategy and actions are taken by the dominant management coalition in which practitioners have no role and they are simply given the task of communicating about the decisions taken by this dominant coalition.

The characteristics of each of these practitioner roles and their implications in terms of public relation's participation in strategic decision-making are summarised in Table 2.1.

16

Table 2.1 Roles of PR practice and their strategic implications

	Role	*Implied strategic role*
Communication technician	Production of communication material for organisation. Dealing with the media.	Not present when strategists define organisational problems and select solutions. Practitioners produce the communications and implement programmes, sometimes without full knowledge of original motivation or intended results.
Expert prescriber	Regarded as the authority on PR problems and solutions. Practitioners define PR problems, and develop and implement the programme. Senior management may take a passive role.	PR may become compartmentalised, often apart from the mainstream of the organisation. PR practitioners may only work periodically with senior management (e.g. in crisis situations).
Communication facilitator	Serve as liaisons, interpreters and mediators between organisation and its publics, maintaining two-way communication and facilitating exchanges.	Overall aim is to provide management and stakeholders with the information they need to make decisions of mutual interest. PR practitioners occupy a boundary-spanning role, linking the organisations and its publics and thereby improving the quality of decisions by facilitating communication.
Problem-solving facilitator	Collaborate with other managers to define and solve organisational problems.	PR practitioners seen as part of the strategic management team, engaged in the formulation of strategies. Incorporates the boundary-spanning role of public relations.

In practice, of course, these roles are not mutually exclusive and experienced practitioners may adopt all of these roles to a greater or lesser degree, but research suggests that a dominant role will tend to emerge for each practitioner. For example, a study conducted among US practitioners (Broom, 1982) found that 48 per cent of respondents rated themselves as dominant in the expert prescriber role, 27 per cent identified the communication technician role as their dominant role, and 14 per cent identified the problem-solving facilitator role as their dominant role. Only 4 per cent identified themselves as operating predominantly in the communication facilitator role and only 7 per cent scored two or three roles as equally dominant.

While this research suggests that a significant proportion of practitioners may consider themselves to be operating in what might be described as a managerial capacity – involved in defining organisational problems and helping to identify solutions to them – such findings need to be treated with a degree of caution, since one might expect that practitioners would tend to enhance the degree of influence that they may claim to have in the organisational problem-solving processes.

It is also perhaps worth questioning whether the finding that only 27 per cent of respondents work predominantly in the communication technician role is an accurate reflection of the predominance of this type of role. If one accepts Grunig and Hunt's (1984) finding that the dominant model of public relations practised in organisations today appears to be the publicity or press agentry model, then the figure of 27 per cent may well underestimate the proportion of practitioners who, in practice, operate largely as communication technicians.

Further analysis of the roles research suggests that there is something of a polarisation between practitioners who score highly in terms of the expert prescriber, problem-solving facilitator and communication facilitator roles, and those who score highly as communication technicians. Cutlip et al. (1994) suggest that these former three roles seem to fit together to form a single complex role, whereas the communication technician role seems to stand alone. Thus, there seems to be a clear division between practitioners who work predominantly as technicians, and those who occupy managerial roles.

While the two-fold classification of practitioner roles as technicians or managers may provide a more readily recognisable and applicable basis for role classification, there is a danger that it may obscure some of the important distinctions between these different roles. Cutlip et al. (1994) go on to suggest that the particular configuration of roles occupied by practitioners may be strongly related to the type of environment in which organisations operate. The communication technician's role is more likely to be found where organisations operate in relatively stable non-threatening environments, whereas communication facilitators tend to predominate in relatively turbulent, but low threat environments. Practitioners are more likely to occupy the roles of problem-solving facilitators and expert prescribers where organisations are perceived as facing more threatening environments. Here problem-solving facilitators are more likely to predominate in environments that, while threatening, are relatively stable, whereas expert prescribers are more likely to predominate in conditions that are both threatening and relatively turbulent.

SUMMARY AND CONCLUSIONS

It has been argued that the environmental conditions which provide the context in which the organisation operates play a major part in determining the degree to which public relations practitioners are allowed to participate in the strategic management process and contribute directly to the formulation of organisational responses to the environment and environmental change. Here, one of the most obvious ways in which practitioners can contribute to the process of managing the organisation-environment interface – a key dimension of strategic management – is through the role of environmental scanning and analysis of the implications of environmental change for organisational stakeholder relationships.

However, the type of roles which practitioners are assigned or adopt within organisations will obviously affect their ability to contribute to the strategic management of the organisation. If practitioners are confined largely to the role of communication technicians, then their role will be confined, at best, to one of informing different publics about the strategic policies determined by management. As communication technicians, they will have little, if any, input into the management decision-making processes and will therefore have little opportunity to influence the type of policies which result from management's deliberations. In contrast, those practitioners who operate in the expert prescriber or problem-solving facilitator roles are more likely to be able to exert some influence on the strategic decisions determined by senior management and may even play a part in their formulation. The extent to which public relations practitioners are able to exercise any influence on decisions concerning organisational strategy will, however, depend largely on their ability to command the confidence and respect of senior management. The evidence to date does not seem to suggest that many practitioners have been successful in securing a regular place within the dominant management coalition in most organisations. This is not to suggest that senior management teams do not value the advice which experienced practitioners may be able to offer, but, in the vast majority of cases, it appears that such advice may be confined to how best to present the policies that management have already determined, rather than accepting that public relations counsel should have a role in determining the policies themselves.

The issue of access to the dominant management coalition in organisations is clearly one which has important implications for the status of public relations and for its claim to be considered a strategically important management function, and is one in which further research is required.

DISCUSSION TOPICS

1 Why should public relations be treated as a management discipline?
2 What are the characteristics of effective public relations?
3 How useful are Grunig and Hunt's models of public relations practice in describing the reality of public relations practice?
4 Is the distinction between craft and professional public relations a useful one?
5 Of what use is systems theory in conceptualising the role of public relations in organisations?
6 Are public relations practitioners in organisations primarily 'boundary spanners'?
7 Is the main role of the public relations function in organisations to interpret the 'enacted' environment for the benefit of the strategic leadership?
8 Are the public relations practitioner roles mutually exclusive?
9 Could our understanding of the role of public relations be increased if we consider the conceptualisations of craft and professional public relations and the public relations practitioner roles in conjunction rather than in isolation?
10 Evaluate the potential role of public relations in organisations today.

CASE STUDY: TESCO HEALTH AND BEAUTY RANGE

The Tesco health and beauty range comprises over 1,000 products for men and women, including body, bath, hair, skincare and babycare. However, there were many misperceptions of the range among key media, who generally did not hold positive attitudes towards supermarket own-label health and beauty products, assuming them to be cheap and of poor quality.

In 1994 Tesco retained Beechey Morgan Associates to promote the health and beauty range. The objectives of the public relations activity were threefold:

1   To enhance the profile and build awareness of the range, achieving a continuous flow of positive media coverage in relevant beauty features.
2   To build media and consumer perception of the authority and credibility of the range as the first choice for health and beauty requirements.
3   To create media and public awareness of the quality of own-brand Tesco health and beauty products.

The strategies to achieve these objectives can be divided into four main areas: the creation of a Tesco Health and Beauty Bureau; a focus on five 'halo' brands; the Health and Beauty Directory; and effective media relations.

The creation of the Tesco Health and Beauty Bureau, with its own dedicated telephone line, logo and press materials, aimed at establishing an authoritative central point of reference for media enquiries. Any press releases were issued on paper with the Health and Beauty Bureau logo. Press briefing notes and a mix of product and lifestyle photography were developed for five halo brands, aimed at increasing media perception of the authority and and credibility of Tesco health and beauty products. An easy-to-use reference guide, the Tesco Health and Beauty Directory, was developed in a filofax-type format covering all the health and beauty range in order to assist the media in planning features. The directory was launched to the media at a press breakfast at The Ritz in London.

The final element of the PR campaign was the operation of a proactive and reactive press office function, focusing on the promotion of the five halo brands and the remainder of the range. This was achieved through sustained media liaison with key writers, distribution of press briefing notes, placement of branded photographs, provision of product samples and the negotiation of sampling opportunities.

Evaluation of resulting media coverage shows that since the start of the campaign Tesco has received positive media coverage across all sectors of the women's consumer press and that Tesco products are being recommended and being compared favourably with branded products. The Health and Beauty Bureau is receiving a steady stream of calls and journalists are using the directory.

(*Source*: Based on 'Tesco Health and Beauty Directory: Making a brand out of own label', IPR Swords of Excellence Awards, 1995, *IPR Journal Supplement.*)

REFERENCES

Aldrich, H. and Herker, D. (1977) 'Boundary spanning roles and organisational structures', *Academy of Management Review,* 2: 217–30.

Axelrod, R. (1976) *Structure of Decision: The Cognitive Maps of Political Elites,* Princeton: Princeton University Press.

Broom, G.M. (1982) 'A comparison of sex roles in public relations', *Public Relations Review,* 8(3): 17–22.

Broom, G.M. and Smith, G.D. (1979) 'Testing the practitioner's impact on clients', *Public Relations Review,* 5(3): 47–59.

Brownlie, D. (1991) 'Environmental scanning', in M.J. Baker (ed.) *The Marketing Book,* 2nd edn, London: Butterworth-Heinemann.

Brownlie, D. (1994) 'Environmental scanning', in M.J. Baker (ed.) *The Marketing Book*, 3rd edn, London: Butterworth-Heinemann.

Cutlip, S., Center, A. and Broom, G. (1985) *Effective Public Relations*, 6th edn, Englewood Cliffs, NJ: Prentice-Hall.

Cutlip, S.M., Center, A.H. and Broom, G.M. (1994) *Effective Public Relations*, 7th edn, Englewood Cliffs, NJ: Prentice-Hall.

Grunig, J.E. (1976) 'Organisations and public relations: testing a communications theory', *Journalism Monographs*, No. 46: 285–326.

Grunig, J.E. (1984) 'Organisations, environments, and models of public relations', *Public Relations Research and Education*, 1(1): 6–29.

Grunig, J.E. (ed.) (1992) *Excellence in Public Relations and Communications Management*, Hillsdale, NJ: Lawrence Erlbaum.

Grunig, J.E. and Grunig, L.A. (1992) 'Models of public relations and communications', in J.E. Grunig (ed.) *Excellence in Public Relations and Communications Management*, Hillsdale, NJ: Lawrence Erlbaum.

Grunig, J.E. and Hunt, T. (1984) *Managing Public Relations*, New York: Holt, Rinehart and Winston.

Harlow, R.F. (1976) 'Building a public relations definition', *Public Relations Review*, 2(4): 34–41.

Jemison, D.B. (1981) 'The importance of boundary spanning roles in strategic decision making', *Journal of Management Studies*, 21: 132–52.

Leifer, R.P. and Delbecq, A. (1978) 'Organisational/environmental interchange: a model of boundary spanning activity', *Academy of Management Review*, 3: 40–50.

Lenz, R.T. and Engledow, J.L. (1986) 'Environmental analysis: the applicability of current theory', *Strategic Management Journal*, 7: 329–46.

Starbuck, W.H. (1976) 'Organisations in their environments', in M.D. Dunnette (ed.) *Handbook of Organisational Psychology*, Chicago: Rand McNally.

Weick, K.E. (1969) *The Social Psychology of Organising*, Reading, MA: Addison-Wesley.

Weick, K.E. (1979) 'Cognitive processes in organisations', *Research in Organisational Behavior*, 1: 41–74.

White, J. and Dozier, D.M. (1992) 'Public relations and management decision-making', in J.E. Grunig (ed.) *Excellence in Public Relations and Communications Management*, Hillsdale, NJ: Lawrence Erlbaum.

3

THE EVOLUTION OF PUBLIC RELATIONS: PRINCIPLES AND PRACTICE

Philip J. Kitchen

CHAPTER AIMS

- to give an outline of the public relations literature in the twentieth century
- to provide definition and exploration of the meaning of public relations
- to describe the functional elements of public relations
- to explore the emergent marketing public relations (MPR) concept
- to indicate the evolutionary process of PR and its emergence as a mature managerial discipline
- to provide case studies indicating the need for PR in practice, but soundly based on well understood theoretical foundations

ILLUSTRATION: 'THE NEED FOR CORPORATE CHAMELEONS'

Information technology research specialist Spikes Cavell recently took a long hard look at the hi-tech PR sector from a client and media perspective. In a survey undertaken in August 1995, the company talked to a cross-section of marketing managers from 105 UK hi-tech companies which retain an external consultancy. Each was questioned about their likes and dislikes, needs and requirements, and asked to assess their agencies skills, attributes and competencies.

A series of discussions revealed an industry dominated by a small clique of 12 specialist consultancies – namely Firefly, Argyll, Harvard, A-Plus, Moores Associates, Bogard, GBC, Insight, Berkeley, BourneRiver, Hunt Thompson, and Noiseworks – who jointly handled around 42 per cent of the client companies interviewed. At the same time, Spikes Cavell MD Luke Spikes points to 'an increasing encroachment by generalists creating specialist divisions and then differentiating themselves by focusing more at a corporate level'.

Interviewers questioned each company about the range of their agency's involvement to see if there was a growing trend for PR agencies being used in a broader marketing context. In reality, while a fair proportion of PR agencies have a role that extends beyond press relations – 60 per cent of the clients questioned said that their relationship with their agency was strategic, with company positioning cited as one of the most important areas of input – the level of involvement at 'board level' tends to be dependent on the size of the company.

Ten per cent of companies questioned said that they relied heavily on their agencies when it comes to marcoms, however, strategic input is limited in Europe by US domination of the market. 'The hi-tech industry is US-dominated with UK companies tending to be regarded more as the sales arm so there is a lot less emphasis on influencing the City than on generating sales,' says Spikes.

While European outlets of most US software companies may have their hands tied in terms of product and marketing development, indigenous service companies are inevitably more likely to involve their PR companies in corporate affairs.

At the same time desktop PC companies seem keen to take advice from agencies on marketing developments. 'It is a maturity issue,' says Spikes. 'Because of the size of companies in the sector, the UK operations have a tendency to be more autonomous and to be able to define marketing strategy for their region.'

Spikes Cavell also spoke to 25 trade titles ranging from *Computing, Computer Weekly* and *Computer Business Review* to *Software Future, Network News* and *Corporate IT Strategy.* Quotes from anonymous journalists include praise for agencies who 'don't pound me with rubbish' and who 'are sophisticated enough to understand their clients'. However, they also complain about lack of targeting and manipulative tactics. No matter how fast the IT sector develops, some things never change.

Spikes Cavell plans to repeat the exercise at the end of 1996.

(*Source*: *PR Week*, 12 January 1996: 16, used with permission.)

INTRODUCTION

Whether one chooses the hi-tech sector, the fast-moving consumer goods sector, or some other sector of industry or commerce, it is becoming evident that public relations – as a communications vehicle, and as a tool of corporate or marketing management – has a vital role to play in developing effective communications or effective relationships with a wide diversity of publics or audiences who could impact on organisational performance. But public relations is not 'new'. As Walker (1988), in a review of the public relations literature, stated: 'To say that public relations is not a profession and has no defined body of knowledge is exploding in the face of skeptics who deny its existence despite mounting evidences to the contrary.'

Moore and Kalupa (1985) supported Walker's position in their textbook on public relations and stated that in their view 'the need for and the acceptance of public relations as both a business and a societal force is . . . seldom questioned'. They contrasted this with earlier days, when opinions about public relations were mainly negative. While public relations is relatively 'new' in its corporate and marketing functions, it has a long history since its early days as 'press agentry'. The literature developed slowly from the early 1900s, but the main sources initially were from the United States. From 1900 to 1928 just two books with PR titles were in print. By 1986–87, the United States library catalogue listed 156 books in print; this was in addition to thousands of articles in academic, professional and trade literature (Cutlip et al., 1985). To give an illustration of the resilience and need for PR literature, Edward Bernays' classic *Crystallising Public Opinion* (1924/1961) was still in print in 1988. Public relations is indeed 'coming of age' but in the light of changing environmental circumstances. Public relations, in a similar way to

23

marketing, could not have retained its earlier form and at the same time remained pertinent to businesses approaching the twenty-first century.

The purpose of this chapter is to provide evidence for the theoretical development of public relations. The chapter will incorporate the following subject areas:

- The development and evolution of the concept of public relations in the light of changing environmental circumstances.
- Definitions and meaning of public relations.
- An outline of the interaction and debate between PR and marketing (which will also be taken up later on in the text).
- The functional elements of public relations including: publicity and press agentry, public affairs, lobbying, issues management, development and advertising (where possible these areas will be linked into current research and trade commentary).
- The concept of marketing PR and a rationale for its inclusion in the arsenal of public and marketing weaponry given.
- The evolution of public relations as a profession toward maturity.

DEVELOPMENT AND EVOLUTION OF PUBLIC RELATIONS

There is a need to accept public relations as a business and societal force. Like other facets of management, development of public relations took time. Publicity or the placing of newsworthy items in the press is no longer the main scope of public relations. Early literature focused on press agentry or publicity under the heading of public relations (Adams, 1902; Smith, 1915; McCauley, 1922; Long, 1924). Soon after, Bernays (1931) appealed for the need to separate the function of public relations counsellor from that of press agent. This position was supported by the need for public opinion measurement as distinct from publicity and became the focus of research by Harvard alumni (Robinson, 1931). It was not until the late 1940s, however, that the first attempts to link PR and management were drawn by Wright and Christian (1949). They quote from a (presumably enlightened) business executive who affirmed with confidence that 'tomorrow belongs to the man who thinks in terms of the public – the public embracing his employees, his stockholders, his customers, his neighbours surrounding his factory . . . and his government'. Here, for the first time, PR is specifically related to different publics – employees, finance, customers, the local community and the need for government interaction. Publicity was seen positively as a tool to create interest in companies and/or their products. Since the 1950s, public relations has become a profession in its own right and a number of textbooks support the growing trend for education (Lesly, 1950; 1983). The first doctoral dissertation on PR was written in 1954 by O'Hare at Columbia University and reflected the growing body of knowledge and publications about PR at that time. In the 1960s and 1970s bibliographies were being produced by Cutlip (1957) and Bishop (1974; 1976), and between 1978 and 1987 the winter edition of the *Public Relations Review* published annual updates of the public relations bibliography. In the first annual update, the bibliographer wrote: 'there are many more listings in this bibliography from periodicals outside PR than from those within the field.' There is 'conclusive evidence for the widespread respect for the importance of public relations by professionals in all fields of endeavour' (Walker, 1978).

During this same period, business organisations were also undergoing change in response to environmental circumstances. The types of environment in which firms operate influence not only corporate and marketing strategies and tactics but also interrelationships with various publics that need to be set up and maintained. Just as human relations deal with studies concerning individual interrelationships, and international relations deal with relationships among nations, so public relations deals with organisational relationships in environmental settings. Thus in the early part of the twentieth century the emphasis was placed on press agentry or telling a story to support company strategy. This was largely seen as one-way persuasive communications designed to facilitate favourable opinion. But at that time few companies could perceive a need for a relationship with various publics save the all-important one of selling. All the factors of later years – government interaction and interference with corporate behaviour; consumerism; communication proliferation, clutter and expenditure; social responsibility; environmental turbulence occasioned by global marketing; and developments in marketing and corporate communications – had yet to take place. Consequently, public relations development was limited. In later years, as the above quotation by Wright and Christian makes plain, the view of business organisations as interacting with various publics started to come to the fore.

The early functions of PR concerned public contact (publicity), then research into public opinion with a view to influencing such opinions favourably. This latter approach is reflected in one of Bernays' books *The Engineering of Consent* (1955). As the title makes plain the aim of PR was manipulative, one-way rather than two-way. This same orientation was reflected in a popular J.B. Priestley novel, *The Image Men* (1953) and in 1961 Mayer wrote: 'Public relations seeks to direct and if necessary distort the media's supposedly undirected and undistorted content.'

During the decades following the Second World War public relations sought to change its image from manipulative and one-way to two-way, reciprocal, and interactive. The Institute of Public Relations in the United Kingdom uses this type of phraseology in its definition of public relations: 'Public relations is the planned and sustained effort to establish and maintain goodwill and mutual understanding between an organisation and its publics' (IPR, 1991).

Establishing and maintaining relationships and goodwill can be defined as the basic premise of public relations in the 1990s. Public relations has come a long way from its early origins in press agentry, which in fact is now used as a derogatory term by most business organisations. As shall be shown later, however, publicity is still a vital component of public relations.

Coupled with the development of public relations as a management tool was the development of public relations departments within organisations. As would be expected initially, such development was fragmentary focusing on publicity, then public opinion, and latterly with a movement toward further specialisms dealing with each public. For those companies unable to afford the expenditure incurred with an internal department, external PR agencies fulfilled a need. An indicative article on the increased relevance and professionalism of PR is entitled 'Press "agents" that became part of a management team' (Rice, 1980) showing the movement away from press agentry toward integration of PR as a management function. The late 1980s witnessed growth in the UK PR agency sector which accelerated from £106m in 1986 to £216m in 1989, a growth rate of 103 per cent. Also during the 1980s UK development took place in the educational sphere as the need for managers to understand and utilise this function developed. Aside from the many further education courses available (IPR, 1991), Table 3.1 below illustrates developments in higher education. Attention is drawn to these courses to indicate the growing respect and attention devoted to public relations in relation to educational developments which in turn are a reflection of market demand. A review of definitions and meaning of public relations is now in order.

DEFINITIONS AND MEANING OF PUBLIC RELATIONS

Just what is public relations? A number of definitions have already been mentioned including that by the IPR. Rex Harlow, who is regarded as an expert, undertook the task of collating and synthesising some 472 definitions of public relations extant at the time of his study (1976). None of these definitions were found to be acceptable and his own definition was developed. The definition adopted for the purpose of this text bears resemblance to that of the IPR (UK) and was given by Cutlip et al. (1985). To justify the reference to Cutlip (a leading American author), conversation by the author with staff at the institutions listed in Table 3.1 found this textbook was

Table 3.1 Higher education developments in public relations

	Qualification/date of inception
Undergraduate	
Bournemouth University	BA in PR (1989)
College of St Mark and St John (degree validated by Exeter University)	BA in PR (1989)
Leeds Polytechnic	BA in PR (1990)
Oxford University	Diploma in PR (1990)
Birmingham University	A series of PR modules in business studies stream (1990)
West Herts College (formerly Watford)	Diploma in PR (1988)
City University	Developing a PR degree (1990)
Postgraduate	
Stirling University	MSc in PR (1988)
Stirling University	MSc in PR (distance learning) (1991)
Cranfield	Extended elective in PR on MBA (1988)
Manchester Metropolitan University	MSc in PR (1993)
Strathclyde University	Corporate Communications Electives on the MBA/MSc (1993)

adopted more than any other. On the other hand, few UK institutions utilised the writing of Jefkins (an English writer on public relations: 1980; 1983; 1988; 1992) at undergraduate or postgraduate levels. Notably, however, Jefkins writings offer little in the way of a theoretical perspective. PR agency practitioners also cited Cutlip et al. (1985:4) as an acceptable standard of definition:

> Public relations is the management function that identifies, establishes, and maintains mutually beneficial relationships between an organisation and the various publics on whom its success or failure depends.

If this definition is explored; it can be said that public relations is:

1 A management function (i.e. it is guided by management in terms of analysis, planning, implementation, and control; it is not the result of *ad hoc* unplanned publicity).
2 It covers a broad range of activities and purposes in practice (i.e. it is not narrow or singular for example press agentry or publicity).
3 It is regarded as two-way or interactive (i.e. it identifies, establishes and maintains mutually beneficial relationships. This suggests a need for monitoring awareness, opinions, attitudes, and behaviour inside and outside an organisation, which in turn suggests big companies have to change the way they talk to and listen to people both inside and outside their businesses (Economist, 1989).
4 It suggests that publics facing companies are not singular (i.e. consumers) but plural (i.e. this would suggest analysing and adjusting corporate and marketing policies in line with the public(s) interest and organisational survival and growth).
5 It suggests that relationships are long term rather than short term; that hazardous firefighting-type activities may be better accomplished in the light of such relationships.

The above definition and the list of meanings of public relations will change as companies, markets, and management functions evolve. The definition does, however, lap over into that of marketing and considerable confusion exists between boundaries of public relations and marketing. This is evident in the literature (Cutlip et al., 1985; White, 1991), but an attempt is made to distinguish between the two areas.

CONFUSION BETWEEN PUBLIC RELATIONS AND MARKETING

Leading marketeers have put forward an argument in which public relations is bracketed with advertising and other forms of promotional communications (Kotler and Mindak, 1978; Kotler, 1986, 1991; Cohen, 1991; Evans and Berman, 1990). However, a careful distinction needs to be drawn between say advertising and public relations. The two areas are separate and distinct though from time to time advertising and publicity may be used as complementary tactics directed towards achievement of communication or promotional goals. Thus, while some concurrence is expressed with the viewpoint that public relations and marketing communications bear correspondence, that correspondence needs to be qualified. White (1991) devotes a chapter to describing the essential distinctions between the two areas and he follows the approach outlined by Cutlip et al. (1985). While the views put forward are debatable they are supported by other academics in the field of public relations. Public relations is considered to be a broader management communications task than marketing while sharing some similarities. Whereas marketing, according to Cutlip et al., is concerned with an organisation's exchange relationship with customers, public relations deals with a wider range of publics involved with or affected by the organisation.

Marketing has been perceived as the central management task over the past two decades, concerned with satisfying individual and organisational needs and building competitive advantage (Sheth et al., 1988). Public relations operates as a complement and a corrective to marketing. As a complement public relations can assist in achieving organisational goals by preparing the ground in which marketing can perform its function of creating exchanges; as a corrective it can bring other viewpoints to bear beside the need to create exchanges. White argues that the full task of management cannot be reduced to marketing, that the marketing approach itself has limitations (as witnessed by the rise of consumerism), and that the perspective on which public relations is based is broader than that of marketing. Public relations and marketing are two major management functions within an organisation, but how they are organised depends upon managerial perceptions, organisational culture, and historical precedent. The role played by public relations staff and marketing management is complicated by a lack of understanding of these two functions by practitioners themselves.

In practice a number of ways of managing the two functions is possible, and organisations will work to the most suitable arrangements. If the viewpoint is maintained that public relations is a complement to marketing, then this facilitates further the argument developed in this chapter. Public relations can operate at different levels in an organisation; at a corporate level it is concerned with interaction with various publics, not necessarily to create exchanges (as with marketing) but to create an environment to support exchanges taking place. Staying at the corporate level momentarily, there will be significant opportunities for interaction with marketing to take place usually either from creating and sustaining favourable imagery or via sponsorship. At the marketing level a significant groundswell of opinion is developing in major textbooks (e.g. Berman, 1990; Cohen, 1991; Kotler, 1991; Zikmund and D'Amico, 1988) that public relations can be utilised to support marketing objectives. A return will be made to this discussion later in this chapter and a more sophisticated review takes place in Chapter 16. Meanwhile, the major functions of public relations are specified.

FUNCTIONAL ELEMENTS OF PUBLIC RELATIONS

If the premise is accepted that public relations, at one level, is responsible for creating a favourable environment from which marketing can create satisfactory exchanges, then this begs the question of how or in what way is such an environment to be created? This is largely a question of creating favourable imagery and this ties in with the earlier definition of PR – identifying, establishing and maintaining mutually beneficial relationships between organisations and various publics upon which organisational success or failure is based. Various activities and parts of public relations can be identified at the corporate level. Before discussing these, a brief outline of what is meant by 'favourable image' is presented.

Creating a favourable image

Firms, in order to create effective and mutually satisfactory relationships with various publics, need a variety of PR functions. With each public, creation of a favourable image is paramount. Companies such as Cadbury Typhoo, Sellafield British Nuclear Fuels, the National Audit Office, and ICI all have one thing in common – the need to create a favourable image or an effective corporate identity (Business Week, 1979a; Kreitzman, 1986). Using the argument adopted by Seitel (1992), 'image' refers to the way the company is perceived in the minds of whatever marketplace (public) is important. Businesses tend to be operating in a 'pressure-cooker' environment characterised by consumerists, environmentalists, civil rights and other activist groups, intensified competition, takeover threats, employee relations and the threat of government intervention. Such an environment equates to a need by organisations to create and sustain favourable images which involves organisations in changing the way they talk to and listen to people both outside and inside their businesses (Economist, 1989). An estimate put forward by *The Economist* (1989) stipulated image management or the time spent by a typical corporate communications department as shown in Table 3.2.

A few examples of creating a favourable image are now considered. When Denys Henderson took over as chairman of ICI from Sir John Harvey Jones in 1987, research discovered most Britons found the company boring and the City took a dim view of the firm, believing it to be subject to booms and busts. Overseas, few had heard of ICI. These perceptions were prevalent despite the previous leadership of Sir John Harvey Jones, which had led ICI to soaring profitability and a leading-edge position in medical advances. A major revamping of the firm including redesigning the company image via logo redesign, a worldwide corporate advertising campaign, and a programme of educational seminars were set up (Economist, 1989). This had the effect of raising the image not only of ICI but also of the public relations department within the company.

In December 1984, an explosion in Bhopal, India, killed more than 2,500 people. Union Carbide, the American firm that owned majority shares in the firm, started to receive more than 5,000 media calls per day. Bhopal Union Carbide was lambasted by the media. The result was the formation of a public relations team. It was

Table 3.2 Managing the image

Area	% of time
Employees	35
Investors	30
Government	25
Media	10

estimated (Economist, 1989) that 75 per cent of the chairman's time was now taken up with communications. Following the Bhopal disaster and a resultant out-of-court settlement, Union Carbide found itself on the receiving end of a takeover bid. The bid was foiled as the result of better communications with appropriate publics and an increased share price value.

In the USA, Ralston Purina Co., an animal and poultry feed giant, tried in 1978 to withhold information in a session with stock market analysts. The analysts in turn touched off a stock market crisis that immediately trimmed more than $100m from the value of Ralston shares (Business Week, 1979b). This was not a case of withholding information of a confidential nature, but merely maintaining a private face to the world. Such a confrontational situation could have been avoided by the effective use of PR. Here in the UK, many companies have been involved in takeover bids, and a significant factor in the fight to maintain independence is media relations. Often companies which have not built a relationship or a favourable image with their publics find themselves without support in takeover battles, in addition to a share price below company value.

The discussion so far has given three examples of firms utilising (or not utilising) public relations to influence key publics and in the main the centrality of corporate public relations has been posited. The argument developed in this chapter, however, is that two types of PR are necessary – both corporate *and* marketing – and that interaction between the two is desirable in order to develop effective external organisational communications. The debate and confusion among academics and practitioners has been indicated. Summarised briefly it can be said that corporate PR is aimed at various publics, primarily employees, suppliers, stockholders, governments, the general public, the City, labour groups, and consumerist movements (Shimp, 1989:488–9). Marketing PR is also concerned with specific publics which, as Cutlip and White make clear, are customers, clients and consumers with whom exchange relations take place. Goldman (1984:xi–xii) makes an important distinction between proactive and reactive PR:

> Proactive PR which tries to enhance a company's image and increase its revenues is counterbalanced by reactive PR which tries to restore the company to the status quo – by repairing its reputation, preventing marketing erosion, and regaining lost sales.

Achieving the tasks mentioned by Goldman can be a function of either corporate or marketing PR and the reality may be that there is, or should be, a close correspondence between the two communication areas. The section below refers to functions carried out via corporate communications by asking the question: which methods, techniques, skills, or activities are most useful in building favourable relationships with publics? The section following then outlines the nature of marketing PR.

ACTIVITIES AND PARTS OF PUBLIC RELATIONS

There is a degree of confusion as to the activities and the parts that make up public relations. Previously, it was suggested that the Cutlip definition of public relations defined publics as pluralistic rather than singular. This in turn suggests a variety of mechanisms need to be utilised in order to develop effective relations. The discussion will focus on the following typology of parts or activities: publicity (press agentry), advertising, public affairs, lobbying, issues management, financial PR and sponsorship (note with this last area there is a very significant overlap with marketing).

Publicity (press agentry)

Twenty-five years ago the term 'press agentry' in effect described PR practitioners as the contact men between client and media who sought to reach the 'publics'. Put more simply, the task was to get clients' names in papers and was used for the purpose of building name recognition and attracting large audiences; as such it would be used more to attract public notice than build understanding. It is one-way rather than two-way communications. Nowadays it is used by circuses, tourist attractions, film makers, concert promoters, and sports, religious and political personalities. While it can be said that all organisations at some point use press agentry, it does not seem of great value to today's modern business organisations. In interviews by the author with senor executives in fast-moving consumer goods firms and a survey with PR agencies there is a movement away from press agentry toward publicity, which can also be termed media relations. The aim of media relations is to build long-term relationships with publics appropriate to the organisation within its social setting. Proactive or reactive publicity is the outcome of such relationships. Publicity is defined as 'information from an outside source used by the news media based on its news value' or information perceived by the media as relevant to its audiences. Thus financial reports and data, scientific findings and developments, statements on strategies and tactics, news of corporate personnel changes, staging of newsworthy events, press conferences, new product launches, and publicity relative to sponsorships all have obvious 'news value' and are arranged primarily for media coverage. Public relations evolved from publicity but the two are not the same. Still, it could be said that publicity events and releases are among major tactics used to achieve public relations objectives.

This discussion makes clear that publicity can be used at a variety of levels and functions in modern business organisations. This would suggest building relation-ships with appropriate media and developing messages through the media as 'news'. It offers significant opportunity to build relationships with target audiences with the added bonus of endorsement by the media vehicle.

Advertising

Where publicity is uncontrolled by the source, advertising is controlled in terms of content, media placement, and timing. Advertising in terms of corporate PR is used in a specific sense to differentiate it from advertising for marketing purposes. In corporate PR terms, advertising can be viewed as a 'strategy option for non-marketing purposes', that is institutional, public service or controversy advertising. Thus ICI (quoted earlier) began a worldwide campaign in 1987 to improve its corporate image. Typically, such advertising seeks to improve goodwill or understanding with specific target groups. Cutlip et al. (1985:foreword), however, states that 'organisations turn to advertising only when access to the editorial sections is limited or when control over message content placement, and timing is too important to be left to chance'. Thus if the opportunity is available to use editorial channels (via media relations and publicity) then this should be taken. Corporate advertising was viewed askance by many in-house public relations practitioners given that corporate messages are more believable through non-advertising mechanisms of communication.

Public affairs

This area of public relations is rapidly becoming almost a separate corporate communications area in its own right, and in the United States has enjoyed significant growth since the 1950s (Post et al., 1982; Andrews, 1985; Marcus and Kaufman, 1988). Public affairs sections in public relations departments concern themselves with 'corporate citizenship' and public policy and as such are concerned to design, to build, and to maintain community relations and governmental relations. In this context, lobbying becomes a subset of public affairs. For the purposes of this discussion, however, the two activities are discussed separately. In some organisations the title 'public affairs' is seen as more acceptable than 'public relations', and this distinction adds somewhat to the confusion over terminology in this area. In this text, public affairs is considered a subset of public relations.

Within public affairs corporate citizenship, community relations, charitable interaction, and social responsibility are the expected types of activities to be engaged in. Two UK companies taking public affairs seriously are British Telecom and National Westminster Bank PLC as reported by Kitchen (1990). British Telecom in a report to consumers (1989) proudly proclaimed its membership of the Per Cent Club, which in 1988 devoted nearly £12m in cash, materials and labour to community projects. While this seems like altruism of the highest order, the resultant PR opportunities support the image of British Telecom as a caring corporation and a good corporate citizen. National Westminster Bank, in a magazine handout available at the counter of every branch, also devotes several million per annum to causes judged worthy of its interests. While the true significance of these activities is debatable there is no doubting their necessity. Such companies hold significant social and economic power and, as market leaders, their aim is to build and maintain competitive advantage. Whatever will contribute to that aim will be – and is – accessed and utilised.

Attempting to justify the development of public affairs is not difficult in the context of changes in the environments faced by organisations. Company performance is not only affected by corporate or marketing strategy but also by change in its markets – i.e. in the wider world. Earlier in the discussion public relations was explained as pluralistic in its activities and parts. That same pluralism extends to society. Keith Davis (1967:45–57) commented on the dawn of social responsibility:

In our pluralistic society, business is influenced by all other groups in the system, and business in turn, influences them. Therefore the business must be socially responsible for its actions. Not only are the parts of modern society more inter-dependent, but the social sciences are giving us new knowledge about how business affects the other parts . . . Business, in the long run, to maintain its position of power, must accept its responsibility to the whole of society.

Writing in 1967 Davis' position was not unassailable by any means, but now a study of most business organisations would indicate that they are taking this very seriously indeed as a fundamental cornerstone to maintaining a favourable image. A reading from virtually any serious daily national newspaper would indicate many articles indicative of this (see also *Daily Mail,* 1989). Of interest here is involvement of firms with various types of charitable endeavour. As an aside, some firms play their involvement in charity down, whereas others attempt to tie charitable giving into corporate and marketing communications.

Lobbying

Lobbying can legitimately be considered a subset of public affairs. Because of terminological difficulties, however, it has been accorded a separate section and Chapter 10 is devoted to this subject. Lobbying is aimed at directing attention to potentially influence legislative and regulatory affairs in government at both a local and national level. It is also directed toward non-governmental publics whose voices are heard by legislators and/or officials in government. At the very least lobbyists within business organisations or employed on their behalf serve as credible advocates and reliable sources of information. In the UK, large firms should play a role in the formulation of new laws or in adapting or influencing European community edicts. There is considerable interaction between governments and the private sector in terms of industrial experts and committee representation, pollution and use of the earth's resources, and the societal impact of proposed new products and consumerism. Lobbying does not primarily involve the one-off petitioning of government decision-makers, but is a long process of building an interactive relationship which ultimately proves of value to business organisations.

Issues management

Several definitions of the term 'issue' exist in the literature of issues management (Jones and Chase, 1979; Heath and Nelson, 1986). For the purposes of this discussion an issue may be defined as: 'a point of conflict between an organisation and one or more of its publics' (Hainsworth, 1990). Issues management refers to a particular proactive as opposed to reactive strategy. Chase (1977:25–6) stipulated that issues management is: 'the process of identifying issues, analysing those issues, setting priorities, selecting program strategy options, implementing a program of action and communication, and evaluating effectiveness.'

Conceptually, as part of public relations, issues management is defined in a manner similar to Chase, that it 'deals with emerging issues and their potential impact on the operations of any type of organisation'. Not all issues, however, can be known to an organisation in advance of their occurrence. But a business organisation can have a coherent and rational plan of what to do in the event of a particular scenario. While issues such as the movement away from red meat, high cholesterol foods, non-biodegradable packaging, and ozone damaging aerosols suggest themselves as interesting examples of issues management, rather than firefighting, the Tylenol case is particularly pertinent.

In 1982, seven people died in the Chicago area of cyanide poisoning as a result of ingesting Tylenol capsules. Many analysts predicted that Tylenol would never regain its market leadership position. Some observers questioned whether Johnson and Johnson would ever be able to market anything under the Tylenol name again. Rather than denying a problem existed Johnson and Johnson acted swiftly to remove Tylenol from retail shelves. A major media PR campaign was launched warning consumers not to ingest Tylenol capsules. Tylenol was then relaunched using innovative tamper-proof packaging and offering free replacements for disposed of products. The result was that Tylenol regained its market share in a short time period and this despite actions by competitors to steal Tylenol customers (Shimp, 1989:498).

Other examples of reactive PR occurred in the case of Rely brand tampons, and Firestone 500 tyres (Gatewood and Carroll, 1981). When Rely brand tampons were found to have a possible link with toxic shock syndrome, Procter and Gamble acted quickly to remove the brand from retailer shelves, and advertising and PR campaigns were utilised to warn and protect consumers. Procter and Gamble's image emerged untarnished. Alternatively, Firestone Tyre and Rubber company only agreed to withdraw its Firestone 500 tyres after heavy pressure from the USA National Highway Traffic Safety Commission and others and this after 41 deaths and 65 injuries which may have been related to tyre defects in the brand. The result was a tarnished image and a $135m product recall cost.

The examples quoted supply ample evidence for the management of issues, rather than firefighting-type reactions. What the Procter and Gamble and Johnson and Johnson examples illustrate is that reactive PR to a particular issue is the result of forethought, planning and policy thought out in advance. Issues management is of increasing relevance to firms in the turbulent environment of the 1990s.

Development

Development, according to Cutlip et al. (1985), is often related to fund-raising and is mainly to do with private, often not-for-profit organisations. This activity calls for annual and special events and is often to do with maintaining relationships with volunteers, alumni, 'friends', members, donors, and prospects. As such, development is peripheral to the mainstream of this text but from time to time business organisations may get involved in fund-raising activities in which case the resultant publicity may add lustre and credence to organisational activity.

Financial PR

Contemporary financial PR goes well beyond 'share-pushing' and is about creating an understanding between an organisation and those in the financial community upon whom it must depend for its long-term prosperity (Good, 1980). Such understanding may involve communicating the merits of supporting or resisting takeover bids (Newman, 1983); explaining company performance against new technology investment and short-term dividend restraint; or discouraging stock market over-optimism if there is a risk of market disappointment. Earlier, Ralston Purina was noted as not being involved with stock market analysts with the result of a major loss in share value, while Union Carbide was in a similar position after the Bhopal disaster. Business organisations need to build appropriate relationships, especially as it is evident that editorial comment and views taken by leading financial commentators serve to influence the opinions of private shareholders and financial intermediaries. As will be shown later in the text, financial PR is of major importance to many firms.

Sponsorship

Sponsorship is an area of activity virtually ignored by the public relations and marketing literature. For example Kotler, who is regarded as an authoritative figure in marketing, does not mention sponsorship at all in his text (1991); the same absence of sponsorship is evident in Cutlip et al. (1985). The view of the author is that sponsorship is an area of communications overlapping between corporate and marketing public relations. Sponsorships are managed by marketing or by corporate PR departments. Goldberg (1983) compared arts versus sports sponsorship and found that the former is very much the lesser of the two. The amounts of money involved are vastly different, media exposure for arts is much smaller, advertising opportunities are less, and the two are generally entered into for different reasons and supported from different budgets. Table 3.3 compares the objectives of sponsoring companies for arts and sports.

Major objectives of arts sponsors linked into corporate public relations in the sense that they were related to corporate image, enhancement of community relations (a subset of public affairs), and promoting brand awareness as well as seeking publicity coverage and exposure. Sports sponsors were also concerned with corporate image, but far more with promoting brand awareness, achieving media coverage, and increasing sales – all elements concerned with marketing PR. Sponsorship seems to be a cinderella-type subject in the academic literature; but it is certainly not a cinderella in the allocation of corporate and marketing PR budgets.

The preceding discussion leads into the debate concerning marketing PR.

MARKETING PR

Public relations is an important tool from a marketing communications viewpoint but until recently it has been viewed as a marketing stepchild according to Kotler (1991) and Merims (1972). As has been suggested, public relations can be utilised

Table 3.3 Objectives of sponsoring companies

	Arts % (rank)	Sports % (rank)
Enhance community relations	51.8 (2)	26.1 (7)
Benefit employees	4.8 (9)	3.5 (9)
Promote corporate image	71.0 (1)	70.1 (1)
Promote brand awareness	39.2 (3)	68.1 (2)
Press coverage/exposure	32.9 (4)	61.5 (3)
Radio coverage/exposure	22.2 (7)	40.4 (6)
Television coverage/exposure	31.0 (5)	53.5 (5)
Increased sales	28.4 (6)	57.8 (4)
Entertaining clients	20.5 (8)	24.1 (8)

Source: Goldberg, 1983, as quoted by Linstead and Turner, 1986, adapted by author.

by marketeers to maximise the co-ordination of its marketing programme. The parts or activities discussed previously may not tie directly into product or brand support and there is debate and confusion over what has been termed 'corporate public relations' and 'marketing public relations'. The argument adopted thus far has stipulated that public relations at the corporate level has been outlined as a function of management seeking to identify, establish and maintain mutually beneficial relationships between an organisation and the various publics on whom its success or failure depends (Cutlip et al., 1985). The publics would include the gamut of supplier, distributor, government, finance, internal staff, trade bodies and so forth and these in turn demand particular, sometimes highly specialised, PR activities. Marketing, on the other hand, is not only concerned with organisational success or failure but also with specific publics with whom exchanges take place. Thus PR in its broadest sense is concerned with a wider range of publics than marketing. *But,* corporate and marketing public relations are not viewed as being mutually exclusive. Rather they are mutually interactive. Public relations is not only an area reserved exclusively for corporate communications, but also is of value at marketing levels. This argument, however, calls for some justification.

Marketing management and PR management may not always speak the same language. One major difference is that marketing is more concerned with the bottom line, whereas PR practitioners may see their task as disseminating communications. Despite language and objectives problems there is a need for marketing-oriented PR. Marketing PR, like financial PR and community PR, services the needs of the marketing department. The rationale for the development of marketing PR is to do with audience fragmentation and rising media costs. Evidence for the development of marketing PR is weak in the UK context but the relaunch of Beechams Brylcream using PR in the first instance, the public relations efforts supporting the 'garden city' concept, and the repositioning of Glasgow as a 'city of culture' spring to mind. In the US market, Kotler (1988) gives several examples of the use of marketing public relations: new product launch (Cabbage Patch Kids), repositioning mature products (New York City), building interest in specific product categories (i.e. milk, eggs, meat, influencing specific target groups (i.e. neighbourhood events), defending products encountering public problems (i.e. Tylenol, Rely), and building corporate image to reflect favourably on product (Lee Iaccoca's speeches).

Marketing public relations seems to be developing more and more, especially in the United States, but some evidence for its development here in the UK has been put forward. Taken with the preceding discussion relating to imagery and parts and activities of PR, marketing PR operates as a complement to existing public relations and marketing communications activities. Public relations seems to be coming of age.

TOWARD MATURITY OF PUBLIC RELATIONS

The review of literature forming the basis for the theoretical framework in this chapter commenced by quoting from Walker (1988) and Moore and Kalupa (1985) as to the seeming essentiality and functionality of public relations in relation to modern business organisations. The development of public relations has undergone a process of evolution since the start of the twentieth century. From a somewhat shady pursuit involving press agentry or plain publicity, public relations has evolved towards becoming a multifaceted and essential management discipline. Its multifaceted nature has been described in terms of evolution of management thought and expression, as shown in the multitudinous literature (both academic and practitioner); in the development of further and higher education; in the diversity of types and activities of public relations; and in the development and value of marketing public relations.

While it would be difficult to show that the principles of PR are consistent and enduring, the practice of public relations has been influenced extensively by social forces, technical and scientific developments, and a continually changing environment. The definition, function and use of PR have undergone significant change and growth throughout the twentieth century. Media costs and audience fragmentation and demassification has meant that PR can be considered and utilised as a marketing tool in addition to its many corporate communication functions. Synergy between PR at both corporate and marketing levels is evident. Public relations seems to be moving toward a state of maturity in the early 1990s.

SUMMARY AND CONCLUSIONS

The argument developed in this chapter has sought to establish a theoretical framework for the development and evolution of public relations and justify this development via the academic and practitioner literature. Such development and evolution has taken place according to findings from the literature in terms of the volume of subject matter, academic course development, changes in competitive environments, developments of in-house PR departments and changes in the PR agency sector. Such evolution was then positioned in relation to definitions and meaning of public relations; a conceptual definition by Cutlip et al. (1985) was given and its rationale explored. In accordance with the definition, functional elements of public relations were explored, posited on the basis of creating a favourable image.

Elements, parts, or activities associated with public relations included publicity (press agentry), advertising, public affairs, lobbying, issues management, development, financial PR, and sponsorship. The rationale for the inclusion of marketing PR was given. Each facet of the argument contributes toward 'setting the scene' and establishing a sound theoretical framework. Metaphorically, this chapter forms a foundation stone or undergirding structure upon which many of the specialist contributions can be based.

DISCUSSION TOPICS

1 Suggest your views as to why much of the current thinking on public relations stems from across the Atlantic.
2 Critically discuss the statement by Moore and Kalupa that the 'need for and the acceptance of public relations as both a business and societal force . . . is seldom questioned'.
3 Explain the difference between press agentry and publicity. Which is more relevant to business organisations in the latter part of the 1990s?
4 Justify the inclusion of public relations as course material for UK undergraduate and postgraduate study. Which factors underpin these developments?
5 Explore the PR definitions by the IPR and Cutlip et al. Why choose Cutlip as an acceptable standard?
6 Indicate why there should be a debate as to the respective parameters of PR and marketing. In what way is the debate 'academic'?
7 Why is image so important to large multinationals? What is image, how is it created, sustained, or damaged?
8 The functions of PR have been defined. Are these functions based on any underlying trends or forces? If so, which?
9 Why is sponsorship a 'cinderella subject'? Which camp (PR or marketing) should legitimately lay claim to sponsorship?
10 Is PR 'mature' or is it still going through the process of development?

CASE STUDY: FILLING THE PR VACUUM AT TORY CENTRAL OFFICE

Eight years as a tabloid hack and an unwavering belief in John Major may not be enough to prepare Charles Lewington for the job of turning around the Tory Party's image.

While the rest of the country was helping itself to its last mince pie, Charles Lewington, former political editor of the *Sunday Express*, was discovering just how tough life can be on the other side of the fence.

Two weeks into his new job as the Tory Party's director of communications . . . . Emma Nicholson jumped ship to the Liberal Democrats leaving John Major with the prospect of a minority government before 1996 was out.

A political journalist of eight years' standing, Lewington certainly seems to have the vital attribute missing in his predecessor Hugh Colver – an unwavering belief in John Major and the Tory Party.

His charm and good looks have been much commented on. But Lewington will need more than a winning smile to steer the Party through the 17 months remaining of this Parliament. Labour has a commanding lead in the opinion polls, the feel-good factor is as stubbornly absent as ever and the internal split in the Tory Party shows signs of escalating into a full-scale war.

The appointment of a newspaper journalist, and a tabloid hack at that, to fill the void left by career PR man Hugh Colver, is a testament to the Tories' continued obsession with Tony Blair's press secretary Alastair Campbell. Major has made great play that Lewington has access to him '24 hours-a-day, 7 days a week' and it is clear the Tories hope to replicate the disciplined, flexible organisation that has worked so effectively for Blair.

One thing Lewington is anxious not to replicate is Campbell's high personal profile – he declined to be interviewed on the record. But as the political editor of one newspaper points out, they are in very different situations. 'Campbell lives and breathes Tony Blair all day long. He's one of Blair's two or three key advisers . . . Alastair can ring up a shadow minister and say you're on ITN in 20 minutes and they will be. Charles just hasn't got that power.'

The envy with which the Tories view Labour's propaganda machine reflects their frustration with their own. Whether, as Colver pointed out, it is the natural reticence of departmental press officers to make political capital out of government business, or that there is no clear line of communication, the fact is that the Tories have consistently lost the initiative to Labour.

The new-look Press office – Sheila Gunn from the *Times* dealing with the lobby, Paul Hooper from the *Sun* handling the tabloids and head of broadcasting Ceri Evans – has been less than entirely successful. Gunn, in particular, was slated after the leaked damaging details about an asylum case in the *Guardian* – prompting a front-page story alleging that the Tories were abusing Home Office files for their own political purposes.

Then there was the story Central Office leaked to the *Daily Telegraph* about a speech in which the Lord Chancellor, Lord Mackay, was to warn judges not to overstep the mark in quashing ministerial decisions. The speech was never made and the story prompted an angry denial by Lord Mackay.

Over the next two or three weeks, Lewington is expected to unveil a series of changes designed to streamline the press office and ensure a more co-ordinated approach. 'There have been too many people putting out the message, we need more co-ordination,' said one party worker. It is not clear whether any heads will roll in the planned shake-up, though one source does speak ominously of 'personnel changes'.

Lewington is determined to make the fact that the Party is in government work for it rather than against it. The aim, says one source, is to 'allow ministers to behave more politically', though Colver's suggestion that there should be a political press officer in each ministry, sitting alongside their civil service collegues, has found little favour.

As one former Tory strategist points out, there is already a whole legion of people whose job it is 'to mesh government and party' – the special advisers. 'It's their job to enable the party machine to understand and be able to use government policy,' he explains. 'It seemed to me significant that the worst cock-up involved the only department which doesn't have a special adviser – the Lord Chancellor's department.'

One thing Sheila Gunn will have learned is that the skills of a good journalist do not automatically translate into good PR handling. And some worry that Lewington will never be more than a good media relations man.

'The party already has a fair amount of journalistic experience but nobody with PR experience,' says one ex-Central Office worker. 'There is a distinction between people who are expert in media handling and those good at undertaking PR activity in support of a campaign. They may feel the lack of campaign managers.'

Former Thatcher adviser Sir Tim Bell's rehabilitation as part of a dream team with Maurice Saatchi and Shandwick chairman Peter Gummer may be a sign that the Tories have recognised there is something missing.

Referring to the press advertisement run over the New Year, a former strategist said 'It was a credible message but there was no news content, no particular PR campaign to back it up, no posters, no press conference. Putting one ad out in isolation does not add up to a campaign. What Charles will be bending his mind to is how to bring the elements together to make a campaign. It's all about control of the agenda by weight of advertising and PR activity – otherwise it's all reactive.'

(*Source*: S. Bevan, *PR Week*, 12 January 1996:9, used with permission.)

REFERENCES

Adams, H.C. (1902) 'What is publicity?', *North American Review*, 175(57), December: 896.

Andrews, P.N. (1985) 'The sticky wicket of evaluating public affairs: thoughts about a framework', *Public Affairs Review*, 6: 94–105.

Bernays, E.L. (1931) 'A public relations counsel states his views', *Advertising and Selling*, January: 31.

Bernays, E.L. (1955) *The Engineering of Consent*, New York: Liveright.

Bernays, E.L. (1924/1961) *Crystallising Public Opinion*, New York: Liveright.

Bishop, R.L. (1974 and 1976) *Public Relations: A Comprehensive Bibliography*, Ann Arbor: The University of Michigan Press.

Business Week (1979a) 'The corporate image: PR to the rescue', Special Report, 22 January: 47–61.

Business Week (1979b) 'Perils of not minding the store', Editorial, 15 January: 56, 82–3.

Chase, H. (1977) 'Public issue management: the new science', *Public Relations Journal*, 33(10), October: 25–6.

Cohen, W. (1991) *The Practice of Marketing Management*, 2nd edn, New York: Collier Macmillan, pp. 502–25.

Cutlip, S.M. (1957) *A Public Relations Bibliography*, Madison: University of Wisconsin.

Cutlip, S.M., Center, A.H. and Broom, G.M. (1985) *Effective Public Relations*, Englewood Cliffs, NJ: Prentice-Hall.

Daily Mail (1989) 23 February.

Davis, K. (1967) 'Understanding the social responsibility puzzle', *Business Horizons*, 10, Winter: 45–57.

Economist, The (1989) 'Corporate eyes, ears, and mouth', 18 March: 105–6.

Evans, J.R. and Berman, B. (1990) *Marketing*, 4th edn, Collier Macmillan: 482–513.

Frazier Moore, H. and Kalupa, F.B. (1985) *Public Relations: Principles, Cases, and Problems*, 9th edn, Richard D. Irwin: p. 1. vi, vii.

Gatewood, E. and Carroll, A.B. (1981) 'The anatomy of corporate social response: the Rely, Firestone 500, and Pinto cases', *Business Horizons*, 24(5), September/October: 9–16.

Goldberg, H. (1983) *Sponsorship and the Performing Arts*, London: Goldberg, p. 125.

Goldman, J. (1984) *Public Relations in the Marketing Mix*, Henley-on-Thames: NTC Business Books, pp. xi–xii.

Good, T. (1980) 'The death of the old ivory tower image', *Campaign*, 22 August: 51.

Hainsworth, B.E. (1990) 'The process of issue development: the distribution of advantages and disadvantages', Working Paper, Brigham Young University.

Harlow, R.F. (1976) 'Building a public relations definition', *Public Relations Review*, Winter: 36.

Heath, R.L. and Nelson, R.A. (1986) *Issues Management: Corporate Policymaking in an Information Society*, Beverly Hills: Sage, p. 37.

IPR (Institute of Public Relations) (1991) 'Public Relations as a Career', pamphlet, London.

Jefkins, F. (1980, 1983, 1988, 1992) *Public Relations*, London: M&E Handbooks.

Jones, B.L. and Chase, H.W. (1979) 'Managing Public Policy Issues', *Public Relations Review*, 5(4): 11.

Kitchen, P.J. (1990) 'Let's hear it for brand X', *The Times Higher Education Supplement*, 16 February: 16.

Kitchen, P.J. (1991) 'Developing use of PR in a fragmented demassified market', *Market Intelligence and Planning*, 9(2), 29–33.

Kotler, P. and Mindak, W. (1978) 'Marketing and public relations', *Journal of Marketing*, 42(4): 13–20.

Kotler, P. (1986) 'Megamarketing', *Harvard Business Review*, 64(2).

Kotler, P. (1991) *Marketing Management*, 9th edn, Englewood Cliffs, NJ: Prentice-Hall, pp. 621–48.

Kotler, P. (1988) *Marketing Management*, 8th edn, Englewood Cliffs, NJ: Prentice-Hall, pp. 655–60.

Kreitzman, L. (1986) 'Projecting an image', *Marketing*, 25 September: 59–61.

Lesly, P. (ed.) (1950) *Public Relations Handbook*, New York: Prentice-Hall.

Lesly, P. (ed.) (1983) *Lesly's Public Relations Handbook*, Englewood Cliffs, NJ: Prentice-Hall.

Linstead, S. and Turner, K. (1986) 'Business sponsorship of the arts: corporate image and business policy', *Management Research News*, 9(3): 11–13.

Long, J.C. (1924) *Public Relations: A Handbook of Publicity*, New York: McGraw-Hill.

Marcus, A.A. and Kaufman, A.M. (1988) 'The continued expansion of the corporate public affairs function', *Business Horizons*, 31(2), March/April: 58–62.

Mayer, M. (1961) *Madison Avenue, USA*, Harmondsworth: Penguin, p. 309.

McCauley, H.S. (1922) *Getting Your Name in Print*, New York: Funk and Wagnalls.

Merims, A.M. (1972) 'Marketing's stepchild: product publicity', *Harvard Business Review*, 36(5), November/December: 107–13.

Newman, K. (1983) 'Financial communications and the contested takeover bid, 1958–1982', *International Journal of Advertising*, 2(1): 47–68.

O'Hare, F.J. (1954) 'A Reference Guide to the Study of Public Opinion', unpublished doctoral thesis, Columbia University.

Post, J.E., Murray, E.A., Dickie, R.B. and Mahon, J.F. (1982) 'The public affairs function in American corporations: development and relations with corporate planning', *Long Range Planning*, 15(2): 12–21.

Priestley, J.B. (1984) *The Image Men*, Allison.

Rice, M. (1980) 'Press agents that became part of a management team', *Campaign*, August: 33–49.

Robinson, C. (1931) 'The new science of public opinion management', *Harvard Business School Alumni Association Bulletin*, July: 232–37.

Seitel, F.P. (1992) *The Practice of Public Relations*, 5th edn, Oxford: Maxwell Macmillan, pp. 301–27.

Sheth, J.N., Gardner, D.M. and Garrett, D.E. (1988) *Marketing Theory: Evolution and Evaluation*, New York: John Wiley, pp. 96–105.

Shimp, T.A. (1989) *Promotion Management and Marketing Communications*, 2nd edn, Forth Worth, Phil.: Dryden Press.

Smith, H. (1915) *Publicity and Progress*, New York: George H. Doran.

Walker, A. (1988) 'The public relations literature: a narrative of what's been published by and about the profession, 1922–1988', *Public Relations Quarterly*, Summer: 27–31.

Walker, A. (1978) 'Public relations bibliography: sixth edition, 1976–1977', *Public Relations Review*, Winter: 1.

White, J. (1991) *How to Understand and Manage Public Relations*, London: Business Books, pp. 94–109.

Wright, J.H. and Christian, B.H. (1949) *Public Relations in Management*, New York: McGraw-Hill.

Zikmund, W.T. and D'Amico, B. (1988) *Marketing*, 2nd edn, New York: John Wiley.

4

A STRATEGIC PERSPECTIVE FOR PUBLIC RELATIONS

Danny Moss and Gary Warnaby

CHAPTER AIMS

- to investigate how the concepts of strategy and strategic management can be applied in the public relations context
- to examine to what extent organisations within the UK treat public relations as a strategically important function
- to examine how public relations can, in practice, contribute significantly to the development of effective corporate and business strategies

ILLUSTRATION: BRENT SPAR – CRISIS COMMUNICATIONS

The strategic importance of the public relations function is perhaps most graphically illustrated when organisations face a crisis which may threaten their competitive position and, in some cases, their very survival. It is at such times that organisations often find themselves exposed to both intensive media and public scrutiny, with every move they make being carefully dissected and subject to critical examination by different stakeholder groups who perceive themselves to have a vested interest in the outcome of the incident. The recent (1995) problems which Shell (UK) faced over the planned disposal of its Brent Spar oil storage platform in the Atlantic Ocean can be seen as a classic example of just such a crisis situation in which the company was widely criticised for its failure to appreciate the strength of opposition to its plans for the disposal of the Brent Spar platform.

The Brent Spar incident saw Shell put on trial in the 'court' of world opinion and found wanting. Shell's problems stemmed not so much from a lack of awareness that environmental pressure groups such as Greenpeace might oppose their plans, but resulted from its management's miscalculation of the likely scale of the public opposition to their plans for the deep water disposal of the Brent Spar platform. The fact that scientific studies had shown that deep water disposal of the platform was the most environmentally safe option appears to have blinkered Shell's management to the fact that such evidence did not impress environmental pressure groups such as Greenpeace. As a result of a high-profile campaign to stop Shell proceeding with its plans to sink the platform in the Atlantic, the company was forced to abandon its original plans and seek an alternative and more costly on-shore disposal option. Had Shell taken more effective soundings among the media and public in the UK and throughout Europe, its management might have realised the likely strength of opposition to its original disposal plans, and might have been better prepared to combat Greenpeace's campaign of opposition.

This case illustrates the potential importance of public relations strategic counsel when organisations are confronted with issues that have the potential to damage their reputation and their standing among those stakeholders on whom they depend for their success or, in extreme cases, their very survival.

INTRODUCTION

Despite the growing volume of literature devoted to the subject of strategy that has emerged over the past thirty years, public relations has rarely been acknowledged by management scholars as having a strategically important role to play within the strategic management function of organisations. In this chapter we will attempt to show how public relations can contribute to the more effective formulation and implementation of organisational strategies at both the corporate and competitive levels. Moreover, we will argue that the nature of the environment in which many organisations operate today, in which increasingly powerful environmental and single-issue pressure groups as well as governments exercise increasing influence over the activities of corporations, has forced organisations to put the management of their communications firmly on the strategic agenda. We will begin this chapter by reviewing how thinking about the concept of strategy and strategic management has evolved in recent years, before going on to examine how the strategic role of the public relations function can be conceptualised. Here we will draw on both management and public relations theories to identify a model which can help to explain where and how public relations can contribute to the strategic management process. Here we will draw, in particular, on the work of Grunig et al. (1992) whose study of 'excellence' in public relations and communications management offers perhaps the clearest articulation to date of a conceptual framework for understanding how public relations can contribute to the strategic management function and also of how public relations itself can be managed strategically.

In examining how the concept of strategy has been treated in the literature, the chapter will review and contrast the linear, adaptive and interpretive models of strategy (Chaffee, 1985), and will attempt to show how thinking about strategy has moved towards a more integrated view of these models. In terms of public relations strategy-making, as will be shown, the predominant view found within the public relations literature is that of strategy as a form of 'strategic planning'. The model of strategy-making suggested in this chapter challenges this predominantly linear perspective and suggests that the strategic role of public relations is far more clearly identified when strategy is considered from the adaptive and/or interpretive perspectives.

In terms of competitive strategy-making, the chapter challenges whether the concept of 'generic strategies' advanced by Porter (1980; 1985) which have tended to dominate thinking about competitive strategy in recent years do, in fact, reflect how most firms approach the task of creating competitive advantage. Here the chapter examines Kay's (1993) arguments about the importance of building successful strategies around the distinctive competencies that firms possess. Kay's distinctive competencies framework is used as the basis for exploring how public relations can help support the development of successful competitive strategies.

In the final section of the chapter, we examine how public relations strategies can be themselves formulated and here we argue that the traditional linear planning perspective, advanced by public relations scholars such as Grunig and Repper (1992), is of limited value in explaining how such strategies may be formulated in all situations.

DEFINING THE CONCEPT OF STRATEGY

One of the major themes that recurs throughout the strategy literature is that of the role of strategy as a continuous and adaptive response to external opportunities and threats that may confront an organisation (e.g. Argyris, 1985; Mintzberg, 1989; Steiner and Miner, 1977). A broad consensus exists within the management literature that strategy is essentially concerned with a process of managing the interaction between an organisation and its external environment so as to ensure the best 'fit' between the two. From this perspective, it can be argued that the public relations function has the potential to make an important contribution to strategic management through its role at the interface between an organisation and its environment. Here, for example, Grunig and Repper (1992) argue that public relations is able to contribute to organisational strategy by helping 'to manage potential conflict and assisting in building relationships with those strategic publics who may limit the autonomy of the organisation [to attain its goals]' (Grunig and Grunig, 1992:312). We will consider how this role of public relations can be best understood in more detail later in this chapter.

First, however, it be may useful to consider some of the more important recent developments in thinking about the concept and process of strategy-making which provide the context for examining the strategic role of public relations. To this end, this chapter examines a number of conceptual frameworks which may help in analysing where and how public relations can contribute to the overall strategic management of organisations and the achievement of their strategic goals. This analysis may help us to define the characteristics of strategy and strategic management in the public relations context.

WHAT IS STRATEGY?

Despite the prodigious volume of literature devoted to the subject of strategy that has emerged over the past thirty years, a comprehensive, consensus definition of strategy has remained elusive. In fact, there are almost as many different definitions of strategy as there are writers on the subject. Hambrick (1983) suggests two main reasons for this lack of consensus: first, strategy is a multidimensional concept; and secondly, strategy is inherently situational and will, as a consequence, tend to vary by industry.

Therefore, rather than striving to identify a single comprehensive definition of strategy, it may be more useful to focus on identifying those areas of broad agreement about what constitutes the basic dimensions of strategy. Here, it may be

45

useful to consider two alternative approaches to defining strategy, namely those suggested by Mintzberg (1991) and Kerin et al. (1990).

In recognising the multifaceted nature of strategy, Mintzberg (1991) accepts that it is extremely difficult to identify a single comprehensive definition of the concept. He thus suggests five alternative, yet related, definitions of strategy which he terms the five 'Ps': strategy as a 'plan', a 'ploy', a 'pattern', a 'position' and a 'perspective'. Here, Mintzberg argues that each of these 'definitions' of strategy holds different implications as to how the content and the nature of the process of strategic decision-making are understood.

In proposing these five alternative, yet complementary, definitions of strategy, Mintzberg (1991:12) looked to extend our understanding of the strategy beyond the frequently adopted 'planning' perspective – the view of strategy as some sort of 'consciously intended course of action, a guideline (or set of guidelines) to deal with a situation'. Thus Mintzberg's five definitions embrace ideas of the sometimes emergent nature of strategy (strategy as a 'pattern'); of strategy as a means of locating an organisation in its environment (strategy as a 'position'); of strategy as a concept within the head of the individual strategist (strategy as a 'perspective'); and the idea that strategy can sometimes be seen as simply a manoeuvre for outwitting competitors (strategy as a 'ploy') (1991:12–17).

Mintzberg (1991) emphasises the interrelated nature of these definitions and stresses that by recognising these multiple perspectives of strategy, it is possible to construct a more complete and coherent picture of the strategy process. This view is echoed by Christensen et al. (1982) who suggest that one of the most difficult aspects of strategic management is reconciling the implications of the different components of strategy into a coherent whole.

Kerin et al. (1990) adopt a contrasting approach. Building on earlier work by Hax and Majluf (1988), they analysed a number of definitions of strategy advanced by various authors from which they derived six key dimensions of strategy which are summarised below (1990:8–10):

1 Strategy is a means of establishing the organisational purpose (in terms of its long-term objectives, action programmes, and resource allocation priorities).
2 Strategy defines the competitive domain of the firm. In other words, one of the central concerns of strategy is defining the business the firm is in or should be in.
3 Strategy is a response (continuous and adaptive) to external opportunities and threats and internal strengths and weaknesses that affect the organisation.
4 Strategy is a central vehicle for achieving competitive advantage.
5 Strategy engages all the hierarchical levels of the firm: corporate, business and functional.
6 Strategy is a motivating force for the stakeholders (such as shareholders, debt-holders, managers, employees, customers, communities, government, and so forth) who directly or indirectly receive the benefits or costs derived from the actions of the firm.

While these six dimensions of strategy are not directly comparable with Mintzberg's five 'Ps', the ideas that they contain are embodied, to a greater or lesser degree, in the alternative definitions of strategy suggested by Mintzberg. Thus, for example, the idea of strategy as 'defining the competitive domain of the firm' is clearly embodied in Mintzberg's definition of strategy as a 'position', and the idea of strategy as a means of establishing the organisational purpose conveys a very similar view of strategy to that of Mintzberg's definition of strategy as a 'perspective'.

PERSPECTIVES OF STRATEGY

Kerin et al.'s dimensions of strategy can be seen to be broadly comparable with what Chaffee (1985) identifies as broad 'areas of agreement' about how strategy should be defined or understood. However, Chaffee suggests that beyond these areas of broad consensus, agreement tends to break down among strategy scholars. Indeed, in recent years some aspects of these so-called 'areas of agreement' have come under increasingly critical scrutiny themselves. For example, Pettigrew (1992) has challenged whether the second of these areas of agreement – the implied separation of content of strategy from the process of strategy formulation – reflects the reality of strategy-making practices, arguing that content and process issues cannot be so easily separated. Recognising the fluid nature of the debate about strategy and the strategy process, Chaffee identifies three distinct 'clusters' of strategy definitions and approaches to strategy – 'linear strategy', 'adaptive strategy' and 'interpretive strategy'. Examining each of these three approaches or perspectives briefly will reveal something of the contested nature of the current debate about how the concept of strategy should be understood.

Linear strategy

The linear approach emphasises the planning aspect of strategy. Strategy is seen as a form of methodical, directed, sequential planning which contributes to a rational decision-making process with the overall aim being the achievement of pre-stated goals. This view of strategy embraces the 'purposeful' dimension of strategy expressed in definitions such as those developed by Chandler (1962). This linear strategy model is based, however, on a number of inherent assumptions which management scholars have increasingly called into question. First, that the organisation needs to be structured in a formal way so that all decisions made at the top can be implemented throughout the organisation. Secondly, it is assumed that organisations are operating in a relatively predictable environment, or that the organisation is well insulated from environmental forces – such conditions being deemed necessary because of the time-consuming and forward-looking nature of the planning process. Thirdly, managers are assumed to act in a more or less rational manner and have access to the necessary information on which to base their decisions. The reality of these assumptions underpinning the concept of linear strategy have been increasingly challenged by authors such as Eisenhardt and Zbaracki (1992) and Pettigrew (1992) who have highlighted the doubts raised earlier by a number of other scholars (e.g. Cyert and March, 1963; Nutt, 1984) about whether managers do, in fact, act in an entirely rational manner in making strategic decisions. Rather, empirical research seems to suggest that most managers tend to act only in 'boundedly rational' manner. As Eisenhardt and Zbaracki (1992) argue:

'these traditional [linear] paradigms rest on tired debates about single goals and perfect rationality, and on unrealistic assumptions about how people think, behave and feel' (1992:18).

Adaptive strategy

The adaptive approach, on the other hand, emphasises the importance of strategy as a means by which organisations seek to respond to the changing nature of their environment. Here, for example, Hofer (1973) emphasises the role of strategy in helping firms to match their existing strengths and capabilities to the opportunities and risks present in the external environment. This idea of strategy as a means of 'matching' an organisation to its environment is a central theme of the adaptive view of strategy.

This view of strategy assumes that the environment is much more dynamic and less susceptible to prediction than is assumed within the linear model and, as a result, the organisation must change, or adapt to, the environment rather than attempt to impose its strategy on it. The adaptive approach to strategy formation is seen as more continuous and iterative than the linear approach and corresponds to the notion of 'incrementalism', first articulated by Lindblom (1959) and later popularised by Quinn (1980). The adaptive model necessarily involves the organisation taking into account a greater number of external variables than might be the case with linear approaches and also requires a greater propensity for change than does the linear model. Strategy-making, from this perspective, also emphasises the importance of the role of the 'actors' in the process.

Interpretive strategy

Like the adaptive approach, the interpretive approach also emphasises the idea of strategy as a means by which organisations seek to manage their relationship with the environment. However, the interpretive approach emphasises the idea of management holding a 'cognitive map' – a 'world view' which colours how managers interpret the changes an organisation faces and the responses they adopt to them (Weick, 1987). From this perspective, the formulation of strategy will be determined to a large degree by the way in which organisational culture and individual value systems affect the management's perceptions of the situation the organisation faces, and type of responses that are seen to be appropriate. The interpretive approach is also based on a 'social contract' view of strategy, portraying the organisation as 'a collection of co-operative agreements entered into by individuals with free will' (Chaffee, 1985:93). Here, the organisation's existence is seen as relying on its ability to attract enough individuals to co-operate in mutually beneficial exchange relationships. This model of strategy can be seen to correspond to the 'stakeholder perspective' of strategy, examples of which can be found articulated in the definitions of strategy advanced by authors such as Andrews (1987) and Chaffee (1985).

The main characteristics of each of these three perspectives or models of strategy in terms of their emphasis, underlying assumptions and the processes involved are summarised in Table 4.1.

Table 4.1 Types of strategy

	Strategy Model		
	Linear	*Adaptive*	*Interpretive*
Emphasis			
	Methodical, directed, sequential, rational planning process	Importance of link between company and environment	Open-systems perspective emphasises role of strategy in shaping the attitudes of stakeholders towards the organisation and its outputs
	Overall aim is the achievement of pre-stated goals	Firms seek to 'match' existing strengths and capabilities to opportunities and risks	Emphasises the idea of managers holding a 'cognitive map' or 'worldview' which influences their interpretation of environmental changes
		Continuous iterative, strategy-making process	Corresponds to stakeholder perspective of strategy
Assumptions			
	The company is formally structured to facilitate implementation of strategic plans	The environment is more dynamic and less susceptible to prediction	Strategy strongly influenced by 'politics' and prevailing socio-cultural characteristics of company
	The environment is relatively predictable, or company is well insulated from environmental forces	The company must adapt to environment rather than attempt to impose its will on it	The company's success/ survival depends on balancing conflicting stakeholder interests
	Managers act in a more or less rational manner	Managers must take into account more external variables	Seeks legitimacy for the company's policies
Processes			
	Rational planning	Logical incrementalism, or emergent strategy	Seeks to deal with the environment through symbolic actions and communications Emphasises negotiation and bargaining to achieve consensus

INTEGRATING THE DIFFERENT APPROACHES

Chaffee (1985) recognised the need to consider these various approaches not simply as distinct alternatives, but as a set of hierarchically related approaches that represented differing levels of sophistication in strategy-making. Thus, Chaffee suggests that organisations might initially rely largely on linear planning approaches, but might then progress to adaptive and then interpretive approaches to strategy-making as they become more sophisticated and adept at strategic management. While little empirical research has been conducted into whether and how organisations may attempt to integrate different approaches to strategy-making, the rationale underpinning the case for such integration is a powerful one. As Chaffee (1985:96) argues:

> It is important to integrate each lower level model with models that represent more complex systems because organisations exhibit properties of all levels of systems complexity. Adaptive and interpretive models that ignore less complex strategy models ignore the foundations on which they must be built if they are to reflect organisational reality. Furthermore, a comprehensive interpretive strategy probably requires some planning as would fit with a linear strategy and some organisational change as would fit with an adaptive strategy; and a viable adaptive strategy may well require some linear planning.

Here, Chaffee recognises that different approaches to strategy and the process of strategic management may not be as mutually exclusive in real-world conditions as some theorists might imply. Indeed, a recurring theme in the strategy literature is the need for the greater consideration of how many of the concepts proposed by strategy theorists can be operationalised. As Chaffee (1985:96) suggests, 'the full value of strategy cannot be realised in practical terms until theorists expand the construct to reflect the real complexities of organisations'.

IMPLICATIONS FOR PUBLIC RELATIONS

When examined from a public relations perspective, obvious parallels emerge between Chaffee's adaptive and interpretive approaches to strategy and strategy formulation and the 'open-systems' perspective of the role of public relations in organisations (e.g. Grunig and Hunt, 1984; Cutlip et al., 1993). Indeed, both the adaptive and interpretive perspectives of strategy are themselves based on an open-systems view of organisations in which the role of strategy is seen as the means by which organisations attempt to respond and adapt to environmental pressures and change within the overall business and social systems of which they form a part. While public relations scholars might argue that this systems perspective suggests an obvious role, at least theoretically, for public relations (as a boundary-spanning function) in 'enacting' the process of adaptation to environmental change, this role is not acknowledged within management perspectives of environmental interaction and strategy. In effect, public relations remains effectively 'hidden from view' with the responsibility for managing environmental interaction being seen as the prerogative of other management functions.

Before we go on to examine in more detail the contribution which public relations can make to the strategic management of organisations and how public relations is itself managed strategically, it may be worthwhile examining yet another, perhaps somewhat controversial view of different approaches to strategy – that advanced by Whittington (1993).

FOUR GENERIC APPROACHES TO STRATEGY

In what is an admittedly provocative and challenging text which emphasises the contested and imperfect nature of strategy, Whittington (1993) analyses what he defines as four 'generic' approaches to (business) strategy: *classical*, *evolutionary*, *processual*, and *systemic*. Whittington suggests that these approaches to strategy differ fundamentally along two dimensions: the *outcomes* of strategy and the *processes* by which strategy is made (1993:2). In terms of outcomes, he suggests strategies vary between, at one extreme, those which are directed towards profit-maximising goals (classical and evolutionary approaches) and, at the other extreme, those strategies that encompass a more pluralistic set of goals (processual and systemic approaches). The processes by which strategy is formulated, Whittington suggests, range between deliberate, calculated planning approaches (classical and to a lesser extent systemic) and unstructured, accidental, or emergent approaches (evolutionary and processual). Each of these approaches, Whittington argues, has quite different implications for how strategy is made and put into action. The characteristics of these four generic approaches are summarised in Table 4.2.

These four generic approaches to strategy identified by Whittington (1993) can be seen to be broadly comparable with the strategy approaches described by Chaffee (1985). However, where Whittington makes perhaps his most significant contribution to the debate about the nature of strategy is in the emphasis he places on the increasing importance of the 'systemic approach' to strategy and in his dismissal of the classical planning perspective of strategy in particular. For Whittington, the systemic approach, which emphasises the socio-cultural 'embeddedness' of strategy and strategy-making, represents the most appropriate and effective approach to strategy and strategy-making in the increasingly competitive and turbulent environments in which many organisations operate today. Whittington argues that developments such as the emergence of powerful Far Eastern economies, the breakdown of the traditional East–West divide within Europe, and the closer integration of Western economies have led to the dominance of the traditional 'Anglo-Saxon' model of strategy being increasingly challenged. These develop-

Table 4.2 Characteristics of Whittington's (1993) four generic strategy approaches

	Classical	Processual	Evolutionary	Systemic
Type of strategy	Formal	Crafted	Efficient	Socially embedded
Rationale	Profit maximising	Vague	Survival	Locally adapted
Focus	Internal (planning)	Internal (politics/cognitions)	External (market-focused)	External (societal focus)
Processes	Analytical planning	Bargaining learning	Darwinian	Socially orientated
Key influences	Economics military	Psychology	Economics biology	Sociology
Key authors	Chandler Ansoff Porter	Cyert and March Mintzberg Pettigrew	Hannah and Freeman Williamson	Granovetter Marris

ments, Whittington argues, have brought about an increasing recognition that 'the Anglo-Saxon model is no longer the archetype, but just one of many variants in an increasingly complex and competitive world' (1993:41). Given the socio-cultural emphasis of the systemic approach to strategy, public relations scholars might argue that it implies a potentially important role for public relations (at least theoretically), in terms of analysing and interpreting social and cultural differences within society and assisting management, in turn, to develop or adapt their strategies to suit them. Whether, in practice, public relations is capable of fulfilling, or allowed to fulfil, this role is, of course, a more contentious matter.

LEVELS OF STRATEGY

In the preceding sections of this chapter, we reviewed the debate about what can be seen as the generic nature of strategy and strategy formulation. However, before exploring how these different perspectives of strategy may influence how the role of public relations is defined, it may be useful to distinguish between the different 'levels of strategy' and to examine, in particular, what has generally been the main area of interest to strategy scholars, namely that of competitive or business strategy.

Conceptually, strategy has been considered in terms of a hierarchically organised structure in which the essential layers of any formal strategic planning process are seen to comprise the corporate, business and functional levels of strategy (e.g. Hax and Majluf, 1991). The articulation of such discrete hierarchies of strategy can be seen as typical of the linear perspective of strategy in particular. However, such distinctions between hierarchical levels of strategy (implicit within the linear perspective of strategy) have been subject to increasing criticism by many strategy scholars who have argued that such distinctions (between different levels of strategy) are becoming increasingly blurred and fail to reflect the reality of strategy-making in most organisations today (e.g. Pettigrew, 1992; Eisenhardt and Zbaracki, 1992).

While acknowledging such reservations, it must be noted that most strategy texts have adopted this hierarchical perspective, if only to provide a convenient theoretical and analytical framework for examining the characteristics of strategy at the corporate, business, and functional levels. Johnson and Scholes (1993) draw the following distinctions between corporate, business and operational or functional strategies.

Corporate strategy

Corporate strategy is concerned with what type of business a company as a whole should be in and is therefore concerned with decisions of scope. Corporate strategy may also be concerned with decisions regarding the acquisition or divestment of businesses or with the allocation of resources between a company's different businesses. Corporate strategy is also likely to be concerned with questions about the financial structure and organisational structure of a company as a whole. In other words, corporate strategy addresses issues which by their very nature affect the totality of the organisation. Hax and Majluf (1991:16) identify the critical importance of such decisions:

These are decisions that cannot be decentralised without running the risk of committing severe sub-optimisation errors. Those who operate at lower levels of the firm do not have the proper vantage point to make the difficult trade-offs required to maximise the benefits for the corporation as a whole, mainly when confronted with situations that affect adversely their own unit in the organisation.

Business or competitive strategy

Business or competitive strategy is concerned with determining how a company should compete in particular markets. Thus while corporate strategy is concerned with decisions about the organisation as a whole, competitive strategy is more likely to be concerned with various business units within the organisation. Here decisions may focus on such issues as whether to compete across a market as a whole or whether to focus on particular segments of the market. Competitive strategy decisions may also be concerned with how best to enter new markets, or how best to combat the threat from competitors in the markets in which the organisation operates.

Operational or functional strategy

Operational or functional strategy is concerned with how the various functions of an organisation – marketing, finance, personnel, manufacturing, and so on – contribute to the success of other levels of strategy. Such contributions can be extremely important, for example, in how the organisation seeks to be competitive. Here, for example, decisions about the quality of the products manufactured and the type of personnel employed can be critically important to an organisation's success. As Johnson and Scholes (1993:11–12) point out 'in most businesses, successful business strategies depend to a large extent on decisions which are taken, or activities which occur, at the operational level. The integration of operations and strategy is therefore of great importance'.

While it is generally recognised that all three levels of strategy need to be integrated closely together in order to ensure that an organisation is able to make optimum use of its resources and is able to compete effectively in its markets, it is undoubtedly at the competitive level that most academic interest has been focused and thus this level of strategy warrants closer examination.

COMPETITIVE STRATEGY

While corporate strategy focuses on determining what could be seen as the scope of an organisation's current and future business operations, competitive strategy, according to Ansoff, is concerned with 'specifying the distinctive approach which the firm intends to use in order to succeed in each of the strategic business areas' (1987:111). Competitive strategy has been described as 'the core level of strategy' because it is at this level that most competitive interaction occurs and where competitive advantage is ultimately won or lost (Montgomery and Porter, 1991:xiv).

Perhaps the most important and influential contribution to thinking about competitive strategy in recent years has been that of Harvard Business School professor, Michael Porter, whose two texts *Competitive Strategy: Techniques for Analysing Industries and Competitors* (1980) and *Competitive Advantage: Creating and Sustaining Superior Performance* (1985) have undoubtedly had a pervasive influence on thinking in this field. For Porter (1985:1), the emphasis on competition is all important:

> Competition is at the core of the success or failure of firms. Competition determines the appropriateness of a firm's activities that can contribute to its performance, such as innovations, a cohesive culture, or good implementation. Competitive strategy is the search for a favourable competitive position in an industry, the fundamental arena in which competition occurs. Competitive strategy aims to establish a profitable and sustainable position against the forces that determine industry competition.

Arguably, Porter's most important contribution lies in redefining the focus of competitive strategy-making away from the earlier reliance on matching external environmental analysis to the firm's internal strengths and weaknesses (i.e. the SWOT analysis), emphasising instead the importance of understanding the forces driving the intensity of competition in any industry. Thus for Porter, creating successful competitive strategies begins with a clear definition of what constitutes an industry and analysis of the forces driving the level of competition within it. The competitive forces he identified as determining industry profitability are: rivalry among existing competitors; the threat of entry of new competitors; the threat of substitutes; the bargaining power of suppliers; and the bargaining power of buyers (1980), as depicted in Figure 4.1.

Porter is, however, perhaps best known for his work on those 'generic competitive strategies', which determine the organisation's ability to create and maintain a level of performance that is above average for the industry within which it operates. Porter (1985:11) explains why firms seeking competitive advantage should pursue one or other of two generic strategies as follows:

> Though a firm can have a myriad of strengths and weaknesses *vis-à-vis* its competitors, there are two basic types of competitive advantage a firm can possess: low cost or differentiation. The significance of any strength or weakness a firm possesses is ultimately a function of its impact on relative cost or differentiation. Cost advantage and differentiation in turn stem from industry structure. They result from a firm's ability to cope with the five forces better than its rivals.

Porter goes on to combine these two basic types of competitive strategies with the scope of the organisation's activities to produce three generic strategy options: *overall cost leadership, differentiation;* and *focus*. Cost leadership and differentiation strategies seek competitive advantage in a broad range of industry segments, whereas focus strategies aim at a cost advantage (cost focus) or differentiation (differentiation focus) in a specific or narrow range of segments. Porter argues that these generic strategies offer the only viable ways of combating the effects of competitive forces and out-performing a firm's rivals in its industry.

54

EXTERNAL ENVIRONMENTAL FORCES

ECONOMIC ENVIRONMENT

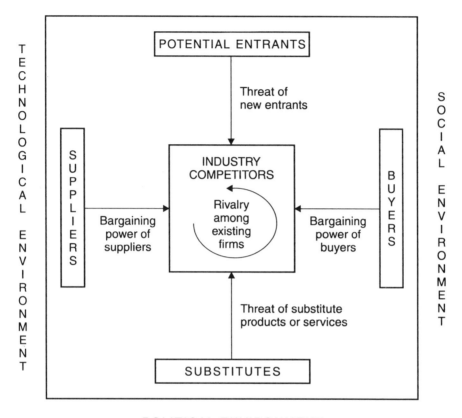

POLITICAL ENVIRONMENT

Figure 4.1 The five forces model for analysing the level of competition in an industry.
Source: Adapted from Porter (1980).

CRITIQUE FOR PORTER'S THEORIES

Despite their widespread use by academics and professionals, Porter's theories have not been accepted uncritically, and, indeed, they have come under fire from a number of commentators in recent years. For example, the five forces model has come in for a degree of general criticism (e.g. O'Shaughnessy, 1988; Speed, 1989; McDonald, 1992). Speed (1989) points out that the collective strength of the five basic competitive forces can vary tremendously in different industry situations, while O'Shaughnessy (1988:55) criticises the choice of the five forces which Porter's generic strategies are supposed to deal with:

Why only five forces? Porter believes that all other forces reflect themselves in his five forces. He even views government action as manifesting itself through these five forces. But could not such an argument be used to justify having fewer than five forces? Some marketers already claim that they implicitly take into account supplier power when fixing profit margins, while likely inroads by substitutes are acknowledged in determining market potential and growth.

O'Shaughnessy also questions Porter's suggestion that a choice must be made between seeking overall cost leadership and differentiation because the pursuit of differentiation inevitably raises costs (1988:55). He argues that there are numerous cases where a firm has gained differentiation through being the technological leader, yet gained overall cost leadership through economies of scale and experience curve effects.

Perhaps one of the most persuasive criticisms of Porter's ideas is found in McDonald's (1992) contention that while marketing tools and techniques such as those offered by Porter make a useful contribution to diagnosis, no one method can provide the solutions required by today's marketing managers. He emphasises the inherent dangers in over-reliance on a single device. While Porter's five forces model and the generic strategies have continued to represent a central focus in contemporary strategic thinking, they should perhaps be considered as representing a valuable set of guidelines rather than being treated as the definitive word on the subject.

GENERIC STRATEGIES OR DISTINCTIVE COMPETENCIES?

An alternative perspective to the conventional views of how organisations achieve competitive success is offered by London Business School Professor John Kay whose work focuses on the concept of 'distinctive competencies' (1993). Kay (1993) argues that corporate success results from careful appreciation of the unique strengths of the firm (its distinctive capabilities) in relation to the economic and market environment it faces.

In arguing that successful strategies are normally based around a firm's distinctive capabilities, Kay challenges Porter's (1980; 1985) ideas that the route to sustainable competitive advantage lies in the pursuit of one or other of what he defined as two main 'generic strategies' (cost leadership or differentiation) open to firms. Here Kay questions the underlying logic of Porter's arguments about the effectiveness of generic strategies, arguing instead that each firm's source of competitive advantage must be, by definition, unique otherwise it would not be sustainable. Here, Kay (1993:64) suggests that a firm can only achieve added value (a key measure of any firm's success) on the basis of some distinctive capability – some feature of its relationships (with customers, suppliers, etc.) which other firms lack or cannot readily reproduce. Drawing on his research among successful European firms, Kay identifies three types of distinctive capabilities which he argues have formed the basis on which many firms have founded their success. These Kay identifies as: *architecture, reputation* and *innovation*. Even where a firm lacks any distinctive capability, he argues it may still achieve competitive advantage, providing it holds a particular strategic asset – e.g. a concession to exploit a resource (De

Beers), or an exclusive licence to supply a product or service (British Gas, British Telecom, Deutsche Bundespost).

The chief characteristics of each of these distinctive capabilities together with an indication of the way in which they can provide a source of competitive advantage are summarised in Table 4.3. In each case, we have suggested the role that public relations may play in both helping to create and sustain these three types of distinctive capability.

Of course, as Kay points out, in order to build a successful strategy around a firm's distinctive capabilities, it is important to recognise that:

> A capability can only be distinctive if it is derived from a characteristic which other firms lack. Yet it is not enough for that characteristic to be distinctive. It is necessary also for it to be sustainable and appropriable. A distinctive capability is sustainable only if it persists over time. A distinctive capability is appropriable only if it exclusively, or principally, benefits the company that holds it. Often the benefits of a distinctive capability are appropriated instead by employees, by customers or by competitors (Kay, 1993:13–14).

Kay goes on to suggest that organisations will often use these distinctive capabilities in conjunction with one another rather than exclusively. Thus, reputations may originate from another source of competitive advantage, such as technological innovation, which may be transformed into reputation with time or may be augmented by it. Architecture, innovation and reputation, in isolation or in combination, are therefore seen as the foundation on which firms can build their competitive success. However, as Kay emphasises, organisations do not exist in a vacuum and a distinctive capability only becomes a competitive advantage 'when it is applied in an industry and brought to a market' (1993:14). The market and the industry have both product and geographic dimensions and these considerations are reflected in the nature of the strategic decisions that have to be made relating to the scope and direction of the organisation's activity, thereby providing the corporate context for these business level decisions.

In exploring the way in which public relations can contribute to the development of successful competitive strategies, we have focused, in particular, on Kay's distinctive competencies framework which not only suggests a more obvious role for public relations, but we also believe provides a more accurate reflection of the basis on which most organisations seek to create and sustain an advantage in the competitive environments in which they operate.

Having explored a number of different perspectives of strategy and examined some of the major debates about how strategy is formulated both at the corporate and competitive levels, we can now go on to explore the role which public relations can play in supporting the strategic management function and to look at how the strategic management of public relations itself can be conceptualised.

THE STRATEGIC POTENTIAL OF PUBLIC RELATIONS

While public relations scholars and professionals continue to make the claim that public relations should be treated as a strategically important function and argue

Table 4.3 Kay's distinctive capability framework for successful strategy development: the implications for the role of public relations (Kay, 1993)

Distinctive capabilities	Descriptive characteristics	Source of competitive advantage	Implications for public relations
Architecture	Comprises the 'network of relational contracts within or around a firm'. These may be: • Internal – e.g. with employees • External – e.g. with customers, suppliers or distributors • Networks – e.g. among a group of firms engaged in related activities	The value of architecture lies in its capacity to create organisational knowledge and routines which can result in more flexible responses to changing circumstances and the rapid and open exchange of information. To be an effective source of advantage, such knowledge must be distinctive to the individual firm. As all firms possess forms of internal and external architecture, it is the unique way in which firms create and use their relationships and network of contacts to enhance their position that gives rise to competitive advantage. Equally, it is the inability of competitors to replicate such architecture that allows the advantage derived to be sustained.	The creation and maintenance of internal and external architecture relies to a large degree on effective communications between the parties involved. Communications can be seen as the essential 'glue' which holds such relationships and networks together. Public relations is, arguably, the function best equipped to handle such communications on both an internal and external basis.
Reputation	The most important commercial mechanism for conveying information to customers and other stakeholders. Can be regarded as a more extensive form of architecture applied on a nationwide or even international scale. Reputation is influenced by: people's experiences of a firm and its products; how the firm presents itself; how employees, others and the media talk about it – the 'sum of the stories that people tell about it'.	The value of reputation lies in its influence on customer and other stakeholder groups' attitudes, perceptions and behaviour towards the firm/organisation. Specifically, in allowing an organisation to differentiate itself and its offering from its competitors and to charge premium prices vis-à-vis competitors products or services. Reputations are not immutable nor are they created easily and once established must be carefully preserved.	The management of reputation is generally recognised as core responsibility of public relations. Here the role of public relations includes: spreading knowledge of an organisation widely; promoting its attributes; and defending its reputation, where necessary, from misrepresentation and attack.
Innovation	Comprises the ability of firms to generate unique products or services that cannot be easily replicated by other firms and to sustain this innovative ability over time.	Undoubtedly the most difficult source of competitive advantage to sustain and can be both expensive and the outcomes uncertain. Success relies on the inability of other firms to replicate or imitate the new products or services introduced by the firm. Thus innovation tends to be used in conjunction with another distinctive capability – either reputation and or architecture.	While public relations may have no obvious role in the process of innovation, it can play an important part in disseminating information about new innovations and their uses and in supporting other distinctive capabilities that may be deployed in conjunction with that of innovation.

that 'public relations should have access to the boardroom', relatively little evidence can be found within the public relations literature of a coherent argument to explain how public relations should contribute to the strategy-making process in organisations or of how public relations itself should be managed strategically. Moreover, where the question of strategy is discussed within the literature, it is almost exclusively in terms of strategic planning.

In what is undoubtedly the most extensive examination of the strategic role of public relations conducted to date, Grunig et al. (1992) set out to present a case for public relations to be treated as a strategically important function and they suggest a model for the strategic management of public relations which, they argue, incorporates the dual role of public relations in the overall strategic management of organisations and in the strategic management of public relations itself (1992:124). However, as we will show, even though this theoretical model can be seen as a major step forward in developing a strategic perspective of public relations, the model has a number of serious limitations.

As has been suggested, the dominant view of strategy found within the public relations literature is that of strategy as a form of planning (e.g. Wilcox et al., 1986; Seitel, 1992; Cutlip et al., 1993). Here, most authors tend to portray the strategic planning process as a logical sequential process – that is, as a form of linear strategy approach. Little, if any, recognition can be found within the public relations literature of more recent debates among management scholars about alternative perspectives of strategy – that is, of adaptive, interpretive or systemic models of strategy. In this sense, public relations scholars have continued to adopt a relatively narrow perspective of the concept of strategy – one that limits the potential scope for public relations to contribute to the strategy-making process. Here it can be argued that when strategy is viewed from an adaptive or interpretive perspective, a more obvious case emerges for public relations having an important role to play in the strategic management process.

As was suggested earlier in this chapter, a central tenet of most strategy theories is the idea of strategy as the means by which organisations attempt to adapt to their environments. However, as we have also already highlighted, there is little, if any, acknowledgement in the management literature that public relations may have a significant role to play in the 'matching process' between environmental actors and forces, and the capabilities and competencies of the organisation. However, in reviewing how management scholars have attempted to explain the process of environmental adaptation or 'matching', Grunig and Repper (1992:122–3) argue that most management theories fail to explain fully how organisations actually go about managing their relationships with the 'environment':

> although writers on strategic management discuss the environment and make lists of its components, they seldom describe how the organisation should diagnose the environment or who in the organisation should observe the environment. Few, if any, of these writers recognise or describe the role of public relations in helping the organisation to identify – to 'enact' – the most important components of its environment.

Grunig and Repper go on to suggest that public relations, when managed as a strategically relevant function, can fill the 'environmental void' in theories of strategic management, but, equally, they recognise the need for public relations scholars to draw more heavily on strategic management theories to 'fill the "void" in public relations theories of how public relations can contribute to effective organisations' (Grunig and Repper, 1992:123).

The absence of any reference to a role for public relations in most strategic management theories points to the fact that for most management scholars, public relations simply does not enter into the 'strategic management equation' – it remains what Bell and Bell (1976) described as a largely 'functionary' activity. Broom (1986) has suggested that one reason why public relations has failed to gain greater recognition as a strategically important function is because of the existence of a 'closed-systems' ideology among the senior management in some organisations. Broom goes on to suggest that this type of orientation has tended to encourage an over-reliance on ritualistic communication in which there is little place for environmental scanning or other externally orientated activities. In such organisations, Broom (1986:16–17) argues, public relations is often isolated from management decision-making and is often 'subsumed by other functions and is cast in the role of technical support staff to implement programmes dictated by others' values and perceptions of the environment'.

However, Broom also suggests that the extent to which an organisation's environment is unstable, threatening, or both, may play an important part in determining the degree to which practitioners are likely to enact a management role and, by implication, be in a position to exert greater influence on the strategic decision-making process. However, given that such unstable environmental conditions are increasingly common today, the question remains as to why public relations appears to have made relatively little progress in establishing a more prominent role within the strategic management processes of many organisations.

THE BOUNDARY-SPANNING ROLE OF PUBLIC RELATIONS

Given that most strategy theories emphasise the importance of strategy as the means by which organisations attempt to adapt to their environments, there is an obvious need for strategic management to have a clear understanding of their organisation's environment and the forces driving environmental change. Environmental scanning is normally seen as the mechanism by which organisations seek to gather and analyse data about their environment. The process of environmental scanning is usually seen as one which is performed by 'boundary-spanning' personnel. This could potentially be one of the main roles carried out by public relations practitioners. White and Dozier (1992) argue that it is as boundary spanners that public relations practitioners are able to make perhaps their most important contribution to the strategic decision-making process, assisting organisations to manage exchanges across organisational-environmental boundaries.

Here, as boundary spanners, public relations practitioners can help support strategic decision-making in a number of important ways. First, because boundary-spanning practitioners operate at the interface between an organisation and its environment, they are ideally placed to assist management to keep abreast of, and alert to, the implications of any changes taking place within the organisation's environment, particularly in terms of identifying how such changes may impact on key stakeholder relationships. In this sense, public relations can be seen to function as the 'antenna' of the organisation, providing an early warning system to detect the emergence of issues which may have significant implications for the organisation's current or future strategies. Boundary-spanning practitioners can also help to bring a stakeholder perspective into the strategic decision-making process, representing the likely reaction of stakeholders to alternative strategy options, and thereby assisting management to give a more balanced consideration to the attractiveness and feasibility of the alternative options open to them.

Boundary-spanning practitioners can also play an important part in the implementation of corporate strategies by helping to communicate the organisation's strategic intentions to both internal and external stakeholders which may help avoid misunderstandings that might otherwise frustrate the smooth implementation of the organisation's strategy.

THE EXCELLENCE THEORY VIEW OF PUBLIC RELATIONS STRATEGY

Perhaps the clearest articulation to date of a theoretical framework for considering the strategic role of public relations is that contained in Grunig et al.'s (1992) work on 'excellence' in public relations. In developing a theory of 'excellence' Grunig and his co-researchers sought to identify a set of general attributes of excellent management which contribute to organisational effectiveness (by implication, organisational effectiveness can be seen as one of the key objectives of strategy), and then to identify their implications for the management of the communications and public relations functions. As a corollary, they sought to demonstrate how the performance of excellently managed public relations functions might contribute to improving an organisation's overall effectiveness (and by implication the achievement of organisational goals). Here, Grunig et al. (1992:65) argue that public relations contributes to organisational effectiveness by 'using communications programmes to build relationships with the strategic constituencies of an organisation – those constituencies that constrain or enhance an organisation's ability to achieve its goals'.

In developing a conceptual framework for understanding the strategic role of public relations Grunig and Repper (1992) adopt an essentially stakeholder perspective of strategy (akin to Chaffee's interpretive model) which implies that organisations recognise the interdependency between themselves and other organisations and groups in their environment. This (stakeholder) perspective implies that organisations will normally accept the need for a more pluralistic set of goals than is predicted by classical or linear planning theories of strategy. Thus, goal setting in such organisations will normally involve an attempt to balance profit maximising or satisficing imperatives against the anticipated social costs of the alternative strategies that might be adopted to achieve these goals. While classical strategic management theories tend to consider the environmental impact of strategies in terms of loosely defined, and often amorphous, concepts such as the 'social, economic and political environments', stakeholder theories of strategy focus more specifically on assessing how alternative strategies may affect a particular organisation's relationships with those stakeholders on whose support it relies. In this sense, stakeholder theories provide a more tangible focus for the assessment of the potential environmental impact of different strategies.

Thus Grunig and Repper see the role of strategy in terms of analysing, interpreting and responding to environmental pressures, while also recognising the need to balance various stakeholder interests. Here, public relations is seen to play a key role in managing relationships with all parts of an organisation's environment, or more specifically, with all key stakeholder publics active within the organisation's environment. Similarly, drawing on Whittington's (1993) analysis, Grunig and Repper's (1992) model of public relations strategy and strategic management can be seen to fit best within what Whittington terms the 'systemic perspective' of strategy, emphasising the need for strategists to remain sensitive to the socio-cultural environment in which their organisations operate.

However, despite the obvious parallels between Grunig and Repper's (1992) theoretical perspective of public relations strategy and strategic management and the adaptive, interpretive, and systemic perspectives of strategy described by Chaffee and Whittington, Grunig and Repper make no explicit reference to these management perspectives. More significantly, having articulated what can be seen as a largely adaptive or interpretive perspective of public relations strategy, Grunig and Repper then go on to suggest an essentially linear or classical model to explain the *processes* by which specific public relations strategies are formulated (see Figure 4.2). They appear to have ignored much of the recent debate within the management literature about the possibility that strategies may be developed in, for example, an incremental (Quinn, 1980) or emergent manner (Mintzberg, 1987; 1991).

This failure to consider alternative perspectives of the process of strategy-making can be seen as perhaps the most obvious weaknesses in Grunig and Repper's (1992) model of strategic management for public relations. In suggesting that public relations strategies are developed through what appears to be an essentially linear approach, the authors appear to have ignored the criticisms that have been voiced by many management scholars about the limitations of such linear perspectives of strategy-making. For example, as has already been pointed out, management scholars such as Cyert and March (1963) and, more recently, Eisenhardt and Zbaracki (1992) have questioned the underlying assumptions about the rationality of management decision-making that are implicit in such linear strategy models.

While it can be argued that virtually all organisations engage in some form of planning, at least in the short-term, management scholars, and perhaps most notably Mintzberg (1994), have argued that 'planning' and 'strategy' are not necessarily the same thing. In fact, Mintzberg (1994) makes a clear distinction between strategic planning and strategic thinking; the former, he argues, is about analysis and the latter is synthesis. Thus, Mintzberg (1994:107) argues that 'strategic planning, as it has been practised, has really been strategic programming, the articulation and elaboration of strategies, or visions that already exist'. While Mintzberg's arguments about the difference between strategic planning and

---

STAKEHOLDER STAGE

Identifying and analysing and managing strategically important stakeholder relationships

---

PUBLICS STAGE

Identifying those stakeholder groups who are affected by or whose actions may affect the organisation and who have recognised that a problem exists and have organised themselves to do something about it

---

ISSUES STAGE

Anticipating and analysing the likely emergence of issues that may arise out of the organisation's relationship with its various stakeholders and developing solutions to them

---

PUBLIC RELATIONS/COMMUNICATIONS PROGRAMMES AND PLANS

Public relations/communications programmes are formulated for different stakeholders or publics at each of the above stages (to maintain relationships with stakeholders; to help manage conflict with publics; and to help resolve issues). The formulation of programmes is seen to take place through a planning approach comprising the following steps:

1 The setting of formal communications objectives
2 Developing formal communications campaigns to accomplish the objectives
3 Implementation of the campaigns
4 Evaluation of the effectiveness of each campaign with respect to the predetermined objectives

Figure 4.2 Grunig and Repper's model of the strategic management of public relations.

Source: Adapted from Grunig and Repper (1992).

thinking have not gone unchallenged (e.g. Ansoff, 1992), they undoubtedly call into question the way in which the traditional role of strategic planning is understood.

On closer examination, however, it would be difficult to challenge the logic of the initial three (analytical) stages of Grunig and Repper's strategic management model (the stakeholder stage, the publics stage and the issues stage), at least from a strategic planning perspective, since they represent what is, arguably, the logical approach to identifying the fundamental problems or issues around which public relations strategies will tend to focus. Rather it is the sequential planning process that Grunig and Repper then suggest should be followed in formulating the specific communications strategies used to tackle these problems or issues that is open to more critical scrutiny. As management scholars have argued, the assumed rationality of such linear approaches does not always tally with the messy reality of strategy-making, in which strategies may sometimes only emerge incrementally, and perhaps only after considerable 'political in-fighting' among members of the decision-making team (e.g. Mintzberg, 1987; Whittington, 1993).

While it can be argued that the linear planning approach to strategy formulation may be a feasible option where organisations are operating in relatively simple and stable environments, as management scholars such as Mintzberg (1987, 1991) have suggested, linear approaches are unlikely to prove so effective where organisations are operating in more complex and dynamic environments. As Duncan (1972) has argued, when faced with highly complex and dynamic environmental conditions, managers are more likely to experience considerable uncertainty about the future, and hence, by implication, they are more likely to resort to more flexible and perhaps incremental approaches to strategy formation. Thus, while, in principle, Grunig and Repper's model of strategic management for public relations may describe a feasible approach to public relations strategy-making in relatively stable environments, it is more questionable as to whether it represents an appropriate model to describe how public relations strategies may be formulated where organisations are operating in more complex and dynamic environments.

It can be argued, then, that Grunig and Repper's model of public relations strategy and strategic management only goes part-way towards providing a comprehensive and positive framework for understanding the nature and process of strategy-making in public relations. Their model requires further elaboration to take on board recent developments in strategic management thinking, particularly in terms of considering the different processes by which strategies may be formulated. Here, we suggest their model not only requires greater recognition of the possibility that strategies may be formulated through emergent or incremental processes, but it also requires a more explicit recognition of the potential influence that internal 'micro-politics' may have on the process of strategic decision-making. There is a need to make more explicit the links between public relations strategy and corporate and competitive strategies. While it may be difficult to incorporate fully all of these considerations within a single model of public relations strategy-making, nevertheless, we believe that it is important to work towards the development of such a model in order to overcome some of the inherent weaknesses in current conceptualisations of public relations strategy-making.

A NEW MODEL OF STRATEGY AND STRATEGIC MANAGEMENT FOR PUBLIC RELATIONS

Drawing on Grunig and Repper's model and other conceptualisations of strategy and strategy-making which have been examined earlier, we have suggested an alternative model of the role of public relations in strategic management (see Figure 4.3) which attempts to overcome some of the chief weaknesses that have been highlighted in Grunig and Repper's model. In advancing a new conceptual model of public relations strategy and strategy-making the aim has been to develop an effective framework that might help in understanding better the nature of public

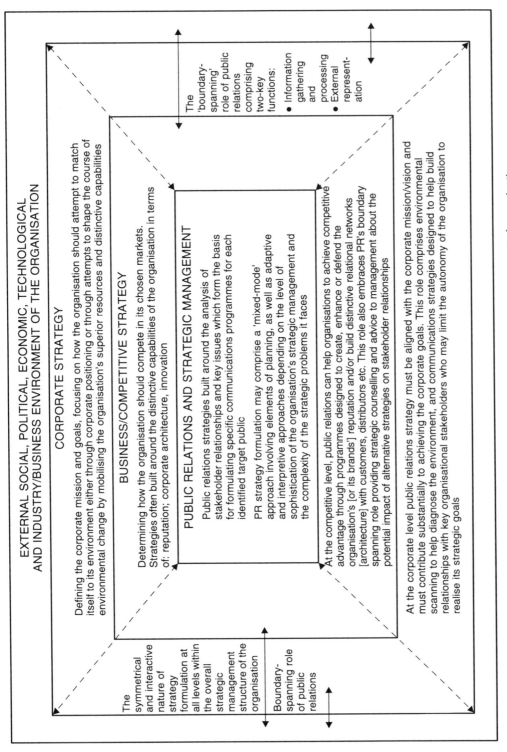

Figure 4.3 The role of public relations in the strategic management of organisations.

relations strategy and its position in relation to corporate and business strategy-making.

We have sought to draw on the work of Chaffee (1985), Kay (1993) and other management scholars whose ideas have been discussed earlier in this chapter, as well as building on the work of Grunig and Repper (1992) themselves. The model which has been proposed attempts to provide an integrating framework linking corporate, competitive and public relations strategy development. In this sense, the model recognises that for most organisations, strategy can be made for different groupings of individuals and tasks within the organisation, yet also recognises that these different *levels* of strategy should be seen as forming part of a coherent whole.

A fundamental presupposition underpinning this model is the belief that most organisations will tend to approach the task of strategy formulation from an essentially 'adaptive' or 'interpretive' perspective, rather than treating the process of strategy-making as simply an exercise in strategic planning. From this perspective, it is also assumed that most organisations will tend to adopt a more pluralistic set of goals, rather than being driven by purely profit-maximising imperatives. Here, the choice of specific strategies is seen as focusing around attempts to 'match' an organisation's distinctive capabilities to the opportunities and threats identified within its corporate and business environments. In this sense, our model builds on Kay's (1993) arguments about the basis on which successful strategies are constructed.

Thus, at the corporate level, public relations is seen as fulfilling an environmental scanning role, helping to identify and analyse important issues and stakeholder relationships which may be critical to the success of an organisation's strategic goals. The 'stakeholder dimension' of this role is seen as particularly important, and involves counselling senior management about how alternative strategy options may affect the organisation's relationships with its key stakeholders in the business and wider social environment. Through this analysis of stakeholder relationships, public relations practitioners can help management to anticipate the likely political and societal reaction to alternative strategy options, and thereby enable management to assess the potential attractiveness and viability of those strategies under consideration. When effectively integrated within the total strategy-making process, public relations/communications programmes can also be seen to act as the essential 'glue' (Grunig, 1992) which holds organisations together and links their corporate level strategies to those developed at the business and operational levels.

At the business or competitive strategy level, the main role of public relations is seen as that of supporting the development of 'distinctive capability-based' strategies (Kay, 1993). Here, public relations strategies will tend to focus around supporting the creation or, more often, the enhancement of those distinctive capabilities that an organisation already possesses (see Figure 4.4). Thus, public relations strategies are seen as directed towards building and maintaining the network of relational contracts (architecture) both within and around the organisation, and/or helping to build and enhance the organisation's reputation and that of its products or services within its target markets. To this end, public relations strategies will tend to focus on the key stakeholder relationships and issues that may constrain or enhance an organisation's ability to maintain or improve its position within its markets, and to achieve its business goals.

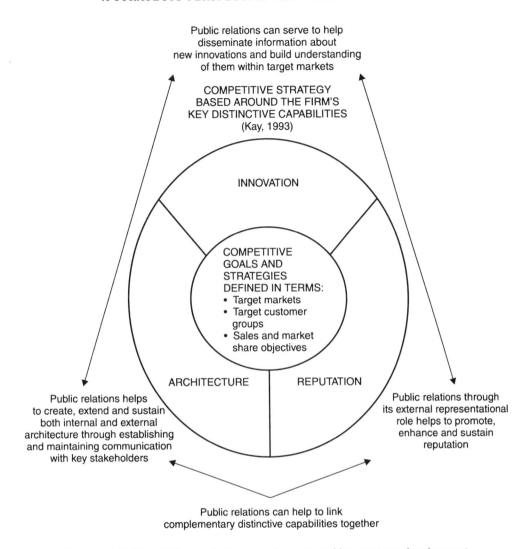

Figure 4.4 Public relations role in supporting competitive strategy development.

The central premise of the model is that public relations strategies should be viewed in the context of the corporate and business strategies from which they derive their essential purpose and to whose success they will ultimately contribute. The operationalisation of an organisation's public relations strategy is seen as focusing around the creation of specific communications programmes that will ultimately aim to build or enhance the organisation's relationships with its strategically important stakeholder publics, or, in some cases, counter or deflect any opposition to its policies from other stakeholder publics. Here, strategically important stakeholder publics are defined as those individuals, groups, or institutions whose support or acquiescence the organisation requires in order to realise its corporate and business goals. While these public relations/communications programmes will tend to be characteristically two-way asymmetrical in nature – using persuasive communication to try to influence the attitudes and, ultimately, the behaviours of particular stakeholder publics – they may also take the form of two-way symmetrical communications which may seek, through dialogue, to resolve areas of actual or potential conflict between an organisation and particular stakeholder publics.

The process of developing these communications programmes will involve the initial identification and analysis of both the stakeholder relationships and 'issues' that are likely to affect the organisation's current and future success. It is recognised that the initial three stages in Grunig and Repper's (1992) strategic management model – the stakeholder, publics and issues stages – provide a useful description of the key stages of analysis around which strategic communications decisions and plans are likely to be based. However, where this model departs from that advanced by Grunig and Repper is in the way in which it views the approach to formulating the specific public relations/communications strategies that will be used to help achieve the organisation's goals. As has been suggested earlier, we believe that the linear planning approach which Grunig and Repper appear to suggest characterises the development of these communications strategies and programmes, represents far too prescriptive a view of the process involved and fails to acknowledge the often fluid nature of the process of strategy formulation. As has been shown, this linear view of strategy fails to acknowledge the influence of factors such as perceived uncertainty about the future (e.g. Duncan, 1972; Eisenhardt and Zbaracki, 1992) or the internal micro-politics within organisations (e.g. Pettigrew, 1992), which will often militate against the adoption of purely linear approaches to strategy formulation.

Although, the model described in Figure 4.3 appears to suggest three distinct levels of strategy-making, we believe that strategy-making at these three levels should be recognised as forming a part of a more or less integrated system of decisions and actions directed towards achieving a commonly agreed set of goals. Thus corporate level strategy provides the context for the formation of an organisation's business strategies, and public relations strategy both contributes to the effective development of these two other levels of strategy, as well as deriving its own rationale and purpose from them.

Of course, like all models, the model of strategy and strategy-making that has been outlined here is inevitably an abstraction of what, in reality, can often be a highly complex process of decision-making and actions. Clearly, we recognise that the model cannot hope to capture fully the potentially wide variations in the way in which different organisations may approach the development of their corporate, business and public relations strategies. In this sense it must be recognised as representing an essentially conceptual view of how corporate, business and public relations strategies may be related in practice. However, we believe that this model does provide a sound conceptual framework for exploring in more detail the reality of how public relations may fit into the overall pattern of strategy-making in organisations. Moreover, we believe that this model does overcome many of the weaknesses inherent in many of the linear strategy models that have been advanced in the literature to date.

STRATEGY FORMULATION – NARROWING THE STRATEGIC FOCUS

In considering how practitioners formulate communication strategies to address organisational problems, we have expanded Grunig and Repper's model extending their strategic analysis stage, in particular, to incorporate three additional elements, organisational/industry context, timing and media pressures, which, while implicit in Grunig and Repper's model, we believe, warrant more explicit recognition (see Figure 4.5). Clearly, the particularly type of organisation or industry in which an organisation operates is likely to play a major part in determining the type of stakeholders and issues which are likely to present the greatest threats to an organisation. Thus, for example, companies operating in the oil or chemical industries are more likely to find themselves in conflict with environmental pressure groups and are perhaps more likely to encounter difficulties in dealing with government organisations than those in less sensitive/high profile industries. Timing considerations are also likely to be an important factor affecting the magnitude of the problems an organisation may be confronted with and the speed of response that is required. Here, for example, an organisation may face situations where there is a need for rapid action to avert an issue escalating into a full-scale crisis, and hence there may be considerable pressure on management to agree on an appropriate response strategy. Finally, the media, as has been acknowledged earlier, have become increasingly influential over the years and are capable of accelerating the development of an issue by giving it the 'oxygen of publicity'. Hence, thorough analysis of the media coverage of emerging issues that may affect the realisation of an organisation's goals should form an integral part of the strategic analysis process.

From this analysis of stakeholders, publics and issues, it should then be possible to narrow the strategic focus of the communications/public relations function to identify the specific problems and priorities for action. Once the strategic priorities and key objectives for public relations have been identified, the task of formulating an appropriate response strategy can begin. Here, as has been suggested, a combination of planning, adaptive/incremental approaches, or, in some cases, more strongly interpretive approaches may be required. For example, where organisations are perhaps dealing with particularly complex and rapidly changing situations, it may be impossible to rely on formal planning approaches, since strategies may have to be developed 'on the run' as events unfold – in an adaptive or incremental mode. Equally, some situations may demand that organisations focus primarily on winning support from strategically important stakeholders who may have the power to prevent the organisation pursuing its goals. Here the prime aim of the organisation's strategy may be to gain legitimacy for itself and its policies in the eyes of these key stakeholder groups. Thus Shell's problems in handling the Brent Spar incident could be seen to have required a strongly interpretive approach in order to combat the widespread opposition to its plans for the disposal of its oil storage rig.

In summary, therefore, the process of strategy formulation which we have

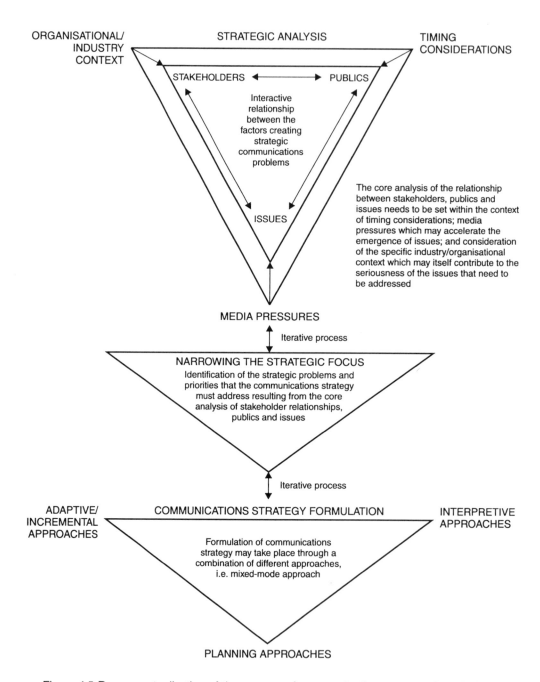

Figure 4.5 Re-conceptualisation of the process of communications strategy formulations.

suggested here is intended to capture a sense of the often fluid nature of strategy formulation which may often involve an essentially iterative approach in which various options are considered and balanced in the light of the prevailing external and internal pressures experienced by strategists. Strategy formulation needs to be recognised as an inherently human decision-making process and, as such, is always likely to be subject to the individual and collective biases and predispositions of the 'human actors' at its centre. It is this fact that makes it almost impossible to prescribe how strategy is or should be formulated in all organisations.

Clearly, there are dangers in attempting to represent such a potentially complex process as strategy-making within any one model. Inevitably there is a tendency to convey the impression that strategy is developed through what may appear to be an essentially sequential linear process, whereas, in practice, as many writers have argued, strategies may often be developed in a far from linear fashion (e.g. Mintzberg, 1987, 1991; Quinn, 1980). However, we believe that the model advanced does, at least, go some way to capturing a sense of how strategies may be formulated in many organisations.

SUMMARY AND CONCLUSIONS

In this chapter we have advanced a conceptual framework for understanding how public relations can contribute to the strategic management function in organisations and for understanding how public relations should itself be managed strategically. We have highlighted the weaknesses in much of the current public relations literature with respect to defining the concept of strategy and strategic management and explaining how these concepts might be applied to the public relations function. As we have argued, much of the discussion of the strategy in the public relations context, appears to be rooted in a rather narrow and somewhat outdated perspective of strategy and strategic management – one that emphasises largely a (linear) planning view of the strategic management process. And we have argued, more recent conceptualisations of strategy and strategic management (e.g. adaptive, interpretive and systemic models) would appear to offer a more realistic view of how organisations approach the task of formulating and managing their strategic development and these perspectives can also be seen to suggest an obvious role for public relations, albeit one that management scholars have, as yet, failed to acknowledge.

DISCUSSION TOPICS

1 What are the dimensions of the concept of strategy?
2 How useful are the various perspectives on strategy in advancing our understanding of the concept of strategy?
3 What are the implications of the linear, adaptive and interpretive strategy perspectives for advancing our understanding of the strategic potential of public relations?
4 From a public relations perspective, does Porter's generic strategies or Kay's distinctive competencies offer the most appropriate conceptualisation of competitive strategy?

5 Why has public relations not been able to achieve its potential as a strategically important function?

6 Evaluate the strategic importance of the boundary-spanning role of public relations.

7 Assess the model of public relations strategy by Grunig and Repper put forward in Grunig's: *Excellence in Public Relations and Communications Management.*

8 From a public relations perspective, to what extent are the levels of strategy mutually exclusive?

9 How far can public relations contribute to competitive strategy?

10 Is public relations a strategically important function?

REFERENCES

Andrews, K.R. (1987) *The Concept of Corporate Strategy,* Burr Ridge, Ill.: Richard D. Irwin.

Ansoff, H.I. (1987) *Corporate Strategy,* rev'd edn, Harmondsworth: Penguin.

Ansoff, H.I. (1992) 'Critique of Henry Mintzberg's *The Design School:* reconsidering the basic premises of strategic management', *Strategic Management Journal,* 12: 449–61.

Argyris, C. (1985) *Strategy Change and Defensive Routines,* Marshfield, MA: Pitman Publishing.

Bell, S.H. and Bell, E.C. (1976) 'Public relations: functional or functionary?', *Public Relations Review,* 2(2): 51.

Broom, G.M. (1986) 'Public relations roles and systems theory: functional and historicist causal models', Paper presented at the meeting of the Public Relations Interest Group, International Communications Association, Chicago.

Chandler, A.D. (1962) *Strategy and Structure: Chapters in the History of American Industrial Enterprise,* Cambridge, MA: The MIT Press.

Chaffee, E.E. (1985) 'Three models of strategy', *Academy of Management Review,* 19(1): 89–98.

Christensen, C.R., Andrews, K.R., Bower, J.L., Hamermesh, R.G. and Porter, M.E. (1982) *Business Policy: Text and Cases,* Burr Ridge, Ill.: Richard D. Irwin.

Cutlip, S., Center, A. and Broom, G. (1993) *Effective Public Relations,* 7th edn, Englewood Cliffs, NJ: Prentice-Hall.

Cyert, R.M. and March, J.G. (1963) *A Behavioural Theory of the Firm,* Englewood Cliffs, NJ: Prentice-Hall.

Dozier, D.M. (1990) 'The innovation of research in public relations practice: review of a programme of studies', in L.A. Grunig and J.E. Grunig (eds) *Public Relations Research Annual, Vol. 2,* Hillsdale, NJ: Lawrence Erlbaum, pp. 3–28.

Duncan, R.B. (1972) 'Characteristics of organisational environment and perceived environmental uncertainty', *Administrative Science Quarterly,* 17: 313–27.

Eisenhardt, K.M. and Zbaracki, M.J. (1992) 'Strategic decision-making', *Strategic Management Journal,* 13: 17–37.

Grunig, J.E. (ed.) (1992) *Excellence in Public Relations and Communications Management,* Hillsdale, NJ: Lawrence Erlbaum.

Grunig, J.E. and Grunig, L.A. (1992) 'Models of public relations and communications', in J.E. Grunig (ed.) *Excellence in Public Relations and Communications Management,* Hillsdale, NJ: Lawrence Erlbaum, pp. 285–325.

Grunig, J.E., Grunig, L.A. and Ehling, W.P. (1992) 'What is an effective organisation?', in J.E. Grunig (ed.) *Excellence in Public Relations and Communications Management,* Hillsdale, NJ: Lawrence Erlbaum, pp. 65–90.

Grunig, J.E. and Hunt, T. (1984) *Managing Public Relations,* New York: Holt, Rinehart and Winston.

Grunig, J.E. and Repper, F.C. (1992) 'Strategic management, publics and issues', in J.E.

Grunig, (ed.) *Excellence in Public Relations and Communications Management*, Hillsdale, NJ: Lawrence Erlbaum, pp. 117–57.

Hambrick, D.C. (1983) 'Some tests of the effectiveness and functional attributes of Miles and Snow's strategic types', *Academy of Management Journal*, 26: 5–25.

Hax, A.C. and Majluf, N.S. (1988) 'The concept of strategy and the strategy formulation process', *Interfaces*, May–June, pp. 99–109.

Hax, A.C. and Majluf, N.S. (1991) *The Strategy Concept and Process: A Pragmatic Approach*, Englewood Cliffs, NJ: Prentice-Hall.

Hofer, C.W. (1973) 'Some preliminary research on patterns of strategic behaviour', *Academy of Management Proceedings*, pp. 46–59.

Johnson, G. and Scholes, K. (1993) *Exploring Corporate Strategy*, 3rd edn, London: Prentice-Hall.

Kay, J. (1993) *Foundations of Corporate Success*, Oxford: Oxford University Press.

Kerin, R.A., Mahajan, V. and Varadarajan, P.R. (1990) *Contemporary Perspectives on Strategic Market Planning*, Needham Heights, MA: Ally and Bacon.

Lindblom, C.E. (1959) 'The science of muddling through', *Public Administration Review*, 19: 79–88.

McDonald, M.H.B. (1992) 'Strategic marketing planning: a state of the art review', *Marketing Intelligence and Planning*, 10(4): 4–22.

Mintzberg, H. (1987) 'Crafting strategy', *Harvard Business Review*, July/August: 65–75.

Mintzberg, H. (1989) 'Strategy formation: schools of thought', in J. Frederickson (ed.) *Perspectives on Strategic Management*, San Francisco: Ballinger.

Mintzberg, H. (1991) 'Five P's for Strategy', in H. Mintzberg and J.B. Quinn *The Strategy Process: Concepts, Contexts, Cases*, 2nd edn, Englewood Cliffs, NJ: Prentice-Hall, pp. 12–19.

Mintzberg, H. (1994) 'The fall and rise of strategic planning', *Harvard Business Review*, January/February: 107–14.

Montgomery, C.A. and Porter, M.E. (1991) *Strategy – Seeking and Securing Competitive Advantage*, Boston: Harvard Business School Press.

Nutt, P.C. (1984) 'Types of organisational decision processes', *Administrative Science Quarterly*, 29: 414–50.

O'Shaughnessy, J. (1988) *Competitive Marketing: A Strategic Approach*, Boston, MA: Unwin Hyman.

Pettigrew, A.M. (1992) 'The character and significance of strategy process research', *Strategic Management Journal*, 13: 5–16.

Porter, M.E. (1980) *Competitive Strategy: Techniques for Analysing Industries and Competitors*, New York: The Free Press.

Porter, M.E. (1985) *Competitive Advantage: Creating and Sustaining Superior Performance*, New York: The Free Press.

Quinn, J.B. (1980) *Strategies For Change: Logical Incrementalism*, Burr Ridge, Ill.: Richard D. Irwin.

Seitel, F. (1992) *The Practice of Public Relations*, 5th edn, Colombus, OH: MacMillan.

Speed, R. (1989) 'Oh Mr Porter! A reappraisal of competitive strategy', *Marketing Intelligence and Planning*, 7(5/6): 8–11.

Steiner, G.A. and Miner, J.B. (1977) *Management Policy and Strategy*, New York: MacMillan.

Weick, K.E. (1987) 'Substitutes for corporate strategy', in D.J. Teece (ed.) *The Competitive Challenge; Strategies for Industrial Innovation and Renewal*, Cambridge, MA: Ballinger.

White, J. and Dozier, D.M. (1992) 'Public relations and mangement decision-making', in J.E. Grunig (ed.) *Excellence in Public Relations and Communications Management*, Hillsdale, NJ: Lawrence Erlbaum, pp. 91–108.

Whittington, R. (1993) *What is Strategy – and Does it Matter?*, London: Routledge.

Wilcox, D.L., Ault, P.H. and Agee, W.E. (1986) *Public Relations: Strategies and Tactics*, New York: Harper and Row.

5

THE INTERNAL COMMUNICATIONS CONTEXT

Heike Puchan, Magda Pieczka and Jacquie L'Etang

CHAPTER AIMS

- to introduce students to key concepts relating to the internal organisational context

INTRODUCTION

This chapter aims to introduce the student of public relations to key concepts relevant to understanding, analysing and researching the internal organisational context. As such, the chapter lays out the necessary preparatory thinking that is required before beginning or changing a programme of internal communication.

The chapter begins with definitions of organisational structure and culture and a discussion of managerial styles and then proceeds to discuss the implications of these concepts for the role and scope of public relations. The chapter proceeds to review approaches to researching the organisation and concludes with a case study of the Royal Bank of Scotland.

First, however, here are some examples of scenarios in which understanding the nature of the internal organisational context becomes very important for strategic management and public relations functions.

ILLUSTRATIONS

Scenario 1

Two engineering companies merge. Management would like what they see as the most positive aspects of both organisations to be welded together in the new organisation. In short, they wish to change the corporate culture in a way that will enhance the competitive performance of the company and develop good relations between those from the two different companies.

Scenario 2

A telecommunications company wishes to reposition itself in the marketplace and as part of this task intends to change its corporate identity to reflect its changing mission and vision.

Scenario 3

An electrical retailer introduces a new programme of customer care which will entail the involvement of all staff and improved communications between various functional parts of the organisation in order to improve the quality of customer relations as well as the response time to customer complaints.

Scenario 4

A large public sector organisation is relocating most of its staff from London to Manchester. Many long-serving staff from London who are unable, for domestic reasons, to move will be offered redundancy and early retirement packages. The majority of the staff in Manchester will be new to the organisation, much younger and relatively inexperienced.

Scenario 5

A medium-sized public relations consultancy specialising in IT accounts and which employs the traditional hierarchy of account handling faces problems in being unable to offer either promotion or a greater range of work to staff who are at the bottom of hierarchy but who have stayed loyal to the consultancy and developed their skills and expertise over periods from two to four years. Now the consultancy faces something of a crisis in that a number of these staff are threatening to leave if they do not achieve promotion.

Issues for class discussion

For each of these cases, you should first specify the managerial as opposed to public relations decisions. Then try to identify what information the public relations in-house practitioner or consultant would need before making specific recommendations for action. How would the public relations practitioner go about obtaining that information?

ORGANISATIONS

It will be useful at this stage to consider the question: what is an organisation? At a simple level we might define an organisation to be a group effort with defined goals, specified tasks and reward structures. As we shall see, however, organisations are much more complex than this because they affect the way we think, the values we hold and the way we behave. Also, our view about what a particular organisation is depends upon our own experience and position within it. One person might see an organisation as a prison while someone in a different position might see it as a source of political power like a small personal fiefdom. Understanding different perspectives within an organisation is fundamental to internal public relations. One organisational theorist who has done much to develop ideas which can help us to access such perspectives is Gareth Morgan (Morgan, 1986; 1992). Morgan develops a number of different metaphors which present different views of the organisation – as a machine, as an organism, as a brain, as a prison – but also argues that there are an infinite number of other ideas about organisations. In his role as management consultant, Morgan has carried out such an exercise with senior managers and employees in order to understand more fully how they see the organisation in metaphorical, often pictorial, terms which can be very revealing in terms of drawing out different perspectives that exist within the organisation.

Class exercise

How do you see your university? Can you think of a metaphor for it? Would your view of the university be the same or different from the views of lecturers and administrators? Why? How would you expect them to be different? Would lecturers in all departments all have the same view? If not, why not?

The French philosopher, Rousseau, claimed that 'Man is born free, but everywhere he is in chains.' In organisation studies there is a commonly quoted adaptation of this which runs, 'Man is born free but everywhere he is in organisations.' What this seems to imply is that organisations are necessary and intrinsic to human society, but that they inevitably restrict individual action. The resulting conflict and compromise implies communication and a role for public relations in enhancing understanding of different positions, developing and articulating arguments and assisting in negotiative processes. Organisational analysis and its implications for public relations entails analysis at the four levels identified by Wilson and Rosenfeld (1990:5): societal, organisational, group and individual. Untangling the connections between these different levels of analysis and drawing out their implications for internal communications is a complex task. We shall now proceed to discuss the influence of structure and culture on the internal organisational context before proceeding to draw out the implications for the role of public relations.

ORGANISATIONAL STRUCTURE AND CULTURE

So far we have defined organisation as a group effort with defined goals, specified tasks and reward structures. A more realistic definition, however, would have to acknowledge what we all know from our various experiences of organisations: as soon as there are a number of people together, there are also a number of different, if not conflicting, interests pursued. In complex organisations, such as virtually any organisation we are likely to come into contact with, the existence of a common goal does not automatically mean that various professional or functional groups will not have their own interests, which often may be more important to them than the organisational goals.

Class exercise

Take the example of your own university or college. Breaking down this big group of people into smaller groups, a first distinction could perhaps be drawn between students and staff. Identify what interests or goals might the teaching staff be actively pursuing? Are they the same as those of students, and university administrators and technical support staff? It might help if you can perhaps remember a recent example of conflict within the organisation: who were the involved parties? What was the bone of contention? Why was it contentious?

It would seem that within any organisation there are two opposing forces at play: one which pulls its various elements together, a unifying force; and another which fragments the organisation, a centrifugal force. The role of management could therefore be seen as balancing these two forces. To understand how co-operation and control are effected in organisations we will focus on two concepts: *structure* and *culture*.

STRUCTURE

The structure of an organisation refers to the socially created pattern of rules, roles and relationships that exist within it (Dawson, 1992:107).

Class exercise

Let us start with a simple example. Think about the work that goes into delivering to you a fresh hamburger with fries within a minute of your ordering one in a fast food restaurant. What necessary tasks could you name? Can you remember how many people seem to have been involved? How were the tasks allocated?

In thinking about structure we might start with the tasks and their allocation (*individual roles*). The next step is to consider how these various individual roles fit together. Then there is the question of setting up control and supervision. Thus, specifying *relationships* in terms of reporting, delegation (vertical) and grouping of individuals into teams (horizontal) is another element in organisational structure. Finally, if our hamburger is to be produced to a certain standard and within a certain amount of time, we need to specify *rules and systems* that will make it possible: procedures, control, communication, terms and conditions of employment, and planning and decision-making.

Thinking about organisations as structures, and – anticipating later developments, one could also say – thinking that structures alone deliver effective balance between individual and organisational goals, is linked to rapid industrial development in the nineteenth century. Mechanisation and mass production changed the nature of work and new ways of managing had to be developed. Thus modern management was born around the turn of this century with theories now referred to in textbooks as classical (Fayol, Mooney and Urwick) and scientific (Taylor) management. Typically, these are often discussed together with Weber's work on bureaucracy (see, for example, Mullins 1994:34–44). In fact, Weber himself saw the process of mechanisation of industry as of the same nature as the bureaucratisation of administration. If management according to the classical approach was concerned with planning, organisation, command, co-ordination and control, Weber saw bureaucracy as:

> a form of organisation that emphasizes precision, speed, clarity, regularity, reliability and efficiency achieved through the creation of a fixed division of tasks, hierarchical supervision, and detailed rules and regulations (Morgan 1986:24–25).

However, it is not by accident that *bureaucracy* today stands for inefficiency and inflexibility. The drive to simplification of complex tasks by breaking them down into small units, designing jobs around a small number of such units, and tight managerial control soon became the accepted rational ways of organising. Gradually, however, a more complex picture started to emerge from various research projects. Taylor believed that money was the most important motivating factor for the work force, but when researchers went into Western Electric Company in the United States (a project known as the Hawthorne experiments, 1924–32) they realised that there were other, social factors that had a bearing on the workers' performance. For example, it became clear that the formal organisational structure was not the only one existing in the organisation. There were also informal groups and these had a strong influence over their members, imposing their own practices and norms, and subverting that of management. Out of this work, grew the Human Relations school, an approach which emphasised 'the primary work group and the importance of supervisory styles in influencing workers' attitudes and behaviour' (Dawson, 1992:9).

Other researchers, such as Selznick (1949), Gouldner (1954) and Merton (1940; 1957), have written about what might be termed the side-effects of bureaucratic organisation: the formation of subgroups pursuing their own rather than organisational interests; the vicious circle of demotivation, caused by strict and formal rules leading to more need for supervision and hence further rules; and the rigidity of behaviour resulting from the requirement of reliability, that is meeting standard problems with standard responses.

Another set of problems to do with bureaucracy and structure which have received a fair amount of attention from researchers has been that related to links between the size of an organisation and its structure (Pugh et al., 1969a; 1969b; Pugh and Hickson, 1976; Pugh and Hinings, 1976; Blau and Schoenherr, 1971; Child and Mansfield, 1972). Researchers found that there was a correlation between two factors: the bigger the organisation, the bigger the need for formal and standardised solutions to problems of co-ordination and control. What also gradually emerged was that there was a wide range of organisational structures, which could be explained with reference to environments in which they existed. This gave rise to Contingency Theory (Lawrence and Lorsch, 1967; Mintzberg, 1979) postulating that organisational structures emerge in response to demands and conditions in the external environment. There is no one best way of organising, no universal solution that would work for all organisations and under all types of external conditions.

A great amount of research effort in the 1960s and 1970s went into studying organisations as complex entities embedded in equally complex environments. Towards the end of the 1970s, however, a new factor attracted researchers' attention. Japan had emerged as an industrial success. Western industry found it increasingly harder to compete against the Japanese, and, naturally, explanations about the roots of this success were sought. What was immediately obvious was that Japanese enterprises seemed very different in the ways in which they managed decision-making, motivation, and workers' involvement (Ouchi, 1981). The term 'culture' began to be used more and more often.

The floodgates were opened by a 1980 *Business Week* article on corporate culture. By 1982, three popular titles appeared: Deal and Kennedy's *Corporate Cultures* (1982, 1988); Peters and Waterman's *In Search of Excellence* (1982); and Allen and Kraft's *The Organizational Unconscious: How to Create the Corporate Culture You Want and Need* (1982). The books were popular both in terms of sales (Peters and Waterman's was a bestseller and has gone through four reprints) and in terms of their style of exposition and language. These were manuals telling managers how to manage this new thing called culture.

CULTURE

The term 'culture' in organisational analysis refers to 'shared values and beliefs' which are seen to characterise particular organisations . . . Culture is . . . in Hofstede's terms [see Hofstede, 1990] 'the collective programming of the mind which distinguishes the members of one group or category of people from another' (Dawson 1992:136).

Interest in organisational culture in the 1980s was equally strong among academics as it was among management practitioners. Allaire and Firsirotu (1984) offered a conceptual framework for organisational culture on the basis of extensive discussion of approaches in cultural anthropology. The framework postulates that culture results from the complex relationships between three constituent parts of the organisation. The first is a *socio-cultural system* encompassing: structure, strategies, policies, management processes, and an ancillary component formed from an organisation's reality and functioning, such as, for example, goals, authority structure, reward, and motivation (Allaire and Firsirotu, 1984:213); the second is the *cultural system*

that embodies the organization's expressive and affective dimensions in a system of shared and meaningful symbols manifested in myths, ideology and values and in multiple cultural artifacts (Allaire and Firsirotu, 1984:213).

The last component is the *individual actor,* who is both an individual and a member of the organisation. Actors are both recipients and contributors to organisational culture as they 'strive to construct a coherent picture to orient them to the goings-on in the organization' (Allaire and Firsirotu, 1984:215).

A much simpler way of understanding culture as 'the way we do things here' comes from an experienced practitioner, Martin Bower, for many years the managing director of the famous management consultancy McKinsey and Company

(Deal and Kennedy, 1988:4). In fact, practitioners seem to have stuck with the view that organisational culture is something the organisation *has*; it is a variable; it can be managed; it is corporate culture. This is a common theme in the popular 'excellence' approach and normally linked to advice on how to create a strong culture, which is seen as a prerequisite to success. For a discussion of an alternative view of culture, as something that the organisation *is*, and which is, therefore, not open to short-term manipulation, students should turn to Smircich (1983), Clegg (1990) and Turner (1990).

IMPLICATIONS FOR THE ROLE AND SCOPE OF PUBLIC RELATIONS

So far we have tried to define organisations, we have looked at organisational behaviour and we have reviewed organisational structure and culture. This section aims to discuss the implications of those ideas and concepts for the role of public relations within an organisation.

For many years internal communications has been regarded as the stepchild of public relations, but today public relations and corporate communication departments in organisations have realised that the 'old' public relations saying is not to be neglected: 'good public relations begins at home'. There are several reasons why internal communication has to be perceived as an important task of public relations. Whereas public relations in a wider context provides an opportunity for a more consensus-oriented and less conflict-oriented society, internal communication in the organisational context can be used as a means to create a more democratic, harmony-oriented organisation. From this perspective the concept of internal relations is closely linked to the concept of human relations discussed above. The central idea is that employees can only work effectively if they can participate in the organisation and they can only participate effectively if they are fully informed. Full information implies that each employee needs to have a complete understanding of the aims and objectives of an organisation. It is also necessary to make clear where the individual fits into the strategy of the organisation and how he or she is contributing to the fulfilment of the organisation's aims and objectives. Another relevant aspect is the importance of communication for the managerial style that leaders in the company are adopting. A participative style of leadership for example involves the implementation of ideas and suggestions of employees when decisions are being made and the generation of feedback on those decisions. Staff who have the possibility to participate and feel that their opinion is being heard are more likely to be motivated and effective in the work they are doing.

Feedback is not only valuable in terms of employee motivation and industrial relations. It can also be useful for evaluating relationships with other publics of an organisation. If we take, for example, customers of an organisation we see that employees such as salespersons or customer relations staff are the ones who are in the front-line of the reactions of customers. They receive complaints, opinions or recommendations from the customers which can complement systematic research carried out by specific departments dealing with customer relations. This example illustrates that employees can be a valuable source of information if appropriate channels to feed back their opinions and experiences are established.

One of the most important reasons why internal communications is a public relations task is that employees are among those groups that are crucial to an organisation. Depending on their perception of the organisation they will communicate positive or negative messages to other important groups of the organisation such as members of the community, politicians and financial supporters.

Having reviewed some of the reasons for the importance and necessity of communication in an organisation the implications for the practice of public relations can be easily established. As we have discussed, communication is crucial and takes places on every level and in every section of an organisation. The task of public relations is to develop and implement manageable communication structures in the organisation which allow communication to become effective; effective communication that takes into account the importance of both internal and external communication, their close relationship and the resulting need for coherent messages. In other words, public relations has to make sure that there are no contradictory messages sent out to different groups important to the organisation.

For public relations to achieve those objectives, research has to be carried out to evaluate internal communication efforts on a regular basis and to advise on necessary changes. Internal communications requires a systematic approach – in other words, a strategy has to be developed. The next question is: what is a good communications strategy and how can it be developed? A good communications strategy will differ from one organisation to another, taking into account the various factors which determine and shape the organisation's appearance. Those are:

- type of business (e.g. car manufacturer, consultancy, charity)
- size (multinational, national, local)
- age of the organisation
- culture
- managerial style
- financial background
- staff
- stability/volatility of its environment.

A good communications strategy will also be strongly linked to the overall business strategy of an organisation as the aims and objectives of the business strategy will be the framework of the organisation. The business strategy will answer questions such as 'what are its values, its stakes, its future?' To support the business objectives, a communications strategy has to be developed in close co-operation with the management of an organisation.

This already shows that however sophisticated the internal communication system, public relations cannot manage internal communication on its own. One aspect which has to be borne in mind is that every employee is a communicator and has to communicate their information and messages to the other parts of the organisation. Therefore, internal communications have to be a combined effort of different parts of an organisation. There are also expert communication tasks that require the input of departments such as personnel, marketing, and so on. One example would be the closure of a subsidiary of an organisation. The personnel department would have to be involved in order to develop a specialised plan outlining how to communicate the changes to the employees.

The complex task of internal communication demands a specialist treatment carried out by a professional who manages the various communication efforts necessary in an organisation. The public relations department's role in this combined effort could be described as a co-ordinator's role.

RESEARCHING THE ORGANISATION

As the above sections will have made clear, understanding and analysing the organisational context with a view to developing programmes of internal communication is not a particularly easy matter. Perhaps this explains why some public relations practitioners and some public relations books emphasise internal communication techniques rather than research. However, we would argue that the occupation of public relations will only gain respect and be regarded as a professional occupation when its practitioners have the ability to carry out that sort of analysis based on theories of organisation and communication. For the public relations practitioner the first step should be evaluation of the existing situation in an organisation in order to develop a benchmark against which to measure change. Sometimes this process is referred to as an 'audit' or 'communication audit', but it should be noted that there is no industry standard for what constitutes an audit and no industry guarantee that public relations practitioners have the necessary skills either to carry out such research or to make a satisfactory purchase on such skills.

Because public relations is a relatively new occupation and because its practitioners have tended to emphasise techniques rather than strategy, there is not a great deal of research in public relations on internal communications and audits. There is, however, a vast amount available within the field of organisational communications which provides a rich source of ideas and research approaches that can help the practitioner to understand a client organisation. According to Jablin et al. (1987) areas that fall within organisational communication include:

- communications implications of systems theory
- communications implications of management theories
- information environments of organisations
- corporate discourse (public relations and issues management)
- communication climates
- organisational culture
- effects of organisational structure on communication
- superior-subordinate communication
- sensory and symbolic bases of perception
- verbal and non-verbal communication
- symbolic performances
- message flow and decision-making
- messages and message exchange

- politics and power
- conflict and negotiation
- networks and channels
- feedback, motivation and performance
- leadership
- new technology.

Ideas about evaluation in organisational communication have been published since the 1950s (Greenbaum et al., 1988) and there was a developing interest in the field into the 1970s when the Internal Communication Association (ICA) developed a standard methodology in order to improve understanding about organisational theory in a way that would benefit industry. The purpose of the ICA audit was to: 'evaluate the organisation's communication system, providing information and recommendations which should help an organisation improve both its communication practices and its overall effectiveness as an organisation' (Greenbaum et al., 1988).

The ICA audit gave a picture of message flow and content, gatekeeping and communication networks within the organisation, organisational climate, extent of interpersonal trust and job satisfaction. It employed a multi-method approach using quantitative and qualitative techniques including:

- interview (structured and unstructured)
- questionnaire
- 'critical incident' where respondents describe what they regard as characteristic communication experiences in the organisation
- diaries
- network analysis in which respondents record social and formal communication
- message tracking.

The CIA audit and communication audits that include a similar range of methodologies provide a more complete picture because they derive information from various parts of the organisation in a number of different ways. This is important because each individual research technique has its strengths and weaknesses: using a mixture of techniques can build a more accurate analysis. Statistics can be used to correlate, for example, motivation with a variety of variables such as satisfactory superior-subordinate relationships, perceptions of involvement with organisational strategy, salary levels and so on while 'stories' of specific organisational relationships in particular departments can give a very graphic and human account of particular experiences. The technique of selecting a range of methodologies is derived from social science and is called 'triangulation'. The use of a single research instrument (such as a questionnaire) can sometimes be delusory in that while it gives the appearance of incontrovertible proof because it is numerical it also has its weaknesses in that the questions answered are those that have been asked by researchers and are not necessarily those of most importance to the respondents.

In researching the organisation public relations practitioners must ensure that their research is rigorous and conforms to standard social scientific practice in presenting to the client a clear account and justification of methodology (including details of sampling procedures, rationale for the development of interview guides and questionnaires, variables to be tested) and data collection that can be checked so that the results and analysis that are derived from that methodology can be used as a benchmark and tested again over a period of time.

SUMMARY AND CONCLUSIONS

In this chapter we have tried to define organisations as complex constructions that are necessary to human society but at the same time restrict the action of individuals. We have looked at the make-up of organisations and identified unifying and centrifugal forces that counteract each other. The role of management can be seen as balancing those two forces. Two main internal phenomena determine the equilibrium of an organisation: structure and culture. Whereas structure is concerned with individual roles, relationships, rules and systems of the organisation, culture is concerned with shared values and beliefs which seem to characterise an organisation. We then discussed the implications of the complexity of an organisation for public relations and the development of an internal communications strategy. Communication in an organisation has to be flexible and multi-dimensional, but co-ordinated. It has to be directly related to the business strategy and requires the input of all different parts of an organisation. Public relations role can be seen as the co-ordinator of a multi-departmental effort. In order to fulfil its role, public relations has to adopt a strategic approach based on the results of on-going research activities.

DISCUSSION TOPICS

1 Contrast the relationships between employees and the public relations function and employees and the human resource function.
2 What issues arise from the interface of the public relations and human resource management functions?
3 What are the dangers of employee participation from a management perspective?
4 There is currently much discussion about the Intranet (internal Internet). Discuss the pros and cons of establishing an Intranet within an organisation.
5 Discuss the concept of 'feedback' from the points of view of managers and employees. How might these two groups define feedback and what differences might emerge?
6 How can managers deliver on expectations raised by the implementation of a full communication audit?
7 What are the implications for the public relations function of a technique as opposed to a research-driven internal communications programme?
8 What is the implication for public relations of a definition of culture as something the organisation is rather than something the organisation has?
9 How do structure and culture affect each other?
10 Returning to each of the five scenarios outlined at the beginning of this chapter, identify the public relations issues and make recommendations for action.

CASE STUDY – THE ROYAL BANK OF SCOTLAND

The Royal Bank of Scotland has undergone an organisational change programme in order to reappoint it in the right direction as a financial services organisation. Part of the change was to improve the communications in the organisation and to enhance the flow of information in all directions from the top to the bottom, from the bottom to the top and sideways – a difficult task in an organisation with about 18,000 employees.

As far as the public relations department is concerned the change programme first of all meant reorganisation. The 25 members of staff – all of them working under the umbrella of the corporate communications department – were split up into different pockets such as internal communication, media relations, and so on. The main objective of internal communications was established so as to ensure that messages are passed throughout the group – including all divisions such as the branch Banking Division, Corporate and Institutional Banking, Personnel and Operations Division – wherever and whenever it is required to send something out. To achieve this objective, the Corporate Communications department established three communication channels: face-to-face communication, written communication and the so-called fast-delivery communication system.

Face-to-face communication includes mainly two communication tools: the cascade and the team meeting system. A cascade takes place when a strategic or policy message, for example concerned with computerisation or a change in the branch system, has to be sent out to all members of staff in the organisation. The first step is to produce a video which includes the core message. The managing director then holds briefing meetings with 250 briefers and delivers the message personally to them in London, Manchester and Edinburgh headquarters. This should provide for a two-way dialogue between the managing director and those people who will deliver the message to the staff. These briefers then go back to their areas and pass the message on to the staff in cascade briefing meetings. Here staff are introduced to the topic by video. A question and answer session follows which should ensure that as many questions as possible relating to the topic are answered. Any unanswered enquiries are fed back in a refer-up system and answers have to be provided back to the staff within 21 days.

The second type of face-to-face communication is the team meeting system. It is used on a monthly basis at a national level to send information generated within the highest management level through the network into the departments to the members of staff. Teams of four to 10 people in each group discuss with a team leader current operational situations. As the core brief leaves the board room it is added to at each level until it reaches the local level, that is a branch or department within the head office. Each leader at each level adds relevant information to the core brief. By the time it gets to the bottom it not only delivers the national news but also news related to each level of the organisation. During this cascade staff are encouraged to discuss and add to the core brief. The strength of the cascading system is the possibility for staff to participate, to consider issues and to present their views. These views will then be fed back upwards through the organisation and also sideways. Altogether there are 2,000 teams spread throughout the country and they will be briefed on a monthly basis. Additionally, there will be a minimum of one other meeting a month dealing only with local issues containing all information any member of staff needs to fulfil his or her function in their organisation.

Another category of internal communication is the written communication. The Royal Bank of Scotland has four main internal printed media. First of all there is *Newsline*, the bank's internal magazine. It is issued bimonthly, six times a year and fulfils mainly a social communication function although it also includes two major items of general interest to the staff. It features sporting events, marriages, charity events, and so on. The second publication is called *Insidetrack*. It is a strategy magazine produced on a quarterly basis for managers and presents articles of leading officials and directors on the future plans of the organisation or contributions of particular managers to the company. *Focus*, the third written communication tool, operates on a daily basis carrying information staff need to know to carry out their job. *Focus* is produced three days a week for delivery in the branches on Tuesdays, Wednesdays and Thursdays. Every day has as specific 'focus': Tuesday's *Focus* concentrates on staff and resources, Wednesday's on customers and Thursday's on operations. *Focus* was developed to co-ordinate the efforts of different departments who send written material out on a daily basis in order to inform their fellow staff members. In the past, this has led to an overflow and finally to a distinct lack of information because staff refused to, or simply did not have the time to, study vast amounts of literature reaching their desks every day. *Focus* provides the possibility of informing employees about specialised issues in a systematic manner. Staff know when and where to look for a specific type of information. Whereas every department has an input, the public relations department is the co-ordinator and makes sure that the items in *Focus* are free of technological jargon and understandable to everybody in the organisation. The fourth written communication produced by the organisation is a magazine called *New Bank Vision*. This publication is dedicated to the change programme and explains how and why changes are being made. It informs members of staff at which stage the organisation is with the programme and where the managers and employees see themselves going in the future.

The third category of communication are the fast delivery systems. There are three types of systems. The so-called System News is linked to the bank's computer main frame and messages can be sent out straight to the bank office screens. It is used on a day-to-day basis to send out urgent messages. However, it is rather restricted, because there are only 36 lines on the mainframe available. The second system is Surefax that allows members of the organisation to send out lengthy urgent messages to the whole area or only parts of the organisation. It is used, for example, to inform members of staff about the half year and annual results before they will be announced in the press. The third system is the 9 am delivery. This is designed to provide every member of staff within the organisation with a letter on their desk at 9 o'clock in the morning. It is used occasionally by the managing director to send out confidential information which affects every individual. It might be used for example in cases of a takeover.

Although public relations has the co-ordinator role within the internal communication system, there is input from every area of the organisation. For example, *Newsline* is produced with the help of freelances with correspondents in every department; an editorial committee existing of a group of managers and directors decide over the content of *Insidetrack*, and so on.

In addition to the feedback mechanisms mentioned above, the public relations department also carries out Key Responsibility Area Surveys (KRA). This quarterly survey investigates with the help of a questionnaire how the line managers are performing in communication, how communication in general is perceived, and so on. Monitoring is also provided on a spot-check basis where members of the internal communications section of the public relations department visit a certain region and talk to 30 to 50 per cent of the staff. The organisation also applies a communications audit system to find out whether messages are being received, if they are arriving in an acceptable form and where possible communication blockages are. In cases of communication blockages produced by individuals, it is the task of internal communications to train and educate those members of staff.

QUESTIONS FOR CLASS DISCUSSION

What are the strengths and weaknesses of the Royal Bank of Scotland's internal communications strategy? What are the communication tools used within the programme? What input do different departments have into the programme? How do you rate the feedback mechanism in the internal communications system? What would you do differently?

REFERENCES

Allaire, Y. and Firsirotu, M. (1984) 'Theories of organizational culture', *Organization Studies*, 5(3): 193–226.

Allen, F. and Kraft, C. (1982) *The Organizational Unconscious: How to Create the Corporate Culture you Want and Need*, Englewood Cliffs, NJ: Prentice-Hall.

Blau, P.M. and Schoenherr, R.A. (1971) *The Structure of Organisations*, New York: Basic Books.

Bryman, A. (ed.) (1994) *Doing Research in Organizations*, London: Routledge.

Child, J. and Mansfield, R. (1972) 'Technology, size and organisation structure', *Sociology*, 6: 211–23.

Clegg, S. (1990) *Modern Organisation – Organisation Studies in the Post Modern World*, London: Sage.

Dawson, Sandra (1992) *Analysing Organisations*, 2nd edn, Basingstoke and London: Macmillan.

Deal, T. and Kennedy, A. (1982/1988) *Corporate Cultures: The Rites and Rituals of Corporate Life*, Harmondsworth: Penguin; first published in Reading, MA: Addison-Wesley, 1982.

Fayol, H. (1949) *General and Industrial Management*, London: Pitman.

Fineman, S. and Gabriel, Y. (1996) *Experiencing Organizations*, London: Sage.

Gouldner, A.W. (1954) *Patterns of Industrial Bureaucracy*, New York: Free Press.

Greenbaum, H.H. (1974) 'The audit of organisational communication', *Academy of Management Journal*, 27: 739–54.

Greenbaum, H.H., Hellweg, S. and Falcione, R.L. (1988) 'Organisational communication evaluation: An overview 1950–81' in G.M. Goldhaber and G.A. Barnett (eds) *Handbook of Organizational Communication*, Norwood, NJ: Ablex, 275–317.

Grunig, J.E. (ed.) (1992) *Excellence in Public Relations and Communications Management*, Hillsdale, NJ: Lawrence Erlbaum.

Heath, R.L. (1994) *Management of Corporate Communication: From Interpersonal Contacts to External Affairs*, Hillsdale, NJ: Lawrence Erlbaum.

Hofstede, G. (1990) *Cultures and Organisations: Software of the Mind*, London: McGraw-Hill.

Jablin, F.M., Putman, L.L., Roberts, K.H. Porter, L.W. (1987) *Handbook of Organizational Communication: An Interdisciplinary Perspective*, London: Sage.

Jablin, F. (1987) 'Formal Organisational Structure', in F.M. Jablin, L.L. Putman, K.H. Roberts and L.W. Porter (eds) *Handbook of Organizational Communication: An Interdisciplinary Perspective*, London: Sage, pp. 389–420.

Lawrence, P.R. and Lorsch, J.W. (1967) *Organisation and Environment*, Boston, Mass.: Graduate School of Business Administration, Harvard University.

Merton, R.K. (1940) 'Bureaucratic structure and personality', *Social Forces*, 18: 560–8.

Merton, R.K. (1957) *Social Theory and Social Structure*, rev. edn, Chicago: Free Press.

Mintzberg, H. (1979) *The Structuring of Organisations*, Englewood Cliffs, NJ: Prentice-Hall.

Morgan, G. (1986) *Images of Organization*, Newbury Park, London: Sage.

Morgan, G. (1992) *Imaginization*, Newbury Park, London: Sage.

Mullins, L.J. (1994) *Management and Organisational Behaviour*, London: Pitman.

Ouchi, W. (1981) *Theory Z: How American Business Can Meet the Japanese Challange*, Reading, MA: Addison-Wesley.

Peters, T. and Waterman, R. (1992) *In Search of Excellence: Lessons from America's Best-run Companies*, New York: Harper Collins; first published in 1982.

Pugh, D.S. and Hickson, D.J. (1976) *Organizational Structure in its Context*, The Aston Programme, Vol. 1, Farnborough: Saxon.

Pugh, D.S. and Hinings, C.R. (1976) *Organization Structure: Extensions and Replication*, The Aston Programme, Vol. 2, Farnborough: Saxon.

Pugh, D.S., Hickson, D.J. and Hinings, C.R. (1969a) 'The context of organization structures', *Administrative Science Quarterly*, 14: 91–114.

Pugh, D.S., Hickson, D.J. and Hinings, C.R. (1969b) 'An empirical taxonomy of structures of work organizations', *Administrative Science Quarterly*, 14: 115–26.

Selznick, P. (1949) *TVA and the Grass Roots*, Berkley: University of California Press.

Smircich, L. (1983) 'Concepts of culture and organisational analysis', *Administrative Science Quarterly*, 28: 339–58.

Taylor, F.W. (1911) *Principles of Scientific Management*, New York: Harper and Row.

Turner, B. (ed.) (1990) *Organisational Symbolism*, Berlin: de Gruyter.

Urwick, L. (1937) *Papers on the Science of Administration*, NY Institute of Public Administration: Columbia.

Van Riel, C.B.M. (1995) *Principles of Corporate Communication*, Hemel Hempstead: Prentice-Hall.

Wilson, D. and Rosenfeld, R. (1990) *Managing Organisations*, Maidenhead: McGraw-Hill.

6

PUBLIC RELATIONS: THE EXTERNAL PUBLICS CONTEXT

Richard Varey

CHAPTER AIMS

- to provide a recognition of the value of clearly identified 'publics' in public relations programme management
- to give a distinction between 'publics' and 'markets'
- to provide a recent example of a spectacular failure to identify key publics, the issue, and to prepare an adequate communication plan to deal effectively with public opinion

ILLUSTRATION

When BP's then Director of Government and Public Affairs sat down in 1990 to consider how to explain the role of public relations to management groups in the company, he constructed a diagram which identified BP at the centre of a network of relationships between groups of people who were important to the company (White, 1991:6).

The company, he argued, must prepare to manage the business within a recognised social network of these relationships. If the company is not involved in these relationships then they may develop in a way that is unfavourable to the company. Central to the diagram were the groups which were close to the company and its business operations – employees, customers, shareholders and suppliers. Other groups with less direct contact included the media, government and pressure groups. The diagram mapped out some of the important relationships between these various groups.

INTRODUCTION

What does the identification of these important groups mean to managers of public relations? If we think in terms of public relations as 'the management of communication between the organisation and its publics' (Grunig and Hunt, 1984), we need to be clear about who these 'publics' are.

While some obvious similarities can be discerned between the notion of targeting publics and the marketer's approach of targeting market segments, it is necessary to distinguish between 'markets' and 'publics'. In identifying key publics we are really addressing the need to consider the groups that affect our ability to achieve our own aims, their key characteristics and communication needs (Parkinson and Rowe, 1977).

One of the significant developments in the field of public relations in recent years has been the recognition of the need to reconsider the nature of 'publics' (Newsom et al., 1993).

CHAPTER OVERVIEW

In this chapter we are concerned with understanding that the organisation does not and cannot exist in a vacuum and the freedom of choice of the management group is therefore constrained by the interests of other groups. Increasingly, it is being recognised by managers that they must have a positive dialogue with other groups if they are to retain the 'licence to operate' as a business.

We will first consider the existence of groups external to the organisation who may or may not be customers, and who can exert some influence on operations and performance. In doing so, we will discuss and dismiss the notion of an 'audience' for public relations messages.

The concept of stakeholders is introduced and some examples of those individuals and groups who may be stakeholders for an organisation are listed. The ethical dimension of public relations activity is highlighted.

The concept of a public is distinguished from that of the stakeholder, and some discussion about how to identify publics is included. Essentially, the marketer's technique of segmentation is the basis for defining publics, but the definition must recognise the dynamics of external groupings around issues and opportunities which change over time.

Some methods for prioritising the wide range of publics as part of a public relations programme is touched upon.

Finally, the Brent Spar problem is discussed in some depth as a case study of the problems that can arise when an issue is not spotted or is ignored and, as a consequence, there is no proactive communication programme plan.

EXTERNAL PEOPLE AND GROUPS

Public relations can be neatly described as the management of reputation, with the purpose of developing understanding in all parties to a situation or issue. One of the founders of the public relations field, Arthur Page, said in the early part of the century:

> All business in a democratic society begins with public permission and exists by public approval . . . the purpose of public relations is to deserve and maintain public approval (quoted in Broom and Dozier, 1990:xi).

Thus consideration of 'publics' by public relations managers essentially concerns the ways in which the behaviour and attitudes of people – individuals, organisations and governments – impinge upon each other (Black, 1993:11).

Musicians and actors have audiences. Advertisers and publicists have audiences. Everyone else has stakeholders – key groups of people or 'publics' whose attitudes and decisions can affect your ability to do what you want to do in your business enterprise. 'Audience' is often an inappropriate term to use since it implies that the corporate communicator is performing in front of others (putting on an act). What must be portrayed is the place of the business organisation member in a complex set of interrelated relationships with identified key publics.

These groups have differing interests, motivations, attitudes, expectations, and sources of information, and are interdependent in their relationships with each other. This can lead to direct and indirect influence on your business. Some people may be members of more than one group, for example, your employees may have local political interests, or a customer may have a particularly close trading relationship with your major competitor! There is increasing recognition of the complexity of the web of influence, as is illustrated in Figure 6.1. We *now* believe that the earth is not at the centre of the universe – an organisation is but part of the web of stakeholders. Table 6.1 shows the location of some key external groups.

All managers of public relations should be concerned with the creation of a *corporate conscience* through constant awareness among managers of the organisation's responsibility to all its publics. Two additional issues must be considered important. First, any public relations activity can potentially generate criticism from any or all of the publics. In addition, there is the ethical question of whether individual public relations practitioners may act to rationalise corporate behaviour and manipulate public opinion, thus hampering rather than helping corporate social responsibility.

The full force of public demand for a balancing of quality of life and economic well-being is deflected by public relations people, in this view, and managers are thereby protected from having to face the realities of the wider situation.

Secondly, other practitioners in the field of public relations will expect

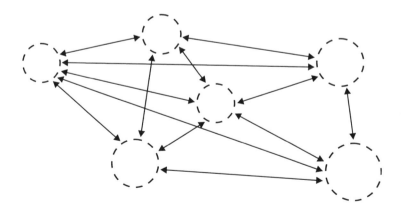

Figure 6.1 The molecular model or 'tangled-web' of stakeholder relationships.

Table 6.1 The location of some key external groups

Location	Group
Local community (and others affected by the factory, depot, quarry, etc.)	residents, including employees' families local authority community organisations and media educational institutions local community leaders
Influential groups/opinion formers (i.e. all those whose opinions may help/ harm the organisation in pursuit of its goals)	activists/pressure groups/environmental lobbyists academics educators and researchers special interest groups/consumer groups 'watchdogs' consultants writers and journalists business leaders students personalities trade unions public officials non-government organisations, quangos
Central and local government	departments agencies and executives political parties MPs and MEPs legislators regulators civil servants, policy-makers
The news media	newspaper editors and reporters magazine editors and contributors journal editors and contributors radio station managers and reporters TV station producers news agencies (international/national/local) trade and financial publication editors journalists and columnists writers other opinion formers
Investors	individual shareholders – past and potential institutional investors – past and potential competitors bankers insurers stockbrokers analysts and investment counsellors fund/portfolio managers financial advisors and their regulators specialist journalists
Consumers, customers and clients	past present future customers' reference groups and colleagues activist groups
Society (as consumers of information)	prospective employees past employees students everyone else! – especially your customers' and employees' relatives, friends, and peers

Table 6.1 (continued)

Location	Group
Business community	distributors/wholesalers/dealers/agents/retailers
	suppliers of materials and services
	competitors
	trade associations
	professional institutes
	partners
	prospective acquisitions
	prospective acquirers
	senior executives in other companies

practitioners to behave in such a way as to earn respect for the practice of public relations. Note that the various key groups are not listed in any assumed rank order. It is for the public relations manager to analyse their own corporate situation regularly to determine the weighting of interest among constituent members of these groups. It is essential that they recognise that these are not mutually exclusive groups. There may be much overlap of membership between some groups, and the communication with one group may spill over into another group. Then, conflicting priorities and differing interpretations may become a major problem for the public relations manager. False impressions are created, whilst perceptions are confused.

The corporate communications management task is to manage positive relationships with a range of overlapping audiences and to help these audiences to understand what the organisation is doing and why. At the same time, in order to achieve this, the public relations manager needs to constantly update and refine their understanding of their different needs and concerns. Is this not essentially what corporate strategy requires?

STAKEHOLDERS

A *stakeholder* is a key group or individual on whom the future of the enterprise depends. They have a stake in its prosperity and/or are affected by the organisation's behaviour. Stakeholders are people affected by the decisions, actions, policies, practices and goals of an organisation, or their decisions and actions can affect the organisation. Most stakeholders are passive. Those stakeholders who are or become more aware and active are *publics*. Once some interests of the organisation and people external to the organisation coincide there is an identifiable stakeholder.

Public relations managers and their organisations have ethical responsibilities to a variety of publics. External publics are not part of the organisation, but have a relationship with it, and can have, in certain circumstances, a substantial impact on the organisation.

THE ORGANISATION'S PUBLICS

Public relations and marketing are two distinct disciplines:

Marketing deals with markets and public relations with publics. Organisations can create a market by identifying a segment of the population for which a product is or could be in demand. Publics create themselves however, whenever organisations make decisions that affect a group of people adversely (Grunig, cited in Briggs and Tucson, 1993).

The distinction between markets and publics is important. Organisations choose their markets, but publics arise on their own and choose the organisation or industry for attention.

Publics form when people face a similar problem, recognise that a problem exists, and organise to do something about it. Publics organise around issues and seek out those organisations that create the issues. They may seek information, redress for grievances, to exert pressure on organisations, or government regulation. As publics move from being *latent* to *active*, organisations have no choice but to communicate with them. Public relations specialists communicate with publics that threaten the organisation's goals or provide opportunities to enhance the corporate mission. Active publics are the only ones that generate consequences for organisations. The proactive public relations practitioner will be communicating in advance in order to prevent a latent public from shifting to an active stance. This is *issues management*, in which an issue is identified and communication is pursued with potential stakeholders and publics before they become active publics.

Active publics engage in individual or collective (activist group) behaviours to do something about the consequence of an organisation's actions. They might wish to *oppose* the organisation through a product boycott, by opposing a price increase, or by supporting government regulation. In other instances, a public may be intent on supporting the organisation; for example, by buying shares or by making a donation.

Active publics are easier to provide information to because they actively seek it, but they will look at many sources and will be much harder to persuade than will be a passive public. *Passive stakeholders* should not be ignored, since they can become active publics. Proactive public relations concentrates on the passive stakeholder before they become active, and it is the aim of issues management to anticipate any possible shift in perceptions and role among stakeholders and publics.

Every grouping of similar ethnic, racial, religious, geographic, political, occupational, social, or special interest origins, interests, allegiance, or orientation represents a potential different 'public' for an enterprise. As in marketing, these represent segments of the total 'general public' who may have a particular orientation towards what you do and say.

Grunig and Repper (in Grunig, 1992) define *latent publics* who are motivated to become *active publics* by:

- becoming aware of a need for information in a given situation
- seeing themselves as limited by external factors rather than being in control; they begin to think that they might be able to change things, and thus begin to seek information with the intention of taking some action
- feeling involved in and affected by a situation.

Publics can be categorised and their communication behaviour predicted by considering their degree of problem recognition, degree of constraint recognition (i.e. to what extent they believe they can influence the problem outcome), and level of involvement (Grunig and Hunt, 1984; Grunig, 1983). To what extent do people passively attend to information or actively seek information? Publics who do not recognise a particular issue are termed *latent*. When a problem is recognised as relevant to their interests, the public is *aware*. If they then seek information or to take other actions, they become part of an *active* public. Communication behaviour analysis can identify publics that cannot be defined by demographic indicators or personal activities or attitudes.

Grunig's research suggests that publics defined in terms of their similarity in *communication behaviour* are not the same as those identified by demographic attributes and attitudes (Grunig, 1983). The *information seeker* is sufficiently interested in a problem or situation to want to know more about it, while the *information processor* is aware of, and may be touched by, a message but does not actively seek the information. Problem recognition increases the probability of communication and information search. Recognition of constraints on the ability to act decreases the likelihood of action, since the person expects limitations and constraints on their own behaviour. The person's perceived level of involvement determines whether they adopt proactive information-seeking or passive information-processing behaviour (see Figure 6.2).

Grunig claims to consistently find four types of publics:

1 Those who are active on all issues
2 Those who are inattentive and inactive on all issues
3 Those who are active on only one or a limited number of related issues
4 Those who are active when an issue enters widespread social conversation.

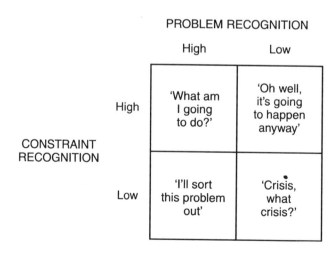

Figure 6.2 Behaviour based on perceptions of the situation.

These definitions of publics go well beyond demographics or psychographics to include relevant indicators of common recognition of mutual interests and features of situations that link certain people, but not others, to specific situations or issues, which in turn determine each public's composition, size, and range of responses. Publics, because they respond to issues, are dynamic. Public relations specialists need to re-define them from time to time by taking account of changes. The group boundaries (which define who is included in a public) need to be defined for each situation or problem.

DEFINING KEY PUBLICS

The public relations manager is interested in identifying key publics in order to develop a programme of communication activities focused on clear objectives. These objectives might be to increase or to decrease a public's problem or constraint recognition or involvement. The public relations manager needs also to take account of the public's resistance or willingness to change. General categories of potential stakeholder groups are of little real help since the planning and implementation of the programme receives little useful information about how people in each of the categories uniquely contribute to or are affected by the problem situation and organisation (Cutlip et al., 1993). Each of the stakeholder categories will have members who are to some degree aware-unaware, involved-uninvolved, or active-passive in a problem situation.

For a definition of a public to be useful to the manager, it must describe the public in relevant actionable terms, including:

- How the people are involved or affected by the problem situation or issue?
- Who they are?
- Where they live?
- What relevant organisations they belong to?
- What they do that is relevant to the situation?

Cutlip et al. (1993:361) and Broom and Dozier (1990:32) describe a range of factors which can be used singularly or in combination to define target publics from the various stakeholder groups:

- *Geographics* – natural or political boundaries and addresses only tell the planner where to find people and provide the data for direct mail.
- *Demographics* – individual characteristics such as age, gender, income are generally of little help in understanding why or how people are involved or affected by situations or issues.
- *Psychographics* – knowledge of lifestyle or psychological factors is only of real value if linked to other attributes relevant to a particular situation or issue. The VALS (values and lifestyles) psychographic segmentation system is based on consumer behaviour research, and considers *attitudes* (disposition or tendency towards something), *opinions* (judgements about something), and *beliefs* (convictions about truth or right/wrong).

- *Covert power* – the behind-the-scenes power and influence exerted by some people can be identified by careful observation and reference to other people.
- *Position* – some people may be identified as important in a particular situation because of the roles they play in positions of influence they hold.
- *Reputation* – opinion leaders and influencers may be defined by people in situations.
- *Membership* – affiliation and membership of a professional association or special interest group may be important because they usually receive controlled media messages from their organisation.
- *Role in the decision process* – seeks to identify those who influence decisions in a particular situation and are most active in making decisions, taking action and communicating.

The main concern in defining publics is to identify how people are involved and affected in the situation for which the programme of public relations activity is to be designed to deal with. The interpretation of behaviour – how people perceive certain situations and how they behave in them – is crucial. Only when the planner understands what various people know about a situation or issue, how they feel about it, and what they do or can do that either contributes or reacts to it, can they set realistic and worthwhile objectives and design strategies to achieve them, for each defined public. It is also important to realise that publics are not fixed unified entities. They vary from situation to situation and over time. They, as a collection of people, and their relationships with an organisation are dynamic.

There is increasing diversity in society. The stereotypes which once permitted mass communication are no longer workable. Individuals have many roles and may belong to more than one public or stakeholder group:

> The author as – parent, motorist, voter, employee, taxpayer, citizen, Yorkshire-man, consumer, personal computer user, husband, book reader, music lover . . .

Various publics may include the same people playing out different roles at different times. Conflict may even exist between two or more publics. Protesters on the Newbury by-pass site tried to protect wildlife and came into conflict with residents and contractors who wanted a safer town and the creation of jobs.

PRIORITISING PUBLICS

Freeman (1984) suggested the development of a *stakeholder map* which identifies all stakeholders through environmental scanning research. The public relations practitioner needs to think through the consequences of the organisation on people and those that people may have for the organisation. Research methods may include:

- public opinion polls
- examination of mass and specialist media, including academic and technical journals
- conference with political and community leaders
- expert advice from issues management committees.

The research activity would include ongoing *issue forecasting*, that is research to collect and interpret information to determine how the organisation and its publics (re-defined if necessary) might react to a future event, trend, or controversy. From this key future publics can be identified.

Once research has provided the facts needed about a given issue, situation, or opportunity, the public relations manager needs to begin exploring the publics involved. Existing profiles of publics should be examined to see how each group of individuals might be affected. By comprehensively examining all publics, areas of conflicting interest between divergent publics may be discovered.

The publics can then be ranked and assigned a weighting to indicate their relative impact on the organisation and/or the extent to which the organisation believes it should moderate its consequences on them. It is also important to identify which are active and which are passive. Prioritising may take into account the specific issue and how the set of publics may act collectively. Quality circles and focus groups methods serve to bring managers and external groups together to review problems. The interpretation of behaviour is another approach, as discussed earlier.

Some methods have been developed to help managers to identify their priority publics. The *P*ublic *V*ulnerability *I*mportance Index (PVI) calculates an estimate of the *importance* of a public to the organisation and to its public relations programmes by summing an estimate of the *potential* of a public to be influenced by the organisation plus the *vulnerability* of the organisation to action from that public. The PR quotient, devised by Muller, uses a list of 40 questions with weighted responses to evaluate the importance of various publics (see *Public Relations Quarterly*, Fall, 1990:11–13).

The priority or 'target' public may be determined by large-scale socio-economic or socio-political changes. The only professional way to go about prioritising publics is to conduct research and to develop sensitivity to their attitudes and to try to imagine how they will feel and react.

Priorities are necessary because of constraints on money, people, and other resources available for public relations work. The public relations manager can then plan an ongoing communication programme by working down the list of priority publics as far as the available resources will go. Priorities must be reviewed regularly; they can change suddenly due to outside events beyond the control of the organisation, for example, when an election of government takes place.

SUMMARY AND CONCLUSIONS

Publics are not the same as markets and have to be treated in a different manner than that used by the marketer. Promotion through advertising and publicity, and persuasion through selling activities, are not appropriate for much of the work that has to be done to build and maintain positive relationships between the organisation and a range of people who may be adversely affected by some management decisions and the behaviour of the organisation.

Table 6.2 is a comparison of the various groups to which managers must pay attention.

The public relations practitioner should plan communication programmes with the various stakeholders and publics at each of the three stages that any individual

Table 6.2 Comparison of various groups

Group	Composition of group
Market (Dibb et al., 1994)	Persons for whom a firm creates and maintains product and service offerings, communication mechanisms, promotional messages, points of delivery of value, to specifically fit the needs and preferences of the group's members.
Stakeholder (Johnson and Scholes, 1993)	A group or individual who may gain or lose from, or have an expectation of, the organisation's performance – this may arise as a result of a specific event or issue – need to map out their expected reactions to a variety of possible changes.
Audience	Passive recipients of a message or performance.
Interest group	People who are prepared to take action on an issue of interest to them.
Public (Newsom et al., 1993)	People tied together, however loosely, by some common bond of interest or concern that has some involvement with the particular organisation.

or group may, at a particular time, and for a particular issue, be located within (Grunig and Repper, in Grunig, 1992:124). The three stages identified by Grunig are: stakeholder > public > issue. Perhaps this is better thought of as a stakeholder being transformed into a public by their own identification of an issue which has importance to them.

It is particularly important to manage planned communication at the stakeholder stage before any conflict occurs, since any public is a potential adversary, and this will depend upon the specific situation. This helps to develop stable, long-term relationships in order to build support from stakeholders and to manage conflict when it occurs. Active publics seek information; then the public relations manager must ensure that the organisation is not engaged only in reactive communication, but has a proactive programme of appropriate communication activity operating effectively with the priority publics and stakeholders. The communication must be two-way with the organisation listening and modifying its practices to create alignment of interests (Duncan, 1995).

The public relations function must monitor its publics and their environments to:

- identify issues
- analyse opinion
- build or rebuild relationships
- measure effectiveness in business terms.

Publics are those groups and individuals who hold expectations and whose behaviour, judgements, and opinions can influence the operation and performance of the organisation. Public relations is about harmonising the interests of the

99

organisation with those of the people on whom its success depends. This may require changes to the organisation's proposed business strategy and plans.

The public relations manager must gauge the organisation's sense of commitment to its various publics, which often have conflicting interests. Every organisation needs to compile a comprehensive list of its stakeholders and key publics, and recognise that at any time any particular public may become the focal point for a public relations effort as a 'target', 'key', or 'priority' public. Research is necessary to define each public's characteristic knowledge, predispositions and behaviours. This information is essential to the understanding and awareness required in setting public relations programme objectives. The most suitable performance standard for public relations work is the degree to which the organisation satisfies the demands of its relevant publics.

DISCUSSION TOPICS

1 In what circumstances do marketing and public relations specialists logically need to co-operate? To what extent is public relations a form of market intelligence?

2 List your own personal issues on which you are part of an active public.

3 For a prominent issue in recent times, list the stakeholders. Identify the priority publics for the issue.

4 When you have read the Brent Spar case study, see if you can define the core issue and can identify other publics. List all of the stakeholders for Shell UK.

5 Public relations may be thought of as essentially about reputation management. Is it possible to have a different reputation with each public? Think of an illustrative example of this.

6 Think of an example of a situation in which unfolding developments would require the re-definition of priority publics.

7 If stakeholders are passive, what is the best way of ensuring that a dialogue takes place with them?

8 Put yourself in the position of the head of public relations at Shell UK. How would you have dealt with the situation over Brent Spar?

9 Why is the use of the notion of an audience for public relations increasingly being discarded?

10 To what extent, and how, might the segmentation activities for markets and publics overlap for a typical product manufacturing organisation?

CASE STUDY: BRENT SPAR – A PLATFORM FOR CONTENTION?

Introduction

When the decision was taken to decommission and dispose of a North Sea oil platform, the managers of Shell (UK) Exploration & Production must have had little, if any, inkling of what was to transpire out in the Atlantic and on the pages and screens of Europe's news media. A perfectly rational judgement based on business and environmental analysis and the best interests of the company had been made following the seeking of a study of possible environmental impact and the approval of the British Government. Unfortunately for Shell (UK) management, there were many other people who were to find the abandonment of the Brent Spar to be of great interest and concern.

The object of attention

The Brent Spar is a 14,500 tonne cylindrical buoy of 20 mm plate steel, some 29 metres in diameter and 137 metres in length, of which 28 metres stands above the water line. The structure has three sections: a helicopter landing deck, crane, tanker mooring, and loading boom, and accommodation for 30 people; six storage tanks capable of holding 300,000 barrels of oil; and a sealed ballast compartment.

The unit was used to store oil and to act as a tanker loading facility in the Brent Oil Field during 1976–91. After some 15 years of service and a 1991 estimate of a likely cost of £90m and two to three months out of commission for refurbishment, it was decided to decommission the unit. Shell (UK) examined several onshore and offshore abandonment options, and decided to sink the unit in an approved deep-water disposal site in the North East Atlantic.

Rudall Blanchard Associates Ltd had prepared a detailed report on the possible environmental impacts of this option in December 1994. At this point it was estimated that the oil storage tanks contained some 48,000 m^3 of sea water, 100 tonnes of oily sludge (of which approximately 10 tonnes was oil and heavy metals), and about 41 tonnes of oil and wax coating to the tank walls.

For the most likely of the three sinking scenarios considered, it was thought that contamination would not spread beyond 500 metres from the point of impact on the seabed, some 150 miles west of the Hebrides in 2,000 metres of Atlantic waters. Corrosion estimates suggested that the seabed resting place would leave the steel structure largely intact for some 4,000 years.

The battle of the Brent Spar – in the public arena

The first news report of the intended disposal at sea of the Brent Spar broke in March 1995. Greenpeace Germany did not stand still and by 10 April members in Hamburg had a plan for direct action. On 27 April as the Brent Spar was being towed out to the licensed dumping ground in the North East Atlantic, the Greenpeace campaign swung into action. Four specialist climbers had been hired to make a daring attempt to board the platform. This they succeeded in doing. They were quickly followed by 26 other activists from around Europe and 20 tonnes of equipment and supplies, including a live satellite link. Greenpeace had begun a £750,000 operation to stop the dumping of the Brent Spar through direct action.

By Sunday, 30 April, Shell had drafted plans to deal with the boarding but these were overtaken by Greenpeace's next move, which was to get a number of journalists onboard the platform. By now some £350,000 of media equipment was also onboard, including a live satellite link which was beaming pictures to German TV within hours. Greenpeace were also simultaneously lobbying at the Fourth North Sea Minister's Conference. In time, due to the efforts of Shell, protesters left the platform but

Greenpeace attempted to re-board Brent Spar on 16 June. Chancellor Helmut Kohl of Germany berates John Major for supporting the company's plans. In late May, Deutsche Shell was visited by a Greenpeace Germany representative delegation.

In June, Greenpeace claimed to have targeted 100 UK Shell service stations with groups of protesters – an estimated 75 per cent of Shell's customers at these sites were turned away, they claimed. Around this time, MPs in the UK were raising the issue in Parliament, while in Leipzig, Germany, officials were barred from signing supply contracts with Shell, and even Dutch Ministers declared that they would not buy Shell petrol. The Lutheran Church boycotted Shell garages. Overall, sales of Shell products fell by around 30 per cent in Germany during this time. Similar boycotts followed in Denmark, Holland, and other North Sea countries, and demonstrations took place in several European cities. Also in June, the Oslo & Paris Commission (OSPAR) voted to ban the dumping of oil installations in the North East Atlantic. The UK Government objected to the decision, which in any case was not legally binding in the UK.

Meanwhile, on 16 June two Greenpeace protesters re-occupied the Brent Spar by being dropped from a helicopter while it was being towed to the disposal site in the North East Atlantic. Shell products were being boycotted in Germany and this was spreading elsewhere in Europe. On 17 and 18 June two Shell service stations in Hamburg, home of the Deutsche Shell headquarters, were attacked. One was destroyed by fire bombs planted by protesters; the other was fired on with handguns. A third service station was attacked with fireworks. This coincided with an announcement from Shell UK that executives would now spend more time trying to 'more fully explain the merits' of the plan.

On 20 June, the about-turn was announced: the UK Chairman had been ordered to make a U-turn on the decision by the Board of the Anglo-Dutch parent company Royal Dutch Shell, headquartered in The Hague. The group Board had never objected to the original decision to abort the planned dumping, which was to have taken place on the 22nd. The Energy Minister, Tim Eggar, told Parliament that the Prime Minister supported Shell's plan. Only minutes later a press release was issued in London announcing that their operation was being halted. Shell had reversed its decision and would cease the disposal operation, insisting that this was due to pressure from other European governments. The UK Government were reportedly infuriated since they had continued to support the original decision. Shell failed to communicate with its most valuable champion, even after receiving powerful public backing by the government.

In August 1995 the Brent Spar could be seen moored in a Norwegian fjord. The Norwegian ship classification society, Den Norske Veritas (DNV) was commissioned to carry out an independent survey.

September was an embarrassing time for TV editors who had to admit that they had, arguably unwittingly, allowed Greenpeace to manipulate their news coverage of the saga. Greenpeace had supplied most of the film which had been used in news broadcasts. On 4 September Greenpeace admitted that their estimate of 5,500 tonnes of oil onboard the Brent Spar was wrong.

Lord Peter Melchett, UK Executive Director of Greenpeace, met with Christopher Fay, Shell's UK Chairman and Chief Executive, and re-affirmed their opposition to deep sea disposal of the Brent Spar. Shell UK was by now studying some 200 options for onshore disposal or re-use of the Brent Spar. Greenpeace confirmed that it had based its campaign on Shell's estimates of 100 tonnes of toxic sludge and 30 tonnes of low level radioactive waste. A further meeting between Shell's Board and Greenpeace was set for October.

DNV published their inventory of the contents of the Brent Spar in October. This was to assist in planning the onshore dismantling of the platform.

Who were the publics?

When the UK Board made the decision to dispose of Brent Spar at sea they felt that a good business decision had been made and that the UK Government was in support of their move. Moreover, from the environmental point of view they considered that deep disposal is the most practicable environmental option from a technical and scientific perspective. Technical considerations and a cost-benefit analysis had shown them the best option and the scientific basis for the decision was well rehearsed.

Over the next few months the Shell UK Board were to realise that a range of publics had put the issue of dumping on their agenda and that many would be outspoken, while others would be prepared to take direct action to vent their feelings. But just who were these publics?

Shell had the support of Prime Minister John Major and agreement, following investigations by the Department of Trade and Industry and the Department of the Environment, that their plan was right and best. The approval of the disposal plan by the UK Government was in line with international agreements, and made sense from a safety and economic point of view. Guidelines set by the International Maritime Organisation (a United Nations agency which oversees sea pollution issues) were met by the plan. The UK Offshore Operators Association (UKOOA) had also been consulted and had not opposed the plan.

The Chancellor of Germany, Helmut Kohl, openly and publicly disagreed with John Major at the G7 Summit in Halifax, Nova Scotia. The German Parliament tabled a debate which called for UK Ministers to abandon and ban such dumpings. Even the German Police refused to use Shell petrol. Consumers, especially in Germany, where reaction against the plan was strongest and severest, applied pressure to the company in the form of product switching and boycotts of Shell petrol stations. Other foreign Governments – the Danish, Swedish, Belgian and Dutch Governments – all applied pressure on the UK Government to stop the planned disposal.

Environmental regulators, concerned with protection – for example the Environment Agency, the European Commission, the European Parliament, and the National Environment Research Council – were key influences on the judgements about the suitability of the disposal plan. The whole issue of environmental protection was once again called into question in the light of increased awareness and sensitivity aroused by the Brent Spar problem. Many business people see the environmental protection system in Europe as costly and bureaucratic. At the same time, other people in Europe seem to want more not less protection of the environment.

Clearly, environmental pressure groups, including those willing and prepared to take direct action, such as Greenpeace, were central in raising awareness. Greenpeace created a high level of media coverage and were able to mobilise people's feelings about the apparent injustice of 'licensed waste disposal' in a way that caught Shell UK and the UK Government in a dilemma. A rational, scientifically sound decision was being halted by public outcry. Their management of this single issue campaign was effective and efficient. They were adamant, despite their mistake over the quantity of waste involved, that the campaign was about the question of moral acceptability of dumping at sea; the Brent Spar was simply a test case for this issue.

Even the public relations industry, through its professional group, the Institute of Public Relations (IPR), joined the debate. The IPR issued a statement saying that such a reversal of the decision to go ahead probably had a negative impact on Shell's public relations position. Their credibility as stewards of the environment in which they operate was called into question and this could damage the company's reputation.

Even employees of Shell did not escape the public spotlight. In Germany, threats were made against some employees of Deutsche Shell. The German subsidiary of RDS were also badly caught out in March 1995 when they had launched a high-profile corporate environmental and community project advertising campaign, which subsequently had to be abandoned. Greenpeace succeeded in creating a public humiliation of the entire Shell organisation; few people realise that the original decision to abandon at sea was made by the UK Board of Directors. The US 50 per cent partner Exxon (with the brand name Esso in the UK) may also have been affected, although many would not realise the relationship. Mr Peter Duncan, chief executive of Deutsche Shell, even admitted that he learned of the plans to dump at sea 'more or less from the television', according to *Der Spiegel*.

One particularly damaging aspect of the nature of publics and their interactions is the convergence of interests between various groups, including those who might be expected to be allies. For example, the oil rig yards spotted a salvage opportunity and perhaps, unintentionally, they fuelled the pressure on Shell UK.

Aftermath

Sales of Shell products were well down in Europe during the Summer of 1995. The Brent Spar is still anchored in a Norwegian fjord awaiting a firm decision on how to proceed.

To save the company from further embarrassment and criticism, Shell was forced to postpone its annual Better Britain awards, having encouraged positive environmental projects for a number of years. The UK Board of Shell has had to admit that it took too narrow a view and failed to translate the debate from science to emotion. Greenpeace's image is in question, especially in the UK where the backlash has been greatest. Did their climb-down on the facts about toxic waste damage Greenpeace's reputation?

Lessons learned?

In a worldwide business group which generates around £4bn in annual profits, surely the £40–50m cost of onshore dismantling is no big deal. Not so, since Brent Spar is only the first of hundreds more North Sea rigs which will have to be disposed of in the years ahead. In financial terms, as we have seen, which are too narrow to consider alone, this may be the case. But perhaps the public relations damage may be much greater and may last much longer?

Why was, arguably, a good rational business and scientifically-based decision, supported by careful preparation and technical planning, including cost-benefit analysis, the cause of so much anger and resentment? The analysis was apparently very thorough. Over four years was spent in getting DTI approval for the plan. It, however, dealt only with whether the environmental measure was worth pursuing and deciding this on cost in a cost-benefit analysis. The feelings of many people were not considered. Shell people had been careful to reach a balance between safety, environmental pollution, and economic factors. Yet, few outside the organisation were ever to understand this.

Company executives cannot ignore public opinion. Managers failed to identify a wide range of publics for this issue – and how they might interact with each other – yet, perhaps ironically, Shell was the pioneer of scenario planning in which efforts to foresee possible future issues and problems is formalised in the planning of the company. Equally, deep sea abandonment is not a new issue in any case. Yet, with 32 similar platforms in the North Sea, and a total of more than 50 oil structures which could be dumped if Brent Spar set a precedent, there was a woeful lack of communication with those who might feel some threat from the decision. Most of those at Shell who were involved in formulating the abandonment plan have trained as engineers. They are, generally, not used to considering emotions in their work and are not exposed to public opinion. Much of the furore which emerged was driven by emotions rather than by so-called 'rational science'. The outcry was on what many saw as a moral issue, rather than a technology issue. Laudably, their work on technical and scientific considerations was thorough and relevant – as would be expected of a worldclass company such as Shell. But even the Chairman had to admit, retrospectively, that they had (obviously) become too introspective in their thinking. Communication outside of company and government circles about the options was only an afterthought – once the fury of the decision had overtaken events.

Shell's effort to debate the issue was too reactive. First, dumping at sea was thought to be a positive option, so they failed to win adequate support by failing to detect the degree of public feeling in Europe. They tried to keep their heads down in the hope that no one would challenge their stance. The company had grown so sure of themselves and their argument (they had lived with it for four years) that they thought the 'scientific facts' would speak for themselves. Clearly, they had forgotten the power of persuasion – Greenpeace had not! The cumbersome, perhaps too complacent, culture of Shell UK had been exploited by a group intent on raising the issue of dumping in a cross-border forum in which the Germans, Dutch and Scandinavians seem to be especially environmentally sensitive. Perhaps managers spent too much effort on convincing the Government and emphasising that they had their approval, and placed too little importance on consulting with the wider stakeholder group – their own sister companies in the RDS group, employees, suppliers, and the various community groups. Increasingly, consumers are taking stands against companies – the connection between consumer spending and politics, in the form of ethical concerns, has never been more obvious.

The Internet was used extensively by environmental activists to communicate with each other. Greenpeace's use of the Internet to feed material to the news media was particularly sophisticated. In contrast, Shell UK had a homepage in the US, but it carried no mention of Brent Spar or Greenpeace.

Clearly, the decision-makers failed to recognise the political implications of their proposals, and consequently the quantity and style of communication was never able to anticipate the nature of the communication problem that faced the company. For example, Greenpeace Germany were publicly concerned with the issue of dumping, not the facts of the Brent Spar situation, right from the start of their campaign. Greenpeace staged a guerrilla war in which they were able to have themselves portrayed as plucky campaigners at the mercy of powerful exploitative opponents. Anti-Shell images were blitzed across the press and broadcast media. The Shell communication effort was consequently almost entirely reactive.

Mr Mike Beard, past President of the Institute of Public Relations, summed up Shell's problem: 'They failed to communicate the benefits of the course they believed to be right . . . now they're having to defend something they don't consider to be defensible' (editorial by D. Summer, *Financial Times*, 23 June 1995). The very act of attempting to abandon the Brent Spar has unnecessarily heightened environmental concern. In doing so, perhaps Shell UK has damaged, to some extent, its own corporate reputation and that of the oil industry (another of its stakeholders).

A clear lesson from the Brent Spar experience is that the oil industry, and companies like Shell UK need to communicate with their stakeholders in order to achieve a balance of interests. Further, companies have much to learn about how environmental issues can impact on their business. A careful, continuously updated, publics review can be of great value in identifying issues and in planning means to constructively deal with them in an honest responsive manner. An Environmental Management System is one approach which could have aided Shell to have anticipated the uproar over the Brent Spar plan. This system would have required provisions for more extensive consultations with environmental groups.

One final question concerns the nature of the Greenpeace campaign. Some have described it as a meeting of piracy, politics and propaganda, in returning to high profile stunts. Estimates of Greenpeace expenditure on the campaign are about £1.4m, of which some £370,000 was spent on communications. Did Greenpeace's methods on this single issue political campaign turn into blackmail? Will the perceptions of the organisation lead to damaged credibility in the long-run? Who are the key publics for Greenpeace? Some have portrayed the confrontation with Shell as like David and Goliath. But, as pointed out by Colin Duncan, Director of Corporate Communications at British Nuclear Fuels plc, in his workshop at the 1995 Institute of Public Relations Conference, perhaps it is nearer the mark to portray

Greenpeace as Goliath. With 43 offices and almost 1,400 full-time staff spending an annual budget of some $150m, with a fleet of ships, and a real-time IT and communications network, their operation is a formidable opponent in any single issue campaign.

Postscript

With 200 platforms in the British sector of the North Sea, several of which are soon to be decommissioned, this problem will not go away easily. Shell UK and other oil companies have since hired a specialist public relations firm to help create a climate of political and public opinion which permits such decisions to be implemented without a public backlash.

In January 1996, Elf Petroleum announced that it was awarding a $15m contract to a Norwegian company to remove and dismantle, onshore, an abandoned oil platform from the Norwegian Continental Shelf.

In March 1996, Shell UK announced the planned onshore dismantling of a further oilfield structure. This follows a report from the UKOOA which concludes that on-land disposal and recycling of oil rigs is preferable to sea dumping, on environmental grounds. This time there was a noticeably quiet press. In the meantime, Shell International have sought advice from outsiders who they feel can offer 'an informed, thoughtful set of external observations on the nature of Shell's situation' (*PR Week*, 15 March 1996). This was not to be seen as an invitation for public relations agencies to make pitches for future business, a Shell communications spokesman added.

ACKNOWLEDGEMENTS

The author wishes to acknowledge the assistance of Professor Doug Newsom (Texas Christian University), Professor Jon White (City Business School), and Colin Duncan, Director of Corporate Communications (British Nuclear Fuels plc), in the preparation of this chapter.

REFERENCES

Black, S. (1993) *The Essentials of Public Relations*, London: Kogan Page.

Briggs, W. and Tucson, M. (1993) *PR vs. Marketing, Communication World*, San Francisco: International Association of Business Communicators.

Broom, G.M. and Dozier, D.M. (1990) *Using Research in Public Relations: Applications in Program Management*, London: Prentice-Hall.

Cutlip, S.M., Center, A.H. and Broom, G.M. (1994) *Effective Public Relations*, 7th edn, London: Prentice-Hall.

Duncan, C. (1995) Corporate Communications as a tool for Corporate Alignment, speech given at the Launch of the BNFL Corporate Communications Unit, University of Salford, 27 November.

Freeman, R.E. (1984) *Strategic Management: A Stakeholder Approach*, London: Pitman.

Grunig, J.E. (1983) 'Communication Behaviours and Attitudes of Environmental Publics: Two Cases', *Journalism Monographs*, No. 81, pp. 40–41.

Grunig, J.E. (1992) *Excellence in Public Relations and Communication Management*, Hillsdale, NJ.: Lawrence Erlbaum Associates.

Grunig, J.E. and Hunt, T. (1984) *Managing Public Relations*, New York: Holt, Rinehart & Winston.

Johnson, G. and Scholes, K. (1993) *Exploring Corporate Strategy*, 3rd edn, London: Prentice-Hall.

Newsom, D., Scott, A. and Vanslyke Turk, J. (1993) *This is PR: The Realities of Public Relations*, 5th edn, Belmont, CA.: Wadsworth Publishing Company.

Parkinson, C.N. and Rowe, N. (1977) *Communicate: Parkinson's Formula for Business Survival*, London: Prentice-Hall.

White, J. (1991) *How to Understand and Manage Public Relations*, London: Business Books.

7

EXTERNAL PUBLIC RELATIONS ACTIVITIES

Richard Varey

CHAPTER AIMS

- to identify and discuss the nature of major external activities of public relations managers and their functions
- to provide insight into the breadth of activities conducted by public relations specialists
- to research emphasis for public relations activity planning
- to provide an understanding that public relations is not concerned solely with product promotion and is not simply 'free' advertising or company promotion
- to give detailed illustration of how external public relations activities are co-ordinated with wider business aims and objectives

ILLUSTRATION

Publicity is but one part of public relations work. Public relations is an extensive field of activities for dealing with creation and maintenance of a positive reputation and goodwill, and of influencing long-term public opinion on issues which affect the business.

For example, consider the small electronics company which gained wide press coverage in trade journals and the national media when they received a visit from Japanese scientists to their UK factory. Domestic sales and product enquiry levels increased as people got the message that the Japanese were trying to learn from this, presumably innovative, company. The media coverage was well in excess of that which the company could have afforded at normal advertising rates, and the reports were perceived as credible because they were written by independent journalists and thus seen as 'news' rather than advertising. But this is not public relations. It is a good example of publicity, and rightly should be thought of as successful promotion, as a part of the company's marketing, and as a tool of public relations.

Contrast this with the situation in which a UK company received a range of complaints from local residents including concerns about heavy lorries, litter and other aspects of site operations. As part of a constructive approach to community relations, the public relations managers decided to hold a public meeting at which the company could hear more about residents' concerns and show a human face in their attempts to deal with them in a constructive manner. This was followed by face-to-face interviews with some of the residents, carried out by a small team of independent researchers from a local university, to help managers better understand the origins and nature of concerns. The information gathered in this non-threatening way was included in further planning of a community relations programme which will serve to bring the company's managers and local residents into a closer dialogue about how and why the site is run in a particular way.

INTRODUCTION

Most people think of 'PR' as a way of influencing the thinking of people who are not members of the organisation, especially customers and others who can influence purchase and supplier selection decisions. In practice, professional public relations is essentially about identifying key publics and interacting in various appropriate ways with them by giving and receiving information, and the forming of policies in co-operation with managers.

Effective public relations involves a wide range of activities, including announcement of expansion plans and new appointments, community and charity donations and expert comment in the media on news items. Public relations is not simply the promotion of the company's selling message – this is publicity. Making sure that the organisation's representatives are involved in public debate, and that key publics are informed, is an essential role of the public relations manager. The establishment and maintenance of a climate of trust and openness is an essential aspect of relationships with all those who can exert power over the manager's right to manage.

The public relations manager has a much wider remit than simply media coverage. While public relations need good press relations, the public relations manager must never forget that a high media profile means that bad news as well as good news will be reported. It is the climate in which 'bad' news is raised that should be a major concern of the public relations function.

Public relations work consists of a range of principal activities (Greyser, 1981; Raucher, 1990) which fit with the overall concept of a managed relationship climate. For example, Panigyrakis (1994) listed the primary activities of the public relations manager in a consumer goods company, ranked by importance:

1 Writing
2 Editing
3 Media relations
4 Special events
5 Speaking
6 Production
7 Research
8 Programming
9 Training
10 Management

A study of public relations by Spicer (1991) identified major activities undertaken by public relations managers, including:

- Writing, editing, and proofing their own and others' work for publication
- Media relations and special events
- Communication management – decision-making, problem-solving, establishing budgets
- Co-ordination of relations and servicing 'clients'
- Speaking to employees and to others outside the organisation.

A further, too often neglected, aspect of public relations management work is the carefully considered and thought-out planning and evaluation of day-to-day activities within a longer-term framework of business aims and objectives.

CHAPTER OVERVIEW

Public relations is identified as part of management and as concerned with the reputation of the organisation. Relationships with publics depend on perceptions of corporate identity and image and have to be constructively managed if the organisation is to retain and justify its 'licence to operate'.

A range of linked, often interdependent, activities are discussed.

The role of the strategic public relations manager is to help favourably position the organisation in the minds of key publics (see Chapter 8) and to create a climate in which understanding and acceptance is sought and achieved.

A public relations management framework is set out. This can help to ensure that public relations activities are appropriate, co-ordinated and meet the communication needs of the organisation and its key publics.

A case study of the visitors centre at the British Nuclear Fuels site at Sellafield in Cumbria illustrates how many activities can be programmed around business aims and objectives.

EXTERNAL PUBLIC RELATIONS ACTIVITIES

Public relations is: 'the discipline which looks after reputation with the aim of earning understanding and support and influencing opinion and behaviour' (Beard in Hart, 1995:xviii). Whether an organisation achieves its objectives can depend on what people think about it, what it does, and what it says, that is on its reputation. Public relations is not simply 'press relations'! According to Jefkins, the public relations task is: 'to present untreated credible facts in order to overcome misunderstanding and the resulting hostility, prejudice, apathy, and ignorance' (Jefkins, 1994).

White (1991) and White and Mazur (1994) view public relations as much part of management as human resource management or financial management – the management of relationships between the organisation and its various 'publics': employees, shareholders, customers, and other interested parties. The 1978 'Mexican Statement' from an international gathering of public relations societies provides a broader and more precise description of the role of public relations:

Public relations practice is the art and social science of analysing trends, predicting their consequences, counselling organisation leaders, and implementing planned programmes of action which will serve both the organisation's and the public interest (Jefkins, 1991:181).

Public relations, then, identifies and anticipates issues likely to affect key relationships and responds for the development of those relationships. Thus public relations contributes to planning, cohesion and effectiveness through managed communication with a range of groups. If only the practice were like this! This attention to all of the members of the web of relationships may result in organisational change if current or intended activities, policies, and plans do not fit with the needs and expectations of other parties. Thus public relations must enter the planning RACE (Marston, 1979; and discussed by White, 1991):

Research > Analysis > Communication (action) > Evaluation

Once a range of groups of individuals (publics) located outside the organisation have been identified the public relations manager may wish to establish and maintain a dialogue with some for various reasons, including community relations, strategic crisis management, customer relations, investor relations, issue management, employee recruitment, supplier relations and government relations.

External communication aims to *ensure positive supportive relationships now and in the future* with those groups outside the organisation who influence access to required resources – this, of course, includes the sale of goods and services, new investment, changes to working practices, or the provision of further financial support in the case of public sector and not-for-profit organisations.

Essentially, advertising and public relations are the two approaches – some even claim that advertising is part of public relations (Hart, 1995:24), whilst traditionally it has been seen as a tool of marketing communications (Jefkins, 1991). Yet marketers are in the communication business, responsible for relationships with customers, product/service promotion, and market research.

Some would observe that essentially external communication is taken care of by advertising on the one hand (i.e. promotional messages) (see Shimp, 1993, for example, who argues that marketing requires both a marketing concept and a promotion concept) and public relations on the other. I would wish to broaden this to include marketing communications which are genuinely two-way. This would include market research, customer satisfaction surveys, teamworking which includes customers, company visits, and so on. Traditionally, marketing communications were seen as one-way promotional efforts via advertising, publicity, personal selling, exhibitions, direct mail, sponsorship and sales promotions (point-of-sale material, offers, etc.). The more enlightened approach now seeks dialogue and emphasises listening to customers' and users' needs and feelings rather more than simply telling them the company message. High-level communication skills have usually been thought of as talking articulately and giving compelling presentations. To what extent do managers concentrate on facilitating the other part of a conversation or dialogue as well as delivering their own? (Dixon, 1993).

CORPORATE IDENTITY AND IMAGE

Corporate communication focuses responsibilities for narrowing the gap between the organisation's desired image and its actual image; establishing a consistent organisation profile; and, the organisation of communication by developing and implementing guidelines for co-ordinating all internal and external communication, and controlling communications. Public relations complements marketing communication in achieving the aims of the organisation among external publics.

Corporate identity is the strategically planned and operationally applied self-presentation of the organisation (the corporate self) on the basis of a desired image. A strong corporate identity:

- raises employee motivation
- inspires confidence among the organisation's key external groups
- acknowledges the vital role of customers
- acknowledges the vital role of key financial groups.

Professor Cees van Riel (1995) suggests that corporate identity is like a 'business adhesive'. When powerful, it increases the likelihood of identification or bonding of internal and external key groups with the organisation.

Corporate identity is often misunderstood by managers and many think it is the same as image. It is best to think of the planned and operational self-presentation of an organisation, both internal and external, based on an agreed organisation philosophy, that is it is developed through the channels and techniques used by management. Indeed, any action of expression of the organisation is either one of:

- *behaviour* – ultimately people are judged by their actions, or
- *communication* – verbal and visual messages can be used tactically (but be warned these had better be consistent with actual behaviour), or
- *symbolism* – this is the recognised design and graphics aspect, including logo, slogans, house style, uniforms, office and shop fittings, vehicle livery, etc., or
- *personality* – the manifestation of the organisation's self-perception.

Corporate image appears cumulatively as recipients of messages interact with the organisation and their interest and involvement grows. They form a mental picture of the organisation and its products. The image develops like a photographic plate, through a series of impressions that the individual experiences. Thus an image is:

> a set of meanings by which an object is known and through which people describe, remember and relate to it. That is the result of the interaction of a person's beliefs, ideas, feelings and impressions about an object (Dowling, 1986).

Garbett (1988) provides a useful checklist on corporate image formation:

$$\text{Reality of the company} + \text{Newsworthiness of company activities} + \text{Communication efforts} \times \text{Time} - \text{Memory decay} = \text{Company image}$$

Companies increasingly have to justify their actions. When the image does not equal reality, people will suspect contrivance. Managers must seek to reflect reality in their corporate image. Corporate communication translates an identity into an image. The organisation's people must understand and accept a clear corporate identity in order to use such media as advertising, public relations, building design, products and their behaviour (effort, expertise and attitudes) to portray it consistently so as to not produce a confused image in the minds of key groups' members. It is not what the media says about the organisation and its people that counts. It is what key individuals and groups believe.

Impression management is a policy of presenting the organisation to key groups in such a way as to evoke in them a favourable image or to avoid an unfavourable image (Giacalone and Rosenfeld, 1991; Bromley, 1993).

Corporate reputation is what people think and say about the organisation, its products/services, and the behaviour of its people. Some argue that public relations really is just about reputation management (Bernstein, 1984; Smythe et al., 1992; Bromley, 1993; Dowling, 1994; Haywood, 1994; Greyser, 1981;; Frombrun, 1995).

Strategic positioning is essentially the conscious choice of a particular basis for competitive advantage – the combination of an appeal to the customer or stakeholder and the competitive considerations that can give a company or brand a distinctive perception or position in the key group's mind(s).

This requires that the organisation is better than the competition in terms relevant to their targeted groups, irrespective of what the organisation's members themselves think is important. The organisation must be perceived to be better, as well as performing better, and it must therefore sell to the right customers based on good knowledge of its strengths and weaknesses and those of other providers. Managers must decide *where* to compete and *how.*

The communication task is then to translate the desired strategic position into behaviour, communication messages and symbols at the organisational, operational and functional levels. Managers must decide clearly how they wish to present the organisation and its offerings, having clearly identified their key groups using stakeholder analysis, to understand what images they have of the organisation. They must then create a corporate image mix which delivers the desired image, while keeping an eye out for changes in competitors' corporate image mixes. The creation of a suitable mix consists of:

- determining communication objectives
- selecting target groups (those customers and publics that matter)
- formulating appropriate message(s)
- selecting media and planning
- organising (co-ordination).

STRATEGIC PUBLIC RELATIONS

As pointed out by Black (1995), the activities of public relations go well beyond many people's perceptions of the PR function. Black is among a growing number of observers and practitioners who argue that PR and public relations have ceased to be synonymous. The former is concerned with getting media coverage (in terms of 'column inches') for a selling message, while the professional would claim that the latter is far more to do with creating understanding among all parties (see, for example, Jefkins' (1994:11) 'public relations transfer process'.

Today, there is so much choice for where and how to communicate with key publics – new techniques have been developed over the years, and there has been a proliferation of communication channels, with the advent of cable and satellite TV, video conferencing, e-mail and personal communications networks (mobile telephones and laptop computers with fax facilities). Ultimately, however, the choice of channels and techniques must rest on objectives and the accessibility of the important publics, before considerations of cost are allowed to limit the options, the needs of the communicators and the measures of desired effectiveness must be considered. The major concern of the public relations specialist must be the use of appropriate media and channels of communication.

The external public relations activities conducted have the objective of defining, developing and managing the company's corporate and/or product brands. Programme planning, monitoring and control should be closely tied to business objectives. Jefkins' Six-Point PR Planning Model (Jefkins, 1994:72) is an appropriate approach:

1 appreciate the situation (research)
2 define objectives
3 define all publics relevant to the programme
4 select appropriate media and techniques
5 set a realistic budget
6 monitor and evaluate the results.

The professional public relations manager must be concerned to communicate with a wide range of audiences in a professional way, thereby safeguarding the company's licence to operate – in an honest and sincere manner – even when there is disagreement, and to actively seek responses and to canvass views on matters concerning the operation of the business.

A range of activities of *strategic public relations* is now discussed.

Media relations, perhaps the most obvious activity, seeks publicity and fosters positive interest by the press and other media in your organisation. Managers can create goodwill and understanding through effective news coverage. The media are not just a *channel* of communication, they themselves are a key group. Managers need to work at earning their respect, appreciating what news is, being truly creative, meeting the needs of journalists and producers, and building their credibility with the media. Journalists typically want:

- Fast reaction to enquiries
- Open and honest media relations policy
- Willingness to deal with unfavourable news
- Accessibility of managers rather than the press/media department
- Understandable and easy-to-use information
- Proactive policy of contact; regular, consistent, personal.

Preparation of news and other press release documents which takes a proactive standpoint and anticipates media interest, in an effort to avoid reactive 'fire-fighting', is a hallmark of the modern public relations office activity. Topics will include marketing developments, company policies, news of general interest, personalities, current developments. Writing may be for feature articles on issue-related topics rather than on self-promotion of the company.

Publicity is the dissemination of purposefully planned and executed messages through selected (unpaid) media to further the particular interest of an organisation or person. Public relations has much more to offer in helping the organisation to meet its long-term business aims and objectives. *Press agentry* creates short-lived news events, while *promotion* is a series of special events or activities designed to create and stimulate interest in a person, product, organisation or cause. Media relations work is distinct from advertising and selling since it seeks publicity for, or responds to interest in, an organisation and/or its products. *Propaganda*, on the other hand, is the effort to influence the opinions of a public in order to spread a particular belief. Public relations has a much greater interest in dialogue between the organisation and its key stakeholder groups and publics.

As Bob Hoskins says in the recent BT advertisements 'It's good to talk'. Managers must be talking with the media even in the good times to prepare the ground: to maintain the right to tell things in their own time at their own discretion; to narrow the gaps between real, declared, and perceived intentions and actions; to ensure that their voice is heard.

Financial relations aims to foster supportive relationships and to handle communication within the financial calendar with shareholders (existing and potential), investors, the City (stockbrokers, merchant banks, analysts) and financial journalists.

Public affairs can cover strategic communications planning and deals with various audiences at the corporate level – government, press, public organisations, the City, shareholders, trade unions and the general public. While many see public relations as a policy-making function of organisations, they may use the term public affairs to include the interaction with groups and government that leads to public policy and legislation.

Lobbying (government affairs) identifies and acts for the particular interests of the organisation at local, national, and international political levels among legislators and government agencies. A realistic presentation of a clear case with sustained pressure over an appropriate timescale requires good long-range intelligence. This is much more than simply monitoring parliamentary activity. The aim is to influence and to thereby set the managers' own agenda on matters that can affect their business performance now and in the future. Liaison with politicians is a vital part of many public relations portfolios and will be especially important in industries where government regulation is significant (Jefkins, 1994).

Industry relations covers communication with organisations within the industry of which the organisation is a part, for example, trade associations and research bodies. Some organisations have found it helpful to conduct *minority relations*, that is communication with individuals and groups of racial or ethnic minorities.

Corporate advertising treats the organisation as the product and is the 'face and voice' of the organisation. Little understood, and sometimes feared by managers, this highly public communications technique does not directly deliver sales and market share and is thus often difficult to justify (Garbett, 1981; Worcester, 1986; Schumann et al., 1991; Gregory, 1991). Research has shown that while expensive, corporate advertising can strengthen image, there must be no significant gap between the organisation's corporate message and their customers' perceptions of their services/products and you.

Corporate social responsibility is clearly on many boardroom and key group agendas in the 1990s (Collins, 1993; Carroll, 1993; Embley, 1993), especially activist/pressure groups. Society expects businesses to make profits, at a cost. Society expects the corporate citizen to give as well as take. *Community relations* requires clear policy for dealing with the concerns and interests of local groups in matters of the organisation's future direction and its corporate citizenship (i.e. acceptance of benefits and responsibilities in the relationship) in the local community.

There has been a resurgent interest in the notion of corporate social responsibility in recent years as a process by which a company manages its relationships with groups which have the capacity, individually and collectively, to influence organisational ability to succeed at its chosen endeavours (see Carroll, 1993, for example). Relationships are symbiotic: the enterprise managers need each other to prosper. The organisation has a relationship whether it is wanted or not; it must be managed. Whether or not such relationships enhance reputation is up to the manager.

The concept of *stakeholders* as individuals or groups with a vested interest in organisational activities is central to corporate social responsibility as a management concern. These people interact with the organisation in some of its activities and their co-operation is required if the organisation is to be successful in pursuit of its business. Managing stakeholder relationships is to be seen as an investment and at the core of business planning and management.

Management of stakeholder relationships does not eliminate conflicting pressures between stakeholders, one of which is, of course, the organisation itself. It recognises the need for trade-offs between differing needs and expectations and develops a clear understanding of the impact of organisation decisions on various groups, and makes the trade-offs more explicit and objective. Above all, it requires managers to respond positively to the needs and aspirations of a wide range of interest groups, by realistically and thoroughly assessing the mutual interdependency of each stakeholder relationship.

Community involvement deals with one especially important key group for the socially responsible organisation. This two-way approach to the organisation's relationship with the local community is part of the broader long-term business investments which are intended to make a positive contribution to the business, and thereby society as a whole.

Public relations specialists are often called upon to represent their company in various local community groups, to assist in gauging local public opinion and to respond with suitable community involvement programmes, as a visible manifestation of managers' sense of corporate social responsibility, although this can be either genuine or cynical, of course.

Sponsorship is where the company buys exclusivity for an event or sports competition, or lends its name to a product, to promote itself through media exposure and/or positive association with the event. In supporting an activity or event, the company's managers will expect a tangible return for their money and effort – engendering goodwill, influencing customers, creating a high profile for the organisation or a product or brand, for example. The public relations manager can hope that their key group(s) remember the company and its offerings long after the financial support has ended.

Information services are an essential part of fostering mutual trust and understanding between the company and other groups. The public relations office should take the lead in co-ordinating the provision of information to the public media about company activities, and this will often include educational material which may aim to increase awareness and understanding of both the company and its industry.

At BNFL Sellafield, such is the interest in the company's plans and operations that a Speakers Panel provides over 1,000 organised talks to a wide range of audiences each year. Since this places managers in the role of 'part-time public relations officers', the public relations team provide speech writing support for managers, to ensure consistency in content and tone. With over 7,000 VIP visitors per year, this is a very important responsibility.

The public relations office in many organisations provides access to an information database to facilitate timely technical responses to questions. This also can provide a surveillance and intelligence service with research and interpretation to assist and advise management decisions. Information can then be fed into the company decision-making processes, and to managers about the company. Research will include public and staff opinion, attitudes and expectations, enabling informed discussion of various concerns and interests to develop better understanding.

Counselling and consulting activities are an important part of many public relations teams. Public relations professionals are increasingly being called upon to advise and counsel on management issues and policies. Increasingly, communication management is being taken seriously as a business competence, and the public relations specialist is called upon to advise and guide managers on how to talk to the 'outside world', and then to facilitate and broker this communication. Rather than being the sole 'mouthpiece' of the organisation, the public relations specialist helps managers to understand how the media works. This may also involve a role in staff training and development, especially in terms of communication skills and relationship management.

Crisis management considers the future in trying to anticipate and prepare for possible events which may disrupt important relationships. This may range from contingency planning to damage limitation, to learning from previous crises, to surfacing and managing manager's assumptions and attitudes, to handling a crisis. *Issues management* is the systematic identification and action regarding public policy matters of concern to your organisation. It differs from crisis management only in timescale and sense of panic. Managers should take care to conceive issues from the various publics' points of view. Public relations should anticipate these issues which arise out of perceived problems, and manage the organisation's response to them.

Issues planning and crisis management require systematic issues audit and proactive media liaison, as well as support and resources (see Jefkins, 1994). Again, rather than simply acting as spokesperson for the management team, analysis of future trends and helping managers to predict their consequences, often called 'scenario planning' (Schwartz, 1991), is a public relations activity. Management of an off-site media briefing centre (including design and testing of emergency arrangements in case of crisis such as an accident) will require that a clear working plan is in place and regular staff training is conducted.

Design and writing of printed materials, including special public relations literature, company brochures, especially the company's annual report and company history, and product brochures may fall to the public relations office, especially where consistency is an important concern. Increasingly, audio-visual materials will be required. Much of this work is intended to be promotional, and may require the marketing and public relations specialists to work closely together to ensure that a consistent corporate identity is created and maintained. This will require consideration of such things as corporate logo, registered trademarks, product names, vehicle livery, uniforms, and the full range of publications. Writing and editing employee and community newsletters and a range of other house journals is also a common function of the public relations team.

Events management is often considered part of the public relations responsibility, since public events present opportunities for company people and others to meet and to create impressions about each other. The public relations office will frequently arrange and professionally handle visits for members of the public, customers, schools, VIPs and opinion-formers, including fact-finding journalists and vocational (professional membership) groups. They will also arrange special events, such as ceremonies for donations and sports and arts sponsorships. Educational links are expanding through a diverse range of scholarships and sponsorships; for example, the BNFL Corporate Communications Unit at The University of Salford was established with a covenant of moneys for a five-year research project. This is part of the company's community sponsorship programme, which has also supported university research in laser and virtual reality technologies. Increasingly, the public relations manager is the guardian of a company's sponsorship policy, and will plan and oversee a range of activities such as competitions and local events run jointly with community groups.

Exhibitions and conferences, and other special events, also present a public face to the company. Stand design and staffing, as well as venue selection, may fall to the public relations manager, at least in an advisory capacity.

Corporate hospitality allows managers to entertain customers, distributors, suppliers, journalists, investors, and other people who can help them in your business endeavours. The human face of the organisation and its operations and people can also be revealed in discussion forums. BNFL, for example, run a series of Round Table events in which interested parties are invited to meet managers and to discuss issues and concerns.

Marketing support may also be a responsibility since it is recognised that public relations has a role in helping to foster a climate in which marketing and selling can take place positively. Product placement and endorsement, and support in the promotion of products and services, are obvious areas of responsibility, but this should not be confused with publicity which promotes products and services, and is therefore actually advertising (Jefkins, 1994). Jefkins has clarified the role of public relations as one of 'market education'. The principle is that people are more likely to respond to a selling message when they understand what is being sold. Market education, or pre-selling, can have the following effect on advertising:

- It will help to make it more readily acceptable and to produce more response.
- It can save considerable sums of money since the public relations activity will cost much less than a commensurate level of advertising.
- The advertising run will be more cost-effective.

Marketing support is a legitimate and logical part of public relations activity, but managers should be clear in their expectations of where marketing ends and public relations begins. In some organisations public relations people are responsible for advertising and direct mail, for example in promoting BNFL's Sellafield Visitors Centre, itself a major part of the company's public relations programme (see case study). In some cases, corporate advertising, in which the company is the 'product' (Gregory, 1991; Schumann et al., 1991), will also fit comfortably within the public relations programme.

Public relations management is an essential aspect of public relations. Often not discussed in sufficient depth, the management of public relations programmes is a key aspect of the public relations manager's work. Just how are the appropriate activities selected and designed, and how does the company know that it has achieved its aims in a professional, cost-effective manner?

A process of systematic research planning, evaluation, and review is essential if the complexity of the total task of public relations is to be handled effectively to ensure that its role in strategic corporate management is fulfilled. This will include realistic and honest reporting of progress in terms of reputation and relationships, and in representing the corporate image and reputation to senior decision-makers and policy-makers in the organisation.

NEW DEVELOPMENTS IN EXTERNAL PUBLIC RELATIONS

Some practitioners and academics would claim that the basic tasks of public relations have long since been clearly defined and that recent and continuing progress is in the degree of effectiveness with which they are carried out. On the other hand, advances have been made in a number of areas.

Increasingly, the ethical responsibilities of managers and public relations specialists are being recognised (Newsom et al., 1993). Many companies have pursued increased community involvement and support, for example by helping with environmental projects. North West Water, for instance, has a major investment programme in projects which improve public access and wildlife preservation in and around its considerable land-holdings.

Managers are exercising their concerns for 'doing good business by doing good' (Embley, 1993) by taking on more high-profile sponsorships which attempt to deal with significant social causes. For example, cash help in the form of a donation for the national Drugline initiative, and providing equipment for helping severely handicapped children.

In terms of management and techniques, many agencies and in-house public relations specialists are trying to integrate public relations, advertising, and direct marketing. For example, advertising is being designed and executed using public relations techniques, such as an 'editorial' style in print advertising.

Corporate identity is receiving much more attention as organisations strive for a greater coherence in order to become distinctive in increasingly competitive markets. Corporate advertising is being more widely adopted and managed using the media planning methods of the advertising agencies to ensure targeting and cost-effective impact on key groups.

Public relations specialists continue to seek greater involvement in business initiatives, so as to increase their influence on management decisions, and to not be cast as just the messenger for the senior management group. For example, in planning improvements in local community support as part of BNFL's Springfields site Total Quality Management 'Business Excellence' Programme, the site public relations manager is the Team Leader. The aim of this initiative is to develop and implement specific community support schemes as part of the public relations strategy and to encourage employees to act as ambassadors.

Perhaps the most prominent development is the growing call for greater recognition of the need for evaluation of public relations management, including the setting of clear communication objectives which are business-driven, media impact analysis which is more sophisticated and relevant than mere 'column inches', and non-media public relations performance measurement. This drive is for the ability to prove to management the true value of managed public relations activity. A relatively new measure of performance is that of community perceptions, and the creation of awareness, resulting in changed behaviour. Favourable media coverage is no longer seen as solely important.

Finally, developments in new technologies, such as video news releases, wire services, electronic distribution of press releases (e.g. via the Internet), teleconferencing, and e-mail, are being heralded by many as a major boost to the public relations manager. The proliferation in the number of channels and means for conveying information and messages may yet prove to be a threat to the PR department which has not yet moved beyond the role of publicist – it may mean that they are out of a job!

SUMMARY AND CONCLUSIONS

The external public relations activities are diverse and many and must be co-ordinated and evaluated to ensure that they meet the communication needs of the organisation and its key publics. Planning is an essential part of the public relations manager's role.

Upon defining a public relations problem, that is a gap between the perceived and desired situation, an issue or opportunity can be defined. A situation analysis requires the systematic gathering of information (research) which informs the formulation of a programme of activities, including those described earlier.

Programme goals must be set, publics defined, and specific objectives determined. Only then can an action plan which sets out responsibilities, schedules and budget allocations be designed. An evaluation of the programme's impact is essential and feedback allows corrective action when objectives are not met. This is the essential activity of the public relations manager.

Public relations is a conscious and targeted attempt to align a company's image. It is:

> the management function which evaluates public attitudes, identifies the policies and procedures of an organisation with the public interest, and executes a programme of communication to earn public understanding and acceptance (adapted from Simon, 1980:8).

Public relations is about reputation – the effect of what organisations do, what managers do, and what others say about them – managers and organisations must deserve a good reputation and then use planned communication to benefit from it.

External communication is essentially about finding out what people think and why they think it, and then behaving in an appropriate manner in both word and deed, because:

Personality > Image > Reputation > Behaviour
(Message > Knowledge > Attitude > Behaviour)

But remember image as perceived by the organisation and as perceived by others may differ markedly! The communication management task is to bring the attainable and desired images as close together as possible. The starting point must be careful research, and this must be followed by monitoring and evaluation of changes, responses, and understanding.

The Public Relations Society of America maintain that their members are concerned with monitoring, evaluating, influencing, and adjusting to the attitudes, opinions, and behaviours of groups or individuals who constitute their specific publics. Thus public relations management is about confronting problems openly and honestly and then solving them – the disclosure of an active *social conscience*.

While this discussion has covered external activities as distinct from internal public relations activities, it is important to consider the need to integrate them into a single function.

DISCUSSION TOPICS

1 What is the distinction between public relations, advertising and propaganda?
2 Why is it that publicity and public relations are so often confused as the same thing?
3 Discuss an example of a public relations programme or campaign which failed due to a lack of good research information.
4 Consider a further example which clearly demonstrates the value of a research basis for public relations planning.
5 How would you envisage emerging new technologies will impact on the external activities of the public relations manager in the coming decade?

6 Consider the likely content of a public relations programme plan. In what areas might there be considerable overlap with a marketing plan?

7 Discuss the notion that a public relations manager has to think like a journalist in dealing with his colleagues, and think like a manager when dealing with the media. Do you see any inherent difficulties in this?

8 In what circumstance would it be appropriate to hire a consultant or agency?

9 Compare and contrast the skills, knowledge, and abilities required by the effective manager and the effective public relations specialist.

10 How are personality, identity, image, and reputation linked? What are the implications for the general manager?

CASE STUDY: THE BNFL SELLAFIELD VISITORS CENTRE – A NEW HOME FOR THE *MIGHTY ATOM*

Introduction

For those who want more than a bus trip around the Sellafield site, the visitors centre was created to communicate vital information and ideas to the general public about the nuclear industry and the business philosophy and aims of BNFL in a professional, effective, and efficient manner. It is the part of the British Nuclear Fuels plc group of businesses which has a high public profile, and is always open to criticism. It acts as the company's 'shop window' and its staff are inevitably ambassadors for the company.

The visitors centre was built at a cost of £5m in 1988 but was literally worn out by its own success in attracting visitors, and a £5m refurbishment project was completed in June 1995. Over 150,000 people have visited the centre each year since 1988, placing it among the most popular tourist centres in the North of England. A staff of eight full-time and 20 part-time public relations professionals are supported by eight staff in the centre's shop and restaurant.

The visitors centre at Sellafield

The only day of the year on which you cannot visit the centre at Sellafield is Christmas Day. Clearly the company's managers believe that the level of commitment is worthwhile. What is the pay-back for such an investment of time, money, and people?

As part of BNFL's corporate communications strategy, the centre's establishment and operation has clear aims:

- to provide a focal point for public relations activities at Sellafield
- to provide a focal point for national corporate advertising
- to assist in the communication of the company's business aims within the context of the nuclear power and reprocessing debate
- to provide a focal point for educational activities at Sellafield
- to be a major tourist attraction in West Cumbria
- to provide an interface between the company and the general public

- to provide a point of enquiry for those seeking information
- to reflect the desired image of the company.

All of this is attempted through the careful design and realisation of educational and entertaining exhibits, many of which are highly interactive and combine humour with information delivery about the history of the nuclear industry, some of its notable people and achievements, and the processes involved in reprocessing and disposing of waste. Whereas the original centre focused on nuclear energy, the new centre emphasises the world energy context and the role of nuclear energy.

The refurbishment was driven by feedback from visitors who wanted more information on current issues such as waste management, and staff who wanted more freedom to work with visitors, and the development of new technology, much of which has been employed in clever lighting and optical effects to create a range of 10 simulated environments and exhibition zones, including the inside of a reactor! Children have been especially catered for with the introduction of the animated character called the Mighty Atom who participates in several of the exhibits to explain various aspects of the nuclear industry and BNFL's business.

The centre, which was officially opened by HRH Prince Philip, Duke of Edinburgh, has a restaurant with a view, a tourist information centre, a gift shop which sells Mighty Atom souvenirs as well as books and local produce. The centre is also the regular venue for showcase exhibitions of art from local school children who concentrate their work on the nuclear theme. It has won several awards including the prestigious Sword of Excellence from the Institute of Public Relations.

Advertising and promotion

In 1994, the corporate communication strategy of the company made a commitment to make a much more strategic use of national and local media. In the national media, including TV advertising, the emphasis was on promoting the visitors centre as a way of explaining what BNFL does and of reinforcing the company's openness by inviting people to find out more for themselves by going to the centre. The audience to be reached was those people who had never been to Sellafield and would be receptive to understanding more about the company. Local media use would promote the centre as a tourist attraction for those already in the area.

Based on extensive opinion research amongst the general public, politicians, the media, and the financial community, the national television advertising campaign was designed to create a favourable context in which to communicate with opinion formers and those in the A and B social grades (the top 13 per cent of UK families as defined by the JICNARS classification by the occupation of the head of household). The aim was to set BNFL's own business agenda separate from that of the general nuclear industry, and to emphasise the company's core strengths as a business. People would be encouraged to visit the visitors centre to find out more and to think of BNFL as willing to share the problem of nuclear waste disposal rather than as arrogantly imposing their own solution.

The visitors centre video

Aimed at people in the international nuclear community, people in the UK nuclear industry, and public relations people generally, the new video was released in the New Year of 1996. As a vehicle for revealing the originality and fun, as well as the information value, of exhibits and activities in the visitors centre, the video programme describes the background to BNFL's change of corporate image and position and shows how this led to the brief for the redesign of the visitors centre. It demonstrates how the underlying aims of the company are met by the centre's exhibition as a whole and by individual features in particular.

A successful public relations focus?

Since re-opening in June 1995, the visitors centre has surpassed even the ambitious objective set for an increased number of visitors. The target for 1995/96 was 200,000, but in the first three months after re-opening, over 60,000 people had passed through the doors. The centre operates well because it is staffed by highly motivated, skilful people who understand the importance of the centre's role and work closely together to ensure that visitors have an enjoyable and informative experience.

What evidence of success? Is it simply a matter of numbers of visitors? Certainly, the new centre has attracted visitors. In the first few weeks after re-opening, over 200 people descended each day, and then only local advertising was running. Further research after the first three months of operating the new visitors centre shows that over 80 per cent of visitors found the centre informative and entertaining, and public opinion about BNFL has been changed. Commentary from experts involved in the formulation and construction of the new visitors centre and interviews with members of the visiting public provide evidence of the effectiveness of the work in the centre.

The approach taken by the public relations team in meeting the requirements of BNFL's corporate communications strategy has demonstrated their awareness of the need to apply a high degree of professionalism, innovation and adventurous thinking to create an entertaining presentation that will capture the emotions and attention of the visiting public, and some of those who don't make the trip to West Cumbria. The Sellafield visitors centre was planned as a sophisticated and effective public relations undertaking, and seems to have helped to develop BNFL's identity as a dynamic company with a human face and a vital role to play in the community at large.

(*Footnote:* The Mighty Atom has proven so popular that a new line of merchandise will be available to the general public during 1996! During the nine months in which the centre was closed for the 68 contractors to complete their work, the public relations staff were not idle. Six of them had babies – two girls and four boys.)

ACKNOWLEDGEMENTS

The author wishes to acknowledge the assistance of Francis Hallawell (The Quentin Bell Organisation), Bob Lawton (BNFL Capenhurst), Dick Marshall (BNFL

Sellafield), Danny Moss (Manchester Metropolitan University), Peter Osborne (BNFL Springfields), and Dr Jon White (City University), in the preparation of this chapter.

REFERENCES

Bernstein, D. (1984) *Company Image and Reality: A Critique of Corporate Communications*, London: Cassell.

Black, S. (1995) *The Practice of Public Relations*, 4th edn, Oxford: Butterworth-Heinemann.

Bromley, D.B. (1993) *Reputation, Image and Impression Management*, Chichester: John Wiley & Sons.

Broom, G.M. and Dozier, D.M. (1990) *Using Research in Public Relations: Applications to Program Management*, London: Prentice-Hall.

Carroll, A.B. (1993) *Business and Society: Ethics and Stakeholder Management*, Cincinnati, OH.: South-Western College Publishing Co.

Collins, M. (1993) 'The challenge of corporate social responsibility', *The Business Studies Magazine*, 6(2): 27–30.

Dixon, P. (1993) *Making a Difference: Women and Men in the Workplace*, Oxford: Heinemann.

Dowling, G.R. (1986) 'Managing your corporate image', *Industrial Marketing Management*, 15: 109–115.

Dowling, G.R. (1994) *Corporate Reputations: Strategies for Developing the Corporate Brand*, London: Kogan Page.

Embley, L.L. (1993) *Doing Well While Doing Good*, London: Prentice-Hall.

Fombrun, C.J. (1995) *Reputation: Realising Value from the Corporate Image*, Boston: Harvard Business School Press.

Garbett, T.F. (1981) *Corporate Advertising: The What, the Why and the How*, London: McGraw-Hill.

Garbett, T.F. (1988) *How to Build a Corporation's Identity and Project its Image*, Lexington, MA.: DC Heath & Co.

Giacalone, R.A. and Rosenfeld, P. (eds) (1991) *Applied Impression Management: How Image-Making Affects Managerial Decisions*, London: Sage.

Gregory, J.R. (1991) *Marketing Corporate Image: The Company as Your Number One Product*, Lincolnwood, IL.: NTC Business Books.

Greyser, S. (1981) 'Changing roles for public relations', *Public Relations Journal*, 37(1): 23.

Hart, N. (1995) *Strategic Public Relations*, London: Macmillan.

Haywood, R. (1994) *Managing Your Reputation: How to Plan and Run Communications Programmes that Win Friends and Build Business*, London: McGraw-Hill.

Jefkins, F. (1991) *Modern Marketing Communications*, London: Blackie Academic & Professional.

Jefkins, F. (1994) *Public Relations Techniques*, 2nd edn, Oxford: Butterworth-Heinemann.

Marston, J. (1979) *Modern Public Relations*, London: McGraw-Hill.

Newsom, D., Scott, A. and Vanslyke Turk, J. (1993) *This is PR*, 5th edn, Belmont, CA.: Wadsworth Publishing.

Panigyrakis, G.G. (1994) The public relations managers' role in four European countries, Proceedings of the 23rd European Marketing Academy Conference, Maastricht, The Netherlands, pp. 707–728.

Raucher, A. (1990) 'Public relations in business: A business of public relations', *Public Relations Review*, 16(3): 17–24.

van Riel, C. (1995) *Principles of Corporate Communication*, London: Prentice-Hall.

Schumann, D.W., Hathcote, J.M. and West, S. (1991) 'Corporate advertising in America', *Journal of Advertising*, 20(3): 35–56.

Schwartz, P. (1991) *The Art of the Long View*, London: Century Business Books.

Shimp, T. (1993) *Promotion Management and Marketing Communications*, 3rd edn, Fort Worth, TX.: Dryden Press.

Simon, R. (1980) *Public Relations – Concept and Practices*, Columbus, OH.: Grid Publishing.

Smythe, J., Dorward, C. and Lambert, A. (1992) *Corporate Reputation: Managing the New Strategic Asset*, London: Random Century.

Spicer, C.H. (1991) 'Communications functions performed by public relations and marketing practitioners', *Public Relations Review*, 17(3): 293–305.

White, J. (1991) *How to Understand and Manage Public Relations*, London: Business Books.

White, J. and Mazur, L. (1994) *Strategic Communications Management: Making Public Relations Work*, Harlow: Addison-Wesley/Economic Intelligence Unit Series.

Worcester, R. (1986) 'Why corporate advertising is the key to public goodwill', *Campaign*, 16th May, pp. 33–34.

8

CORPORATE SOCIAL RESPONSIBILITY: LINKING BEHAVIOUR WITH REPUTATION

Shirley Harrison

CHAPTER AIMS

- to give an outline of the social responsibilities of organisations
- to provide a rationale as to why companies should consider their social responsibilities
- to show how companies can discharge social responsibilities effectively
- to introduce a discussion concerning ethical implications in undertaking social responsibility programmes

ILLUSTRATIONS: PROCTOR AND GAMBLE; SHELL

Proctor and Gamble . . . now provides about £1.5m (mostly in kind) to 40 [Tyneside] organisations. There is advice on regeneration; training in business skills for senior secondary school teachers; training in quality management for voluntary and public sector workers; sponsorship for leisure schemes and involvement in special social projects. Employees can also apply for £500 grants to help them develop voluntary community work in their own time (Meikle, 1995:25).

An independent report into the conflict between Shell and the community concluded that 'the Shell Petroleum Development Company has been indifferent, insensitive to the requests and plight of the people of Ogoniland [Nigeria]' and that 'the conflict could have undoubtedly been averted if Shell Petroleum was responsible and conscious of her social obligation to the host community.' . . . Shell says that private companies cannot get involved in the political situation of the country in which they operate (Rowell, 1995:6).

INTRODUCTION

These two case vignettes appeared a few pages apart in an edition of the *Guardian* dated 8 November 1995. They provide a clear example of the importance to organisations of considering the issue of corporate social responsibility. How companies act and how they are reported and thus perceived by their publics is possibly the greatest factor in the management of their reputation.

Milton Friedman's view that the business of business is, simply, business needs some clarification in the 1990s. The rise of consumerism; the increasing public awareness of environmental and ethical issues assisted by sophisticated pressure groups; the understanding by business that a competitive edge can depend on reputation and not simply on products, price or services; all these factors lead to the conclusion that companies ignore corporate social responsibility at their peril.

So what exactly are the social responsibilities of organisations? Why should companies consider their social responsibilities? How can they discharge them effectively? What are the ethical implications for companies in undertaking social responsibility programmes? The discussion of these questions forms the basis of this chapter.

THE SOCIAL RESPONSIBILITIES OF ORGANISATIONS

Companies are not the state and they are not there to provide services and facilities which should properly be provided by the welfare agencies and paid for out of taxation. But companies are part of the society in which they operate and they need to consider their corporate behaviour as part of their role in society.

The impact which businesses have on the communities in which they operate has been likened to the effect of a stone dropping into a pond (Figure 8.1), where the initial impact is at the lowest level. The first two levels cover most of what respectable companies think is their responsibility to society and the communities on which they have an impact.

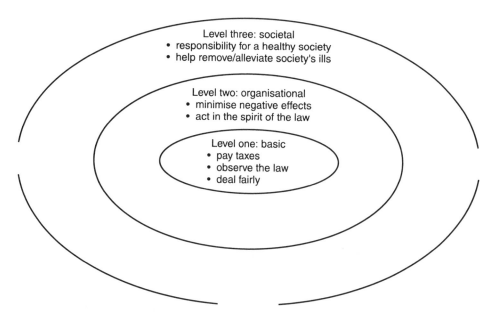

Figure 8.1 Impact of business on its environment.

Source: Adapted from Peach (1987:191–3).

At the most basic level, a company fulfils the legal requirements laid upon it: it pays its taxes, observes the law and deals fairly with its stakeholders – its staff, suppliers and shareholders, for example. At level two, the company takes account of its responsibility as an organisation and considers any negative effects it may have. For example, what are the potential effects of the company's existence, processes and products on the environment? It may seek to reduce these effects as far as possible by setting criteria for its location, by controlling emissions or changing its production methods to reduce pollution, or by setting stringent controls on the sale of its products so as to avoid misuse. A company operating at this level is likely to act in the spirit rather than simply to the letter of the law, and is more likely to anticipate trends in public awareness and legislation, leading by example.

The company operating at level three is less common. This type of organisation sees itself as having a responsibility for a healthy society and accepts the job of helping to remove or alleviate problems in society.

WHY ORGANISATIONS SHOULD CONSIDER THEIR SOCIAL RESPONSIBILITIES

Let us examine Friedman's views a little more closely. He argues that 'the very foundations of our free society' would be undermined if 'corporate officials' accepted any social responsibility other than 'to make as much money for their stockholders as possible' (Friedman 1962:133). However, Davis (1967:49) believes the corollary to 'no responsibility' is 'no power'. If organisations wish to maintain their positions of power in a pluralistic society, they must accept their societal responsibilities. There are other reasons for the interest in and growth of social responsibility in companies, including the wish of companies to maintain a favourable reputation; behaving responsibly is the best way to fend off government intervention; and public opinion is in favour of more responsible action. Let us look at each of these reasons in turn.

Pluralism

We live in a pluralistic society, where many diverse groups exist and where power and responsibility are shared. Every business institution has some power over, and thus is responsible to, a number of groups of which its stockholders are only one: they include staff and the wider community. These groups also have a responsibility to the business institution, which arises out of *their* power to affect it. This power-responsibility equation can be expressed as 'the social responsibilities of business arise from the amount of power they have'. Looking at social responsibility from this perspective helps to clarify managerial obligations.

Reputation

A company's reputation can be seen as the sum of the public's beliefs about it, based on their own experience of its products or services, what they have read or heard about it from others, and the way in which it – through its front-line and top level staff – is seen to behave. So an organisation may have a reputation for fast service, good quality and consumer care with its customers; for fair dealing with its suppliers; and for solid achievement with its shareholders. Companies may have a good reputation, a bad reputation, or no reputation at all, because they are not well enough known.

A good reputation has to be earned. In a survey carried out by Loughborough University for *The Economist* in 1991, 1,800 British business people were asked what qualities contributed to a good, positive reputation. They came up with the following list, which includes community and environmental responsibility (Harrison, 1995:72):

- community and environmental responsibility
- quality of management
- financial soundness
- quality of products and services
- value as long-term investment
- capacity to innovate
- quality of marketing
- ability to attract, develop and retain top talent.

Marks and Spencer (M&S) was the company which was felt to have the best reputation. M&S was especially admired for the way in which it had transferred its good name, earned in quality clothes and food, to financial services, because it is trusted as a company by its customers.

In a survey carried out in 1993 among opinion leaders in the City of London, the top six qualities of the 'ideal' company could all be said to reflect corporate social responsibility, as shown in the following list (OLR, 1993:7):

- high standard of corporate ethics
- is a good employer
- committed to training
- committed to equal opportunities
- investment in research and development
- respected for community contribution.

Avoiding government intervention

At the time of writing the Press Complaints Commission (PCC) is taking every opportunity to show that it can regulate its own industry and thus that there is no need for the government to pass legislation proscribing any of its activities. Since 1993, the press has had to consider the threat of a press privacy bill, a tougher regulatory body with the power to impose fines and the appointment of an ombudsman. The PCC has managed so far to avoid these by ensuring that it governs itself properly. It takes its lead from the advertising industry which itself managed to avoid statutory regulation in the 1970s. The Advertising Standards Authority (ASA) ensures that the British Code of Advertising Practice is upheld. Its provisions can be summed up in three statements:

- all advertisements should be legal, decent, honest and truthful
- all advertisements should be prepared with a sense of responsibility to the consumer and society
- all advertisements should conform to the principles of fair competition generally accepted in business.

There is some tension between the advertising industry and the press, however, as the ASA's chairman indicated in a speech at the launch of its 1993–4 annual report when he said that some media were willing to publish advertisements that 'ought not to be published. It would be regrettable if willingness to breach the rules in a few areas damaged the generally very good name of the industry's self-regulatory system as a whole.'

The demands of public opinion

In pursuing issues management, the subject of Chapter 14 of this book, a company demonstrates its interest in what concerns the public, and how issues of the future may impact upon the company's interests and reputation. So, for example, Rhône Poulenc Agriculture has identified the use of agrochemicals and the public's concern about factory farming as an issue which it needs to address. It has done so, in part, by instituting a 10-year research project into the effect on wildlife of organic and conventional farming methods at its farm in Essex (see Harrison, 1995:57–61). The company has identified key publics at whom this programme, Operation Country Practice, is aimed, including farmers, conservation organisations and the environmental and food trade media. One of the objectives of the programme is to build relationships with these key publics in order to influence public opinion.

Sometimes, however, a company's business behaviour can become an issue to publics other than those who seem to be directly affected by it. Thus companies need to consider what public opinion will make of their actions in other spheres. For multinational corporations, such as Nestlé and Shell, this can be especially important.

The Nestlé company is the world's largest manufacturer of infant formula (baby milk). The company's championing of formula in preference to breast feeding, and its aggressive marketing tactics in developing countries, led to protracted hearings in the US Senate and the formation of the Nestlé Infant Formula Audit Commission which began in 1982 and has continued into the 1990s. A consumer boycott has been in operation for almost 20 years, apart from a short break during which Nestlé agreed to abide by World Health Organisation guidelines (see Frederick et al., 1992:560–73).

The Shell oil company has sufficiently alienated public opinion that its petrol stations have been boycotted twice in one year, and over different issues. The first was the decommissioning of the Brent Spar, a redundant oil platform in the North Sea. Shell wanted to ditch the platform and its associated waste *in situ*. The environmental campaigning group Greenpeace alerted the public to what they saw as a potential environmental disaster and, with the help of a successful media relations campaign, had the Brent Spar moved to Norway for dismantling on land.

Although Shell was subsequently shown to have been right in opting for deep-water decommissioning, the company was forced, apparently because of boycotts of their petrol stations in Germany and other European countries, to bow to public opinion.

The second Shell boycott of 1995 has arisen because of the company's role in Ogoniland, Nigeria, highlighted in the quotation at the beginning of this chapter. In a radio interview[1] Shell's representative in Nigeria, Ryan Anderson, indicated that the company's chairman had felt obliged by world opinion to write to the Nigerian head of state asking for clemency for nine Ogoni protesters who had been sentenced to death. Shell had been engaged in oil exploration activities in Nigeria for 37 years under 11 different regimes, he said, and had never before felt the need to interfere. The appeal for clemency was not, in fact, heeded and the protesters were executed the following day, provoking the devastating use of Shell's logo in a newspaper cartoon (Figure 8.2). A report in the same newspaper claimed that

> Shell rejected suggestions that Body Shop, Greenpeace and other groups should be taken on directly on the grounds that it 'would play into the hands of the groups' and 'bring the matter more into the public domain'.
>
> When the seriousness of the situation became apparent, Shell issued a report down-playing Ogoniland's importance to the company and pointing out it had given large sums of money to Ogoni community projects. Privately, officials conceded these donations never reached their intended destination (*The Guardian*, 13 November 1995, 8).

Figure 8.2 The use of Shell's logo in newspaper cartoon.

Source: *The Guardian*, 13 November 1995.

only consider own interests	19	1	shares international concerns
should withdraw from Nigeria	13	1	should stay in Nigeria
exploits community	10	5	acts to improve community
partly responsible for human rights abuses	5	1	not responsible for human rights abuses
ecologically sound	4	4	ecologically unsound
politically involved	3	4	not politically involved
causes pollution	2	2	does not cause pollution

Figure 8.3 Shell's involvement in Nigeria, by volume of messages.

Source: Adapted from PR Week (1995:6).

Two weeks later a survey by CARMA International evaluated press coverage of Shell's decision to continue with a gas project in Nigeria. The results, based on analysis of 34 articles, indicated overwhelmingly negative coverage, as Figure 8.3 shows.

The ethical customer

Chasing the ethical customer has become a growth activity over the past decade. The principle that the customer would rather not do harm to his or her environment or to society at large has spawned environmental friendliness in products and the growth of ethical investment. The green pound may be spent by a customer who travels by non-friendly car to a supermarket built on formerly open countryside, but it is still a pound spent. There has been immense growth in products which claim to be eco-friendly, from washing powders to pest control in the garden.

The Body Shop is a frequently cited example of a company which seeks to gain a competitive edge in the crowded toiletries market by displaying a commitment to its responsibilities to society. Starting with its campaign to eliminate unnecessary packaging, in a business where the box and the bottle were traditionally more important than the contents, the Body Shop went on to encourage recycling of its containers to avoid waste. The company has run a campaign against the use of animals for testing toiletries which has been so successful that most other cosmetic companies have been forced to follow suit simply so that they too can advertise 'this product was not tested on animals'. Body Shop also prides itself on its trade-not-aid attitude to suppliers, scouring underdeveloped parts of the world for natural ingredients which it can buy from local farmers at a fair price.

Although the company has come under periodic attack for not always adhering to the high principles it proclaims, it has continued to thrive and expand and now operates its retail outlets all over the world. Clearly, the Body Shop has found its adoption of corporate social responsibility to be a highly profitable strategy, and possibly even Friedman would see that the bottom line can be served by companies who prefer to discharge their responsibilities to society.

McDonald's, the global hamburger restaurant chain, has developed and published customer information on its environmental policy. This is widely believed to be in response to the boycotts and demonstrations which greeted its arrival in some parts of the UK in the late 1970s and early 1980s. Demonstrators stood outside the Lancaster branch, for example, for weeks holding placards and distributing material which claimed that McDonald's was contributing to the destruction of the Amazon rain-forest because of the company's appetite for burger meat. At the time of writing the so-called McLibel trial is continuing into its second year at the High Court in London, where McDonald's is seeking damages from two unemployed activists who have questioned the company's healthy eating claims.

Significantly, the 1990s have seen the arrival of business ethics experts in the field of management training. A recent seminar on utilising corporate values 'to win, satisfy and retain' the ethical customer included contributions on 'Developing a responsible approach to retailing: how the Co-op is responding to the ethical expectations of its customers' and 'Instilling consumer confidence in the ethical claims your product makes' from the managing director of Beauty Without Cruelty.[2]

A licence to operate

Davis's Iron Law of Responsibility states that 'those who do not take responsibility for their power ultimately shall lose it' (Davis and Blomstrom, 1966:174). The RSA's Inquiry into Tomorrow's Company makes a similar point: 'Business success will only be sustained if there is a supportive operating environment' (RSA, 1994:21). This can only be achieved by companies who understand and are understood by the communities in which they operate and whom they affect. These communities or influences, shown in Figure 8.4, give companies their licence to operate.

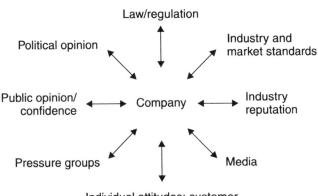

Figure 8.4 Key influences of the licence to operate.

Source: Adapted from RSA (1994:21).

The 'licence to operate' can be an opportunity rather than a threat if it is handled imaginatively. A company, industry or business community in any country can act to enhance its 'licence to operate' by creating positive relationships, or damage it by the wrong behaviour. For example, companies which take the initiative in environmental auditing may help to determine the shape of regulations in line with the needs of their business. Conversely, companies which are insensitive to shifts in public opinion may suffer variously from public opposition, diminishing sales, rising costs, reduced flexibility and blocked opportunities.

DISCHARGING THE ORGANISATION'S SOCIAL RESPONSIBILITIES

Once convinced of the need to discharge their social responsibilities, organisations have to make decisions about how they are going to do so. They need first to do two things: balance interests and set criteria. A major function of the public relations professional is to advise organisations on how to balance the interests of the varied publics whom they wish to address, and to remind them of the importance of the public interest.

Balancing interests

It may be that a company is faced with a dilemma in resolving conflicting views about how society's interests will be best served. An example is furnished by the Cadbury company in South Africa during apartheid. At the time anti-apartheid campaigners were trying to persuade companies to disinvest in South Africa.

In considering its position as an influential and (historically) highly principled company operating in a country run by a morally repugnant regime, Cadbury considered its stakeholders, both the shareholders (who might take a loss or a gain on divestment) and its employees. The staff who worked for the company in South Africa had the most direct stake in its continuing or leaving and, Cadbury believed, the voice of its staff was least likely to be heard outside South Africa.

In arriving at the decision to remain in South Africa, the company took account of its record there, which included an effective training programme for black South Africans. This was of particular importance because, without management skills and experience, it was not going to be possible to change the balance of economic power within the country. 'A further example was that we were either the first, or one of the first, companies to include all our employees in our pension scheme, regardless of race. The company felt therefore that there was advantage to the employees and to the community in our continuing to manage the South African business in the way we had' (Cadbury, 1995).

Cadbury continued to operate its South African subsidiary throughout the period of apartheid, but never attracted the kind of public opprobrium, which, for example, attached to Barclays Bank.

Setting criteria

Organisations need to plan their corporate social responsibility programmes in line with their corporate objectives and this is best achieved by formulating policy and setting criteria as to what types of projects they will undertake or support. This is a responsibility which should be taken at board level and on the advice of the organisation's public relations consultant.

A company may want to position itself as a good community neighbour, and thus its policy may include involvement with environmental projects. One criterion set for acceptance of a project may be that the project has to be locally based. Perhaps the company's target market is young people, in which case another criterion may be that the project is run by or for young people, or that it rewards young people for environmental responsibility.

A company which wants to promote entrepreneurship and independence may choose to give grants only to help new projects to get off the ground. The criterion will be 'pump-priming, not recurrent, support'. Alternatively, it may want to encourage self-help, in which case it may only offer support on condition that the project provides, or attracts from elsewhere, matching funding.

ETHICAL IMPLICATIONS

If companies are fulfilling their obligations to society by undertaking corporate social responsibility programmes, then it might be assumed that there are no adverse ethical implications. However, it is important to consider a number of issues raised by this chapter so far.

Motive

In looking at why companies shoulder their responsibilities to society, the importance of motive depends to a great extent upon the individual's point of view. Views may range from the opinion that it does not matter what the motivation of the company is, as long as the outcome is desirable, to the opposite extreme: actions taken purely for the self-interest of the company are worthless. However, the importance of public opinion and the maintenance of good stakeholder relationships might lead us to conclude that the perceived motivation of a company is vital. The company which is seen to be using philanthropy as a cloak to hide misdeeds, or as a way of buying itself out of regulatory control will, generally, get the reputation it deserves: that is, a poor one.

Procter and Gamble give as their motive for corporate community involvement on Tyneside 'to attract the highest calibre recruits to the region, make staff feel good about living there and prove that it is a responsible "corporate citizen"' (Meikle, 1995). Tate and Lyle's motive for encouraging employee secondments is their belief that 'not only can this make a worthwhile contribution to community activities, but, in doing so, the experience will enable volunteers to develop their own management potential' (Newman, 1995:99). United Biscuits' motive is a clear combination of moral duty and good business sense: 'Our commitment to community involvement stems from our strong sense of social responsibility combined with the realization of the commercial benefits that it brings. Good operating principles – involving ethical dealing, strong people values and a generous and far-reaching sense of community responsibility – are essential to effective long-term business performance' (Newman, 1995:99).

Susceptible targets

In addition to considering their motivation, or 'why?', companies need to consider their target publics, the 'who'. Ethical considerations here are based on the susceptibility of the target audience for the company's message. This may be to do with the age of the target public, and recognition that young children and the elderly need special consideration. For example, sponsorship of events for charitable purposes, a common activity of companies, might be aimed at school children. If the child is expected to pester parents to make unnecessary purchases, or a competitive element is introduced which favours children from well-off families, the ethical wisdom of the company may be questioned.

The target public may be over-susceptible for other reasons. For example, a woman who has just given birth may not be at her most rational. Yet until recently she would, while still in hospital, be overwhelmed by 'gifts' to 'help' her with the new baby – a Bounty box sponsored by the manufacturers of various baby care and feeding products, containing a potent mixture of advice notes and free samples. The boxes are now available for the mother to collect at a later stage from her local baby clinic.

The footloose sponsor

This chapter has necessarily concentrated on companies who have given some thought to their charitable giving and sponsorship, and who have clearly defined the criteria for their policies. However, the footloose sponsor – the company which does not have a long-term or considered policy, but which takes opportunities as they arise – can create some ethical problems.

Favouritism and cherry-picking

Where a company is involved with its local community it is especially important for it to make clear the criteria it uses for determining whom it will help, with how much and for how long. If some community groups are simply picked out and given help while others are rejected, the company will have accusations of favouritism levelled at it. If the company is clear about its motive and its objective, if these are transparent to groups applying for help, and if those who are unsuccessful know why, this problem diminishes.

Similarly, companies can be accused of cherry-picking, that is taking on the most attractive causes and not supporting those that are low profile or unpopular. Marks and Spencer, on the other hand, 'supports those charities which do not usually generate major public support but which reflect the needs of the communities where it has stores' (Clutterbuck et al., 1992:175).

Over-reliance on sponsor

A further ethical problem caused by the footloose sponsor is that of over-reliance by the recipient. The company that wants to act ethically will ensure that it does not pull the plug on a cause which will sink without it. The company's policy may be that it only offers support to any recipient for a limited period, as a pump-priming mechanism, or it may be to offer long-term involvement. Either way, it is important that the company thinks through the implications of its effect on the recipient and makes clear what support the recipient can expect to get for how long.

Dubious associations

Commercial sponsorship arrangements are subject to a contract, in which there is usually a clause allowing the arrangement to be terminated if either party fails to deliver. But the situation can arise in which there is no failure, but the wrong message is delivered. Both the sponsoring company and the recipient need to be aware of the messages given out by the other party and to be sure that the association between them is appropriate and consistent. The company may simply be attempting to use their association with a good cause as a fig leaf to cover its poor image. Conversely, the company will want to assure itself that the activities and objectives of the recipient are in keeping with its own, and that there is a shared sense of values.

Letting others off the hook

One criticism of charitable donations is that they take the place of 'proper' provision. Surely, the argument goes, if we stopped giving donations to stave off hunger in famine-stricken areas, then world leaders would have to take responsibility and change their aid and economic development policies accordingly. A similar criticism can be levelled at corporate community involvement, especially when it is seen as an alternative way of providing welfare services or essential equipment.

Companies need to consider the ethical implications of providing goods or services as an act of charity, if that provision is deemed to be a fundamental right of all citizens. Is the company that donates teaching materials to a school colluding with the government on its under-funding of schools? Or is it letting the local council get away with spending money earmarked for education on some other project? Or is it simply providing 'extras'?

The purpose of raising these ethical implications is not to denigrate the way in which companies fulfil their corporate social responsibilities. It is, rather, to suggest that both companies and the society in which they operate need to understand what they are doing and why. For while it is indeed relevant material for a chapter in a book on public relations, corporate social responsibility is not simply a minor branch of the public relations business.

SUMMARY AND CONCLUSIONS

This chapter has considered various facets of social responsibility. Specifically, the clear importance of corporate social responsiblity has been illustrated in terms of how companies act and more importantly the perceptions of those acts by various publics. In other words, the role of business is no longer business alone in the sense of sales, profits, market share, and so on. Social responsibility provides a mechanism whereby the more overt aspects of 'business' can be supported and sustained. Firms need to consider their role in the wider society in which they operate (see Figure 8.1). Firms should take their wider role seriously given issues such as pluralism, reputation, likelihood of government intervention, public opinion demands, and, sustaining an unwritten 'licence to operate'. Inevitably, in order to discharge such a wide role, firms need to balance a number of interests, and align social responsibility programmes with corporate objectives. They also need to consider both the ethical considerations of the wider societal framework in which they operate and the ethical aspects of the social responsibility programmes themselves. An example of the policy of one company, Yorkshire Electricity, and how this is translated into specific initiatives is given in the case study. This is followed by a number of case vignettes which may serve as a basis for in-class discussion.

DISCUSSION TOPICS

(*Note:* *The contextual circumstance for each topic will be found in both the above text and the following case study and case vignettes.*)

1 Should social responsibility be a marginal corporate activity?
2 Why should firms take social responsibility seriously?
3 Argue for or against Friedman's view that 'the very foundations of our free society would be undermined' if corporate officials accepted any other social responsibility than the fiscal one.
4 Why are firms faced with a dilemma when trying to determine how societal needs will be best served?

CASE STUDY: YORKSHIRE ELECTRICITY

The company

Yorkshire Electricity, formerly the Yorkshire Electricity Board and a publicly owned utility, is one of the largest companies based in Yorkshire and Humberside. It aims to be a good corporate citizen through development of a programme of region-wide activities which emphasise that it plays a leading role in supporting the community.

Policy

Company policy on donations and sponsorship is determined by the Donations Committee, a sub-committee of Yorkshire Electricity Group's main board. Its objective is 'fully to meet the company's responsibilities as a major corporate citizen'. It focuses on four key areas:

- the disadvantaged
- young people
- environmental issues
- economic development.

Guidelines

The company has devised criteria for dealing with requests for support, of which it receives thousands each year. These indicate that Yorkshire Electricity will support any cause provided:

1 requests support its main areas of involvement: disabled people, the elderly, young people, environmental issues, economic development and commercial sponsorship opportunities
2 it has relevance to Yorkshire Electricity's licensed area of Yorkshire and humberside and its customers
3 It is a registered or recognisable charitable or community organisation
4 such projects should demonstrate the benefits of Yorkshire Electricity's support.

In addition, the company runs a staff fund-raising scheme. Individuals or groups of staff who take part in fund-raising activities on behalf of registered charities can have their efforts matched pound for pound up to a maximum of £1,000.

Examples of projects supported

Poles and trees campaign

Two thousand trees have been planted in the region by local people and children as part of this campaign, run in association with the British Trust for Conservation Volunteers. It is part of the company's commitment to plant a tree for every new pole it erects.

Dyslexia institute

Yorkshire Electricity provides bursaries for children and young adults to receive special training at the Dyslexia Institute in Sheffield.

Building on ability arts awards

Cash awards are made to help develop the talents of people with disabilities who 'put something back into the community'. Recent awards included recognition of a water-colour artist keen to progress into painting with oils and a drummer who regularly entertains elderly citizens in residential homes with his musical skills.

Support for new business

The Prince's Youth Business Trust launched a £1 million appeal to help unemployed young people get small businesses off the ground in the area. Yorkshire Electricity made the first donation. Its executive director said that the appeal helped the company to fulfil two of its commitments: to help bring investment into the area and to help young people.

Grimsby International Jazz Festival

This annual three-day event is sponsored by Yorkshire Electricity because it provides a stage for local artistes and young performers to mix with 'some of the international jazz greats'.

Keepsafe project

This project is an important part of the Rotherham Crime Reduction Programme. Yorkshire Electricity's support has helped to provide better locks and security for elderly people.

Guidelines for rejecting requests

Certain types of requests are automatically rejected if they do not fall within the existing policy. These fall into 15 categories:

1. support for projects outside the region
2. financial support for an individual
3. support for visits outside the region, especially overseas
4. donation of second hand vehicles and support for minibus appeals
5. support for individual schools
6. joint fund-raising with other commercial organisations
7. general advertising where Yorkshire Electricity does not sponsor the project
8. political/lobby pressure groups or trade union activities
9. individual team sport sponsorships, unless used as a role model portraying excellence
10. donations for general appeals
11. core funding of projects (running costs and funding individual posts)
12. support for building, renovation or electrical installation work
13. raffle and tombola prizes
14. donation of furniture, equipment or any 'in kind' support
15. donations to local clubs and community groups, e.g. play groups, youth clubs, and local branches of regional or national organisations.

Publicity

Yorkshire Electricity is keen to exploit opportunities to publicise its corporate community involvement. In detailing the benefits of sponsorship to both parties, the company says:

> Most sponsorships are controlled by marketing/public relations managers, who will use their organisational and publicity skills to benefit the sponsorship ... before a commitment is made the sponsor will establish which project offers the best potential value for money in terms of media coverage and awareness profile amongst its stakeholders.

This is clearly a consideration in selecting projects to support under its flagship Building on Ability Programme, which aims to enable people with disabilities to participate in a wide range of sports, arts, environmental and cultural activities, regardless of their ability. The Sheffield wheelchair basketball team, the British champions, were an ideal project as they could achieve high quality media coverage for their sponsors.

Yorkshire Electricity's Community Relations section began in August 1995 to produce a newsletter, *Community Matters*, a six-page A4 gate-fold format on glossy paper and in full colour. Its first issue led with a story headlined 'National Award Honour for Yorkshire Electricity' which reported that the company had received an award for its sponsorship of a programme to increase access to sport for people with disabilities.[3]

CASE STUDY VIGNETTES: CORPORATE SOCIAL RESPONSIBILITY IN ACTION – FURTHER ILLUSTRATIONS

Secondment

In 1991, Boots piloted a secondment scheme of 'development assignments' as part of its graduate development plan. Among the assignments undertaken was Jane Murray's involvement with the Indian Community Centre at Basford. She produced a business plan for the centre, established accounting and budgeting systems, and recruited and trained an accounting clerk. The centre's manager said that her assignment 'significantly enhanced Boots' image amongst the local Indian community, and is a substantial step forward in race relations' (Clutterbuck et al., 1992:180).

The success of the scheme was such that it has now been extended to all graduate trainees. Boots' view is that the secondments are worthwhile not only for the community support they offer, but also because they provide an excellent training opportunity for their staff.

Secondment is more trouble than simply signing a cheque for a donation and companies may feel unable to spare their staff for extended periods. The Nationwide Building Society surmounted this problem by developing 100-hour secondments, releasing staff for one or two days a week for a couple of months. The society was able to raise its profile in the community while widening the horizons of some of its employees.

Sponsorship

W H Smith has sponsored the annual Young Writers' Competition since 1977. Entries from writers aged 16 and under are judged by an independent panel of writers, chaired by the Poet Laureate, Ted Hughes. About 100 prizes totalling more than £7,000 are awarded – 30 to schools who have submitted entries of a high standard overall, and the rest to individual children. Several hundred 'commended' certificates are also awarded. An illustrated paperback book containing all the stories and poems by winners and runners up is subsequently published.[4]

This sponsorship is a strand of the company's Arts in Schools programme, which includes Music for Youth and support of the Welsh Schools Choral Competition. As the UK's major book and record retailer, W H Smith has chosen sponsorship activities which fit very well with its core business.

Voucher schemes

The supermarket chain Tesco pioneered the use of voucher schemes as a form of providing computer equipment for schools. Every £25 spent at the check-out entitled the shopper to a voucher, which could be donated to any participating school. The school could redeem these vouchers: 200 for a software package and 4,000 for a computer. This campaign received immense publicity and has run on more than one occasion.

A similar scheme was set up by Tesco rivals Sainsbury's, called the School Bags scheme. In this case, however, vouchers were not provided on the basis of the amount of money spent in the store. Vouchers were given to Sainsbury's shoppers according to the number of carrier bags re-used by the shopper. The vouchers could be collected by schools to pay for a range of equipment from the School Bags catalogue.

Grants and donations

Barclays Bank receives over 40,000 requests for money a year. It is moving away from a position of reacting to requests towards approaching target charities and requesting them to come up with suitable projects. Among the company's policy decisions are to give where the benefits are clearly visible and to avoid political issues. As Brian Carr, head of Barclays Community Enterprise, explains 'These days it is not enough just to do good, you have to be seen to be doing good in the community and that is what we try to achieve . . . We would rather give money to people to make things happen than to campaigning-type organisations. For instance, we would not give to a local action group campaigning against putting effluent in a river because they could be protesting against the activities of one of our customers.'

National charities are supported by the company's headquarters, regional charities through its regions, and branches can make small donations from their own budgets to local good causes. At every level the decision about whether or not to donate is made after considering the following questions:

- does it fit in with company guidelines?
- does it overlap with support for an existing project?
- has the company supported it in the past and what was their experience?
- how effective is the charity?

(Clutterbuck et al., 1992:176)

Education centres

Severn Trent Water is establishing a network of Education Centres across its region which covers 6,000 schools and over 2m pupils. The centres are in effect well-equipped classrooms staffed by qualified teachers, seconded from the local education authority and expert in environmental education. The centre in Cropston, Leicestershire, is converted from a Victorian pumping station and comprises meeting rooms, an audio-visual suite and a weather-proof viewing platform on top of the pumping station chimney, as well as the central classroom. The visitor centre also includes a 'Come and See' centre offering free visits to organised groups. The site boasts examples of all known tree species which can grow in this climate, as well as badgers, foxes and a wide variety of birds.

The most recent centre to be opened by the company is at Minsworth, one of Europe's biggest sewage treatment works. It provides an opportunity for the study of a range of scientific and environmental subjects on the national curriculum (Foweather and Stillwell, 1994:12–13).

Community investment

IBM's community investment programme has three major objectives:

- to contribute towards a favourable social and economic environment for IBM's business
- to be recognised by selected target audiences as a leader in corporate community involvement
- to promote the morale and motivation of employees.

These objectives, and how they are to be achieved, are reviewed annually in conjunction with the staff. The four focus areas for involvement are education and training; voluntary sector empowerment; support for people with disabilities; and the environment. Support takes various forms but the most effective, both for IBM and for community organisations, seems to be employee involvement (Portway, 1995:226).

ICI Pharmaceuticals in Macclesfield found a novel way of involving employees when the company won the Queen's Award for Industry. It asked employees how they would like the money spent. They suggested donating two ambulances to a local charity that operates transport services for elderly and disabled people. The company was looking for a project related to health care, and which was visible in the community so that everyone could feel proud of the gift.

The retired employee who suggested the idea originally approached ICI for a small grant towards running the fleet. He is now treasurer of the charity. ICI gained positive press coverage for this project as it was 'the first time any of the 2,688 award winners have put the award to such imaginative use' (Clutterbuck et al., 1992:166).

Crime prevention

The high street chain Dixons announced in 1994 that they were to spend £20m to combat 'ram raiding', a form of robbery in which a vehicle is driven through the frontage of a store, loaded with goods and driven away. Dixons is willing to shoulder its responsibility to society for crime prevention and detection, and it has chosen the type of crime which most affects its business. Ram raiding is a direct cost on the business and it illustrates the importance of having a stable society (RSA, 1994:22).

The Kingfisher Group also takes an interest in combating criminal activities, which are estimated to cost the retail industry £2 billion a year and to affect many staff who are the victims of crime at their place of work (Clutterbuck et al., 1992:199–200). Two thousand companies have been involved in sponsoring the charity Crime Concern, according to its chief executive, because 'A safe community is good for business and companies can play an important part in tackling the crimes which affect their staff, customers and premises' (ibid.).

Combating age discrimination

The legal system in the UK militates against discrimination in recruitment and promotion on the grounds of sex or race. However, there is nothing to stop employers discriminating against older people. Downsizing and delayering with the 'incentive' of early retirement have meant that older people have been greatly affected by unemployment in recent years. B&Q have chosen to staff their entire Macclesfield store with over-50s and this pilot was so successful that they extended it to a store which opened in Exmouth in 1990. 'We have found that older staff not only bring increased stability, expertise and social skills, but also compare favourably in performance terms with younger staff at our other stores' (Clutterbuck et al., 1992:88).

Although the socially responsible company may want to ensure that the older people in society receive fair treatment as part of its level three commitment, such companies do have an eye on the rewards they reap. Tesco's campaign Life Begins at 55 attracted many older staff who, in a survey conducted by the World Health Organisation, were found to be 'better with customers, more reliable, more responsible and less likely to take time off sick than their younger colleagues' (ibid.).

NOTES

1 BBC Radio 4 programme Today interview, 10 November 95.
2 The Ethical Customer, 25–26 January 1996, The Berners Hotel, London.
3 Extracted from material provided by the Community Relations section of the Yorkshire Electricity Group.
4 Extracted from W H Smith's explanatory material *A Focus on Education: Arts in Schools.*

REFERENCES

Cadbury, Sir A. (1995) Letter to the author, 17 October.
Clutterbuck, D., Dearlove, D. and Snow, D. (1992) *Actions Speak Louder,* London: Kogan Page.
Davis, K. (1967) 'Understanding the social responsibility puzzle', *Business Horizons,* Winter: 45–50.
Davis, K. and Blomstrom, R. (1966) *Business and its Environment,* New York: McGraw-Hill.

Foweather, R. and Stillwell, S. (1994) *SCIP News*, 37, Warwick: University of Warwick, SCIP.

Frederick, W., Post, J. and Davis, K. (1992) *Business and Society*, 7th edn, New York: McGraw-Hill.

Friedman, M. (1962) *Capitalism and Freedom*, Chicago: University of Chicago Press.

Harrison, S. (1995) *Public Relations: An Introduction*, London: Routledge.

Meikle, J. (1995) 'Take a gamble for charity', *The Guardian*, 8 November.

Newman, W. (1995) 'Community relations', in N. Hart (ed.) *Strategic Public Relations*, Basingstoke: Macmillan.

OLR (1993) *Business and Community: A New Partnership for Mutual Benefit*, London: Opinion Leader Research.

PR Week (1995) 'What the papers say: can anyone be sure of Shell any more?' *PR Week*, 24 November.

Peach, L. (1987) 'Corporate responsibility', in N. Hart (ed.) *Effective Corporate Relations*, Maidenhead: McGraw-Hill.

Portway, S. (1995) 'Corporate social responsibility: the case for active stakeholder management', in N. Hart (ed.) *Strategic Public Relations*, Basingstoke: Macmillan.

Rowell, A. (1995) 'Trouble flares in the delta of death', *The Guardian*, 8 November.

RSA (1994) 'Tomorrow's Company'. Interim report of the Inquiry. London: RSA.

9

FINANCIAL AND INVESTOR PUBLIC RELATIONS

Geraldine Hanrahan

CHAPTER AIMS

- to outline recent developments in financial services which make public and investor relations so important
- to describe the multi-layered and interconnecting web of publics that financial corporations deal with in retail, wholesale, investment, capital and money markets
- to provide a framework for strategies in relation to financial markets
- to outline research and its applications to financial and investor public relations

ILLUSTRATION: VOLATILE MARKETS

Executive Life, a large American insurance company, failed in 1991. This was another blow to confidence in the industry which caused the National Organisation of Life and Health Insurance Guaranty Associations to bid to pay up to $2bn to make up losses. The motivation was to restore public confidence and to avoid further regulation. But official Californian regulators wanted to accept the offer by the French group, Altos Finance, to take over the company because over 97 per cent of investors would not be adversely affected. This assumed that bond and annuity holders had subordinate legal rights to insurance policy holders. At the time of writing, the California regulator and the courts are still disputing this issue.

However, credit rating companies, for example Moody's, then started downrating other insurance companies. Aetna Insurance was in trouble with reduction in property values and therefore book assets. Selling off profitable areas seemed to be one solution to getting out of this problem. Another was to drastically reduce the work force: Aetna laid off 10 per cent of its work force saving $200m per year in 1994 (Gart, 1994).

INTRODUCTION

The public relations issues involved in maintaining Executive Life's public profile during this crisis were complex. The company had to deal with all of its stakeholders simultaneously. It can be very difficult to develop and deliver a consistent message to several audiences, particularly if the public relations function is not the responsibility of one department. In the UK public, corporate and investor relations can be the responsibility of many departments and managers in different segments of the company. Agencies are also used to deal with issues and crisis management. In financial markets, agencies are increasingly used to organise the communications aspects of buy-outs, mergers and takeovers (see Table 9.1).

The main issues which communications strategies address in the 1990s are confidence, competition and competitors. Rapid changes in financial market regulation have created unstable conditions where information is at a premium. A large corporate organisation needs to develop comprehensive strategic alternatives to deal with on-going financial and investor publics as well as changing numbers and status of employees. Communications strategies draw on the expertise of public relations agencies, but they, in turn, are recruiting more personnel from the financial sector to improve their understanding of these highly complex markets. This chapter will also outline academic research into individual and group attitudes and perceptions and how people respond to different medias. This is an essential

Table 9.1 FTSE 100 financial public relations (concerned with major financial companies in the FTSE 100 and the provision they make internally and externally for financial and investor relations)

Financial company	In-house IR [IR = Investor Relations]	Consultancy
Abbey National	IR Department	None declared
Bank of Scotland	Finance Dept	Lowe Bell Financial
Barclays	IR Dept	Mak. Cowell: Brunswick
Commercial Union	IR Dept	Citigate
General Accident	Finance Dept	Financial PR
Guardian Royal Exchange	IR Dept	Dewe Rogerson
Hanson	IR Dept	Lowe Bell Financial
HSBC Holdings	IR Dept	None declared
Legal & General	Corp. Comm.	Dewe Rogerson
Lloyds	IR Dept	None declared
National Westminster	IR Dept	Cardew and Co.
Prudential	Corp. Comm.	None declared
Royal Bank of Scotland	Finance Dept	Financial Dynamics
Royal Insurance	Corp. Comm.	Gavin Anderson: Shandwick
Schroders	Corp. Comm.	Financial Dynamics
Standard Chartered	IR Dept	Lowe Bell: Financial Dynamics
Sun Alliance	Corp. Comm.	Brunswick
TSB Group	IR Dept	None declared
SG Warburg	IR Dept	Maitland Consultancy

Key: IR Dept – internal investor relations department
Finance Dept – investor relations dealt with by finance department, board, company secretary or treasurer
Corp. Comm. – investor relations handled as part of corporate communications

Source: PR Week, 9 December 1994.

process on which strategy development relies. The intuitive skill of the successful public relations manager in the financial sector needs to be underpinned by learnable protocols. Understanding how different publics perceive situations, develop attitudes towards companies and act on those beliefs and perceptions is a vital part of the research of public and investor relations.

BACKGROUND

Until the mid-1980s, competition among various types of financial institution was severely restricted by law. The regulated structure of the financial sector on both sides of the Atlantic ensured the necessary confidence in the integrity and future of a highly segmented market. In the USA banks were restricted to state boundaries and financial products did not generally travel across different types of financial institutions.

Between 1985–92 the average number of bank failures in the USA exceeded one hundred compared to an average of six for the 1945–80 period. In 1991 the recession reduced the value of the portfolio of assets held by larger banks, also threatening insolvency. Many were only saved by merger. Larger banks began to emerge in the USA and new financial products were introduced to support the global movement of funds. For example, banks and other retailing and manufacturing corporations set up non-bank banks to deal with credit card services across the US and international markets.

Market deregulation in the USA and other competitive innovations, such as instant access - interest paying accounts, led to an insolvency crisis in the US FDIC (Federal Deposit Insurance Corporation). Today financial institutions, previously limited to only one segment of the market, are engaged in expanding their activities across the whole financial spectrum. For example, insurance is sold by retail banks as well as insurance company's agents and brokers. It is also being sold direct to the public through tele-access facilities created by such companies as Direct Line.

Traditionally thrift societies in the USA and building societies in the UK only dealt in mortgages and long-term loans. In the mortgages sector throughout this period there was a large increase in non-performing loans. There was also a sharp increase in non-performing loans from third world governments. The collapse of many regional banks in the United States through the property and stock market recessions of the late 1980s was matched in the UK by many bank mergers and takeovers. Retail banks, aggressively searching for related business, moved into mortgages and many building and thrift societies have responded by developing credit and short-term loan facilities.

A major strategic issue for these larger retail financial organisations is to reassure the purchasing public that they are sound, trustworthy and able to survive in the long term. Confidence in financial products and in the institutions that delivered them has been shaken by numerous examples of instability, collapse and insolvency.

On 27 October 1986 the London Stock Exchange transferred to electronic instant dealing and removed trading from the floor of the exchange. This was called the Big Bang and has had wave-like repercussions around the globe and through all layers of the financial world. At the same time the UK government has been involved in extensive privatisation deals, beginning with British Telecom and British Gas. Public relations consultants, Dewe Rogerson, handled the British Telecom flotation, with the strategic objective of increasing the numbers of the shareholding public. One of the ways in which financial public relations differs from other forms of public relations is that the 'product' is very sensitive to changes in confidence. Share prices are volatile and can create predatory behaviour from global companies looking to expand their portfolio of financial instruments. Media over-exposure can be fatal and can cause a stampede in the market. Insider trading is an offence which is hard to prove but which can seriously undermine the value of a company on the brink of a major deal.

In 1987, stock markets around the world collapsed, unable to cope with re-alignments in market structures and instant information with on-line computers and satellite trading. Exchanges, themselves, are now in competition and need a public relations facility to address their institutional and brokering publics – to emphasise stability, volume of traffic and long-term viability. The London Stock Exchange plans to set up a wholesale market. As global capital and credit markets pass through a profound transitional phase, stock markets are also in competition as major financial centres. London, Paris, Frankfurt and Brussels are contenders in the race for the location of a European Central Bank. According to Rybczinski (1994:211) London has a much larger securities and stock market. Attempts by the French to start a Euro-list to capitalise firms in ECUs which would then automatically appear on individual European country member's exchanges would save costs, particularly on media translations.

Competition in market making around financial instruments such as those created around CDs (Certificate of Deposits) and junk bonds (non-investment bond issued for re-loans) will require sophisticated techniques of audience identification, information and communication strategies and evaluation.

The currency markets were first affected by the collapse of the Bretton Woods fixed currency exchange rates system in 1971. Together with the oil crisis of 1974, they created fluctuations in exchange rates which caused global currency and trading markets to develop rapidly. Many large corporations internalised their currency and financial management and investors went global, following the highest return. This was all made possible by technology. National regulations did not affect international markets. The pressure to deregulate caused an ensuing shake-up in financial markets and many bankruptcies. Banks remained regulated for a time but new credit providers, that is General Electric, General Motors, Sears and American Express, entered the market for credit as non-bank banks.

The Price Waterhouse Cecchini Report, which investigated the costs of non-Europe for financial services in 1988, compared price differentials across European countries and found them to be considerable. European legislators had concrete evidence that deregulating the financial sector would make financial services cheaper. One example of such deregulation was in Spain. In 1987, a new IRA (Individual Retirement Account) law was passed to encourage private retirement provision through investment funds and savings.

The financial public relations function, which is escalating, has been a direct result of this deregulation. The consequent transfer of responsibility for confidence and credibility in the financial system rests with the major players in the industry. This has created a gap in the capacity of such organisations to present themselves effectively to their publics – informing and being informed about their mutual concerns. Financial public relations agencies also have to learn to deal with instant information systems like Posit and Instinet.

Yet deregulation and other business environmental factors have caused a dramatic increase in the size and geographical spread of the international financial sector. Apart from privatisation policies by governments, expanding East European and South East Asian markets and rising recourse to capital markets by public sector bodies, growth has been caused by private sector finance through stock issues rather than banks. Increasingly, non-financial organisations are getting involved directly in their own risk management, issuing stocks and shares, to obtain cheaper and more flexible lending. In this capacity they also need to reassure their publics that their financial viability is enduring and stable.

Financial public relations must address increasingly sophisticated audiences who are interested in issues of liquidity, internationalisation, growth in company size, flexibility of capital market funds, rapid privatisation and relative importance of institutional investors. Some institutional investors with large holdings in investment companies are giving advice on governance and management. Efficiency, effectiveness and ethics are major issues.

THE WEB OF INTERESTED PARTIES

'New publics emerge and combine with existing ones the way atoms combine to form molecules' (Oxley, 1989:51). This is certainly the case in the financial sector where deregulation, globalisation, technology and service innovation have caused mass re-alignments of corporate financial holdings and dealings. Publics of interest to the financial public relations manager cannot be viewed in isolation. There is an overall need to promote a constant image and to provide consistent information across public groupings.

Identifying publics is complex as many people wear several public hats. A merchant banker, dealing on a client's behalf in a merger or takeover deal, is looking for information and forming impressions about different companies in the wholesale financial sector. He or she is also a private investor and requires banking, credit and insurance services in the retail financial sector. He or she is a non-executive director of another company and owns shares in yet another. Mergers and acquisitions are creating financial giants that are operating in many financial sectors, requiring a corporate image that is consistent with expectations in all these markets.

All publicly quoted companies need to consider their image in the financial world as investor confidence, share price and asset value depend on this. Certain French corporations have recently taken some innovative steps towards improving investor relations by introducing shareholder committees (Jack, 1995). Variations on this theme include shareholder circles, information lines and a free telephone enquiry service. In the UK and the USA the annual report is still a key vehicle to reach both institutional and private investor alike. In a recent study by Hutchins

(1994), a majority of a sample of institutional investors and chief financial officers thought the annual report a useful vehicle for information about the company in which they had a stake. Other studies (e.g. Clarke, 1996) have found marked differences in the messages sent via the Chairman's statement, related to the financial results and mission objectives.

PUBLICS FOR STOCK AND CURRENCY MARKETS

Public relations managers, attached to stock and currency markets, promoting the image of their institutions must consider the needs of institutional investors, brokers, financial analysts and the media. Large institutional investors such as governments and supra-government agencies require information about the regulatory health of these markets. The Singapore Stock Exchange was taxed by the Barings collapse which emphasised the need for a reliable policy system that investors and external regulators can refer to. The public relations requirement is to make known and understood procedures for the legal and effective working of the exchange and to manage the interaction with the media when a crisis does occur. A concern for brokerage companies is the growing trend of investment and unit trust companies to deal directly with the share-buying public rather than through the exchange and their once exclusive distribution rights. The pattern of dealing on a one-to-one basis with a few clients and gatekeepers is not always feasible. Appropriate messages have to be delivered consistently through the media to the general public. In this way, the third person effect (Pavlik, 1987) filters through to government and other major political institutions.

PUBLICS FOR INSURANCE

Life insurance companies were thought to be safe havens for retirement, health, disability, annuity and death savings provision. Two of the largest insurance companies in the USA, Executive Life and Mutual Benefit Life, failed in 1991. Between 1969–90, 372 US insurance companies were declared insolvent. The main causes were over-capacity and underwriting losses. This has also been the case in the UK where underwriting losses have caused serious problems for Lloyd's of London, a major, global underwriting market.

Rises in life insurance insolvencies particularly in the USA have breached confidence, exposing healthy companies to the danger of a run. Equitable Life, another large insurer, had similar weaknesses because of investments in property; it also attracted media attention. Public focus on the problems of life insurers has meant that the entire industry has suffered from a loss of consumer confidence. The public relations requirement is to generate accurate information consistently and continuously to counter the rise in speculation resulting from prior upheavals in the US retail banking sector. One result has been that much corporate insurance has been internalised to insurance departments and this trend is expected to rise.

PUBLICS FOR SAVINGS AND INVESTMENT

In 1975 the fixed rate commission on the sale of securities in the USA was abolished. Emerging brokerage firms, specialising in new technology services, are addressing an audience of growing independent financial advisors who are retailing asset and financial management services to the general public. Income from commission is dependent on stock market performance, but this can be the result of runs caused by rumour and innuendo arising in another part of the globe. Countering rumours is a complex and difficult operation involving crisis management techniques.

Securities companies have also been affected by the decline in the volume of new issues needing underwriting services. Underwriting income is cyclical and dependent on new debt and equity activity. If new issues replace loans as a risk and debt management facility for manufacturing and service corporations then potential clients for underwriting services will increase. This demonstrates the need to be flexible when identifying publics because, in a volatile environment, publics come and go.

The old divide between merchant banks and investment companies is fading; investment companies acting as merchant banks have their own funds to lend to clients. As banks and investment vehicles merge, new audiences need reassurances that reputation, image and future are sound. New capital has been raised by selling an interest to foreign firms. For example, Goldman Sachs sold 12.5 per cent interest to Sumitomo Bank. Shareholders have become powerful stakeholders to address and the task of strategic public relations requires diplomacy on the sale of nations. Subsidiaries must consider parent companies in their information dissemination process.

Pavlik (1987) suggests that a public relations audit should be designed to evaluate an organisation's standing with its relevant publics. One method to deal with a fragmented audience is to weight the importance of press reports by the subjective assessment of their impact on various publics. For example, institutional publics read the *Financial Times, CFO* (Chief Financial Officer) and *Investment Quarterly*, among others, whereas the individual investor is likely only to read the *Financial Times*. Identifying publics and rating their importance is a first step in strategic public relations. Grunig (1986) argues that information is individually processed in two ways – actively and passively. Passive messages are usually received as entertainment and are less likely to be internalised and remembered.

FUND MANAGER PUBLICS

Changes in the character of the financial services market are emerging with internationalisation and the disappearance of the wholesale/retail divide. Institutional investors own three-quarters of UK equities and two-thirds in the USA. The structure of capital markets (apart from non-financial companies doing business in primary markets) consists of fund management departments or companies and financial intermediaries.

Types of fund managers include:

- *Large* – vertically integrated investment units which use Posit or Instinet for direct access to stock and currency exchanges; for example in-house financial risk management.
- *Medium* – units not large enough to be fully independent which can take advantage of some technology. This includes insurance companies, and unit trusts. This type has been subject to mergers and suffers from lack of full market information.
- *Small* – niche market operators. This is an expanding sector where advice and market management are offered by product or by type of purchaser.
- *Dealers* – and agencies which use new products from different niche managers such as derivatives and synthetic instruments.

According to the hierarchy of effects model (Ostrom, 1969; Ray, 1973) the publics for financial services are likely to have a high involvement in the subject and a clear differentiation between possible behaviours, indicating a learning hierarchy response to information. This has encouraged the development of new financial instruments such as Certificate of Deposits which offer yields tied to the performance of stock markets. There has also been a restructuring in various financial sectors to take advantage of these changes. For example, building societies, such as the Abbey National and the Halifax/Leeds, are merging and converting to stock companies.

RETAIL PUBLICS

Bank regulators in Europe and the USA are balancing the objectives of promoting efficiency through deregulation with maintaining public confidence in the financial system through regulation. Regulation Q, which fixed interest rate ceilings in the USA, was finally abolished in 1986. Individual companies have to use their public relations instrument to improve public confidence, drained by deregulation and shock incidents such as Black Monday. Deregulation and financial innovation have led to a shift away from relationship banking towards price-sensitive services. While one-to-one dealings may survive in institutional markets, increasingly the knowledge and information function has to reach a wider audience.

Political lobbying is now much more important with a lack of rules and regulation. New mergers across sectors such as Prudential (insurance) and Bache (stock brokerage), and Metropolitan Life/Aetna, mean that new corporations now operate across the product divide and in wholesale and retail markets. Other retailers, for example JC Penney and Marks and Spencers, have also become very active in financial services – knowing that it is better to keep customers, costing more to get new ones. Even more will enter the financial services industry as technology reduces entrance costs. Selling insurance was very expensive through agents. Insurance services are being re-aligned to take advantage of computer database back-up, but it is a complicated 'product' which needs clarification to customers as insurance is very price-sensitive.

The trend towards direct financing is important for public relations as it is part of a media-pull strategy. Corporate imaging is fundamental to direct marketing activities such as tele-banking and Prodigy (computer banking) from Sears and IBM. Many insurers have loyal customer bases indicated by name, for example USAA caters for mainly military people; they gain competitive advantage by selling directly through computers. The products are undifferentiated but they can expand their product range to include other money market investments. Another major issue for financial and investor public relations is the public interest in the ethics of the financial sector. People are concerned with fraud in such cases as BCCI and the Salomon Brothers.

Finally, some communications instruments such as the annual report are directed at all publics: shareholders (institutional and private), financial journalists, investment analysts, distributors, potential investors, employees, MPs, business studies lecturers, visitors, competitors, and inward investors to name some of the interest parties.

PUBLIC RELATIONS STRATEGIES

The argument for a corporate public relations function is strengthened when large financial organisations are jostling for position in markets with fewer and fewer players. As financial institutions become larger to fulfil global strategies, the public relations function becomes more complex. To regularly assess what publics to address Pavlik (1987) suggests that a public relations audit be designed to include:

1 An audience identification study
   Four basic steps identify relevant publics:

   • identify issues of concern to potential publics
   • measure their perceptions and attitudes
   • evaluate organisation's present standing with these people
   • measure the power of each public.

2 A corporate image study

   • familiarity of each public with organisation
   • attitudes towards organisation
   • personality characteristics each public associates with organisation.

Different publics can include the financial press, investment analysts, fund managers, shareholders, institutional investors and arbitrageurs: raiders who buy in anticipation of a move by a real predator.

Defensive strategies

Defensive strategies are needed when crises occur or when the corporation is being subjected to hostile external influences. The management executive need a defensive strategy to counter rumours and incorrect or exaggerated press reporting as MacDonald (1991) clearly outlines (see Figure 9.1).

These are needed if a company is closing down, has made a major loss or is guilty of illegal activity such as insider trading. Such a strategy may include a separate

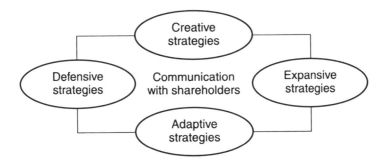

Defensive strategies: crisis management; damage limitation
Expansive strategies: pseudo-events; press releases
Creative strategies: developing long-term corporate images
Adaptive strategies: dealing with mergers; aligning the communications globally

Figure 9.1 Types of public relations strategy.

report refuting the incorrect one made available to all publics as well as the local stock exchange, particularly if the original publication refuses to run a correction. Great sensitivity is necessary when a commercial organisation is caught up in diplomatic crossfire between nations and considerable negotiating skills are required.

Hostile takeover bids can be successfully resisted if shareholders are kept fully informed and if their views are known prior to such a bid. For influential shareholders this may require one-to-one communications.

MINI CASE STUDY: SURVIVING THE GIANTS

When Executive Life Insurance failed in 1991 it caused another blow to the confidence in the industry. The National Organisation of Life and Health Insurance Guaranty Associations made a bid to pay up to $2bn to make up the losses. The motivation was to restore public confidence and to avoid further regulation. This did not stop credit rating companies, such as Moody's and Standard and Poor, from downrating other insurance companies. MONY, a smaller player, took out full-page advertisements to reassure investors and provided a free telephone number for queries. These mainly came from pension fund managers who realised they must act more quickly to retrieve their funds undamaged.

Expansive strategies

Where globalisation and diversification are overall strategies, then the public relations manager needs to consider appropriate measures for achieving this. Many Dutch, Swiss, Japanese and French companies have now moved into the US financial services market. Similarly, many banking and insurance companies are now moving into investments, funds and money management. Product proliferation means that competitive advantage can only be gained at the edge of public relations operations. In the financial sector, examples of planned and sustained activities to become recognised, accepted and trusted in a new environment and with new publics include:

- serving on public interest and regulatory committees
- drafting technical papers
- speaking to study groups and conferences
- writing articles for financial periodicals
- giving evidence to legislative committees
- arranging public visits of executives.

Sponsorship can act as a shortcut by creating associations with an event and networking with other local event planners. This will make a difference to licence applications, acquisitions, disposals and lay-offs (MacDonald, 1991).

Another expansive strategy is to arrange for quotation on the local stock market. This can significantly raise the profile of the listed company. In the USA, prescriptive disclosure for bond issues is required, so the annual report will need to be updated quarterly which can be expensive. In Japan, companies must place themselves in the hands of a sponsoring securities house which gives briefings to the press and analysts and arranges individual institution meetings to encourage take-up.

Creative strategies

The problem of rapid product obsolescence is characteristic of extremely competitive environments and has implications for market share and investment. Creative financial public relations strategies will make use of new technology to improve reputation in retail markets. Global television gives economies of scale in promotional material but does not take account of cultural differences. However, non-verbal communication with the corporate name gets the image across internationally. Cable News Network of America, the NHK (Japan Broadcasting Corporation) and Channel 4 are all linked. O Globo (Rio de Janiero, Brazil) has the largest audience of any television company in the world. The implications for interview strategies are that they can go to all audiences around the world. This requires a knowledge of and ability in diplomacy and selective commentary.

In retail banking a successful strategy will make use of existing names, for example, HSBC Midland. In major financial centres such as London, Tokyo, New York, San Francisco, Hong Kong and Sydney where foreign exchange is traded, the corporate identity can be used with financially sophisticated publics. A substantial knowledge of the international media is necessary to be able to develop creative strategies. Hard copy of newspapers such as the *Financial Times* and the *International Herald Tribune* compete in dealers' offices with electronic news from Reuters, AP-Dow Jones, and Knight-Ridder. Information and analysis is now instant; dealers look to newspapers for comment.

The *Wall Street Journal* (USA), Agence France Presse (France), *Handelsblatt, Frankfurter Allgemeine Zeitung; Börsenzeiting* (Germany), *Neue Zuricher Zeitung* (Switzerland), Jiji Press wire service and Nihon Keizai Shimbun (Japan) all cover global financial events. The public relations executive takes account of local practices in market and media segments. For example, US reporters do not usually include their own opinion in editorial copy, relying on different sources to build up a story. Public relations strategy should account for opportunities like this which allow the company or client to act as market commentators. In this way, they can create attention disproportionate to the size of the firm. In Japan, on the other hand, news releases go through press clubs, for example Bank of Japan club for banking news; Tokyo Stock Exchange club for securities news; permission being required from the club chairman in advance.

Adaptive strategies

Adaptive strategies are necessary when two companies have merged, when a company is moving into a different geographic area or when it is moving into related service delivery fields. It is particularly important to have a flexible approach if these overall strategies are accompanied by hostile reporting or volatile market trading as was the case in the 1980s when there was an explosion of securities trading consequent on privatisation and trends in global deregulation.

Legal and moral issues such as insider trading and illegal buying of treasury issues, for example Salomon Bros in 1991, give rise to adaptive strategies for different markets. The media in some markets will dwell on an issue longer than in others. Public relations must measure the level of trust in its financial customer base because when customers lose trust in an established firm, the firm can be destroyed. This is when a thorough knowledge of different publics pays off. Publics with great weight can be approached on a one-to-one basis to provide reassurance. German and Japanese banks have traditionally had more stake in their corporate clients' stock and therefore have a longer term view of these companies' survival. Corporate advertising and imaging is an integral part of the international public relations role in finance. The level of language translation and destination newspapers are important considerations. Cultural and local differences built into a transnational campaign are better than standard adverts around the world which can do more harm than good, deterring rather than encouraging business relationships. Local agents may be used to adapt messages. Overseas financial advertising costs much more to compete with indigenous advertisers and it may be better to train local managers in the public relations function.

RESEARCH

Impression formation

The Classic Information Processing Model of general attitude and behaviour change (Hovland et al., 1953) suggests identifiable and distinct participants in the communications process, that is source, message, channel, and receiver. Moreover, their research demonstrated that 'credibility of a source influenced the persuasiveness of the message being delivered'. McGuire (1981) added 'destination' to the model as the final outcome sought by the source, that is attitude or behaviour change. He developed the Persuasion Matrix to include exposure, attention, liking, learning, agreement, remembering, behaviour. To enhance attention and memory, special consideration should be paid to the working of the first sentence and then the headline of any news item or press release, editors sometimes preferring to write their own headline. Research has shown there is an order effect on retention of a message and also that source credibility is a multidimensional concept including trustworthiness, expertise and power. Message persuasiveness is also aided by source-audience similarity. Many old financial institutions can tap a tradition of trustworthiness and power which came as a part of their quasi-establishment role prior to deregulation. New companies and alliances make use of these old well-known names, retaining country company titles in an international conglomerate.

Message characteristics should be simple, localised and personally relevant. For financial news releases, using simple language, avoiding legal terms and preparing separate versions for different countries/regions is appropriate. Target audiences will look at and listen to specific issues, particularly if they are repeated often and consistently. Effectiveness is also enhanced when presented in novel ways, employing an appropriate appeal. Rational appeals are directed at cognitive outcomes and emotional appeals intensify motivation. Financial services at all levels are complex and a rational approach to marketing them is essential but the public relations message, dealing as it does with security and confidence, can also be delivered effectively by an emotional message. In particular, positive appeals have been found to be more effective for message retention and targeted behaviour outcomes.

The effectiveness of the communication is closely reliant on the compatibility of the organisation's image with the target audience. For example, the Co-operative Bank has launched a TV campaign to emphasise its commitment to environmental issues by actively seeking ways to promote these issues in its financial services business. Public relations communications should be compatible with the overall social environment and one effective method of generating social support is by mobilising or restructuring community resources, i.e. sponsorship. On the other hand, unknown sources can be more believable as there is no sponsoring identity to include in the evaluation. News items have higher levels of believability than sponsored messages and therefore require fewer exposures.

Channel selection for corporate advertising also involves demographically and psychographically segmented audiences. Financial sector companies use media coverage by providing comment in news slots and sponsoring public debates on pertinent issues. This is relevant to channel selection as more and more print and television media are working on segmented audience blueprints. Grunig (1979) found that people typically use mass media for entertainment, that is low involvement news consumption which should be taken account of in campaign planning. Other research, however, is conflicting. Comstock et al. (1978) suggest that in the USA television is the main entertainment medium but principal source of national news for the general public. Research by Hofstetter et al. (1978) and Reagan and Ducey (1983) found those who prefer newspapers tend to be more knowledgeable. Yet Wilson and Howard (1978) found television reporting to be more accurate than newspapers or radio. In the USA, public television is the main source of news for white, affluent, well-educated audiences.

160

Information and research in this area is changing rapidly as technological developments keep pace with lifestyle changes. For instance the audience for Chinese television is approximately 100 million and at present is relatively inexpensive. Corporate advertisers can identify suitable visual, non-verbal images to reach this audience as soon as possible. New media methods such as cable television will present opportunities for 'narrowcasting' to more selective audiences. In financial public relations this will allow more intensive coverage of current issues of concern to smaller influential groups such as institutional investment, directors or finance officers. Research indicates that one of the most effective tools for public relations is maximising interpersonal contact with the public (Hesse, 1981). This re-enforces the two-way process of public relations, which is characteristic of the activities of public relations executives in the merchant banking and brokerage sector.

Situational factors

Grunig and Grunig (1986) found that demographics were not that useful in identifying individual attitudes and opinions. The argument for media pull rather than marketing push strategies in financial markets depends on this type of research. Grunig's situational theory identifies four important factors which will affect an individual's reception of a message:

- Level of problem recognition. Do you stop and think about the issue?
- Level of constraint recognition. Do factors outside your control limit your action?
- The presence of a referent criterion . . . a piece of knowledge or experience from a previous situation acting as a decision rule.
- The level of involvement, that is the extent to which a person perceives a connection between the self and the environment. The stronger the connection the more likely the communication will be received successfully.

This model provides a way to identify publics according to the extent and methods a person uses to communicate about an issue.

Applied research using this model indicates that investor relations messages could give information about ways to eliminate behavioural constraints to enable targeted audiences to solve a savings problem. A case in point is the increasing resort to personal equity plans to replace national and company retirement insurance. As a new service, many publics were unaware they had a problem and were unable to identify possible solutions. Identifying the relationship between communications and certain cognitive strategies such as hedging and wedging is also appropriate for campaign planning and corporate advertising strategies. Hedging is a cognitive strategy in which a person holds two or more conflicting views on a solution to a problem, increasing the chance of being a winner. This strategy is likely to be used when the person lacks a referent criterion. Wedging is a cognitive strategy of firmly holding one position. This is used by people/publics highly involved with an issue. Financiers are familiar with these terms, adopted from the risk management literature.

Evaluation of added value

Pavlik (1987) has highlighted the need for public relations to shift to less powerful intermediate objectives in the information-processing model. Raising issues for public debate is a measurable activity, whereas persuading people to change their minds is a vague objective, difficult to measure. Social scientists studying the media have found consistent evidence that the media rarely changes attitudes and behaviour, especially among adults. Media channels are conduits for information only. Conversely, Lippmann (1921) argues that behaviour is a response to and based on pictures in our head of the outside world shaped by the mass media. People use the media as a form of social radar. They survey the world through the press, TV and other mass media. Lasswell (1972) differentiated between 'knowledge about' and 'acquaintance with' an issue. Media-based campaigns change acquaintance with an issue not knowledge about it. It would be difficult to understand the success of propaganda if it were impossible for the media and the message to change attitudes. More research is necessary to understand the process of argument and persuasion.

However, the press is successful in telling readers what to think about: they are good at agenda setting. So public relations campaigns can aim to raise the salience or awareness of an issue. Measurable objectives include changing awareness, knowledge or perception rather than behaviour. To raise the public's level of interest and information about an issue will give them a referent criterion when they need to act in the future. Since all individuals and all businesses must deal in finance at one time or another, setting measurable objectives for all audiences is important.

Four types of agenda have been identified: interpersonal (shared and discussed with others) and intrapersonal (individual opinions that shapes personality), community agenda and mass media agenda. Do different media have different effects on different agendas? Newspapers tend to be prime movers by determining what will make the daily agenda. Television acts more like a spotlight. Revitalised media channels like commercial radio can also be evaluated by their contribution to the different agendas. In general, the issue must remain on the media agenda for a long time for it to make the public agenda. Lang and Lang (1983) suggest prominence gives visibility to facilitate attention. So media coverage builds awareness of an issue and if there is heavy media emphasis it can move onto people's personal agenda. It can also influence priorities placed on existing issues. Finally, issues do have life-cycles.

Who sets the media agenda? While the press make decisions about what is newsworthy it may be necessary to avoid an issue coming to the public attention. Many areas of journalism are dependent on press releases for reliable information, although some editors consider that public relations consultants are ignorant of reporting formats and timings. Donohue et al. (1973) proposed a knowledge-gap hypothesis to frame the distribution of knowledge in society. Pathways to possession and control of knowledge are critical references for valid public relations strategies and evaluation. Persons with high socio-economic status know more about public affairs which persons of low status are only acquainted with. This may be because they use different media; the high status population use newspapers (knowledge media) and the low status, television (entertainment media). Barriers to information flow over media boundaries create opportunities for effective control of damage in financial crises, such as a collapse in share prices or exchange rates.

It is this limitation of knowledge which has successfully kept wholesale and retail financial audiences separate. This is changing with mass information technologies such as global television, the Internet and the increase in competition driving companies to reach new audiences.

Another thesis which is useful in developing and evaluating continuous public relations objectives is the cognitive complexity gap (Grunig and Ipes, 1983). Different audiences will initially have a varying number of ideas about an issue. Knowledge of the typical audience member's hierarchy of beliefs about a topic aids in the development of a message which will be successfully targeted. In investor relations, annual reports are central to the communications process but different sections of the report can be more successfully tailored to the audiences that read them. Associationist attitude theory has been applied in financial public relations, particularly in the non-bank retail credit sector, for example, American Express. Associations are based on images created through advertising messages. Denbow and Culbertson (1985) concluded that an organisation's image could be altered by associating it with desirable objects and visa versa.

Another extremely important area for research is internal relations for two reasons:

1 Effective communications with staff about corporate goals enhance their ability to do the job effectively
2 Effective internal communications mirrors a corporation's image with a large group of its stakeholders.

Jeffres (1975) reports that people are purposeful in their use of internal media. Many large insurance and banking concerns in America have had to communicate continuously with their staff about redundancy programmes and public relations staff have themselves been included in these reductions in staff.

Finally, Jones (1975) suggests a public relations audit to identify the gap between the target audience's knowledge and what the company wants them to know. The reduction in this gap by means of the campaign can then be effectively measured. The research indicates that for public relations, communications can build mutual understanding rather than persuade, that traditional goals are unrealistic to achieve and evaluate and that there is a need to integrate theory and practice.

SUMMARY AND CONCLUSIONS

This chapter has highlighted the particular nature and background of financial and investor public relations. The volatility of the market, deregulation, global trends and the growth of new financial instruments have caused dramatic upheavals and opportunities for the PR discipline. More intense competition in the financial sectors has created a need for all stakeholders including market organisers themselves to identify, monitor and communicate more specifically with their targeted audiences.

A more rigorous approach to developing strategic communications policy at the corporate and divisional levels in international and global companies will provide a more significant contribution to overall corporate objectives. Four strategies were outlined: creative, expansive, adaptive and defensive. Some examples of the situations in which these were likely to be useful have been given, but they are by no means prescriptive.

Finally, the public relations function in financial markets can benefit by reference to a substantial body of behavioural and audience research. This research can form the basis of a more detailed analysis of audience identification, communications objectives and methods of and criteria for evaluation.

DISCUSSION TOPICS

1 Provide a report to the investor relations department of a UK insurance company, outlining the main environmental factors it should consider in its corporate communications strategy.
2 How would a communication between a bank and its many audiences differ in content and method of delivery?
3 How should the public relations department of a merchant bank treat financial analysts?
4 Identify the main publics to be addressed by the annual report of an investment company.
5 How can the public relations agent of an international financial services corporation identify strategic objectives?
6 Design an audience identification study for a company of your choice. What criteria would you use to weight the importance of each audience?
7 Devise a corporate image research project for a financial services corporation specifically detailing how you would measure audience knowledge of the company.
8 As a project team of a financial public relations agency, devise a common compatible communications programme for all audiences both national and global, internal and external, which explains the insurance corporation's recent takeover of a major building society.
9 How would you best distribute a communication from headquarters to all international divisions which indicates a merger with another bank and consequent redundancies.
10 Create a headline to counter a rumour that your investment company is being declared insolvent.

CASE STUDY: CLASSIC CITY STRUGGLE

When shareholders decided on 23rd January to accept Granada's £3.8 billion bid for Forte, both PR camps heaved a huge sigh of relief that the two month campaign was all over. Seldom has a City takeover excited such popular interest, even from the tabloid press. The resources that both sides put into the fight is a testimony to the importance they attached to a vigorous PR campaign.

Both companies called in their retained consultants: Citigate for Granada and

Brunswick for Forte. The campaigns were serviced from inside as well as by the agency. Citigate's deputy managing director led a team which included Granada's public affairs director and the group managing director of the rental division. Brunswick partners teamed up with Forte's public affairs director, public relations director and corporate public relations manager.

The campaign was more than getting column inches in a newspaper. The PR expertise was used to judge timing of announcements, appropriate press releases, reacting to circulars, advising on when to be on the front or back foot and keeping people's mind on the bid right up to the last day.

The battle lines of a contested takeover are determined by the 60-day timetable laid down by the Takeover Panel. This provides the framework for a defence or attack strategy and allows both sides to plan the timing and content of messages to shareholders, analysts and press.

Granada's hostile bid for Forte began on 22nd November with the formal publication of its bid document outlining the details of its initial £3.2 billion offer. The PR battle began on that day and finished on Day 60 (23rd January) when shareholders voted on the offer. Key points within that period included the closing date for Granada's initial bid on 15th December, the publication of Forte's defence document on 2nd January and Granada's increased offer to £3.8 billion on the 9th January.

Granada had been considering an attack on Forte for over a year and Citigate planned a communications strategy three months before the initial offer was announced. City observers were, however, surprised at the speed and effectiveness of Forte's defence, which at least until the revised offer in January, appeared to put the bidder on the defensive. One of their key successes was to put the spotlight on Granada. Forte called into question Granada's stability, prospects and management, undermining the value and attractiveness of the bid. At the same time they showed they were prepared to put their own house in order by selling the restaurant business to Whitbread and initiating an £800 million share buy-back.

Forte's defence also included attacking Granada's chief executive, Gerry Robinson, for attempting to create an old-fashioned unwieldy conglomerate while simultaneously agreeing to split Forte's chairman and chief executive's role which had both been held by Sir Rocco Forte. Granada was momentarily caught off guard but by early January had recovered lost ground, partly saved by timing. They had deliberately timed the initial bid so that the last day for Forte's defence document was the end of the Christmas holiday (2nd January).

The huge press coverage that Forte fired was missed by holidaying analysts and shareholders. By the time Granada issued its final bid on the 9th January the pendulum of opinion had swung back in its favour. Although Forte's campaign was more creative and dramatic, they put all their eggs in the shop window at one time and lost the initiative.

It is the analysts and shareholders not the press that make or break a deal. The pivotal role played by Mercury Asset Management, which owns roughly 15 per cent of Granada and Forte, shows how important it is to persuade institutional investors of the merits of the case. They are more concerned with the financial details of the bid. Private shareholders get most of their information from the financial press and circulars and that has an impact on how they perceive the bid.

The cost of the takeover was more than £155 million; for underwriters, bankers, brokers, lawyers and consultants. Citigate's fee was £1 million not including the success fee. Brunswick's fee was reputed to be £2 million. But the costs of a hostile takeover can be much higher for those involved in an unsuccessful defence. Granada only plan to keep eight people out of the three hundred at Forte's corporate headquarters, so Forte's public relations director and corporate communications manager were fighting for their jobs.

(*Source*: John-Pierre Joyce, *PR Week*, 26 January 1996, used with permission.)

REFERENCES

Chase, W.H. (1975) 'How companies are using corporate advertising', *Public Relations Journal*, 31(11): 26.

Clarke, G. (1996) 'Investment companies: the content of the chairman's letter', in G. Comstock, S. Chaffee, N. Katzman, M. McCombs and D. Roberts (1978) *Television and Human Behaviour*, New York: Columbia University Press.

Comstock, G., Chaffee, S., Katzman, N., McCombs, M. and Roberts, D. (1978) *Television and Human Behaviour*, New York: Columbia University Press.

Denbow, C.H. and Culbertson, H.M. (1985) 'Linkage beliefs and diagnosing an image', *Public Relations Review*, 11(1): 29–37.

Donohue, G.A., Olien, C.N. and Tichoner, P. (1973) 'Mass media, knowledge and social control', *Journalism Quarterly*, 50: 652-9.

Gart, A. (1994) *Regulation, Deregulation and Reregulation – The Future of the Banking, Insurance and Securities Industries*, New York: John Wiley.

Grunig, J.E. (1979) 'Time budgets, level of involvement and use of mass media', *Journalism Quarterly*, 55(1): 109–18.

Grunig, J.E. (1982) 'Developing economic education programmes for the Press', *Public Relations Review*, 8(3): 43–62.

Grunig, J.E. (1983) 'Washington reporter publics of corporate public affairs programmes', *Journalism Quarterly*, 39(4): 603–14.

Grunig, J.E. and Ipes, D.A. (1983) 'The anatomy of a campaign against drunken driving', *Public Relations Review*, 9(2): 36–52.

Grunig, J.E. and Grunig, L.S. (1986) 'Applications of open systems theory to public relations: Review of a program of research.' Paper presented to the meeting of International Communication Association, Chicago.

Hesse, M.B. (1981) 'Strategies of the political communication process', *Public Relations Review*, 7(1): 32–7.

Hofstetter, C.R., Zirkin, C. and Bass, T.F. (1978) 'Political information and imagery in an age of television', *Journalism Quarterly*, 55(3): 562-9.

Hovland, C.I., Janis, I.L. and Kelley, H.H. (1953) *Communication and Persuasion*, New Haven, CT: Yale University Press.

Hutchins, H. (1994) 'Annual reports: earning surprising respect from institutional investors', *Public Relations Review*, 20(4): 309–17.

Jack, A. (1995) 'A question of trust', *Financial Times*, 29/12/95.

Jeffres, L. (1975) 'Functions of media behaviours', *Communication Research*, 2: 136–62.

Jones, J.F. (1975) 'Audit: a new tool for public relations', *Public Relations Journal*, 31(7): 6–8.

Lang, G.E. and Lang, K. (1983) *The Battle for Public Opinion*, New York: Columbia University Press.

Lasswell, H.D. (1972) 'The structure of communication in society', in W. Schramm and D.F. Roberts (eds) *The Process and Effects of Mass Communications*, Urbana, IL: University of Illinois Press.

Lippmann, W. (1921) *Public Opinion*, New York: Macmillan.

MacDonald, A. (1991) 'Financial public relations in a global context', in M. Nally (ed.) *International Public Relations in Practise*, London: Kogan Page.

McGuire, W.J. (1981) 'Theoretical foundations of campaigns', in R.E. Rice and W.J. Paisley (eds) *Public Communications Campaigns*, Newbury Park, CA: Sage.

Mendelsohn, H. (1973) 'Some reasons why information campaigns succeed', *Public Opinion Quarterly*, 37(1): 50–61.

Nally, M. (ed.) (1991) *International Public Relations in Practise*, London: Kogan Page.

Ostrom, T.M. (1969) 'The relationship between the affective, behavioural and cognitive components of attitude', *Journal of Experimental Social Psychology*, 5: 12–30.

Oxley, H. (1989) *The Principles of Public Relations*, London: Kogan Page.

Park, R.E. (1923) 'The natural history of the newspaper', *American Journal of Sociology*, 29: 273–89.

Pavlik, J.V. (1987) *Public Relations: What Research Tells Us*, Newbury Park, CA: Sage.

Ray, M.L. (1973) 'Marketing communication and the hierarchy of effects', in P. Clarke (ed.) *New Models for Mass Communication Research*, Newbury Park, CA: Sage, pp. 47–176.

Reagan, J. and Ducey, R.V. (1983) 'Effect of news measures on selection of state government', *Journalism Quarterly*, 60(12): 211–17.

Revell, J. (ed.) (1994) *The Changing Face of European Banks and Securities Markets*, Basingstoke: Macmillan.

Rybczynski, T. (1994) 'The development of European capital markets: the main trends and their implications', in J. Revell (ed.) *The Changing Face of European Banks and Securities Markets*, Basingstoke: Macmillan.

Wilson, C.E. and Howard, D.M. (1978) 'Public perception of media accuracy', *Journalism Quarterly*, 55(1): 73–6.

10

GOVERNMENT AND LOBBYING ACTIVITIES

Kevin Moloney

CHAPTER AIMS

- to give a competing political perspective on lobbying
- to provide a theoretical perspective underpinning lobbying activities
- to describe and analyse governmental activities and lobbying from the dual perspective of politics and public relations
- to give a view of PR practice from a non-market perspective
- to explain the relation of lobbying to UK society and public relations
- to provide an understanding of the main elements of lobbying and measurement of its (potential) effectiveness of consequences

ILLUSTRATION: THE RAIL LINK AND CHANNEL TUNNEL

One example is the route of the rail link to the Channel Tunnel. Local authorities in East London and cement manufacturers Blue Circle, the owner of disused land in Kent, all lobbied ministers in order to attempt to influence the route of the new railway. The pay-off of a favourable decision for those groups lay variously in job creation; attracting firms to locate in specific areas; building a station and/or an industrial park; or starting up construction works. Successful lobbying tends to offer significant benefits.

INTRODUCTION

'Government' and 'lobbying' are two terms which are often used together when we talk about current affairs. For public relations people, the next breath usually delivers phrases such as 'government relations', 'corporate affairs', 'corporate communications', 'public affairs'. This chapter aims to describe and analyse relationships between these terms in such a way that they can be understood from the twin perspectives of politics and public relations. This analysis should provide insight into a significant segment of public relations practice: that part which does not deal directly with markets, which is usually called by one of the titles above, and which has lobbying inside it as a component. By the end of this chapter readers should be able to take a view on how lobbying fits into UK society, and how it relates to public relations, and be able to understand its main elements.

What issues are at stake when lobbyists lobby government and what processes are involved? The range of matters lobbied on is inevitably wide because lobbyists go to work when the organisations they represent believe their interests can be expanded or reduced by some act or omission by government. Moloney (1994) has listed some 50 issues that relate directly to the United Kingdom. They include, for example, issues as diverse as supermarket development in and out of towns; building regulations for steel and concrete; European work councils; packaging; the National Lottery; regional airports; the price of fragrances. His list was limited inasmuch as it was drawn from the business sector, and left aside issues which concerned people in social, voluntary and professional occupations.

Issues share certain features. They are located in organisations (or groups as they shall be described henceforth); they are affected in some way by public policy; they are perceived as either an opportunity or a threat to that group; such organisations believe that government can enhance opportunities or serve to reduce threats. The underlying assumption is that government(s) can be influenced to legislate favourably from an organisational context.

In this chapter we are concerned to ask questions related to the location of a 'mental map', provision of a discursive model, and to provide a theoretical perspective in political and public relations studies which may offer a valid explanation of what lobbying is. The chapter then offers a definition of lobbying, explains what this entails, and who is responsible to carry out this function. The chapter also explains the relationship of lobbying with public relations and its perceived effectiveness (from the author's perspective, it is a specialised activity inside the broader discipline of public relations). The chapter concludes with a summary, and offers an extended case study of the British Gas transition from the public to the private sector.

COMPETING POLITICAL PERSPECTIVES

Lobbying can be defined in the first instance as persuasive activity to change public policy in favour of an organisation by groups of people who are not directly involved in the political process. This definition will bias the following excursus in two ways. First, it situates lobbying as a collective activity which seeks to achieve common goals, such as building an extra terminal at an airport. The definition excludes the activity of an individual (and his or her lobbyist if he or she hired one) to persuade government to adopt a personally favoured policy. An example would be the financier Sir James Goldsmith who wants the European Union (EU) to be trade protectionist. We might say – rightly in conversation – that he is lobbying Brussels with that view. However, that persuasive activity by him is excluded here because he speaks for himself. Another exclusion would be Baroness Thatcher lobbying John Major for a reduction in welfare spending. Lobbying, as defined in the literature, and, as carried out in practice, relates to groups, what they may want and, if government controls what they want, how they might persuade government to agree with them. Secondly, the definition above of lobbying is very broad in its definition of groups. It includes – to give UK examples – ICI, Greenpeace, the Church of England, the Trades Union Congress, and Outrage (the homosexual equality campaign).

Thus lobbying is done by all sorts of organised entities, in all sectors of public life and by groups of all sizes and reputation. This chapter most frequently uses the word 'group' to identify the entity which causes lobbying to happen. The word is used to include what is known in the literature as pressure groups and interest groups, cause groups and sectoral groups. That meaning is extended to cover private companies and publicly funded bodies such as schools, universities, and hospital trusts. Sometimes the word 'organisation' is inserted as an alternative to 'group' for stylistic simplicity.

It is not possible to disentangle lobbying from politics: to say, for example, 'ICI is lobbying' is semantic shorthand for the fuller expression 'ICI is lobbying government'. Groups operate in the public domain of our lives as opposed to the private and that domain is affected by government. This does not imply either that government 'controls' the public domain or has only a minimum role to play in it. Either of those conditions could be empirically valid for any particular government: rather the statement asserts that in contemporary liberal market economies at the end of the twentieth century, government cannot avoid some degree of involvement with the public areas of our lives. The following examples illustrate the systemic nature of government involvement. The UK Conservative Government declares that it wants to reduce the 'red tape' (i.e. regulation) affecting business. But reduction cannot mean zero regulation for international treaties and membership of the EU imposes regulation on the UK acumen – say, in the matter of noxious emissions – whatever the British Government may wish ideologically. Therefore ICI does lobby London and Brussels about emissions from its chimneys because the amount and quality of externally imposed emission controls adds or subtracts significantly to or from costs.

Government may declare – rightly – that the sexual preferences of citizens is their private choice, but it cannot ignore the public consequences of individual choices. These consequences include questions of public taste and decency; or job and lifestyle discrimination; or, the rights and safety of minors. Public opinion may pressure government to legislate on all or any of these questions and so set boundaries to private choices. A more local example is the West Southbourne Tennis Club. This recreational body may never have talked to its local council MP for the past 50 years. But that reticence will rapidly evaporate should parking be banned in the streets around its courts.

Groups seek to achieve the purposes for which their members came together: purposes such as making a profit; pursuing a public good, such as free health service; promoting a cause; following a recreation; removing a perceived wrong. In our society, government – supranational, national, regional and local – can help or hinder those purposes and in some cases it has intervened to establish a body to achieve a purpose, for example the National Health Service. Because of their purposes, groups have varying degrees of power and influence: ICI creates a significant amount of material wealth and employment for the UK; local or regional tennis clubs may contribute to help keep the employed, mothers, the retired and the semi-fit in reasonable physical health by providing a form of physical recreation.

Groups lobby to ensure that government is at least neutral about their purposes and at best, supportive. This definition of lobbying can be recognised as a description applied to public relations of what students of politics call pluralism. This political perspective (and the variants which have sprung from it) have been the leading paradigm for explaining US and UK politics since the 1960s. Challengers of that paradigm are Marxist and corporatist explanations and the relationship of the three perspectives to policy-making are set out in Smith (1993) as well as the strengths and weaknesses they have for explaining group/state relationships and interactions.

Truman (1951) and Dahl (1961) are two US writers who developed the basic features of classical pluralism of power widely dispersed in society among groups which were unequal in status and resources. The latter summed up the fundamental question (intriguing to both public policy-makers and lobbyists) that he explored in the first sentence of his very readable book *Who Governs*. He wrote that 'In a political system where nearly every adult may vote but where knowledge, wealth, social position, access to officials and other resources are unequally distributed, who actually governs?' Jones (1991:506) states the pluralist view that government is 'a more or less neutral referee' between groups.

Lobbyists have to engage with this refereeing question in an operational way when they set out to influence government on behalf of a group. They want 'access' to the decision-makers who will decide a matter for or against them and in the UK context they are Ministers, senior civil servants, special advisers to Ministers, MPs or senior European Commission staff or MEPs. Norton and Grantham (1986) conceptualised 'access' as a hyphen, linking government and interests in society. They argue that the outcome of such linkage is better public policy because the hyphen works both ways, with government being told how policy works when applied and groups having influence on policy.

Pluralism has greatly influenced public relations in the US and the UK. Most North American textbooks have taken the stance – implicit or explicit – that lobbying (the public affairs part of public relations) is a guarantor of pluralism. Baskin and Aronoff (1988); Crable and Vibbert (1986); Cutlip et al. (1985); Grunig (1989); Lesley (1991) and Pearson (1992) are in the US pluralist school while White (White and Lazur, 1994), the most influential UK author on public relations, adopts a very similar stance.

Lindblom (1977) developed the neo-pluralist variant of classical pluralism with the view that, of all the groups in society, the most influential in a liberal, market economy was business and it was privileged by government over all other interests. This is a pertinent development for lobbyists because in the UK perhaps most lobbying by public relations people is done for and on behalf of business interests. Earlier pluralist writers admitted that not all groups in a liberal market acumen were equal in power, influence and therefore 'access' but they did not go so far as to unequivocally identify the most powerful. Lindblom argued that elected governments in market economies need prosperity to win elections, that business is a major generator of prosperity, and that government therefore has to satisfy many of the needs of business groups to develop prosperity among electors. This gives business groups what is called structural power – power that flows directly from fundamental features of a society, in this case the power of capital to create and satisfy markets and command resources. Lindblom further noted (1977:141) that groups 'remain grossly unequal in wealth . . . some can hire a supporting organisation; some can hire public relations consultants, broadcast time, newspaper space, or other public platforms; others cannot'. Overall, he offers an explanation of why business is a major lobbyer of government in Western liberal economies and why a relatively new type of lobbyist – those for hire, also known as commercial lobbyists – are mostly employed by business. He provides an account of why non-business and anti-business groups are generally not as well resourced as business for lobbying and why governments tend not to fully satisfy the purposes of these groups.

Grant (1995) has explored most of the issues raised by the business/government interaction in policy formation. In particular, he reviewed the well-established division between 'insider' and 'outsider' groups (where the distinction is in terms of more or less access to decision-makers) and how the distinction affects the sorts of lobbying done by groups and the outcomes therefrom. An example is the Institute of Directors and the Transport and General Workers' Union in the UK since 1979. Other examples are landowners and farmers who are far more influential than their numbers suggest. Government listens carefully to police chief constables when they talk as a group. In contradistinction, the unemployed or consumers, because of their numbers and dispersion across the country, find it hard to organise into groups and lobby as an organised bloc. Black groups frequently talk about exclusion from policy-making because of racism while gender equality groups allege anti-feminist or homophobic discrimination. Lindblom (1987) explores this question of asymmetrical access to government.

Such asymmetrical distinction is crucial for lobbyists because it is a major determinant of their chances of success: 'outsider groups' do not usually get government to accept their policies. The distinction is also the first step in a critique of lobbying which has its foundations in a Marxist view of group activity in a liberal, market acumen. Smythe (1981) has argued that public relations is part of a 'Consciousness Industry' creating acquiescence to monopoly capitalism. Gandy (1982) has developed an explicit theory of how this acquiescence is achieved – the concept of 'information subsidy' – and it is one which involves public relations people. For him, the ultimate 'insider' groups in a liberal capitalist society are major businesses which make information favourable to their interests freely and easily available in ways which do not require research, time or energy on the part of the enquirer. This is 'the information subsidy' paid for by business interests and 'It is the modern public relations firm that plays the central role in the design and implementation of information subsidy efforts by the major policy actors' (Gandy, 1982:64).

For academics like Smythe and Gandy, public relations and lobbying are techniques which keep already powerful groups in their positions of dominance over other interests in a liberal capitalist society. Unlike them, classical pluralists believe that there is competition between interests in society and that business group interests may not always prevail. These authors point to the success of Greenpeace in June 1995 in stopping Shell, a very powerful multinational oil company, dumping the Brent Spar oil storage rig in the North Atlantic and they hail this outcome as an example of competition between groups yielding unpredictable outcomes. The neo-pluralists take a middle position between these two schools saying that business interests are privileged but challengeable – in other words, business interests do not always have their way with government.

All the authors referenced so far identify a place for lobbying in public policy-making. Pluralists welcome it to varying degrees and the neo-Marxists condemn it as part of the apparatus of capitalist domination. There is one author who sees no place for it all in liberal, capitalist societies and excludes it on moral grounds. The American Olasky (1987) declared that he was addressing 'political conservatives and libertarians' in writing that contact between government and business is inimical to free enterprise, competition and political freedom. Contact, whether public relations or lobbying, was a negative he called 'corporate collaborationism'.

LOBBYING: THE PRACTICE OF A PUBLIC RELATIONS SPECIALISM

So far lobbying has been broadly defined as persuasive activity by groups to influence government policy-making. This definition was adequate while the argument focused on groups and their needs as the causation driving lobbying activity. This can be described as an excursus at the macro level of political perspective, centred on a major phenomenon – organised interests – in liberal, capitalist society and it provided competing views for the evaluation of lobbying in terms of political values and beliefs. Attention now switches to lobbying at an operational level – the level of the practice of a specialised public relations activity – and hopefully to a more appropriate definition.

The literature reveals a wide choice of definitions and, at this operational level, it is worthwhile beginning with a lobbyist's view. Charles Miller told the House of Commons Committee on Members Interests (House of Commons, 1987–88:6, 416) that lobbying was 'the business of advising organisations on understanding, monitoring and dealing with the system of government'. This is a formal, textbook definition in that elsewhere *The Government Report*, written by a lobbying firm, urges that 'You have to see lobbying as a battle'. Grantham and Seymour-Ure (1990:66–7) have also noted this element of contest. Well-informed and well-disposed senior civil servants, Ministers and MPs are sought out by the lobbyist but they do not seek their passive support. MPs are often encouraged to table Questions and Early-Day Motions and, where relevant, amendments to Bills, and advance a specific case in debate and through meetings and correspondence with appropriate Ministers.

Miller's (1987) definition, however, is worth perusal as it has the important value of portraying lobbying as a series of discrete but linked activities. Two other lobbyists have offered the same sort of definition. Wedgewood (1987) said his work was both intelligence-gathering (broken down into monitoring, interpretation and research) and operational roles (planning, passive representation and active representation). Smith (1992) stated that lobbying was combined communication and pressure, with any particular lobby being a variable, composite mix.

This chapter borrows from these definitions and defines the practice of lobbying *as monitoring public policy-making for a group interest; building a case in favour of that interest; and putting it privately with varying degrees of pressure to public decision-makers for their acceptance and support through favourable political intervention.*

Lobbying is inside public relations practice because it is a communications-based activity centred on a group (or organisation, in the language of management studies) which seeks to persuade and negotiate with those of its stakeholders in government on matters of opportunity and/or threat. Lobbying is done by individuals in one of two employment categories: in-house lobbyists directly employed by the group and by hired lobbyists contracted in for certain tasks over usually short periods of time. Heinz et al. (1993) estimated that for every one hired lobbyist in Washington DC, USA, there were four in-house lobbyists at work. It is probable that similar proportions apply in London, the location for the great majority of British lobbying. Moloney (1994) reported industry estimates that about £25million was spent in 1993/4 on hiring lobbyists alone'. In-house lobbyists are most often known as public affairs or corporate communications managers and are in a staff, as opposed to line, relationship with their representative boards. Those whom lobbyists, whether in-house or hired, report to in a group are known here as their principals.

WHAT DO LOBBYISTS ACTUALLY DO?

One of the values of the definition above is that it allows insight into lobbying as a range of different activities, activities which can be coupled and decoupled into patterns best suited to achieve intended objectives or goals. For example, at the time of the privatisation of the UK electricity supply and distribution industries, Électricité de France engaged a London lobbyist to monitor and report privately on developments. At the same time, another lobbying firm was drafting, for The Shopping Hours Reform Council, a strategy document on how to revive the flagging campaign for Sunday supermarket opening, and how to build public support in the face of a strong counter-campaign, and compiling lists of supportive, hostile and neutral MPs. Smith (1993:1–76) described how politicians and civil servants are active and competing players in decision-making with their own agendas and how lobbyists have to take this policy network into account.

Such diversity of lobbying activity flows directly from the nature of the operational environment in which groups find themselves when assessing opportunities and threats. In regard to the UK, Western Europe, and North America, lobbyists operate in a relatively open system of markets and of ideas where there are usually multiple decision-makers having an input into public policy. Groups also have material and ideological competitors influencing their operational environment. All these factors produce what Lindblom (1977) has described as 'polyarchy' where politics (formally the public policy-making decision process) is a process relatively accessible to a variety of interests but is done among players of unequal influence.

The consequence for groups is that they have to adopt a contingency approach to lobbying by which they must be ready to use any tactic, legitimated by the rules, or combination thereof, or form any alliance with other groups and public decision-makers if they are to gain their objectives. In this way, lobbyists pick and choose techniques from their repertoire and fashion them into what they hope will be a winning campaign. The need to monitor (reconnoitre) and respond to (counter-attack) events is crucial. It is by not accident that *The Government Report* (Public Policy Consultants, 1987) turned to a military simile to describe lobbying.

Moloney (1994) has argued that the tasks lobbyists do can be grouped under four headings. These are each discussed in the following sections.

Providing access to public policy-makers

It is a sine qua non of all lobbying that there be contact with public decision-makers. This is why entertaining is so important to lobbyists: it is an informal means to increase their contacts with civil servants, Ministers, special advisers, and MPs. These contacts represent the professional capital of lobbyists for they must be able to say to their principals: 'I can get you in front of the decision-makers.' Entertaining also has two other benefits for lobbyists: it introduces their principals to decision-makers and it adds to the lobbyists' stock of knowledge about a policy area. The latter is especially important for some lobbyists who present themselves as policy experts (see below). Looked at from a communication perspective, lobbying can be viewed as a specialist form of networking in the field of public policy-making and access can be characterised as points of linkage between separate groups of actors in the field.

The provision of access results in the ability of the group for whom the lobbyist works to make its case to a decision-maker. Access has two forms: it is either personal and individual in that the principal and/or his or her lobbyist meets the decision-makers; or it is impersonal and electronic in the form of a telephone call, fax or e-mail. The form does not matter as long as access is achieved, but operationally human preferences come into play. Some principals insist on meeting the Minister in the belief that personal presentation of the group's case will carry the day. Lobbyists may be keen to effect this on the grounds of impressing their principal. A Minister, with an over-crowded diary, may prefer a case argued on a single A4 page.

Most 'insider' groups, for example ICI, the National Trust and the National Farmers' Union, do not need a lobbyist to provide access. The Chairman of ICI can probably telephone directly to the Prime Minister, given the contribution of the company to national production, while there are few officials in the Ministry of Agriculture, Food and Fisheries who would not break off a midday meeting to lunch with the National Farmers' Union president. Working for such groups, the lobbyist may be no more than the diarist noting such access. Mention of these powerful groups reminds that government on many issues wants access to groups. Successful policy-making is developed with a clear understanding of the field in which it will be operated. Groups operating in the field are the source of both data and opinion. In many instances, the lobbyist seeking access is pushing at an open door. In part, this 'open door' is one of the consequences – beneficial for lobbyists – of a well-observed feature (Jordan and Richardson, 1982; 1987) of the UK policy process: it is highly consultative.

Making representations to decision-makers

Once access has been gained, what does the group or its lobbyist say to the senior civil servant dealing with policy? (The First Division Association, the trade union for senior civil servants, reports that the principal and assistant secretary grades are the most frequent interlocutors with lobbyists.) The most cogent case for the group's interest has to be put: in the jargon of Westminster and Whitehall, 'representations have to be made'. Moloney found that in the case of lobbying firms, their clients (overwhelmingly large businesses) personally present their own cases in the person of the chairman or managing director. This is in line with the preferences of most hired lobbyists who do not want to be in the firing line of sharp questioning from Ministers and civil servants in policy areas where they, the lobbyists, are not expert (see below). This preference, however, is overturned when the client is too nervous, inarticulate, or ignorant of the policy process.

In the case of in-house lobbyists, there is no reason to assume that the position is different about who presents the case: it is likely to be the chairman or nominated director making the case in front of decision-makers. This is in line with the wishes of decision-makers who want to talk to the holders of power inside groups. This conclusion reminds us that the work of 'lobbying' is done by two sets of people from groups. There are those who do lobbying work on a full-time, professional basis and those senior people from groups who, because of their policy-making responsibilities, present the case of the organisation to powerful players in the public policy-making process. Overall, therefore, the lobbyist is the secondary spokesperson in these formal meetings: effecting introductions; taking notes; making supportive contributions; a source of information and reassurance. But there is one qualification to this secondary role for the professional lobbyist. Many lobbyists know a lot of MPs, Ministers and civil servants and meet them on the entertainment circuit, at clubs or conferences where they can put their case informally. It is not uncommon to hear established London lobbyists of either sort say that they 'know the Cabinet by first name terms' and that they 'can pick up the phone and talk straightaway to the Assistant-Secretary in my policy area'.

One aspect of 'making representations' or 'putting the case' to decision-makers is worth separate mention. Wherever the policy expertise comes from, the argument that is put in favour of the group must have several qualities. It has to be intellectually coherent, it has to demonstrate a public interest dimension, and it has to go with the prevailing drift of government policy. The second point is important in that decision-makers are extremely unlikely, for either public service ethos reasons or political survival reasons, to concede advantages to vested interests with a balancing public interest benefit. In so far as they do and it is known, they are open to an easily mounted critique in Parliament or the media. For their part, lobbyists have to show that there is the 'added value' of a strengthened public interest in any agreement by a Minister or civil servant which favours their respective groups rather than others. The tactical skill of lobbying is to align an enhanced public interest with satisfied private interest.

This emphasis on the cogent case to be put to decision-makers reinforces a self-image many lobbyists hold: that they are political advocates, doing as lawyers do but in the 'high court of politics'. This identification with high-status professionals, such as barristers, leads to some friction between some lobbyists and the broader public relations industry.

Lobbyists as policy advisers

Many lobbyists are experts in their fields. They have usually worked for a business, trade association, trade union or pressure group for a long time. The London lobbying firm Charles Barker has a long association with the greyhound racing industry; the Department of Trade and Industry has consulted a lobbying firm in St Albans which specialises in packaging, and an MEP asked the same firm to draft a Bill. Another London firm, Market Access, has a specialist unit on transport while a London and Brussels based lobbying firm specialises in the European plastics industry. The lobbyist for the glassmakers, Pilkington, had spent his entire career with the company. The lobbyists for ICI and BP are invariably people who have previously had an in-company career, and their public affairs posts are usually in the middle or at the end of their service. Being a lobbyist gives the postholder an overview of the organisation he or she represents and policy knowledge is relatively easily come by. This privileged position is usually reinforced by the organisational chart: lobbyists are attached to chairmen, managing directors or report directly to the executive committee just below the board. Generally, policy expertise is more likely to be found with in-house lobbyists than hired ones. This bias is an inevitable consequence of the employment status of hired lobbyists: they move from client to client inside and across sectors of activity. Their expertise more usually lies with knowledge about the processes and personnel of policy-making.

Lobbyists as administrative support group leaders

Lobbying is popularly perceived as a rather sybaritic activity, which involves mixing with high status individuals at elite venues in central London. No doubt the perception is good for recruiting. (One senior civil servant told the author that an attraction of lobbyists' lunches was the good-looking women they employed.) But access to these political salons is only for established lobbyists. The great majority of lobbying work is mundane and does little to quicken the pulse. It is akin to background research and devilling in the sense that developing somebody else's case has the ubiquitous certainty that one's ideas or fact finding will not be acknowledged. Where this research assistant work is not required, the tasks are often the detailed administration needed for the meetings, conferences and public statements of principals. For example, lobbyists have to monitor Parliamentary Bills; Hansard; Whitehall reports; the output of think tanks; the written works of the EU from Brussels and Strasbourg; relevant documents from technical and professional opinion-makers and the papers of their principals.

This document monitoring is the staplework of the trainee lobbyist and for many with degrees and MBAs, such spadework is not relished. It is, however, the daily reality in all lobbyists' offices and it reflects the first element in the preferred

177

definition of lobbying. British Steel have hired lobbyists for 'a lot of day-to-day spadework' and for relief from 'part of [the] day-to-day burden' while Vauxhall have used them in a reconnaissance role as 'eyes and ears'. Where lobbyists become involved in public campaigns led by media specialists, their role is often background liaison and administrative support at press conferences and special events such as marches, photo-calls and staged events.

How many and how much of these services principals ask of their lobbyists (hired or in-house) can be converted into a quantitative scale of usage and it can be conceptual and operationally helpful to talk of groups being 'heavy' or 'light' consumers of lobbying. Another useful analytical device is to conceptualise lobbying as either of the '*backgrounder*' or '*foregrounder*' type and so categorise the lobbying used in any campaign. These are ideal types in the Weberian sense – conceptually pure categories of rational action and not therefore personified by any lobbyist in practice – which allow comparison and analysis.

The *backgrounder* lobbyist works as an unseen adviser: monitoring documents in the passive sense of spotting references and issues; giving policy control completely to his or her principal; drafting documents for others; suggesting the relevant cast of decision-makers; effecting an introduction administratively and present but silent at meetings. The *backgrounder* gives advice on processes of policy-making and is comfortable with minimal autonomy *vis-à-vis* his or her principal. *Foregrounder* type lobbyists in contrast work as the visible advisers and are active spokespersons for their groups. They are policy experts: monitoring the groups' environments; ready to be policy formulators; prepared to represent the client alone in front of decision-makers; comfortable with media campaigns. Their tendency is towards more autonomy from their principals. There is some convergence here with the lobbyist-as-barrister self-image and while it cannot be that any individual lobbyist is either a complete *backgrounder* or *foregrounder*, the balance of evidence from lobbying practice suggests more behaviour fits the first type.

LOBBYING STYLES

Lobbying is regarded by the majority of its UK exponents as a discreet, at most semi-public, activity. It relies on personal contacts with senior public post-holders at private meetings, not publicly listed as having occurred, high levels of discretion about what was said at such meetings, and confidentiality on information exchanges and any agreements or conflicts. As such, lobbying fits snugly with a well-observed feature of UK government – what Smith (1993:97) and other authors have called the 'secretive character of the British political culture'. This helps explain why there is tension between some lobbyists and other public relations practitioners. These lobbyists point to the word 'public' in public relations, its reliance on media relations (what one lobbyist told the author was 'megaphone diplomacy') and the use of mass demonstrations outside Parliament, public petitions, stunts at pseudo events, third party testimonials from high profile people. This public disportment of a cause does not come easily to those who see lobbying as the private application of persuasion and pressure and this recoil applies to nearly all lobbyists working for business, 'insider' groups, and for London lobbying firms.

Their instinct is that such public displays are a sign of weak powers of persuasion and influence and that where they have to be resorted to, as for the sake of an alliance with other groups, the work is for 'public relations people'. The Greenpeace and Shell contest over the disposal of Brent Spar is a clear example of the strengths and weaknesses in what could be titled 'discreet' and 'megaphone' lobbying. The contest currently rests at a point where the three years of private lobbying Shell did to establish its case for deep-sea dumping with the Government was rendered null by three months of media relations and consumer boycotting by Greenpeace. An operational lesson can perhaps be learnt from these contrasting styles: lobbying is contingency-driven in terms of its tactics and these should be shaped to deliver optimal outcomes from whatever circumstances confront the group.

There are, however, other lobbyists likely to feel comfortable with 'megaphone' lobbying – those working for 'outsider' groups, for charities and cause groups who are often without easy access to decision-makers. Radical environmental groups like Earth First and animal welfare campaigners against exports on the hoof are either contesting declared policy or are pushing against the drift of policy. Ministers and senior civil servants would see little point in consulting these groups and their lobbyists are unlikely at present to get access to more than MPs from constituencies affected. Public lobbying techniques are suitable tactics for such groups while charities such as Age Concern, Actionaid and Friends of the Earth use both private and public lobbying. This is largely because, even though they are 'insider' groups, they have committed supporters around the country by whom they want to be seen as active. Dubs (1989) has written a comprehensive guide to public lobbying for voluntary sector organisations.

BACKGROUND, TITLES AND REPUTATION OF LOBBYISTS

The identity of lobbyists can be gauged in at least two ways: by various occupational features and by reputation. About the first, the literature shows that a significant number of lobbyists were previously involved with government as either research assistant to MPs, political party worker, civil servant or as MPs. Grantham and Seymour-Ure (1990:50, 56) looked at the chief personnel of seventeen of the largest lobbying firms and it reads like a list of people who have changed their roles inside the public policy-making process. The implication is that lobbyists are likely to be very familiar with policy processes and personnel and that their principals employ them because of this knowledge and their contacts. Jordan and Moloney (1993) reviewed the literature on the background of hired lobbyists and also noted this 'insider' status. Undoubtedly, the implication is that you could not lobby without knowing the policy-making system and its personnel first. This assertion has implications for the professionalisation of lobbying. If such a state became widespread, it could mean that access to decision-makers was through a small number of paid experts and that the door to elected politicians was shut to low resource groups.

In-house lobbyists work under titles such as 'public affairs', 'government relations', 'corporate relations', 'Parliamentary liaison' while hired lobbyists work for firms calling themselves 'public affairs consultants', 'corporate communications specialists', 'public relations consultants' or 'political and regulatory advisers'. For reasons given below, few lobbyists formally title themselves in public as 'lobbyists'.

By popular reputation, as a group lobbyists do not attract high social prestige. Jordan (1991:13) summed this up with his reported anecdote about the US lobbyist who complained that his mother used a host of titles to introduce him to her friends but never the words 'my son, the lobbyist'. Generally, lobbyists do not like to be called lobbyists. Their personal cards and literature avoid the term, but in conversation they use 'lobbying' as a general descriptor for the activity they do. Jordan concluded that hired lobbyists had a 'naughty and nice' image, while Alderman (1983:264) noted that they give rise to 'more unease than a cause or a company putting forward its own case'. Dubs (1989:193) feared that they can 'buy' influence because they have 'much greater resources than social lobbyists' while Rush (1990) was concerned about 'pressure politics' being available only to powerful groups with resources to pay for extra lobbying. The source of these concerns about lobbying lies in the perceived power of some groups. These groups, usually business ones, are feared by the public to be seeking even more influence through private, unaccountable channels. This build-up of influence is perceived as against the 'public interest' or against the interests of less powerful groups. In such a scenario of unequal distribution of power in society, lobbying can be viewed as a lightning rod which attracts to itself (maybe in some cases accurately) fears about a powerful, particular interest being privileged over the public interest.

How could lobbyists, themselves concerned liberal citizens, respond to these fears? A reply rests on two foundations. The first is that lobbying as a functional term for a job of work becomes the right to petition government and the right of redress for a citizen when the debate is translated into constitutional terms. In these terms, the liberal (and democrat) would find it extremely difficult to ban lobbying as it has been described in this chapter. The second point of rejoinder is the acceptance that groups in society are unequal in resources, status and access to government. There is a tension between these two foundations if it is accepted that government represents a generalised, society-wide, economy-wide interest (as it should) rather than a set of particular interests. The resolution of this tension lies, among other things, in openness about government's dealings with groups and their lobbyists, and in the accountability to the electorate of elected politicians and appointed public servants for their dealings and agreements with groups and their lobbyists. The remedy lies in more transparent and accountable government. This is the transformation into constitutional terms of the emotive call which ended the classic work on UK interest groups and which drew attention for the first time to public relations involvement with lobbying. Finer (1966) ended *The Anonymous Empire* with the call for 'Light, more light'.

A consequence of more open government will be changes which affect lobbyists as well as politicians. For example, the Nolan Committee on Standards in Public Life (1995) has adopted openness as one of the seven principles of public life and has called on Parliament to stop MPs doing paid work for lobbying firms with multiple clients and has asked for a more detailed public register of their outside interests. In July 1995, the House refused to vote in favour of the former and it also refused to vote on those parts of a new, fuller register dealing with declaration of earnings.

More votes of the full House are likely to be taken in the autumn before this issue of regulating MPs' dealings with lobbyists is settled. These votes are a reminder that lobbyists operate insider rules of behaviour and procedure set by politicians as well as inside a political culture at Westminster, which is largely influenced by politicians' attitudes and behaviour. This implies that any reform of lobbying should be done at the politicians' end of the activity because lobbyists work in a political climate and in a set of formal and informal rules which they do not prescribe. A society gets the sort of lobbying its politicians permit.

There is, however, also a more individual significance in the Commons debates. They are about the competing claims on MPs to choose between particular, and at times, personal interests and a general, more collective interest. Where, if at all, does a sense of the public interest come into an MP's judgement if he or she accepts payments from a lobbying firm or from a business as a director or consultant? And if there are these choices about particular and public interests to be faced by MPs, there are the same choices for lobbyists at the personal and professional levels. Lobbyists should also ask how the interests of the group they represent relate to the public interest.

DOES LOBBYING ACHIEVE ITS GOALS?

It is extremely difficult to give a generalised answer to the question: does lobbying achieve its goals? The research literature does not give one, not least because there is no agreed methodology for evaluation. The difficulty is that the question is dependent on the larger issue of 'are groups effective in achieving their goals?' and Grant (1995: 128) has developed a typology of factors influencing pressure group effectiveness which can be extended to all categories of groups. The pluralist scenarios described above suggest unspecific answers: where groups of unequal influence are in competitive struggle for advantage with other groups, also of varying influence, and are facing powerful state institutions, the answer is entirely dependent on the particular circumstances of the case in question. The neo-pluralists would concede that the general business interest (the aggregation of individual businesses) in liberal, capitalist society achieves more of its goals than, say, the general labour interest, as expressed in, for example, the British TUC. They would also concede that consumers and the unemployed fare less well than business interests. And it is clear that some individual businesses gain advantage over others, for instance only one of three competing consortia will finance and build the Channel Tunnel rail link. But they could not conclude much beyond the prediction that business interests prevail more often than not.

Heinz et al. (1993) came to a similarly unspecific and weak conclusion in their study of US lobbying. The title of their work, *The Hollow Core*, was self-consciously chosen for their decade-long study of group lobbying in Washington. They found that 'power countervailed power' and that 'in any real contest, it is problematic to predict outcomes with certainty' (Heinz et al., 1993:391). They did not find a stable cast of powerful players at the centre of policy-making achieving their goals. They found, instead, a 'hollow core' which 'is something like the opposite of a power elite'. In the UK literature, Richardson (1993) found that the increasing complexity of group/government connections made prediction of outcomes less certain. Grant (1995:125–215) concluded that assessment of effectiveness is 'difficult' and that 'one has to be very cautious about generalising from a particular example'. But this caution has not stopped certain lobbying campaigns from being identified as effective. Rush (1990) has listed the defeat of the 1986 Shops Bill on Sunday trading and technical aspects of the 1986 Budget as examples. There are also short case studies about a defence of the takeover panel and a legislative change in favour of Tottenham Hotspur soccer club (pp. 70–72). Moss (1990) has added as effective examples the lobbying of Sheffield Forgemasters; copyright for photographers; lCI's handling of the CFCs and ozone layer issue; and also bus deregulation.

The argument so far has concentrated on effectiveness (achieving pre-declared goals through own agency) at the level of successful policy outcomes. In essence, this is a debate about groups achieving their goals. But the effectiveness debate can look at individual lobbyists and conclude that they are effective in their personal capacity. That is, they do gain employment and their principals and the decision-makers they deal with say that they are persuasive, making strong cases, and so on. This is effectiveness at the level of good individual behaviour by lobbyists. There is a literature on this, dominated by Americans with Cates (1988) being a recent expositor. In the UK, Moloney has added to it by listing attributes clients, decision-makers and lobbyists themselves identify as associated with 'good' lobbying. These attributes include the recognition that lobbying is a mutual activity and that in return for access, decision-makers expect information not otherwise available, ability to master a brief and present it in terms appealing to the listener, and a sense of timing about the stages of policy-making.

SUMMARY AND CONCLUSIONS

This chapter has concerned lobbying as a highly specialist subdivision of public relations. An overall definition of lobbying in a theoretical and practical sense has been given. Different competing political perspectives on lobbying have been provided. A rationale for the inclusion of lobbying within public relations was necessitated by the pluralistic nature of Western-style liberal economies. The tasks that lobbyists carry out were described in four crucial sections before indicating styles of lobbying and the background, titles, and reputations of lobbyists. The question of effectiveness has been answered affirmatively, but tentatively. As we move toward the twenty-first century the current balance of power toward business interests may be redressed.

It has been argued that the need of groups (broadly defined) to gain material, legislative or ideological advantage in competitive settings leads to the lobbying of government in those situations where government holds the key to advantage. Lobbying is a public relations specialism with its own body of knowledge and skills and should be seen as a series of interrelated activities. These activities are combined in different ways for different lobbying campaigns. Indeed for some situations needing a public relations response, groups should not use lobbying to gain advantage.

DISCUSSION TOPICS

1 State the case for group needs being the cause of lobbying. Give examples.
2 Does the power of business in liberal, market economies mean that non-business lobbyists are powerless?
3 Analyse a successful lobbying campaign known to you.
4 What significance, if any, does a pluralist explanation of lobbying allocate to elections and political parties?
5 Should groups employ their own lobbyists or hire them? What are the advantages and disadvantages of either option for groups?
6 What benefits could a group expect from lobbying?
7 How would a group evaluate its lobbying campaign? Would the evaluation be different if done by a civil servant or Minister?
8 Would a lobbyist recommend that his or her principal appear on television to explain the group's lobbying?
9 Assess the proposition that lobbying is political advocacy and not public relations?
10 Write the knowledge and skills profile of the lobbyist you would prefer to employ.

CASE STUDY: BRITISH GAS, OPPORTUNITIES AND THREATS OF CORPORATE TRANSITION – 1994–96: AN AGENDA FOR LOBBYING

Introduction

Lobbying strategy and tactics flow from an analysis of the opportunities and threats facing a group in pursuit of its goals. British Gas (BG) underwent particularly turbulent experiences in the year from Summer 1994 to Summer 1995 as it moved further away from its public service culture. They were experiences which would test the ability of any lobbying team to turn trouble to advantage. Perhaps such a turn was impracticable and endurance and marginal amelioration were the best to be hoped for. Below is the agenda of issues the BG board and its corporate affairs team faced. Some were more likely to be turned to advantage by media relations or community relations than by lobbying. The agenda, therefore, illustrates an important point about lobbying and its linkage to other public relations specialisms: lobbying offers no panacea. From the viewpoint of a group's leadership, public relations presents a menu of techniques through which to gain advantage and techniques must be matched to the task in hand.

The corporate affairs team were experienced and active lobbyists, having good contacts and policy knowledge at the level of Cabinet Ministers; senior civil servants; think tanks; energy specialists in universities and also with the Opposition front bench. Reading for this case study should be supplemented by reviewing the media for the same period where you will find the public (lobbying?) responses of British Gas to their critics.

- What would your responses to the issues below have been and why?
- On what matters would you have lobbied; how and why?

Corporate reputation

British Gas probably lost corporate reputation with some stakeholders and opinion-formers over its handling of the pay rise for its chief executive, Cedric Brown. 'Probably' is an important part of the above sentence for although the tone of media and political comment was overwhelmingly critical, corporate reputation is difficult to measure. Its measurement can take multiple forms and its relationship to monetary values, such as share price, is problematical. Mr Brown's pay rise was, on one calculation, only 28 per cent but it was taken up by the media as a 75 per cent increase. He lost a performance-related element in the new remuneration package which made his actual increase the lower figure, but the basic salary without the bonus scheme did rise by 75 per cent. Since the original publicity about the rise, a new longer-term performance scheme has been announced which could in the long run increase his remuneration further if the company does well. The media heavily reported the rise during the period September 1994 to February 1995. Share price held steady.

Environmental matters

BG has a good environmental record. Gas is the cleanest fossil fuel but there are problems with contaminated land on which gas was manufactured from coal. This contamination could affect subsequent use of the sites, many of which BG still owns, for new developments such as housing. Also, some scientists have argued that BG is contributing to global warming through release of methane gas by leakage from its pipes and other facilities. Methane gas is 30 times more powerful as a global warming agent than carbon dioxide. So only a relatively small amount of direct leakage of unburnt methane would counteract the advantage that natural gas has over other fossil fuels through producing significantly less carbon dioxide. But BG surveys suggest that its leakage rates are not large enough to outweigh the inherent advantage of gas with regard to global warming.

Consumer standards

Complaints registered by the Gas Consumers' Council have been rising. Standards of consumer service are measured by 39 indicators (e.g. are calls answered within three rings of the telephone in its customer query section?). In October 1995, the Government sought performance improvement in this area within a year's time or BG risks losing its Chartermark, an official seal of satisfactory standards towards consumers.

Markets

The 1996 Gas Act introduced more competition for supplies of gas to the domestic market. BG publicly welcomed the competition but only if it was done on a level playing field of equal obligations and regulations. The Act raises the question of whether BG wanted to defend its current market share against all-comers or, instead, be selective and concede parts of the market it does not find profitable. Alternatively, it could get out of supplying gas to the domestic market entirely and concentrate on providing pipeline transmission services to all the other companies that choose to compete in that market.

If BG wishes to stay in domestic gas supply, does it want to supply all the UK, town and country, business and domestic users alike? Competition means market costing and market pricing and the effect of these is to force prices to be more closely related to costs. In the past, big users used to subsidise smaller users through the use of a common tariff with an unrealistically small fixed charge, while users near gas reception terminals on the coast used to subsidise those far from the terminals through postalised pricing (one national rate). That was the public service ethic. The board asked the question why BG should continue postalised pricing and what are, in effect, subsidies to small users over the whole domestic market. Decisions in this area are market and politically sensitive: they touch on which interest does BG serve first.

Compared with domestic consumers, industrial customers always tend to be more price sensitive and the competitive market that already existed for gas supplies over 2,500 therms per annum showed just how strong these sensitivities in the industrial market could be – BG has already lost over 50 per cent of this market.

A core business in pipelines?

BG sees the pipeline network transporting gas around the country as a core business (with a rate of return of 7–8 per cent) essentially determined by the gas industry regulator. It is a monopoly defended by extremely high capital costs and by technical problems hindering competitive entry. Competition could be introduced by allowing other companies to operate parts of the system (there are a number of competing gas pipeline companies in the USA). Notably, BG does not want any attention drawn to this area.

Gas showrooms

Market disciplines were affecting showrooms. BG cross-subsidised these in the past – more, lower priced cookers and fires sold meant more gas consumed. BG used to reckon that only one out of seven people paying bills in showrooms wanted to buy something, the rest wanted to pay gas bills or make enquiries about service, and so on. Appliance retailers Comet and Dixons objected to what was an effective subsidy to BG appliance prices. BG's new privatised structure required it to eliminate cross-subsidies; it closed nearly half the showrooms (the ones unlikely to make a profit on appliance sales) and called the rest Energy Centres where a range of home appliances is sold (including electric ones). They and the appliance servicing centres have to make a profit. But they were the public face of BG and consumers were sensitive to showroom closures. Often this translated to higher prices in the Energy Centres, fewer distribution outlets, and fewer and poorer services.

Bill payments

The showroom closures led to an outcry after BG stopped payment of bills there. The media took this up as a public service issue for the old and poor. But there were only 500 showroom payment points and under the new system people could pay at 19,000 post offices. BG believes that the benefit of more choice never surfaced in the media coverage. As regards payment systems, market pricing was an issue because BG wanted more direct debit payers and it offered a 1.5 per cent discount to these payers because it costs less to collect their money. But many of the old, unemployed, sick and unmarried parents do not have bank accounts, and, if they do, the accounts are often finely balanced and unable to cope with payments called off at fixed dates by an outside agency. These market-led developments could be read as BG favouring the well-off and discriminating against the poor.

Safety

A safety issue is leaks from distribution pipes. Now that BG has replaced most of the vulnerable cast iron pipes with plastic, these new pipes bend with earth movement and do not fracture. Moreover, plastic does not corrode. The resulting reduction in leaks justified a 90 per cent reduction in the leakage search budget but this was reported unfavourably by the media.

REFERENCES

Alderman, G. (1984) *Pressure Groups and Government in Great Britain*, London: Longman.

Boskin, H.A. and Aronoff, T.S. (1988) *Public Relations: The Profession and the Practice*, 2nd edn, Dubuque: William Brown.

Cates, P. (1988) 'Realities of lobbying and government affairs', in R. Heath et al. *Strategic Issues Management*, San Francisco, CA: Jossey Bass.

Cutlip, S., Center, A. and Broom, G. (1985) *Effective Public Relations*, London: Prentice-Hall.

Crable, R. and Vibbert, S. (1986) *Public Relations as Communication Management*, Edina: Bellwether.

Dahl, R. (1961) *Who Governs?*, New Haven, CT: Yale University Press.

Dubs, A. (1989) *An Insider's Guide to the Parliamentary Process*, London: Pluto Press.

Finer, S.E. (1958, 1966) *Anonymous Empire: A Study of the Lobby in Great Britain*, London: Pall Mall.

Gandy, O. (1982) *Beyond Agenda Setting: Information Subsidies and Public Policy*, Norwood: Ablex.

Gandy, O. (1992) 'Public relations and public policy: the structuration of dominance in information age', in E. Toth and R. Heath, *Rhetorical and Critical Approaches to Public Relations*, Hove: Lawrence Erlbaum, pp. 131–63.

Godwin, R. (1988) *One Billion Dollars of Influence*, Chatham, NJ: Chatham House.

Grant, W. (1995) *Pressure Groups. Politics and Democracy in Britain*, Hemel Hempstead: Harvester Wheatsheaf.

Grantham, C. and Seymour-Ure, C. (1990) 'Political consultants', in *Parliament and Pressure Politics*, Oxford: Clarendon Press.

Grunig, J. (1989) 'Symmetrical presuppositions as a framework for public relations', in C. Botan and V. Hazelton Jr (eds) *Public Relations Theory*, Hove: Lawrence Erlbaum.

Heinz, J., Laumann, E., Nelson, R. and Salisbury, R. (1993) *The Hollow Core*, Cambridge, MA: Harvard University Press.

House of Commons (1987–88) *Select Committee on Members' Interests. Parliamentary Lobbying*, HC 518 2, 4–6.

Lindblom, C. (1977) *Politics and Markets*, New York: Basic Books.

Jones, B. (ed.) (1991) *Politics UK*, Hemel Hempstead: Philip Allan.

Jordan, A.G. and Richardson, J.J. (1982) 'The British policy style or the logic of negotiation?' in J.J. Richardson (ed.) *Policy Styles in Western Europe*, London: George Allen and Unwin.

Jordan, A.G. and Richardson, J.J. (1987) *Government and Pressure Groups in Britain*, Oxford: Clarendon.

Jordan, A.G. (ed.) (1991) *The Commercial Lobbyists Politics for Profit in Britain*, Aberdeen: Aberdeen University Press.

Jordan, A.G. and Moloney, K. (1993) 'Why are lobbyists successful: God, background or training?' For a symposia at London School of Economics held 24 March, organised by Politics Department, Newcastle University and Hansard Society. Paper available from authors.

Lesley, P. (ed.) (1991) *The Handbook of Public Relations and Communications*, London: McGraw-Hill.

Miller, C. (1987) *Lobbying Government*, Oxford: Blackwell.

Moloney, K. (1994) *Lobbyists for Hire*, Aldershot: Dartmouth.

Moss, D. (ed.) (1990) *Public Relations in Practice*, London: Routledge.

Nolan Committee (1995) First Report of the Committee on Standards in Public Life HMSO, Cm 2850–1, Vol. 1: Report.

Norton, P. and Grantham, C. (1986) 'The hyphen in British politics? Parliament and professional lobbying', in *British Politics Group Newsletter*, No. 45, 4–8.

Olasky, M. (1987) *Corporate Public Relations: A New Historical Perspective*, Hove: Lawrence Erlbaum.

Pearson, R. (1992) 'Perspectives on public relations history', in E. Toth and R. Heath (eds) *Rhetorical and Critical Approaches to Public Relations*, Hove: Lawrence Erlbaum.

Public Policy Consultants (1987) *The Government Report*, London: PPC.

Richardson, J. (ed.) (1993) *Pressure Groups*, Oxford: Oxford University Press.

Rush, M. (1990) *Parliament and Pressure Politics*, Oxford: Clarendon Press.

Smith, M. (1992) *Lobbying*, London: Government Policy Consultants.

Smith, M.J. (1993) *Pressure, Power and Policy*, Hemel Hempstead: Harvester Wheatsheaf.

Smythe, D. (1981) *Dependency Road: Communications, Capitalism, Consciousness and Canada*, Norwood: Ablex.

Truman, D. (1951) *The Governmental Process*, New York: Alfred A. Knopf.

Wedgewood, D. (1987) 'Dialogue with Whitehall and Westminster', for Conference on Corporate Communications, London International Press Centre, 15 October, organised by Tolloy Conferences.

White, J. and Lazur, L. (1995) *Strategic Communications Management*, Wokingham: Addison-Wesley.

11

CORPORATE ADVERTISING: THE GENERIC IMAGE

Ralph Tench

CHAPTER AIMS

- to review definitions of corporate advertising
- to evaluate corporate advertising as a communications tool in the 1990s
- to develop the understanding of corporate advertising away from the North American experience
- to consider the psychological factors affecting its success
- to analyse corporate advertising in the context of brand values
- to provide an update on who is involved in corporate advertising in the UK
- to consider the future for the practice and the implications of new technology
- to evaluate corporate advertising's success through case study experiences
- to promote critical thinking of existing research and case studies

ILLUSTRATION: 'MANAGING THE PRIMAL SCREAM'

The NatWest story is a fascinating example or study in how to approach the (corporate) advertising task. It is a story about trust and communication. The ads themselves, as well as being creatively appealing, are an exciting point of departure from run-of-the-mill financial services advertising.

For those who haven't seen them, they comprise three twenty-second commercial 'teasers' showing the atypical Canning family going about their usual days in a grimy London suburb. Brief glimpses of the NatWest Logo are the only clues as to what the ads were for. The daily scenario was followed up by two commercials – one showing the family on a farm holiday and falling in love with and buying the dream house; the other showing the house overrun by sheep once move-in has occurred. The advertisements fulfil a threefold aim: to communicate that NatWest is 'more than just a bank, that it offers mortgage and insurance services, and that customers can deal with NatWest over the phone.

The Canning family was developed as the medium to communicate these messages because they are warm and friendly, their situation is easy to identify with, and because there is ample opportunity for them to demonstrate the range of NatWest products and services.

(*Source*: Adapted from Simms, J. (1996) 'Managing the Primal Scream' in *Marketing Business*, Issue 52, September, pp. 39–40.)

INTRODUCTION

Corporate advertising is not a neutral subject. From time to time battle lines have been drawn up. And although the battles may seem outmoded, the shadow of their lines affects our thinking and approach (Shannon, 1983).

Corporate advertising: what is it?

Most of the research and writing on corporate advertising comes from North America where the importance of advocacy and corporate personality advertising is highlighted through industry case studies and academic research (see Cutlip et al., 1986:385–8). The UK picture is more fragmented, based mainly on practitioner experience such as those of Angus Maitland (1984). The UK experience of corporate advertising is therefore less tangible with few hard and fast figures as to its size, effectiveness or prevalence among major companies, public bodies and non-profit organisations. What is acknowledged is public relations role in devising corporate advertising policies (Grunig and Hunt, 1978). These authors also outline the primary goals of corporate advertising in the context of US research (Grunig and Hunt, 1984) which have been supported and adapted by contemporary academic writing (Schumann et al., 1991):

- improving consumer relations
- presenting stands on public issues
- improving stockholder/financial relations
- improving trade relations
- community relations; employee relations
- 'image' and representation.

Defining corporate advertising can be problematic for students and practitioners of public relations, although Grunig and Hunt (1984) give broad definitions of non-product advertising as being concept; general promotion; goodwill; image; issue; personality; and responsibility advertisements which they collectively call *public relations advertising*. We will go on to discuss this in more detail as we will the issue of 'brands on the balance sheet' whereby in the UK we see some evidence of a trend towards making corporate owners more closely associated with the brands they control.

So, product and corporate messages are not mutually exclusive, particularly in the context of commercial management. This and other issues will be discussed with the aim of encouraging the reader to develop critical thinking about the use of corporate advertising.

Because they are often couched in simple, friendly terms, one may overlook the rhetorical sophistication of corporate image adverts. This form of public relations is hardly 'empty' but rather more often it is a rich and well orchestrated crescendo of symbols (Toth and Heath, 1992).

Key questions therefore remain. How do we define corporate advertising? Who's involved in the activity? What is effective corporate advertising? What are the

189

psychological processes which make it work? Are there brand implications for corporate advertising? What does the future hold? These are the outline areas we aim to discuss within the limitations of this one chapter.

DEFINITIONS OF CORPORATE ADVERTISING

In 1983, the UK Institute of Practitioners in Advertising (IPA) noted (IPA, March 1983:1) that 'blue chip' companies were:

> spending substantial sums on corporate communications with a complex of specialised publics; extending far beyond investors to Government, the media and other opinion formers, trade unions, their own staff, and potential employees . . . [corporate advertising] has less to do with pushing a company's goods or its shares, than to establish or preserve an environment in which the company can go about its lawful business.

In the same IPA report, Wolfe drew a clear link between corporate advertising and public relations. He argued that while companies needed to defend their reputations against external pressures and criticisms, conventional public relations techniques such as media editorials were sometimes not 'active' enough to provide such defence. The paid-for advertising medium, on the other hand, provided a consistent, precise and controllable channel of communication to opinion formers and the general public.

If this is an advertising person's definition of corporate advertising, how do public relations academics and practitioners define the medium? This section explores the definitions of corporate advertising, and the sectors in which it is applied.

PUBLIC RELATIONS ADVERTISING: THE US PERSPECTIVE

Public relations advertising, as it is known in the United States, has been recognised as a tool to disseminate information or promote opinion change since the early 1900s (Cutlip et al., 1986). But it was not until the 1930s, when Warner and Swasey began a series of advertisements that stressed the importance of US business in the nation's future, that public relations advertising took root (Seitel, 1995:251). Since then, many organisations have employed advertising within a public relations context; perhaps most notably the Mobil Corporation, which, since the 1970s has sustained public comment on a range of economic and environmental issues (Cutlip et al., 1986; Seitel, 1995).

Grunig and Hunt (1978) define non-product advertising as 'concept advertising'; 'general promotion advertising'; 'goodwill advertising'; 'image advertising'; 'issue advertising'; 'personality advertising'; and 'responsibility advertising'. Seitel (1995) adds to the list: 'institutional advertising' and 'public service advertising'. The last definition implies that advertising can be used by any organisation to create a public image, to defend a reputation, or to address an issue.

190

CORPORATE ADVERTISING: THE UK PERSPECTIVE

Corporate advertising in the UK is almost universally interpreted as the positioning of the company to build public awareness of, or to defend, the company's activities. One of the earliest campaigns, according to Burdus (1980), was Tate and Lyle's anti-nationalisation campaign in 1949. Also in the 1940s, ICI began 'prestige' advertising to enhance its corporate reputation and has continued promoting the company identity, through advertising, to this decade (Wolfe, 1978).

In public relations texts, it is the non-product advertising of companies which is the focus for discussion (e.g. Hart, 1984; 1994; Howard, 1982). King (1978), however, widened the definition of corporate advertising to advertising employed by 'institutions desperate to explain themselves'. Such institutions, said King, include nationalised industries, governments, trade unions, civil servants, trade associations and political parties. Using King's definition, we could add to this list pressure groups, charities and voluntary organisations – institutions which have become more prominent in the UK during the 1990s. Greenpeace, Amnesty International, the Labour Party, to name a few institutions, all use 'corporate' advertising to address issues of public concern, and to establish their own image in the public mind. Selected examples of campaigns by some of these organisations are cited later in this chapter.

In summary, all kinds of institutions and organisations use corporate, or public relations advertising. Corporate advertising is used to influence public opinion surrounding an issue relating to the organisation. It can be used to defend an organisation's reputation or to build awareness of an organisation where public awareness is low.

WHO IS INVOLVED IN CORPORATE ADVERTISING: A UK PERSPECTIVE

To understand which companies are active corporate advertisers it is important to appreciate how the sector has developed through the last four decades. Fill (1994) gives a summary in which Stanton (1964) highlighted goodwill as the main function of corporate or institutional advertising in the 1960s, followed in the 1970s by issue and advocacy advertising to support and promote political and social ideas. The financial expansion of the 1980s saw privatisations, mergers and takeovers proliferate and, therefore, an increase in the use of 'umbrella' advertising often to support a range of products or brands.

In advance of the new millennium, it has been argued that corporate advertising in the 1990s has reflected industry's concentration on core operating business with a focus on the organisation's strategic aims and objectives (see Fill 1994:398). This enables corporations to reduce advertising budgets across the organisation as brands and corporate image are brought together (contemporary examples discussed later in this chapter include Heinz, Cadbury, Crosse and Blackwell). Research demonstrates that reducing overall product advertising spend need not have a detrimental effect on the recognition of products and services supported by corporate advertising. Well documented research by Yankelovich et al. (1979) supports this point. They gained evidence that the more budget organisations had for corporate advertising then these organisations experienced recall scores equal to corporations using mainly product advertising. Importantly, this required less overall budget for the corporate advertisers.

UK RESEARCH

To obtain a measure of the importance of corporate advertising in the UK a sample of top 100 private companies, FTSE 100 companies and charities/non-profit organisations were written to and asked to respond to a postal questionnaire. The total number of organisations contacted was 204 with a response rate of 41 per cent. Some respondents declared corporate policy reasons for not completing the questionnaire. Others from the charity sector only partly completed the question-naire due to missing information. Consequently only 31 per cent of questionnaires were used in the analysis. For simplicity the three sectors will be referred to as private (the top 100 private companies), FTSE (to represent the FTSE 100 sample) and charity (to cover the charity/non-profit sample).

Due to the profile of the organisations consulted it was no surprise that the turnover for 50 per cent of them is over £1,000m. With regard to corporate communications management it was also interesting to note that 76 per cent of the sample (all employed as public relations staff or equivalent title) claimed to be involved in corporate advertising decisions for the organisations. Also 22 per cent of respondents claimed to contribute to some of the advertising copy. Of further interest in the context of contemporary high profile UK campaigns was the importance placed by charities (71 per cent) on presenting stands on public issues.

The categories chosen for the types of corporate advertising were adapted from Grunig and Hunt's (1984) goals for corporate advertising. When the sample was asked to categorise the types of non-product advertising, respondents for all three sectors consistently selected recruitment as one of the main types of non-product corporate advertising employed (private 65 per cent, FTSE 79 per cent and charity 71 per cent). The full sample's response to which types of corporate advertising they would use demonstrated no spread of application but also a concentration, not surprisingly, on 'support for product/services' and 'recruitment'. Tench and Yeomans (1995) give the following details:

	%
Improving consumer relations	49
Presenting stands on public issues	40
Improving stockholder/financial relations	35
Improving trade relations	24
Community relations	43
Employee relations	24
Sponsorship	56
Recruitment	71
During change or transition	19
Support for product/services	71

As far as targets for non-product/corporate advertising there were some more interesting and consistent results, particularly for the private and FTSE companies. From these groups the majority from each category (80 per cent private, 70 per cent FTSE) consistently selected customers as one of the key target audiences: perhaps raising the question once more about whether product/corporate advertising are converging.

The media used by the sample gave some predictable responses for which are the most commonly used, namely newsprint. However, there was interesting reinforcement that only FTSE companies used TV advertising, probably due to air-time and production costs. Also, the growing use of the Internet was highlighted by respondents and this will be discussed later in the chapter when we consider mediums for corporate advertising.

Growth can therefore be seen in new technology areas but also in corporate advertising in general. From the sample, 51 per cent claimed their use of non-product advertising had grown over the last 10 years and when asked whether they considered the sector was still growing, 41 per cent agreed.

Findings on the extent of corporate advertising by sector demonstrates that the large FTSE companies spend the most on non-product advertising (17 per cent of total advertising budget), private companies second (30 per cent of advertising budget) and charities third (10 per cent of resources). All groups clearly recognised non-product/corporate advertisements and were able to differentiate their use.

What does all this information tell us? Clearly this research is only an opinion test of communication professionals in the identified sectors, but it does reinforce academic research to date. First, that organisations target audiences through the use of non-product advertising with the objectives identified by Grunig and Hunt (1984) in our introduction. The results also demonstrate a continued commitment to this form of corporate communication although the media are changing in line with technological advancements, particularly regarding on line access to information.

MEDIA FOR CORPORATE ADVERTISING

There are a range of media through which organisations can buy time or space in which to communicate their corporate messages to opinion formers and target publics. These include the usual channels for product advertising of TV; newspapers; journals and magazines; radio; posters; cinema; and new technology which is being adapted for corporate advertising, the Internet.

Up-to-date figures on which are the most frequently used are difficult to obtain but the authors' recent research revealed some interesting trends. First, the use of the traditional tool of financial corporate advertising, the newspaper, is still the most popular with 91 per cent of the survey naming it as one of the media they use. Journals and magazines are second most popular with 67 per cent followed by TV 30 per cent (Tench and Yeomans, 1995):

	%
TV	30
Newspapers	91
Journals/magazines	67
Radio	29
Poster	29
Cinema	8
Internet	10

On a broader scale, therefore, it is important that attention is given to the changing market of advertising in general. TV advertising has been a consistent marketing tool since the launch of independent television advertising on 22 September 1955, and the market has grown significantly, with £431m spent on making TV commercials in 1994 (Advertising Association, 1994). Despite this evidence of expansion, the future of TV commercials is uncertain. Technological advances and influences such as satellite broadcasting and new terrestrial channels have fragmented the market and offered increased choice to the viewer.

In this context, advertisers are looking for new and more exciting techniques for communicating both brand and corporate messages. These new techniques include increasingly sophisticated direct mail methods to e-mail and the Internet. This last category is already being accepted by corporate advertisers as the authors discovered with recent research (Tench and Yeomans, 1995). One of the interesting technological references this research revealed was that a greater percentage of major blue chip British companies such as BP are already using the Internet for corporate advertising purposes (see the case study).

EFFECTIVE CORPORATE CAMPAIGNS

One of the key functions of any corporate advertisement is to build awareness for the organisation. A well-documented example of one of the most powerful yet effective print corporate advertisements is McGraw Hill's 1950s one which offers the image of a potential customer sitting looking at the reader. Alongside this image are the statements:

> I don't know who you are
> I don't know your company
> I don't know your company's products
> I don't know what your company stands for
> I don't know your customers
> I don't know your company's record
> I don't know your company's reputation
> Now, what was it you wanted to sell me?

(Adapted, Dowling, 1994)

This powerful, long-standing advertisement does one key thing: it gets the message across to the reader that we all like to buy, sell and work with people (companies and organisations) that we know.

Some managers and executives criticise corporate advertisements for lacking creativity which makes them tired, uninspiring and dull. Bland statements of intent, commitment to product development, societal support and so on, can promote a 'so what' reaction from supposedly active readers of print advertisements, but this need not be the case.

BP launched its 'for all our tomorrows' campaign in 1989 to emphasise the company's commitment to positive research and product development with an acknowledgement of the increasing emphasis on 'green' issues. One advertisement in this campaign was the 'Ladykiller' advertisement which highlighted a new

Figure 11.1 'You can't sink a rainbow.'

Source: Greenpeace (1995); reproduced with permission.

product which would enable crop weedkillers to function without unnecessarily killing wildlife and insects, such as ladybirds. This campaign – with the arresting image of a dead, upturned ladybird and the forward thinking, considered strap line 'for all our tomorrows' – was commended by the *Wall Street Journal*. In fact, this advertisement, nicknamed 'Ladykiller', measured a 93 per cent recall by readers of the newspaper, the highest in the paper's history (Price, 1992:22/3).

Greenpeace

A further example of the effectiveness of print advertisements has as much to do with the news agenda as strategic positioning. Greenpeace do not commit large budgets to the production of advertisements but take a great deal of care in their placing and positioning. In 1995, this led to a positioning of the 'You can't sink a rainbow' (Figure 11.1) on the front page of *The Guardian* in July of 1995. This was the 10th anniversary of the sinking in 1985 in New Zealand of the campaigning ship the Rainbow Warrior by French SAS troops. The advertisement was booked over six months in advance and appeared on the front page on the same day that French troops surrounded and boarded a second Greenpeace ship in New Zealand following confrontations and protesting about planned nuclear testing by the French Government in September 1995.

Ordinarily, editors would avoid such a situation of an advertisement appearing on the front page beneath a headline story which elicited sympathy with the organisation. However, as Greenpeace's direct marketing manager confirmed to the authors, the advertisement was one of only a small number placed in *The Guardian* each year and its impact was high, although very fortuitous.

Shell/Nigeria

Probably one of the most interesting recent corporate advertising print campaigns – which turned into a battle of words – occurred on 19 November 1995. Three full-page advertisements were placed in *The Observer* by different organisations making public statements about the social and environmental action of Shell in the Ogoniland region of Nigeria in the aftermath of the execution of the campaigner Ken Saro Wiwa and his colleagues.

The advertisements were placed by Shell ('Clear thinking in troubled times'); Amnesty International ('He was prepared to die for his ideals. What are you prepared to do for yours?'); and three sponsors The Body Shop, Friends of the Earth and Greenpeace ('Dear Shell, this is the truth and it stinks'). Individually, the advertisements were simple and hard hitting and conveyed the messages of the organisations with clarity.

Furthermore, in the context of heated media debates at the time about social responsibility and business ethics it was the opportunity for both the opposition campaigning groups and the multinational, Shell, to state their case. Shell's commitment to this venture was highlighted with the sign-off line from the advertisement 'We'll keep you in touch with the facts' – a point disputed at the time by Wura Abiola (*The Guardian*, 20 November 1995), the daughter of Nigeria's

196

imprisoned winner of the last official election in Nigeria, who claimed to be misquoted in the advertisement.

Brent Spar

The Shell/Nigeria example shows the importance to organisations and influence of corporate advertisements in times of political, economic and environmental crisis. What this example also goes to prove is that accuracy of information is also vital. Greenpeace learnt this lesson themselves during another campaign against Shell during 1995 with the protests over the Brent Spar oil platform. Lobbying by Greenpeace and the use of advertising and scientific research sponsored by the group contributed to Shell's decision not to dump the platform at sea. The campaigning group later confessed that it had got its facts wrong about the most suitable form of dumping for the oil platform and they agreed with Shell that sea dumping was not the worst option. Interestingly, this turnaround in Greenpeace's stance appeared to have little negative public relations impact for the group at the time. More importantly, the incident raised questions from journalists about the accuracy of research and information supplied through video news releases (VNRs) for national news coverage (Purvis, 1995).

PSYCHOLOGICAL PERSPECTIVES ON CORPORATE ADVERTISING – WHAT MAKES IT WORK?

The advertising industry has strong links into psychological studies as academic research and theories have been used to try to understand the workings of the human mind. Studies linking advertising with psychology date back to the turn of the century when Professor W.D. Scott published *The Psychology of Advertising* in 1908 (see Leiss et al., 1990:138). From 1946 much of the research and writing about advertising and its effectiveness has focused on a number of linear models of consumer behaviour including the often cited and still used AIDA (Awareness, Interest, Desire and Action) model and the hierarchy of effects model, DAGMAR (Defining Advertising Goals of Measured Advertising Results) see Brierley (1995).

Attitudes and behaviour

From this position of measuring awareness and an assumption that this affects behaviour, studies then moved to focus on attitudes and persuasion. Attitudes are used by psychologists in experimental settings to predict behaviours (Fishbein and Ajzen, 1975). These authors developed a complex attitude model which helps to demonstrate the correlation between a positive attitude and image for an object and a positive behaviour toward the object.

What does this research tell us? First, the original objective of brand advertising was seen as aiming to change or shape behaviour (Hovland et al., 1953). Brand advertising uses the creative process of advertising to change consumer brand preferences – and to change them quickly. However, corporate advertising has a more difficult job because of its long-term nature and as psychological research demonstrates, changing attitudes is a complex process. Theories on how this may be achieved vary from self-perception theory (Bem, 1972) to cognitive dissonance theory (Festinger, 1957) and impression management theory (Tedeschi and Rosenfeld, 1982). These theories have relevance in the world of communications, particularly corporate advertising which is attempting to change receivers' attitudes towards the organisation. Attitude research derived from these studies therefore leads us to question whether advertising has short-term and long-term successes in changing attitudes. White (1988) argues that although attitudes may not be changed by advertising, it may modify them in the short term. Whether this then leads on to long-term behavioural change is the question to which no conclusive research proof can be provided.

Media campaigns and attitude change

Psychological research (Maccoby et al., 1977) goes on to support the activities of media campaigns in changing attitudes. The researchers found that the main problem was in reaching the intended audience because people will expose themselves to opinions they agree with and avoid messages they disagree with. However, in Maccoby's large-scale, two-year health awareness campaign aimed at changing habits in order to reduce heart disease, the research showed how the media can be very influential and effective.

Bearing in mind the extensive social scientific research into attitudes and behaviour, the effectiveness of corporate advertising is scientifically debatable, which can put people off the cause or question the benefits. However, as Yankelovich et al. (1979) have shown, the practical rewards can be worthwhile with corporate advertisers having to spend less, on balance, in support of their products in advertising.

The creative influence

In the context of psychological studies, corporate advertisers, like their colleagues in product advertising, are looking to influence behaviour by changing attitudes towards the organisation. Corporate advertising is similar to product advertising as Dowling, from a marketing perspective (1994:119), stresses when he identified four main processing responses as being attention, learning, acceptance and emotion. How the advertiser promotes and maintains attention with a corporate advertisement to encourage learning and hopefully acceptance of the message about the organisation is critical. Dowling emphasised how the fourth processing response, emotion, can be critical in encouraging both learning and acceptance. It is the creativity of the advertiser to put the corporate values, or messages, over in an emotional way which is the process that is most difficult to achieve. Just hearing how great or environmentally concerned an oil company is would not be enough to pass an audience through the learning and acceptance processing stages. However BP's 93 per cent recall for its 'Ladykiller' advertisement has been highlighted as an effective combination of creativity in communication.

One of the dangers for corporate advertising is to appear dull and unimaginative, and therefore not to make an impact on our emotions. This is a potential problem highlighted by Van Riel (1995:202) from an analysis of chemical companies which all used environmental awareness in differing degrees as a key theme to their campaigns. Similarly, almost all companies in the sample focus on their achievements to support the images adopted for the campaigns. This focuses on a potential problem for the corporate advertiser of repetition and the need to differentiate using creative techniques. It is the role of the advertising planners and campaign designers to provoke thinking and emotion if the advertisements are to be effective.

Certain themes can be detected throughout successful campaigns. Advertisers often use intrigue, humour and interest to influence our emotions and maintain attention. For example, Crosse and Blackwell embarked on a product campaign in 1995 for Branston Pickle which associates the product with the corporate parent by using images of famous personalities who have different stage names (Bobby Davro, Gary Glitter) with the strap line holding the sentiment, 'also known as . . . ' to include the star's original, unfamiliar name.

BP has used humour in a number of its corporate campaigns but this was particularly evident in one of the early TV advertisements which asked what nationality was the company which had achieved a range of activities first. The voice-over asks the viewer to 'sit down, stand away from fragile objects' before stating that it is in fact a *British* company – 'BP – Britain at its best'.

Brands on the balance sheet: branding strategy and brand equity

Branding strategy

A company may choose to adopt one of three branding strategies:

- the corporate, or monolithic, approach where all the products of a company are branded with the company name. An example is Yamaha which uses the corporate name to cover everything it sells from motorcycles to organs.
- the branded or discrete approach where a company seeks to develop individual brand images for its products. In this case, the company name will be hard to find. An example is Pizza Hut owned by Whitbread.
- the endorsed approach; also known as portfolio brand management. This is where the name of the parent company is added to the product brand name. An example is Cadbury's which is used to endorse its Dairy Milk, Wispa and Time Out products. The company name may be subtly applied (as in Nestlé on Kit Kat bars) or dominant (as in Ford on its motor car range), depending upon the relative strengths of the company brand and product brand.

In recent years, there has been a trend towards the endorsed branding strategy, where the company name – hidden to many of its target publics – has begun to raise its profile in product packaging, sponsorship and advertising. Levy noted in the UK business magazine *Management Today* (1990:101) that the word 'Lever' had begun to appear in Persil advertising. Commentators (e.g. Mitchell, 1994:22) have noted that the increased promotion of the corporate brand reflects both a growing consumer concern about company ethics as well as the company's ability to compete in international markets. Thus, if a public company has a strong corporate image among financial institutions, competitors and opinion formers, it might enjoy a stronger market position.

Brand equity

Strong brands are vested with an enduring power which can contribute to the survival of the company – even if the products themselves fail. The Triumph brand and its sub-brands, the Trident, the Tiger and the Bonneville, has survived a number of product failures and business disasters over the decades. In 1993, under new ownership, a new range of motorcycles was launched to meet expanding demand from the UK and overseas. According to *The Times*, 'With so many historic names to draw on, it was always going to be easy for the new company to create that vital model identity' (Futrell, 1993:18).

Buying a major brand is often more cost-effective than spending money on brand-building from scratch and the marketing that it entails. Therefore, a company is viewed by financial institutions and competitions not only in terms of its tangible assets, or 'book value', but in terms of its intangible assets – its brands and their associated personalities, images and symbols. One such case is Nestlé which paid $4.5bn, more than five times Rowntree's book value, to acquire the confectionery firm that made Kit Kat, After Eight and Polo Mints (Interbrand, 1990). More recently, Granada has been successful in its hostile takeover of the Forte hotel group for £3.9bn to strengthen its leisure group (*The Guardian*, January 1996:16).

As discussed earlier, corporate advertising can be used to build equity by creating awareness of the company's name and visual identity among financial institutions and competitors, and creating awareness of its portfolio of brands. However, a survey report in *Admap* (1990:25) revealed confusion among City professionals about the intentions of corporate advertising – even boredom – reinforcing the need, perhaps, for effective targeting, campaign evaluation and creativity in campaign strategy.

Another good reason why the company should want to position itself as a brand in its own right is that among the world's top 10 brands, eight are company brand names. These are: Coca-Cola, Kellogg's, McDonald's, Kodak, IBM, American Express, Sony, Mercedes-Benz (Interbrand, ibid:22). One might speculate that with the opening up of global markets, it is the corporate brands that will be best positioned to enter these new markets.

THE FUTURE OF CORPORATE ADVERTISING

If free market ideologies continue to influence government policy in both the public and private sectors of the economy in the UK, then it is likely that privatisations will continue, giving rise to further corporate re-positioning using advertising as a tool. In the public sector, local government reorganisation will compel new councils to establish their identities in recruitment advertising. And pressure brought about by the National Lottery will force charities to revisit their identities and corporate images in the battle for public donations.

A new Labour government, on the other hand, may be influential in encouraging the 'inclusive' approach to stakeholders recommended by the Royal Society of Arts in its Tomorrow's Company Inquiry (1995). Such an approach places an emphasis on organisations – particularly FTSE listed companies – building alliances with strategic publics such as City institutions, shareholders and employees. For corporate communications, this could lead to a drop in big impact 'image' advertising resulting from a more consultative approach between parties.

Advertising on issues of public concern is likely to continue as public awareness of environmental and health issues heightens. However, as scepticism towards environment-friendly statements increases (Reed, 1992), companies will be forced to communicate on environmental issues only with the support of consumer organisations and other pressure groups.

New trade agreements between nations globally, the opening up of new markets in the former Eastern bloc, and the Single Market Act provide increased business opportunities for companies in the UK. Effective channels for corporate communication across geographical and cultural boundaries will be vital for business to succeed. As we have said, technology – including e-mail and the Internet – is already playing a significant role in corporate communication. As newspapers and magazines go on-line, the Internet is likely to be the growth area for corporate advertising. There is evidence that corporate advertising for recruitment purposes is expanding (Clancy-Kelly, 1995), but the Internet also presents opportunities for companies wishing to enter global markets to publicise their credentials to publics such as governments, financial institutions and potential industrial clients.

CRITICISMS OF CORPORATE ADVERTISING

It is argued that large institutions of any kind – from the government to large multinationals – have the resources at their disposal to create propaganda messages through advertising to influence public opinion. Since the ultimate goal of corporate advertising is 'effectiveness', there is an assumption that advertising messages should have an effect on public opinion and attitudes because such an effect would serve the strategic objectives of the company.

If a government department chose to use corporate advertising to reposition itself (for example, the Department of Trade and Industry called itself the Department for Enterprise under Lord Young in the 1980s), would the advertising serve the taxpayer's interests or the ideological goals of politicians? Similarly, if a large oil company used advertising to defend its position on environmental practices overseas, how could customers be sure that the company was telling the truth? In entering these discussions, we begin to enter wider, well-researched debates concerning the nature of propaganda, the social effects of advertising, and the issue of corporate social responsibility. These points are outside the scope of this chapter. However, while acknowledging the potential harmful effects on society of irresponsible advertising, Burdus (1980) saw companies fulfilling an educative social role through corporate advertising.

To have industries speaking with confidence and producing a more informed public, has to be in the interests of society. It is also part of my personal philosophy that only informed people can exercise choice, and that choice is the heart of freedom.

SUMMARY AND CONCLUSIONS

Corporate advertising is defined in many different ways: among these definitions are public relations advertising; issue advertising; and image advertising. Institutions within the profit and non-profit sectors use corporate advertising. While UK research shows that most corporate, or non-product advertising is used equally for recruitment purposes and for supporting a product or service, a significant proportion is used for sponsorship, improving consumer relations, community relations and for presenting stands on public issues. The most popular media for corporate advertising are newspapers, journals and magazines, followed by television advertising. However, a significant and growing number of advertisers use the Internet to communicate their corporate messages.

Case studies demonstrated that effective corporate advertising works in much the same way as product advertising: it aims to influence public perceptions, opinions and attitudes through the creative use of messages and images, timed to fit in with topical debate (e.g. Greenpeace) or a long-term strategy of reputation building (e.g. BP). There is an increasing trend for companies to use the corporate name in their branding strategies, as this adds to the value of the product brand.

Three factors are likely to affect the future of corporate advertising. These are: the development of communications technology; the globalisation of world economies; and increasing awareness of environmental and health issues. On a domestic level, the respective political ideologies of Conservative and Labour governments are likely to influence relationships between organisations and their stakeholders.

DISCUSSION TOPICS

(*Note: The following questions are based on some of the issues and problems raised in this chapter.*)

1 Think about a corporate advertisement from TV; newspapers (daily); specialist magazines (*Economist*) and consider who the advertisers are trying to target. Are the corporate advertisers aiming for particular audiences and why?

2 Technology is one area that research has shown could influence corporate advertising in the future. What are the dangers and benefits of corporate advertising on the Internet?

3 Bearing in mind the advances of new technology will this have an effect on the consistently high use of print (newspapers) as a preferred medium for corporate advertisers?

4 Collect three 'issues-related' corporate advertisements from newspapers/magazines. What do you think the key objectives of each advertisement were?

5 Collect three 'brand-related' corporate advertisements from newspapers/magazines. What do you think the key objectives of each advertisement were?

6 Using the six examples you have collected consider the different psychological process of each advertisement. What are the advertisers trying to achieve: awareness raising, changing opinions, changing attitudes or changing behaviour.

7 With reference to case studies cited in this chapter and those that you collect, what do you think are some of the criticisms that can be levelled at corporate advertising as a communication tool?

CASE STUDY: BP

The company

BP is regarded as one of Britain's biggest companies and amongst the largest in the world. It is ranked as number three in the league table of publicly traded oil companies, employs approximately 60,000 people and holds assets worth over US$60bn. Commercial interests for BP include oil and gas exploration, refining and marketing of oil and the manufacture and marketing of petrochemicals.

The background

Until 1979, BP had traded effectively without involving itself in serious corporate advertising campaigns. However, due to political, environmental, economic and resource questions at the end of the 1970s, the company realised, through market research, that it was not receiving positive public and opinion former perceptions despite being the UK's biggest company.

Continued research from 1969 was carried out by the company through MORI (Market & Opinion Research International) to track its corporate image. Up until

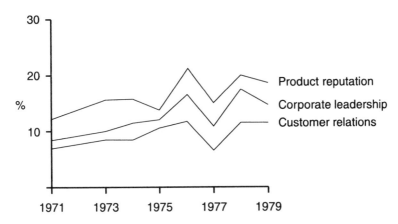

Figure 11.2 BP corporate image trends, 1971–9.

Source: Adapted from Drake et al. (1981).

Table 11.1 Which oil company do you think . . .?

	Is well ahead of competitors		Makes a big effort to avoid polluting the environment		Has products, the quality of which can always be relied on	
	1980	1990	1980	1990	1980	1990
Esso	10	6	9	13	80	90
Shell	12	11	10	20	44	42
BP	11	48	9	27	26	43

Source: Adapted BMRB, 1990.

1976 this showed a strengthening of the image but there was a negative impact in 1977 (see Figure 11.2). Blame for this drop was placed on BP's lack of communication about its activities compared to competitors.

Audits carried out for BP by its advertising agency, Saatchi & Saatchi, in 1979 established that internal and external public perceptions were negative with the main concerns involving nationalisation, state intervention and low consumer understanding of the organisation (Drake et al., 1981).

The research

In-depth research by The British Market Research Bureau (BMRB) established that competitors in 1979 were ranked ahead of BP on marketing capability and corporate attributes. But on a more positive note, successes for British companies were not seen as exploitative if they were British company successes (see table 11.1). BP's target publics were identified as a diverse group including suppliers, customers, shareholders, existing employees, pressure groups, local and national government.

The corporate campaign objectives were:

- to improve the public level of awareness of BP and its activities
- to improve BP's corporate image, in particular
  - to sharpen the company's identity as a successful British company
  - to inform the public that BP is not just an oil company
- to improve the public's attitude to BP as an employer
- to improve the public's attitude towards BP as a source of information
- to support staff in their endeavours and boost morale.

(Adapted from Drake et al., 1981)

Initial campaign

From the research findings a bold, 'proud to be British' campaign was developed by Saatchi & Saatchi and launched in the UK in 1980. Its aim was to highlight, unapologetically, the success of the major British company. The initial campaign slogan was 'BP – Britain at its best', and included strong elements of humour in the copy and creative style of the advertisements. The campaign ran for eight years using six TV corporate advertisements in short, heavy bursts on TV.

> By 1988 we had achieved and maintained our leadership and were clearly seen as the leading and most successful oil company in the UK.
>
> (Ivor Goudge, corporate advertising manager, BP – Price, 1992)

Campaign development

After 1988, BP corporate objectives were re-defined with the aim of extending the company's influence to be seen as a major global company. Following further international research the company discovered it was well perceived in the UK and Australia but was a sleeping giant in the rest of the world. The research also highlighted a lack of optimism for the future, particularly relevant to oil companies which are dealing with finite resources of a natural material. This led BP to develop its socially responsible 'For all our tomorrows' campaign.

Again developed by Saatchi & Saatchi, this campaign was launched in 1989 and used TV in the UK and press advertisements in full colour in leading international English language business publications. The advertisements incorporated arresting images and well thought-out copy which reflected the company's consideration for and interest in the natural environment from which its products are sourced and refined. The advertisements also reflected the company's endeavours to research and invest in development programmes which offered consideration to their wider environmental and societal impact.

Targets for the press advertisements were: *The Wall Street Journal Europe*, *The Asian Wall Street Journal*, *Newsweek*, *Time*, *The Economist*, *National Geographic*, *Business Week*, *International Management*; and the *Far East Economic Journal*, *Scientific America*, *Asian Week*, *Fortune*. These advertisements were supported by cable and satellite spots on CNN; FTTV Europe; Discovery; CNN Asia; Super Channel. The campaign ran until 1992.

Evaluation

The 16-year corporate advertising campaign has achieved the corporate objectives outlined by BP. The initial campaign changed perceptions in the UK in terms of quality, market position and environmental concerns. The environmental factor which was highlighted in early market research has proved to be of considerable corporate concern for many corporations in the 1990s and particularly oil companies. This was acknowledged in BP's early corporate advertisements from 1979 and built on in the 'For all our tomorrows' campaign. A measure of the effectiveness of the 'For all our tomorrows' campaign is reflected in its impact and recall figures in business trade papers as BP's corporate advertising manager, Ivor Goudge, confirmed: 'The ladybird adverts had a 93 per cent recall in *The Wall Street Journal* – the highest in the history of the paper.' (Advertisements are shown in Figure 11.3a and b.)

Weedkillers needn't be ladykillers.

As any conservationist will tell you, weeds aren't the only things that weedkillers kill.

Because more often than not, weedkillers are made of a concentrate which has to be mixed with water. And the resulting mixture has a nasty habit of getting washed into lakes and streams.

Or being blown off target onto innocent victims like birds and insects.

The sad result is a lot of dead wildlife, much of which would have done a great deal to improve the environment.

Ladybirds for example are a major consumer of aphids throughout the world.

For literally millions of harmless living things therefore, a new oil which BP has developed is a lifesaver.

Added to existing products at formulation stage, it ensures that weedkillers can be sprayed more accurately. And it makes certain that once sprayed, they stick only to the intended victim.

Which means that the ladybird can go on ridding us of aphids in exactly the way that nature intended.

Whilst weedkillers will only destroy the things they were designed to destroy.

Helping to conserve nature is one of the things BP is doing today, for all our tomorrows.

For all our tomorrows.

(a)

Thanks to BP solar lighting, Colin's future looks considerably brighter.

Colin can read by sunlight even after the sun has gone down.

Colin lives in a remote African village.

He has no light to study by at home, so after a full day of classes he remains at school to finish his homework.

You may wonder where he gets the energy.

Actually it comes in the form of electricity generated by solar modules.

BP began distributing solar technology in Africa in 1981. Since then we've supplied solar-powered vaccine refrigerators and water pumps to clinics, and lighting systems to schools throughout the continent.

Solar technology may never eclipse conventional power sources. But it already promises the children of Africa a brighter future.

Supplying solar power to remote parts of the world is one of the things BP is doing today, for all our tomorrows.

For all our tomorrows.

(b)

Figure 11.3 (a) 'Weedkillers needn't be ladykillers.'
(b) 'Colin can read by sunlight even after the sun has gone down.'

Source: BP 1990 (reproduced with permission).

206

CASE STUDY: BNFL

The company

BNFL plc is rare in that the company's sole shareholder is the British government. It is also a successful company. In 1994/95, its operating profit was £86m. The nature of its business, nuclear fuel manufacture, fuel reprocessing, waste disposal and decommissioning, means that BNFL has remained at the centre of public debate since the company was founded in 1971.

Corporate advertising

Corporate advertising became part of the BNFL's corporate communications strategy in the mid-1980s following accusations by pressure groups and the media that BNFL was behaving irresponsibly by not cleaning up nuclear waste discharges. The company was perceived as ignoring important environmental issues at a time of worldwide concern about nuclear energy and nuclear waste disposal.

Come and see for yourself

In 1986, a national advertising campaign was launched primarily to attract the public to BNFL's visitors centre at Sellafield. The opening of a small Exhibition Centre symbolised a new era of openness for the company. The Exhibition Centre was not only symbolic for BNFL, it was a vehicle that enabled the company to advertise without promoting its product. It was prevented from doing this because the Advertising Code of Practice did not permit advertising surrounding nuclear power because it was seen as too political.

The response to the Exhibition Centre was overwhelming. On occasions the centre was described by the company as 'bursting at the seams', so the decision was made to build a new £5.4m visitors centre, which opened in May 1988.

The big environmental issue

Between 1986 and 1990, BNFL's corporate advertising developed away from simply attracting the public to its visitors centre, to tackling some of the issues surrounding the nuclear industry. In 1990, three press advertisements were run on the issue of waste disposal, attracting a high response for follow-up literature. Meanwhile, the visitors centre attracted over 150,000 visitors a year.

The creative strategy for the advertising, devised by Young and Rubicam, focused on the 'human' face of BNFL, represented by one of the centre's guides, Enid Winter. As an employee of BNFL, Enid featured in successive television advertisements aimed at a national public. While evaluation of this campaign revealed a high recall, visitors (who were often touring the Cumbria region) were found to travel less than 75 miles to Sellafield.

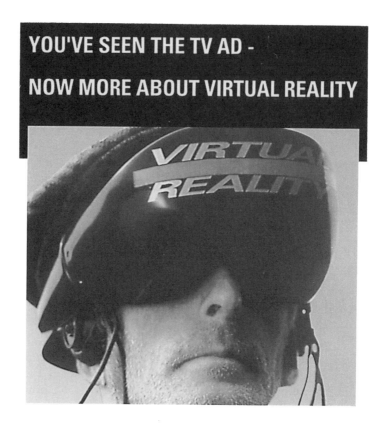

**YOU'VE SEEN THE TV AD –
NOW MORE ABOUT VIRTUAL REALITY**

Mention Virtual Reality (VR) to almost anyone, it seems, and a description will follow of an individual decked-out in a futuristic helmet and wearing strange gloves bristling with wires and movement sensors.

Technologies such as these are typically used to immerse users into a three-dimensional, computer-generated environment, allowing them to interact with objects in the virtual world by using natural abilities such as hand gestures, speech, head and even eye movement.

VR is no longer the exclusive use of science fiction writers and vendors of so-called 'high-tech' entertainment systems. It is fast becoming accepted as an important tool in the commercial and technical armoury of industries across the globe.

Figure 11.4 Virtual reality.
Source: BNFL 1995 (reproduced with permission).

Tourism

In 1991, the campaign was re-focused regionally, with commercial radio being the most successful and cost-effective medium in attracting visitors to the centre. Another reason for BNFL to re-focus its strategy partly owed to criticism regarding the high level of expenditure involved in plans to refurbish the visitors centre. To counteract media criticism of BNFL's 'slick PR machine', the company saw the necessity of getting the tourism industry on its side in promoting not just Sellafield, but Cumbria and the Lake District. The resulting television, press and cinema campaign, known as 'Views', highlighted the beauty of the Cumbrian landscape, after which a seasonal photographic competition was promoted to the general public, attracting 2,000 entries.

Re-positioning in 1995

In 1995, BNFL launched a new corporate communication strategy which included a new corporate visual identity, a refurbishment at the Sellafield visitors centre and a new corporate advertising campaign, devised by CDP. The strategy was to build the company's corporate reputation by:

- re-positioning BNFL as an expert, international company people could trust.
- divorcing BNFL from the anxieties surrounding the nuclear debate.

This was a turnaround as far as BNFL was concerned. This was because research had shown low awareness of the company among the public, but high awareness of nuclear issues. The company also sought to differentiate itself from other parts of the 'nuclear business' such as the soon to be privatised companies, Nuclear Electric and Scottish Nuclear.

New message strategy

The new strategy placed emphasis on internal as well as external communications. It was important for employees to feel involved with the company and proud to be working for it. The inclusion of employees and ex-employees in the advertising continued the approach adopted in the 1980s campaigns, but the advertising messages switched emphasis. In the new campaign, the corporate messages took equal priority with the messages to visit the visitors centre. The corporate messages concentrated on BNFL's technological expertise (for example, corrosion expertise, and virtual reality systems) being put to use in other areas of business.

REFERENCES

Bem, D.J. (1972) 'Self perception theory', in L. Berkowitz (ed.) *Advances in Experimental Social Psychology, Vol. 6*, New York: Academic Press.

Bernstein, D. (1984) *Company Image and Reality: A Critique of Corporate Communications*, London: Cassell.

Burdus, A. (1980) 'Communicating confidence: will the big corporations please speak up?', *Advertising*, Summer 1980; reprinted in *Corporate Advertising: A Selection of Articles and a Bibliography of Recent Developments*, London: Institute of Practitioners in Advertising.

Clancy-Kelly, S. (1995) 'Hooked into a whole new world', *People Management*, 31(5): 34.

Cutlip, E., Center, N. and Broom, B. (1985) *Effective Public Relations*, 6th edn, Englewood Cliffs, NJ: Prentice-Hall.

Dowling, G. (1994) *Corporate Reputations: Strategies for Developing the Corporate Brand*, London: Kogan Page.

Drake, P., Penny, J. and Sammuels, J. (1981) *Britain at its Best: Researching the Effectiveness of a Major Corporate Image Advertising Campaign*, Amsterdam: ESOMAR Congress.

Festinger, L. (1957) 'A theory of cognitive dissonance', Stanford SU Press 577,584.

Fill, C. (1995) *Marketing Communications: Frameworks Theories and Applications*, Hemel Hempstead, Prentice-Hall.

Fishbein, M. and Ajzen, I. (1975) *Belief, Attitude, Intention and Behaviour*, Reading, MA: Addison-Wesley.

Futrell, J. (1993) 'Leader of the Pack', *The Times*, 16 October: 18.

Garbett, E. (1981) *Corporate Advertising the What, Why and How*, Maidenhead, Berks: McGraw-Hill.

Grunig, J.E. and Grunig, L.A. (1992) 'Models of public relations and communication', in J.E. Grunig (ed.) *Excellence in Public Relations and Communication Management*, Hillsdale, NJ: Lawrence Erlbaum, pp. 285–327.

Grunig, J.E. and Hunt, T. (1984) *Managing Public Relations*, Holt, Rinehart and Winston, p. 22.

Hart, N. (ed.) (1994) *Strategic Public Relations*, Basingstoke: Macmillan Business.

Horsfall, J. (1990) 'Corporate advertising: a city view', *Admap*, 26(6): 25.

Hovland, C.I., Jarvis, I.L. et al. (1953) *Communication and Persuasion*, New Haven, CT: Yale University Press.

Interbrand (1990) *Brands*, London: Mercury Business.

King, S. (1978) 'Public response: the key to corporate advertising', *Advertising*, Winter; reprinted in *Corporate Advertising: A Selection of Articles and a Bibliography of Recent Developments*, London: Institute of Practitioners in Advertising.

Leiss, W., Kline, S. and Jhaly, S. (1990) *Social Communication in Advertising*, 2nd edn, London: Routledge.

Levy, L. (1990) 'Brand aid for Britain', *Management Today*, September: 101.

Maccoby, N., Farquhar, J.W., Wood, P.D. and Alexander, J. (1977) 'Reducing the effect of cardiovascular disease: effects of a community based campaign on knowledge and behaviour', *Journal of Community Health*, 3: 100–14.

Maitland, A. (1984) 'Corporate advertising', in N. Hart (ed.) *Effective Public Relations*, Maidenhead: McGraw-Hill.

Mitchell, A. 'In good company', *Marketing*, 3 March: 22–3.

Price, B. (1992) 'Corporate adverts make BP's mission possible', *Media International*, June 1992, 23–5.

Purvis, S. (1995) 'From an address at the CAM/TAS lecture at Trinity and All Saints' College, Horsforth, West Yorkshire.

Reed, D. (1992) 'How the green sell has failed', *Campaign*, 4(9): 28.

Schumann, D.W., Hathcote, J.M. and West, S. (1991) 'Corporate advertising in America: a review of published studies on use, measurement and effectiveness', *Journal of Advertising*, September 1991 (3): 35–56.

Seitel, F.P. (1995) *The Practice of Public Relations*, 6th edn, Englewood Cliffs, NJ: Prentice-Hall.

Shannon, C. (1983) *Corporate Advertising: A Selection of Articles and a Bibliography of Recent Developments*, London: Institute of Practitioners in Advertising.

Tedeschi, J.T. and Rosenfeld, P. (1982) 'Impression management and the forced compliance situation', in Tedeschi, J.T. *Impression Management Theory and Social Psychological Research*, New York: Academic Press 585.

Tench, R. and Yeomans, L. (1995) 'Corporate Advertising a UK Perspective', unpublished MS.

Toth, E.L. and Heath, R.L. (1992) *Rhetorical and Critical Approaches*, Hillsdale, NJ: Lawrence Erlbaum.

Van Riel, C.B.M. (1995) *Principles of Corporate Communication*, Hemel Hempstead: Prentice-Hall.

White, R. (1988) *Advertising: What is it and How to do it*, London: McGraw-Hill.

Wolfe, A. (1978) 'How to adapt research techniques to design and assess corporate image advertising' (ESOMAR seminar, Barcelona); reprinted in *Corporate Advertising: A Selection of Articles and a Bibliography of Recent Developments*, London: Institute of Practitioners in Advertising.

Wolfe, A. (1983): Preface to *Corporate Advertising: A Selection of Articles and a Bibliography of Recent Developments*, London: Institute of Practitioners in Advertising.

Wood, D. (1982) 'Types of media', in W. Howard (ed.) *The Practice of Public Relations*, Oxford: Heinemann Professional Publishing.

Yankelovich, P. and Partners (1979) Corporate advertising phase II an expanded study of corporate advertising effectiveness conducted for *Time* magazine, *Time* Inc.

Yankelovich, P. (1993) Leveraging corporate equity: a pilot investigation, *Fortune* magazine.

12

ISSUE AND CRISIS MANAGEMENT: FAIL-SAFE PROCEDURES

Michael Regester and Judy Larkin

CHAPTER AIMS

- to analyse the rationale for planning and management of issues and crises
- to illustrate the importance of managing communications in issue and crisis situations in order to protect and enhance corporate reputation
- to outline effective managerial characteristics and attributes in crisis scenarios to provide minimal risk processes and systems
- to indicate how to maximise on opportunities created by issue scenarios

ILLUSTRATION: 'DESPERATE BID TO BUILD CONFIDENCE FOR WICKES'

A quart pint of gloss would not be enough to put a shine on the tales of woe coming from DIY chain Wickes. They lasted a full week as further details emerged that the source of the allegations of false accounting was a disgruntled ex-employee. The board was seen to be acting in a timely manner as two directors resigned with alacrity.

Luckily there was a prominent scapegoat in the form of chairman and chief executive Henry Sweetbaum, and he went quietly at the same time as England made their exit from 1996.

However, there is a large job to be done to shore up the company's reputation – if it survives. Speculation mounted throughout the week that the group, which was revealed to have seriously overstated profits to hide trading deficits, was about to be pounced upon by the likes of B&Q and Boots.

As *Sunday Business* said: 'with zero credibility, the heart of the company has gone'. Now the accountants and lawyers are pawing the remains of yet another fat cat.

[It was reported by Carma International that on the basis of 60 articles from 26 June to 1 July 1996 awareness of the DIY troubles affecting Wickes went from 15 per cent on 26 June to peak at 36 per cent by 30 June.]

(*Source: PR Week*, 5 July 1996, 6, used with permission.)

INTRODUCTION

Given the increasing recurrence of issues and crises affecting major firms such as Wickes, this chapter will examine why planning for the management of issues and crisis situations is a crucial part of the strategic planning process, and the importance of managed communication in working with issues and crises to protect and enhance corporate reputation. It will consider some of the:

- characteristics and attributes that are important for effective management of issues and crises
- processes and systems that should be put in place to minimise risk and maximise the opportunites provided by emerging issues and, sometimes, crises.

It will describe the life cycle of an issue, from potential threat through to the crisis stage and the *management response model* that organisations can put in place to anticipate and tackle issues effectively; it will also describe systems and training programmes that can be put in place to minimise damage to corporate reputation when the *instant* crisis strikes.

ISSUES MANAGEMENT

> An issue ignored is a crisis ensured.
>
> (Dr Henry Kissinger)

Ruminating on the consequences of Shell's decision to do a 'u-turn' on the planned disposal of the Brent Spar North Sea platform, in June 1995, following a massive publicity campaign by Greenpeace, Shell UK's director of public affairs wrote:

> businesses will now have to include in their planning not just the views and rational arguments of all concerned – whether opponents or supporters – but will also have to come to grips with an area of deep-seated emotions, subconscious instincts and symbolic gestures.

The *Financial Times* noted: 'in hindsight, Shell failed to detect the extent of public concern in continental Europe or to win adequate support for its argument that the best place for the Brent Spar was in a deep trench in the Atlantic . . . as a result, years of careful cultivation, by Shell, of an environmentally friendly image, have been thrown away'.

The attack by Greenpeace upon Shell forms part of the evidence that corporate and institutional behaviour is under far greater scrutiny. Additionally, there has been a significant increase in activism. Well-organised and well-funded special interest groups are running powerful single-issue campaigns, for example, against the tobacco industry and the nuclear industry. There is a growing trend for activists with similar agendas to link up across national borders to influence the European Union as well as national policy-making.

A consumer rights' movement is growing in line with corporate unpopularity, tackling issues associated with food health and safety, the environment, animal welfare, trading standards, disclosure of information, and so on.

The environment in which we exist today and our changing attitudes as consumers and constituents means that organisations are under much greater pressure to demonstrate understanding of these changes and to communicate continuously in a way that anticipates and responds to changes in public opinion.

In today's complex environment, organisations are under much greater pressure to understand and respond to rapidly shifting public values, rising expectations, demands for public consultation, and an increasingly intrusive news media.

Corporate and institutional behaviour is under much closer scrutiny, consumer activism and advocacy campaigning are on the rise and there is a growing expectation, on the part of a broad range of stakeholder groups, that organisations should perform and behave in a more open, socially caring and responsible way. These principles are even more important in times of intense pressure, for example, where there is a *real* or *perceived* risk to public health, safety, or the environment.

The so-called *Risk Society Thesis* identifies new patterns of political and public anxiety and conflict brought about by continuous societal change and uncertainty, constant industrial and technological innovation, reductionist scientific approaches to evaluating innovation, and a trend towards greater individualisation. In combination, these factors are intensifying a host of *risk issues.*

Traditional reliance on the judgement of *experts* to interpret levels of risk in using new products and processes is now paralleled by a growing public ability – reinforced by modern media – to challenge political and corporate reassurance couched as scientific or technical *fact.* The perceived risk of contracting CJD through BSE-infected cattle is a current (1996) example of the potential and real *business impact of exaggerated public fear.*

Risk is a measure of the adverse effect of an issue. It is about assessing and communicating the possible hazards associated with a particular process relative to the safeguards and benefits which it offers. Risk assessment is essential when a new risk emerges, the degree of existing risk changes, or a new perception of risk occurs as in the case of current discussion about the risk of contracting CJD through BSE-infected cattle or sheep.

There are a number of dilemmas facing organisations endeavouring to understand and manage the dynamics of a risk issue:

- First, *risk means different things to different people.* Sensational risks, such as flying, are over-estimated while common risks such as driving a car are under-estimated. An employee working with aerial sprays may be statistically safer in the factory than at home, but a worker's spouse has far too great an emotional investment in the idea that home is a safe place to be convinced.
- Second, *fundamental attitudes are hard to change.* They are forged by a range of social and cultural factors and reinforced by contact with and opinions advocated by friends, colleagues, family members and others. These attitudes shape the way new risks are interpreted, understood and acted upon.
- Third, *the public is not looking for zero risk.* Everyone constantly makes risk/benefit choices, consciously or unconsciously, but there is a basic unease about two things: where is the benefit? and can I trust these people to manage the risk? This

is particularly true in areas of food and health safety, for example in the fields of biotechnology and chemical usage.

- Fourth, *the source of information about risk is crucial.* Research in the UK indicates that consumers are totally confused about who to trust on food safety and a MORI public opinion survey after the Brent Spar incident in 1995 asking 'who did they trust?' gave an 82 per cent score to Greenpeace, 48 per cent to Shell and 28 per cent to the UK Government. A similar question in the same environmental issues poll to assess public confidence in scientists gave a 97 per cent rating to scientists working for environmental groups, compared with 77 per cent for government scientists and 64 per cent for industry scientists. In other words, third-party expert allies play a critical role in risk issue management.
- Finally, *emotion* is the most powerful change-maker of all. Emotional symbols – water cannon jets aimed at Greenpeace activists attempting to occupy the Brent Spar; aerial shots of the oil spill heading for Alaska; the cloud hanging over Chernobyl; a cartoon of a cow as a biotechnology-controlled milk-making machine – can overwhelm and *totally negate scientific fact.*

For organisations which are facing emerging risk issues, some of the principal guideposts for effective risk communication are:

- To understand the dynamics of public emotion and the working practices of advocacy groups and the media who may strive to raise and legitimise a stance on an issue for public debate and, ultimately, public policy formulation.
- To familiarise the organisation with the cyclical development of an issue (see Figure 12.1) and to focus appropriate resource on early identification and monitoring of information relevant to the emerging issue and organised activity for response, including a clearly defined policy formulation and associated communication strategy.
- To appreciate that it is not realistic to change public opinion about the *size* of the risk and so for the organisation or industry.
- To establish and build *trust* about the commitment to *control, reduce and contain it.*

All too often, when bad news does break, the resulting corporate image is full of negative factors. This may frequently result from a misinterpretation of events by the media, but, whatever the cause, a retrospective look at the company's news-handling process in such cases usually indicates questionable judgement and inadequate preparation. No organisation can afford to fail in this respect. If a company at the centre of a crisis is seen to be unresponsive, uncaring, inconsistent, confused, inept, reluctant or unable to provide reliable information the damage inflicted on its reputation will be lasting – and measurable against the financial bottom-line.

Just as crises can be anticipated and planned for operationally, so can the organisation's communications response be anticipated and planned for. Why have crisis communication planning? Because the consequences of not planning are damaging to profits, share price, employee morale and every other aspect of an organisation's life. The consequences of any unplanned for occurrence, however calamitous, can always be less costly and less traumatic when crisis communications are thoroughly planned in advance. And when the unexpected does happen, be

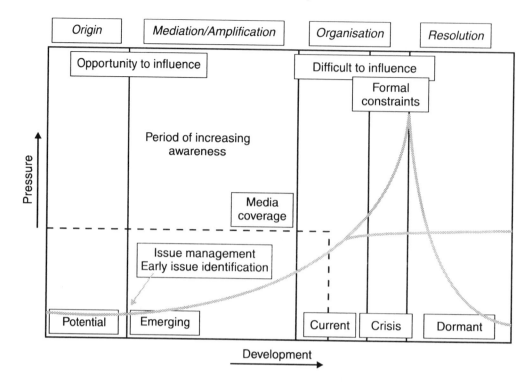

Figure 12.1 Risk issue life cycle.

sure to apply the cardinal rule of crisis communications: *tell it all, tell it fast, and tell it truthfully.*

Journalists are under fierce pressure to file their stories in a crisis situation. If *you* do not feed them the information that they need, or do not feed it to them quickly enough, they will rely on other sources that will be less well informed and less accurate – but, nevertheless, will offer them their livelihood: a story.

PLANNING TO COMMUNICATE IN A CRISIS

Many issues management PR agencies work alongside well-known organisations in helping them to become as prepared as possible to manage risk issues and crisis. But often, their first reaction is to question the need for such preparation since 'it will never happen to us' (usually, the prevailing attitude) and, in any case, 'we have neither the budget nor the manpower to implement what is/may be suggested'.

The agency response is to ask how much they spent last year in promoting their corporate reputation, as well as that of their products and services, and how much management time was taken in looking after that promotional activity.

If the light bulb is to go on, it is generally then that it does. Because time and money spent in preparing to communicate in the event of a crisis is like paying an insurance premium – the effort and expenditure is made to protect an investment often running into millions, paid out over a long period of time. Often such PR agencies are paid out of the marketing or safety budget.

Planning for communication in a crisis is simply a logical process which, like planning to manage issues, can pay huge dividends if the preparation is ever needed to be put into action.

THE 'RISK' AUDIT

The first step is to identify the risks. For public relations purposes, one definition of a crisis could run as follows: 'an event which causes the company/organisation to become the subject of widespread, potentially unfavourable, attention from the international and national media and other external groups (e.g. customers, shareholders, politicians, trade unionists, families of employees, environmental pressure and other activist groups) as well as from employees'.

The task here is to draw up a list of potential risks that would meet the criteria of this definition – and then try to prioritise them. This can be done in a number of ways. For example, by looking at:

- What has happened to the company in the past? (lightning can strike twice in the same place).
- What has happened to other companies in the same industry? (if it has happened to them it can happen to you).
- What is the company planning to do in the future? (crystal-ball gazing can help identify potential problem areas, e.g. construction of a new plant in an environmentally sensitive area; 'downsizing' that might lead to industrial action, and so on).
- What would be the impact on the bottom-line of the identified risk?
- Who would be affected by the identified risk? Who are the audiences or public who could be affected?
- What has the issues management process identified as being potentially threatening to the organisation?

In this way, a prioritised list of potential crises can be drawn up which is 'credible' when presented to management.

DEFINING THE AUDIENCES/PUBLICS

From the list of identified risks, consideration can be given to who would be demanding information given any particular situation, who would do the 'communicating' and by what means.

Thought can also be given to whether or not audiences need to be prioritised. In the example of the Braer, as far as the owners of the oil were concerned, the shareholders were the most important immediate audience to be communicated with. They were wrong: ultimately, crisis communication is all about business survival.

PROCEDURE DEVELOPMENT

Having identified the risks and defined the audiences, crisis communications procedures can be drawn up. These must identify who will be responsible for managing all aspects of the communications process, who will act as the main spokespeople, where will they need to be, who will handle the deluge of expected telephone calls (Occidental Oil took 5,000 telephone calls from the media alone in the first 48 hours after the Piper Alpha tragedy in the North Sea in which 167 people lost their lives), how can these key people be reached 'out of hours'? Crises, sad to relate, have a habit of developing on Christmas eve or first thing on a Sunday morning.

The crisis communications procedures should *not* be a thick, complicated plan, beautifully bound and left to gather dust on an office shelf or in a filing cabinet. It must be an easy-to-read, carefully indexed, working document that enables those responsible to 'hit the ground running' when and if a crisis breaks. Remember, too, that when a crisis does break it is *always* different to the ones that had been anticipated. A great deal of flexibility and judgement is needed in responding to the communications requirements of a crisis situation.

TRAINING

From now on the work begins in earnest. Identified spokespeople need to be trained to handle successfully:

- television interviews
- radio interviews
- telephone interviews
- press conferences

all of which may prove to be potentially hostile. Crisis 'scenarios' need to be developed against which the training can take place so that candidates 'feel the heat' of pressurised Jeremy Paxman-like interviews.

The training of spokespeople should not be restricted to just a few senior members of management, based at Head Office. If Head Office is in London and the company plant outside Manchester has blown up, the press will go to Manchester. Site managers need also to be media trained in order to 'hold the fort' until reinforcements can get there. With television, it is particularly important to restrict the spokesperson to one individual who remains in that role for the duration of the crisis. Having a raft of different spokespeople popping up from the same company on television makes it more difficult to maintain a consistent message (part of Shell's downfall) and makes it more difficult for the viewer to identify with the 'human face' of the company.

In a very serious crisis, involving large loss of life or extensive pollution, 'best practice' dictates that the company chairman or chief executive should act as the main spokesperson – as Sir Michael Bishop, Chairman of British Midland, did in the aftermath of the Boeing 737 crash at Kegworth, alongside the M1. This only holds true, however, if the most senior person is a *good communicator*. If he is not, then the next most senior person should fulfil the role. In such a case, a *role* must be found for the most senior person that is directly concerned with the crisis, such as 'being on site to take personal charge of the tragedy'. The most senior person cannot be in Rio taking his/her winter vacation.

While television is the most crucial medium for communicating in crisis situations, the telephone can often be the second. Not every journalist can get to the site of where it has happened and sometimes there is nothing to see – as in the case of the demise of Barings, Britain's oldest merchant bank, brought to its knees by one of its traders in Singapore in 1995.

Companies must expect to receive hundreds, if not thousands, of telephone calls not just from the media but from all audiences affected by the crisis. The problem here is that, however large the organisation, it will never have a press office or a human resources department or a customer services department which is large enough to cope with the expected deluge. And there is little point in staffing up for something that may never happen.

The solution is to train employees from other disciplines within the organisation to fulfil these response roles. This is precisely how Occidental Oil had prepared itself to deal with a disaster of Piper Alpha proportions – a disaster which they faced in 1988.

A team of 40 such 'responders' (mostly secretaries, who are generally excellent at fulfilling this demanding role) had been especially trained at the firm's Aberdeen offices while a back-up team of another 20 had been trained in the London offices. They were split into separate teams to handle calls from the media and distressed relatives of employees.

Many other companies, across a variety of industries, have adopted this method of preparing themselves to deal with major crises that might involve major loss of life, such as airlines, firms in the chemical and pharmaceutical industries, and of course, the North Sea oil industry. Manning the telephone lines with competent people is as crucial as successfully appearing on television if a company is to tell its own story, and if it is to establish itself as the *single authoritative source of information* about what happened, what the company is doing about it, and how the company feels about it.

TESTING – THE ALL-IMPORTANT EXERCISE SIMULATION

Many companies get as far as producing their crisis communications procedures and put them happily on the shelf to await the dreaded day when the crisis happens. This is like saying: 'Let's wait until the crisis happens to see if our clever procedures work!'

They *must* be tested beforehand to see if they do indeed work and that the various training programmes have been effective. Some of the programmes the authors run for clients like Scottish Hydro-Electric, Thames Water and the gold mining industry in South Africa resemble the staging of a West End production, involving dozens of role-players acting out the parts of all of the 'victim' organisation's audiences – camera crews arriving unannounced, demands for a press conference, employees' relatives weeping in front of the cameras (and demanding compensation!) – in short, testing every aspect of the company's communications response capability.

The 'scenario' for the crisis simulation is developed secretly with one or two members of the client's management. It has to be entirely 'credible'. If it is flawed in any way, managers who are expected to play their part in the simulation stop 'playing' because they say 'this could never happen in real life'. The utmost attention to detail must be given to the preparation of the scenario.

When all is ready, the company is informed that one day during a certain month there will be a crisis simulation (the exact date is not revealed). 'It will be codenamed Exercise Osprey (or some other appropriate code name). When you receive notification that Exercise Osprey is "live" you should drop everything and play the role expected of you in a crisis situation'.

The exercise can take place at any time of day or night and will normally run for four or five hours. It should be immediately followed by a verbal debrief (a 'hot washup' as we call them) in which everyone who has taken part has an opportunity to say how things went for them; we then provide an objective, third-party assessment of how well events were handled and provide additional recommendations, as required, in a follow-up written report.

Only in this way can organisations be certain that they are as prepared as possible to defend and safeguard that most precious of corporate assets: the hard-won reputation of the company, its products and services.

SUMMARY AND CONCLUSIONS

This chapter has sought to provide an overview of how firms need to plan for potential and issues which could impact on sales, profits, return on investment and market share. Each firm possesses an image or reputation which may have taken years or even decades to develop. Such an image or reputation can easily be shattered unless the firm has a clearly defined, structured and comprehensive set of planning procedures of how to act in particular situations. This should not be seen as an academic exercise but be supported and underpinned by a close link with overall corporate strategy and by being practised (through skill training) at regular intervals. Management in every organisation need to develop a managerial response model that is understandable and in which each persons knows their place and delimits of authority.

DISCUSSION TOPICS

(*Note: the following should be answered in the context of both the text and the case study.*)

1 Why should corporate communicators plan for issues and crisis situations?
2 Compare and contrast the product life cycle (introduction > growth > maturity > decline) with the life cycle of an issue. What lessons can be drawn?
3 Comment on the so-called 'risk society thesis'. Can this thesis be defended? Attacked?
4 In relation to a real disaster such as Chernobyl, Brent Spar, or BSE, to what extent does this relate to 'exaggerated public fear'? What implications might these 'fears' have in relation to developing an overall comprehensive plan, strategy, and tactics for crisis or issues management?

5 Illustrate the dilemmas facing organisations confronted by a major issue or crisis (give examples).

6 Critically analyse the Risk Issue Life Cycle (Figure 12.1).

7 Drawing upon recent examples illustrate how and in what way(s) issues and crises impact upon corporate activities.

8 Indicate the strengths and weaknesses associated with a 'risk audit'.

9 In the future significant weight will be placed upon a) planning and b) training for crisis communications when necessary. Discuss.

10 Which lessons, if any, from the Chernobyl experience, can be applied to large multinationals in similar fields of activity?

CASE STUDY: 'WE COME NOT TO BURY CHERNOBYL, BUT TO EXPLAIN IT'

There can be no place in PR for those who want to disguise tragedies, cover up reality or misrepresent the truth. But what about those of us who have to communicate the realities behind such a disaster as Chernobyl? What should guide the ethics and approach that an industry should adopt to communicating the reality behind one of the world's man-made disasters?

The problem I was faced with was that public perceptions were a long way from the reality of the situation. A vested interest, such as the nuclear industry, was in a difficult situation to tackle this problem. The role of nuclear communicators had to be to act as conduits for the independent, credible third-party bodies whose integrity was beyond reproach.

The first step we took was to create an International Chernobyl Task Force, which could co-ordinate the nuclear industry's response to Chernobyl across [national] frontiers. As the chairman of that body I helped ensure that the tenth anniversary was used as an opportunity to pool together the international implications of the tragedy and for the industry to agree a common response.

It was the view of the Task Force that the role of nuclear communicators was to explain what had been learnt as a consequence of Chernobyl. And we as an industry have learned a lot from it. Chernobyl established safety at the top of the agenda in the former Soviet Union and opened up their plants to our expert scrutiny. The formation, after the accident, of the World Association of Nuclear Operators (WANO) shared best safety practice across the globe and raised standards in every country.

It was by a strange irony that the main organisation which was to put into perspective the health impact of the disaster was the United Nation's World Health Organisation (WHO). This was the very same body that rightly brought to the attention of the world the massive increase in thyroid cancer in Ukraine, Russia and Belorussia. WHO has relentlessly condemned those that have exaggerated the health impact of Chernobyl: it claims that the death toll is currently 41 with the worst still to come and that there had been no increase in deformities or leukaemias in the Chernobyl region.

In order to ensure that there was as rational and informed a debate on Chernobyl as possible, the British Nuclear Industry Forum made great efforts to familiarise journalists with the facts. Fact sheets were produced, press trips to Ukraine and Chernobyl were organised for major national newspapers and the broadcast media. The industry explained the safety improvements made at Chernobyl since the accident, but never became apologists for the plant.

The tenth anniversary of Chernobyl was very much a trust building exercise for the international nuclear industry. Building up our credibility with journalists, challenging some myths, clarifying the lessons of the accident, we believe, has had an impact on how the quality press and broadcast media reported the accident.

Public relations must never become an apology for a disaster. It must, however, encourage rational debate so that public perception can come as close to reality as is humanly possible. That was the challenge. The argument could never be won, but our role was to even up the odds, so that the issue was seen in proper perspective.

(*Source:* Roger Hayes, Director-General, British Nuclear Industry Forum, in *PR Week*, 17 May 1996:9, used with permission.)

REFERENCES

'Desperate bid to build confidence for Wickes', *PR Week*, Haymarket Publications, 5 July 1996:6, used with permission. (Students are strongly encouraged to read *PR Week* as part of their public relations course.)

'We come not to bury Chernobyl, but to explain it', by Roger Hayes, Director-General, British Nuclear Industry Forum, *PR Week*, Haymarket Publications, 17 May 1996:9, used with permission.

13

THE INTERACTION BETWEEN PUBLIC RELATIONS AND MARKETING

Philip J. Kitchen

CHAPTER AIMS

- to provide an outline of the debate between public relations and marketing
- to explore research which explores and positions the debate in the context of UK fast-moving consumer goods firms
- to introduce an exploration of the relationship between CPR (corporate public relations) and MPR (marketing public relations)
- to outline major firm views on what is meant by MPR and integrated marketing communications (IMC)
- to give illustrative case material on the relationship between PR and marketing

ILLUSTRATION

The following brief case history highlights Pielle's approach to public relations:

- *Client:* Findus launch of Lean Cuisine range of calorie controlled frozen recipe dishes, described by a leading competitor as the biggest thing in frozen food since frozen food and already a market leader in the USA under the Stouffers brand.
- *Objective:* awareness and understanding of a new product concept and product range to encourage product trial.
- *Audience:* Britain's female adults who are actively conscious of their weight – some 60 per cent of British women diet regularly.
- *Activity:* – small group briefing lunches for national opinion-forming consumer journalists
  - consumer media product sampling using special delivery Leanograms
  - direct mail to Britain's 3,000 slimming club organisers
  - slimming club Lean Team product demonstrations and sampling operated in parallel with in-store demonstration and sampling programme
  - Lean Lifestyle Report of Britain's attitudes perceptions and changing lifestyle.

These programme elements were directed specifically to the slimmer target audience and were part of a comprehensive marketing support campaign covering a broad spectrum of trade and consumer audiences.

- *Results:* – consistent high media visibility
    - 70 per cent product trial among slimming club members with 60 per cent continuing regular repeat purchase
    - 90 per cent brand awareness amongst the slimmer group and 80 per cent awareness amongst consumers
    - Year One sales of £15 million were 50 per cent above target.

(*Source*: The author gratefully acknowledges the source of this mini-case: Pielle Public Relations Consultants, Museum House, 25 Museum Street, London WC1A 1PL; used with permission. Pielle is the UK arm in European Communication Partners.)

INTRODUCTION

What does public relations contribute in relation to achievement of marketing objectives? Where does the boundary lie between public relations and marketing? Is there, in fact, a boundary? Is the boundary one created by differentiated functional specialisms from both marketing and public relations or is it largely about academic debate? This chapter will explore the interaction between public relations and marketing. It would be correct to state that the interaction or relationship has always been ambiguous and controversial. The chief controversy hinges around outlining the roles and boundaries of the two functions. Both marketing professionals and academics have tended to treat public relations as a subset of the marketing mix – a subset largely concerned with simply generating publicity in support of marketing goals. This view largely ignores the more strategic role envisioned for public relations and espoused by public relations practitioners and academics who see public relations as fulfilling a mediating function between an organisation and key stakeholder publics within its environment (Grunig and Hunt, 1984; Grunig and Grunig, 1992; Kitchen and Moss, 1995). The first part of this chapter reviews the extensive literature and comments upon the development of public relations; the second part describes the research design and the findings obtained from a qualitative study, carried out with seven major fast-moving consumer goods firms in the United Kingdom. With each firm, responses were obtained from both senior public relations/public affairs *and* marketing executives – the aim being to compare and contrast the responses. In the event, differences between the two groups were minimal suggesting that there is not, as yet, a clearly identifiable and established relationship between the two functions within this sample of firms, but rather that substantive differences exist both within and between firms. These differences underline the ambiguous nature reflective of research in this unexplored yet highly critical area, essential to communications in today's turbulent competitive environment.

AN OUTLINE OF THE DEBATE BETWEEN PUBLIC RELATIONS AND MARKETING

Public relations and marketing necessarily relate to a view of communication with publics, audiences, or markets internal or external to organisations. Public relations in itself has many different definitions as lamented by Heilbroner (1985) who said that 'public relations is a brotherhood of some 100,000, whose common bond is its profession and whose common woe is that no two of them can ever quite agree on what that profession is'. A more useful definition adopted in this text was developed by Cutlip et al. (1985) that 'public relations is the management function that identifies, establishes, and maintains mutually beneficial relationships between an organisation and the various publics on whom its success or its failure depends'. This would imply a) the selection of target publics b) the design of appropriate messages or communications c) the choice of appropriate media vehicles to deliver the messages. The word 'management' necessitates the usual skills: analysis, planning, implementation and control over time. Marketing constitutes another management function whose definition, according to the American Marketing Association, is 'the process of planning and executing the conception, pricing, promotion and distribution of ideas, goods and services, to create exchanges that satisfy individual and organisational objectives' (*Marketing News*, 1985). Under this definition marketing is charged with creating exchanges and satisfying needs (whether individual or organisational). Such exchanges are invariably founded on communicating with target audiences, a function which again is managerially oriented and requires analysis, planning, implementation and control. So far, so good. Both functions are needful, both need to communicate effectively and efficiently with public or audiences, and both require key resources from an organisation.

However, over the past 10 to 15 years a significant debate has developed concerning the respective boundaries of both public relations and marketing, a debate summarised by Philip Kotler (1989) in a position paper prepared for the Public Relations Colloquium in San Diego. The Colloquium was titled 'Public Relations and Marketing: Dividing the Conceptual Domain and Operational Turf'. In this paper, Kotler drew attention to perhaps a mistaken premise, namely that the two disciplines are adversarial. The word 'dividing' suggests once-and-for-all decisions as to which tools, techniques, principles and procedures belong to public relations and which belong to marketing. Kotler suggests that public relations and marketing are better viewed as corporate allies rather than adversaries, a view supported by Kitchen (1993) who sought to illustrate areas of commonality between the two communication areas, and focused on the ambiguity and confusion characterising their role in business organisations. Despite these papers and ideas, admittedly from what may be perceived as a biased marketing perspective, there is strong resistance by public relations academics as to marketing playing a significant role in public relations, and especially the recent move toward the latest conflation of terms, if not techniques, known as 'marketing public relations'. Such resistance has been potentially inflamed and fanned by the 'traditional marketing view' of what public relations is or should be. (For a more substantive review of the marketing and PR perspectives see Kitchen and Moss, 1995.)

225

The traditional marketing view of public relations recurs throughout the marketing literature. For example, Shimp and Delozier (1986) saw public relations and publicity as activities that serve 'to supplement media advertising, sales, and sales promotion'. Schwartz (1982) maintained that public relations is little more than another form of 'consumer oriented sales promotion'; and Kotler (1978, 1982, 1986, 1991), a prolific and influential author, while acknowledging that public relations and marketing are two separate disciplines, has continued to subsume public relations under the control of marketing throughout most of his writings. For example, Kotler (1986) in the *Harvard Business Review* article 'Megamarketing' reiterated his view that public relations was simply an additional element of the marketing mix. For Kotler, public relations serves primarily as a communications function and, as such, plays a far narrower role than marketing in defining and achieving business goals.

This predominately reductionist view of public relations can be found either explicitly or implicitly in the marketing literature (Bernstein, 1988; Gage, 1981; Kreitzman, 1986). There is increasing evidence of a blurring in the distinction between public relations and marketing in the professional public relations literature where a number of articles posit the viewpoint that public relations *and* public relations practices are recognised as 'integrated and converging concepts' (Goldman, 1988; Novelli, 1988). While the focus of these articles has been on the role of public relations in marketing support, they reflect a growing tendency for convergence (Kitchen, 1993) between the two disciplines. The most striking evidence of this trend has been the emergence in both the marketing and public relations vocabularies of the term 'marketing public relations'.

Harris (1991), in a text which examines this development, argues that the 1980s saw the emergence of marketing public relations (MPR) as a distinct new promotional discipline comprising specialist application public relations techniques that support marketing activities. Harris argues that this specialised form of public relations should be differentiated from 'general public relations' and from 'corporate PR' in particular. Taking Harris's comments to a logical conclusion, MPR would be treated as part of the marketing communications mix which can be perceived by PR purists as belonging again to the 'reductionist school'.

In a series of articles considering the development of public relations, Kitchen (1991, 1993, 1995) stipulates that considerable development has taken place in relation to public relations development in UK fast-moving consumer goods (FMCG) firms, both in *a marketing and corporate communications sense*. This development can be traced to several underpinning factors in the 1980s specifically. From a marketing perspective changes in the promotional environment have led to changes in the promotional mix with budgets and programmes literally being driven 'down the line'. As stated by a public relations director (quoted in Kitchen, 1993):

> The television media has become very cluttered; over the past three decades the net supply has hardly changed; this creates significant pressure on prices. If you cannot spend marketing money via classic advertising it has to go down the line; and one way to do this effectively is via product PR, but the reasons for utilising this tool are based on physical economics.

Quite literally, marketeers are being forced to consider PR's applicability to marketing products, brands and services. Why? Advertising costs are burgeoning, sales promotional activities are questioned, and sales forces are being slimmed down. Clearly, marketeers must seek for new opportunities to promote products in a cost-effective way. At the corporate level the number of public relations tools have diversified and expanded as indicated by a PR manager (quoted in Kitchen, 1993):

> In today's highly competitive and geographically expanding marketplace, a company's image and corporate identity are vital elements in the communication process. How a company is perceived and how it presents itself can have a marked effect on business success.

However, despite public relations growth in either a marketing or corporate sense, debate concerning boundaries still continues. Several important issues remain unexplored or unresolved. The following questions seem crucial:

- What is the relationship between public relations and marketing as viewed by public relations and marketing executives in UK firms?
- What relationship exists between corporate public relations and marketing public relations?
- What does *marketing PR* mean to public relations and marketing executives in FMCG firms?
- What does *integrated marketing communications* (IMC) mean to the two types of executives?

This chapter seeks to explore these issues.

RESEARCH METHOD

The research findings will explore the four questions noted. Firms manufacturing FMCGs were contacted to provide a sample for an exploratory study. Choices of firms for inclusion in the study were based on the Top 100 Advertisers 1993 (Marketing Pocketbook, 1994). Why this choice of companies? Of the top 20 UK advertisers, 10 are FMCG firms with an average advertising expenditure of £45m. The top three advertisers in the league table are all FMCG firms with an average expenditure of £74m. If public relations is making inroads into these companies at both marketing and corporate levels, then this would (at the very least) suggest a basis for the real growth that is taking place in public relations in the United Kingdom.

A questionnaire was developed, pre-tested, and mailed to named executives from both public relations and marketing in 10 firms in late 1994. Of these 10 firms, seven sets of comparative data were obtained. Thus while the sample was small, the findings not representative of all such companies, and statistical tests inapplicable, the research method is useful for this exploratory work. However, such a method cannot guarantee a clear and unambiguous interpretation of the findings. The exploratory research therefore rests on a judgement sample, which, while not representative, does serve to generate ideas and insights, one of the primary purposes of such research (Churchill, 1991). While anonymity was guaranteed for the seven firms who participated in the survey, it is worth pointing out that they are all ranked in the top 30 firms in the United Kingdom. The method is of value in the context of exploring the issues involved: the relationship between marketing and PR; the emergence of marketing PR; and the emergence of integrated marketing communications – within the context of seasoned executives in major UK FMCG firms. The findings describe general perceptions among sample firms respondents and are potentially indicative of trends in the FMCG sector.

RESEARCH FINDINGS

The seven firms operated in the following areas of business: food (2), spirits and beer, OTC (over the counter) pharmaceuticals, confectionery, food/soft drinks, and pet food/supplies. Average turnover was in excess of £3bn, average number employed was in the order of 17,000, with geographic coverage extending from national to Pan-European, and/or global.

Six of the seven firms had a separate public relations/public affairs department. The one firm which did not had a hybrid arrangement for national PR which involved a Director of Planning or the Marketing Team with the planning director and/or external PR agencies as needed. The average number of employees within internal PR departments was 19. A wide divergence of titles was given to senior public relations executives which included public relations director, public affairs director, head of PR, head of corporate relations, director and senior vice president of corporate affairs, head of external relations and public affairs manager. Of these, it was stated by PR executives that two reported to a marketing director, one to a deputy chairman, and two to a group chief executive officer. According to marketing four senior public relations executives reported to a marketing director, and only one to a corporate affairs director. Thus there is a mismatch as perceived by senior executives within these firms, but early evidence supports the view of an interrelationship between PR and marketing. All firms employed PR agencies to assist with PR activities. For these firms usage of PR agencies was seen as necessary, whether to carry out communications at brand/product or corporate level.

For PR functions, such as media relations, product publicity, employee communications, corporate advertising, public affairs, government relations, community relations, sponsorship, event management, issues management and dealer relations, firms use either their own PR staff, and/or the services of a PR consultancy or agency. Community, government and trade relations, and employee communications were performed by PR staff. The remaining activities were either carried by PR consultancies or shared between staff and consultancies. Issues management, followed by internal employee communications, formed crucial areas of importance within these companies. Firms also indicated other areas of activity such as presence marketing, charitable activities/donations, direct marketing, heritage marketing, investor relations, and branded events though it is emphasised that each of these activities were specific to individual firms. With the exception of direct marketing, all were carried out by internal PR staff and did not rely heavily on PR consultancies.

Several areas of public relations practice, as perceived by PR and marketing executives, have become more important over the past three years. PR executives indicated that three areas are more important now. These include employee communications, government relations, and issues management. Only one of these, the first, was rated in the same way by marketing. Media relations has become much more important to marketeers over the past three years. Product/service publicity became less important for one firm. The findings suggest a wide degree of interaction and cross-fertilisation of PR activities, with some activities staying unchanged such as media relations, product/service publicity, and community and dealer relations. Other areas such as sponsorship and event management, had become less important.

The most important audiences for marketing were regarded as customers/consumers, employees, trade unions and dealer/trade relations. For PR the areas are employees, media, customers/consumers, government and trade unions. However, while there are differences between the two groups of responses, it was recognised by both groups that PR is focused on a wider range of target audiences or publics than marketing. Executives were asked a series of open questions concerning perceived responsibility for promotional activities. The primary responsibility for the main promotional activities (i.e. the promotional mix of advertising, sales promotion, personal selling) are under the domain of marketing. Alternatively, publicity in general, events/exhibitions and, potentially, sponsorship are under the domain of PR. But in a number of areas the primary responsibility appears to be shared, i.e. sponsorship, publicity, trade dealer promotions and customer relations. Thus there is interaction taking place between public relations and marketing at the promotional level. Neither PR nor marketing, as yet, appear to be in a superior or subordinate role.

The idea of marketing or PR in a subordinate or superior organisational position is not new. The initial rationale for the proposed interrelationship was put forward by Kotler and Mindak (1978) and revisited by Kotler (1989). As perceived by PR and marketing executives in this research two statements found a degree of correspondence. The first was that PR and marketing enjoy separate but overlapping functions. This suggests that marketing and PR practitioners each manage a distinct set of activities which they can carry out in relative independence, though not complete independence of each other. However, a further statement also found five executives agreeing. This was 'public relations can be seen as part of the marketing function'. Given the earlier comments concerning hierarchical accountability, it seems that in some companies PR is part of a wider and dominant marketing function. It would seem at this time, therefore, that the two functions are not integrated – they have separate and overlapping functions – and, marketing has more importance than PR in most, if not all, respondent companies. This was born out by the ratio of marketing to PR budgets in these firms. The seven PR respondents rated this at 65 to 1 in favour of marketing, while the marketing estimate was more conservative at 20 to 1 on average. Thus, from a financial perspective, marketing carries a far greater importance than PR in these organisations. This, it could be argued, is legitimate given that it is marketing's responsibility to create profitable exchanges that satisfy individual needs and organisational objectives. Without such exchanges the public relations function would be redundant. Supporting this, executives were asked for their opinions concerning statements about the relationship between PR and marketing. Broad agreement was expressed with the view that marketing has greater status and importance than PR in these organisations. However, broad disagreement was expressed from both PR and marketing over views that would marginalise and peripheralise PR as an adjunct to marketing. These findings would indicate that PR and marketing are not normally rivals for company resources (i.e. they are separate but overlapping functions), PR extends beyond the simple generation of media coverage, and PR can be utilised by marketing as well as being utilised as a corporate communications function.

Public relations has increased rapidly in importance over the past three years according to 11 of the 14 respondents. For the other three respondents, PR is about the same in importance as it was three years ago. The reasons for the increased importance of PR are shown in Figure 13.1.

Virtually all the PR executive perceptions are related to corporate issues, particularly corporate imagery, or the raising of a corporate profile. From the marketing perspective, public relations is seen as an additional integrative tool to be utilised for marketing purposes. At the same time marketing does not deny the validity of PR as a corporate communications tool. No respondents anticipated any decline in PR spend over the next two years, five anticipated the same budgetary spend, while nine anticipated increased expenditure (PR + 20 per cent; marketing + 12 per cent).

Questions were asked pertaining to which areas of PR are likely to become more important over the next two years. From PR, these included in rank order: issues management, employee communications, corporate communications/advertising, international communications, public affairs, government relations/lobbying,

---

As perceived by PR executives:

* Focus on targeting
* Greater emphasis on corporate branding
* Animosity toward . . . industry, plus probity, and cost containment in time of recession
* Growing need for corporate positioning and managing change
* The establishing of corporate profile

As perceived by marketing executives

* More educated marketeers, successful PR campaigns/opportunities for marketeers to participate in PR planning activity and can see results.
* Building greater accountability; strategic focus measures; growing consumer sophistication; media fragmentation; development of brand marketing.
* It can provide a very cost-effective means of challenging managers while being a visible manifestation of a company's culture/mission statement.
* Growing recognition of the importance of consumer attitudes to the company and their perceptions of the value added by company activities.

Figure 13.1 Rationale for increased importance for public relations.

financial PR, and finally marketing support activities. Thus, marketing support, as seen by PR executives, was not expected to increase in importance. This point, however, was negated by marketing executives where five of the seven executives indicated that marketing support activities, as an area of PR, *was expected* to increase in importance over the next two years. No other area was as heavily weighted as this. So, again, there appears to be mismatch of opinion. Marketers are clearly indicating PR has to assist marketing in achieving promotional and relational objectives. For PR executives the need for marketing support services was not considered an area of increased importance. Rather issues management, employee communications, international communications and corporate communications/advertising were perceived pertinent in this context. Again, this would underline the view that marketing and PR have separate but overlapping functions, with PR's brief to create and sustain mutually beneficial relations with publics beyond the domain of marketing.

Executives' perceptions of statements concerning interaction between corporate PR and marketing support PR (MPR) were considered. Corporate PR and marketing PR enjoy some degree of interaction and synergy. They are not separate and distinct, as could for example be perceived by 'purist' PR theorists. Nevertheless, much of the impetus for the use of PR for marketing purposes is derived from marketing, not necessarily PR. Corporate and brand images interact to enhance overall ambience and both forms of PR influence the bottom line. There is evidence that both MPR and CPR must work together in an overall communications programme, and while this may be a desirable objective it is difficult to achieve in practice. PR executives indicated that corporate PR affects propensity to purchase, a view not whole-heartedly shared by marketeers. Executives from both areas agreed that the gap between what is perceived to be corporate and marketing PR is closing as companies perceive the need to unite core product and company values through both types of communication. But what is 'marketing PR'? Both types of executives adopted a differential perspective and these perspectives are illustrated in Figure 13.2.

While the term 'marketing PR' is not part of the current language, virtually all respondents suggest that PR can be related to marketing in terms of brand or product support which is extending the more usual support role of PR in marketing. However, many firms have been using the term 'integrated marketing communications' as defined by Schultz et al. (1992) – the ideal of 'building a synchronised multi-channel communications strategy that reaches every market segment with a single unified message'. Figure 13.3 indicates to what extent executives in UK FMCG firms agree with this. Words such as 'message coherency' and 'optimisation of mix elements' bear correspondence to the definition given by Schultz et al. The aim of IMC is to try to ensure that each message delivered through a variety of media impacts on the audience in the same way and 'speaks with one voice'. Thus while marketing PR may not be clearly delineated at this time by this particular group of respondents, IMC is readily recognisable. Moreover, PR executives recognise that public relations is viewed as a coherent part of IMC. The question as to whether PR is part of IMC, however, can be seen through the lens of executive perceptions (see Figure 13.4).

Public relations perspective

* Not seen the term used
* Brand related PR
* Product support
* Generalised promotion beyond USP for products
* Support for brands or products through publicity programmes mainly but not exclusively editorial
* PR connected with commercial activities such as trade communications, etc.

Marketing perspective

* The development of core themes by marketing that are exploited through all mediums to achieve brand communication objectives – from advertising, brands publicity, promotion – in a chain reaction!
* Apart from the latest 'buzz word' – it is concerned with a greater understanding of the marketing function – PR's usual support role has to include more elements of the mix and greater involvement in the process of marketing
* I understand marketing to be the whole process of determining and satisfying customer demand. I would take marketing PR to be a corporate contribution to this – using the company's image/values, etc., to influence customer choice

---

Figure 13.2 Meaning of marketing PR.

Executives from PR and marketing agreed to more than one of the five statements in Figure 13.3. The majority of respondents (13) agreed with statement 5, a further eight agreed with statement 3, and six with statement 4. Statement 2 received two agreements, and statement 1, one. Thus, integrated marketing communications (IMC) is perceived as containing within its remit public relations. And this, in order to ensure that a more appropriate message is delivered to the target audience. Figure 13.4 explores the issue as to why PR is part of IMC.

For the majority of respondents public relations is seen as part of the new trend toward integrated marketing communications. Such communications must, as it were, 'speak with one voice' and draw upon a variety of communication tools (including PR) to deliver appropriate 'one voice' messages to diverse target audiences or publics. In other words, for these organisations, communication, not necessarily a focus on where such communications should be derived, is the major issue. Thus is the debate purely 'academic'? The following section discusses the findings in the context of the original four questions, and attempts to arrive at a coherent conclusion to this chapter.

DISCUSSION

The relationship between public relations and marketing, as perceived by PR and marketing executives in this small exploratory work with FMCG firms, is not a derivation of the academic literature. For this sample, firms' public relations and marketing work hand-in-hand to communicate effectively with audiences or publics

---

Statement:

1 IMC is simply a means of improving the co-ordination between the different elements of the marketing communications mix
2 IMC involves a totally new philosophy of marketing communications
3 IMC is an attempt to carry out marketing communications in a way which will ensure a more coherent message is delivered to the target audience
4 IMC is concerned with optimising use of the different elements of the marketing communications mix
5 Public relations is part of IMC

Figure 13.3 Integrated marketing communications.

Public relations

* Because it is necessary to market our corporate brand
* PR can support other disciplines, giving it independent endorsement
* PR is better at dealing with complex messages
* PR is not restricted to marketing, it has other strategic roles
* It is about communicating values
* Brand PR is an important part of the marketing mix
* It is not needful to have two separate messages when communicating a marketing strategy

Marketing

* Marketing has to become aware of the interrelatedness of the marketing mix in achieving brand communication objectives; in turn brands publicity has changed to respond to marketing needs by catalysing integrated solutions
* Marketing set the objectives. PR is merely one of several variables e.g. advertising that is undertaken to achieve these objectives
* PR can add value to any marketing investment/activity/event. Budgets are always under threat – you have to maximise any marketing involvement by concentrating on core objectives/strategies/activities, etc.
* There is still confusion about the role of PR and what it can achieve for a brand/product, etc. The media diversity, direct mail/marketing, etc., and proliferation of media opportunities are more suited to targeted PR

Figure 13.4 Why is PR part of IMC?

perceived as important in their competitive domain. Considerable agreement was expressed with the view that marketing and PR have separate but overlapping functions *and* the viewpoint that public relations could be seen as part of the marketing function. However, this relationship appears to be changing as the concept of integrated marketing communications takes hold. Admittedly PR would appear to be in a subordinate function because of the necessity for quid pro quo exchanges. However, it seems that PR tools, techniques, principles and tactics can be adapted and used quite readily by marketeers who are accessing this tool for product/brand promotion. Thus from a corporate perspective, the image of an organisation impacts on its marketing (Friend, 1993). This image – developed, sustained and communicated by varied corporate PR tools – impacts necessarily on marketing. But equally, the firms brands, products, services, pricing, distribution and promotional techniques deployed impact on corporate image. Thus PR and marketing are not adversaries within these organisations, but corporate allies – a view supported earlier by Kotler (1989).

There is a *significant relationship between corporate public relations and marketing public relations*. Leaving aside the latter terminology for now, it is evident from this research that both types of communication contribute to organisational success. Both areas of communications access a number of differentiated communication tools. However, the focus of such communication *is different*. Marketing focuses on the need to create exchanges with customers and consumers and, according to this research, borrows or uses PR tools for usage at the marketing level. Public relations has a wider brief to create and maintain mutually beneficial relations with publics who could impact on business success. To do this PR adopts and uses a number of diverse tools. Few would argue with the view that PR is growing in importance in large organisations, but it is growing in two related, interactive and synergistic dimensions for both publics *and* audiences. Thus public relations would appear to contribute directly to business performance. In a recent report supporting this view, UK companies in general saw PR as a vital component of marketing and internal/external communication strategies, and thus contributing directly to bottom-line performance (Farish, 1994).

Marketing PR does not mean a great deal as yet to executives in UK FMCG firms. While the term may not be readily recognisable, its usage is marked. Despite some resistance to PR being used in a marketing support role, its use is well entrenched at the marketing level, though not in the mainstream areas of advertising, sales promotion, or selling. In many other related areas, PR is recognisable and needed given a scenario of declining promotional budgets, media fragmentation, the need for cost-effectiveness, the growing need for integrated marketing communications, and the numbers of criticisms raised concerning promotional effectiveness. Marketing executives expect the PR support role to increase in importance. However, the real need is for all promotional activities to be interactive and synergistic, thus PR can be expected to play a greater role in marketing in the future.

Integrated marketing communications offers, as its terminology suggests, potential for integrating promotional elements of the marketing mix, and strives to ensure that coherent messages are delivered to target audiences. However the term 'integrated marketing communications' extends beyond marketing to corporate activities also. For many FMCG firms, there is a significant need to *market the corporate brand*. Thus while PR can be utilised by marketing, marketing can also be utilised by PR.

SUMMARY AND CONCLUSIONS

Public relations and marketing together form the avenues for communication within organisations. The two form not a competitive disequilibrium but a corporate and marketing equilibrium. The placing of PR or marketing in separate or discrete boxes or compartments adds little or nothing to understanding the complex organisational interactions involved. Public relations is of significant value in the marketing domain. But its role extends beyond marketing. Likewise, however, marketing extends beyond creating quid pro quo exchanges and is of value and relevance to corporate communications activities. There does appear to be some evidence of a moving together of techniques, tools and organisational coupling, that is the movement toward integration. It is too soon from this research process to tell whether marketing PR is the 'new discipline' as proclaimed by its adherents. On the other hand, the emergence of integrated marketing communications seems to herald the juxtaposition of marketing and PR skills. At the risk of criticism it may be worth concluding in the words of one erstwhile marketing executive:

> If one accepts marketing as the whole process of determining and satisfying customer need, the contribution of many different functions in the corporation can be aligned. Any function not focussed on [this definition of] marketing needs to have its continuation closely examined.

Thus, while both PR and marketing are necessary in today's large multi-faceted organisations, marketing is still charged with the responsibility to create exchanges. For the foreseeable future, marketing, essentially, will remain *the driving force* underpinning business progression, development and growth. But public relations has an important and significant role to play in terms of communicating and building relationships with various publics beyond the domain of marketing, and also in terms of its usage as a crucial promotional tool in the promotional mix.

DISCUSSION TOPICS

1 In what circumstances would public relations be useful in the marketing domain?
2 List your own personal views as to the debate between PR and marketing.
3 Provide a recent example as to the use of PR in marketing. List the advantages and disadvantages of such an approach.
4 When you have read the positioning statement from Carol Friend (at the end of the chapter) critically analyse it, and indicate whether you agree or disagree with it.
5 What did Heibroner (1985) mean when he observed that 'no two members of the [PR] brotherhood could ever quite agree as to what the profession is'.
6 'Public relations and marketing: dividing the conceptual domain and operational turf' (Kotler, 1989). Does the conceptual domain have to be divided? Can the operational turf be the same for both disciplines?
7 What distinctions, if any, do you see between marketing or PR executives with regard to the increased importance of PR?
8 'Public relations is part of IMC.' Do you agree or disagree?
9 Indicate how and in what way(s) a close relationship may develop between CPR and MPR.
10 Under what heading should the disparate functions of an organisation be aligned?

CASE STUDY: A PRACTITIONER'S VIEW OF THE RELATIONSHIP BETWEEN PR AND MARKETING

Public Relations and Marketing – the Synergy and the Separation: A position paper developed for the Institute of Public Relations by Carol Friend, FIPR, Managing Director, Pielle Public Relations, Past President The Institute of Public Relations.

Definitions

Public relations and marketing are each misunderstood and misused terms, yet both are well defined in their breadth and depth. Each addresses particular audiences – marketing, the customers it targets; public relations, the various groups which have a stake in the organisation – from employees and shareholders to legislators, supplier, and customers.

Public relations

The definition of the Institute of Public Relations is:

> The planned and sustained effort to establish and maintain good will and mutual understanding between an organisation and its publics.

In modern practice, public relations is a management function, concerned with the management of reputation.

Marketing

The definition of the Chartered Institute of Marketing is:

> Marketing is the management process responsible for identifying, anticipating, and satisfying customers' requirements, profitably.

The role of reputation in marketing

The reputation of an organisation, business, brand, or service, of course, impacts on its marketing. Public relations, therefore, impacts on marketing.

A brand or company reputation for low technology would not support high technology product marketing – no matter how good that product. The customer would be left wondering – technically known as 'cognitive dissonance' or 'perceived risk'.

The role of public relations in marketing

Public relations does not only help to provide the appropriate 'reputation environment' in which professional marketing can take place. The broad range of techniques that public relations employs makes a valuable contribution to marketing, communicating with trade and end-user customers through, for example:

- print and broadcast media relations
- event organisation (site facility visits, exhibitions, briefing meetings)
- communication materials (print, visuals, audio and video tapes)
- sponsorship.

With promotion as a key element of marketing – ensuring that customers are aware of and understand the benefits of a particular product, service, brand, or organisation – public relations has a real role to play in the marketing mix.

Public relations – beyond marketing

Public relations makes an equally valuable contribution to other functions of an organisation using the same techniques – and more:

- finance (City and investor relations)
- human resources (internal communication)
- planning (issue monitoring and Parliamentary monitoring)
- corporate management (Government relations, corporate presentation, issue management, and crisis communication).

At the senior level, the public relations function frequently takes responsibility for the community and social responsibility aspects of an organisation's strategy and actions. This broader responsibility demonstrates why public relations, per se, is not a marketing function, no matter how broadly one defines the term 'customer' in the marketing definition.

Public relations is, however, a very valuable tool of marketing as it is an essential function of best management practice throughout an organisation.

ACKNOWLEDGEMENTS

This chapter was first presented as a paper by P.J. Kitchen and D. Moss at the ESOMAR Seminar on Advertising Sponsorship and Promotion: Understanding and Measuring the Effectiveness of Commercial Communications, Madrid, Spain, March, 1995. Permission for the use of this material has been granted by the European Society for Opinion and Marketing (ESOMAR) J.J. Viottastraat 29, 1071 JP, Amsterdam, The Netherlands.

REFERENCES

Bernstein, J. (1988) 'PR in top communication role', *Advertising Age*, 59, 27 November: 28.
Churchill, G.A. (1991) *Marketing Research: Methodological Foundations*, 5th edn, Chicago: The Dryden Press, pp. 34–138.
Cutlip, S.M., Center, A.H. and Broom, G.M. (1985) *Effective Public Relations*, Englewood Cliffs, NJ: Prentice-Hall, p.4.
Farish, S. (1994) 'DTI report endorses the use of PR', *PR Week*, 9 December: 1.
Friend, C. (1993) 'Public relations and marketing – the synergy and the separation.' A position paper developed for the IPR, Managing Director, Pielle Public Relations, (unpublished 2pp report).

Gage, T.J. (1981) 'PR ripens role in marketing', *Advertising Age*, 52, January: S-10–11.

Goldman, T. (1988) 'Big spenders develop newspaper communications', *Marketing Communications*, 13(1): 24.

Grunig, J.E. and Hunt, T. (1984) *Managing Public Relations*, New York: Holt, Rinehart, and Winston.

Grunig, J.E. and Grunig, L.A. (1992) 'Models of public relations and communications', in J.E. Grunig et al. *Excellence in Public Relations and Communications Management*, Hillsdale, NJ: Lawrence Erlbaum.

Harris, T. (1991) *The Marketeers Guide to Public Relations: How Today's Companies are Using the New PR to Gain a Competitive Edge*, New York: John Wiley.

Heilbroner, R. Chapter 1 in Cutlip, S.M, Center A.H., and Broom G.M. (1985) *Effective Public Relations*, 6th edn, Englewood Cliffs, NJ: Prentice-Hall.

Kitchen, P.J. and Proctor, R.A. (1991) 'The increasing importance of public relations in FMCG firms', *Journal of Marketing Management*, 7: 357–70.

Kitchen, P.J. (1993) 'Public relations: a rationale for its development and usage within UK FMCG firms', *European Journal of Marketing*, 27(7): 53–75.

Kitchen, P.J. (1993) 'Towards the integration of marketing and public relations', *Marketing Intelligence and Planning*, 11(11): 15–21.

Kitchen, P.J. and Moss, D. (1995) 'Marketing and public relations: the relationship revisited', *Journal of Marketing Communications*, 1(2): 105–19.

Kotler, P. and Mindak, W. (1978) 'Marketing and public relations', *Journal of Marketing*, 42(4), October: 13–20.

Kotler, P. (1982) *Marketing for Non-profit Organisations*, 2nd edn, Englewood Cliffs, NJ: Prentice-Hall.

Kotler, P. (1986) 'Megamarketing', *Harvard Business Review*, 64(2), March/April: 117–24.

Kotler, P. (1989) 'Public relations versus marketing: dividing the conceptual domain and operational turf', a position paper prepared for the Public Relations Colloquium, San Diego, 24 January 1989, unpublished.

Kotler, P. (1991) *Marketing Management*, 9th edn, Englewood Cliffs, NJ: Prentice-Hall, pp. 621–48.

Kreitzman, L. (1986) 'Balancing brand building blocks', *Marketing*, 13 November, pp. 43–6.

Marketing News (1985) 'AMA board approves new definition', 1 March: 1.

Marketing Pocketbook 1994, Top 100 advertisers derived from Register Meal Data, pp. 78–9.

Novelli, W.D. (1988) 'Stir some PR into your communications mix', *Marketing News*, 22 December: 19.

Schultz, D.E., Tannenbaum, S.I. and Lauterborn, R.F. (1992) *Integrated Marketing Communications*, Chicago: NTC Business Books, pp. 2–13.

Schwartz, G. (1982) 'Public relations get short shrift from new managers', *Marketing News*, 16(4): 8.

Shimp, T.A. and Delozier, M.W. (1986) *Promotion Management and Marketing Communications*, New York: Dryden Press, pp. 493–94.

14

THE EMERGENCE OF MARKETING PR

Philip J. Kitchen and Ionna Papasolomou

CHAPTER AIMS

- to provide greater analysis concerning the PR/marketing debate in relation to the emergence of marketing PR
- to consider the marketing perspective of public relations
- to consider the PR view of public relations
- to discuss whether PR can be seen as a corrective or a complement to marketing
- to analyse the extent to which marketing and PR can be seen as corporate allies
- to explore the emergent MPR concept, definitional issues, MPR in the marketing mix, whether MPR can be perceived as a distinctive new discipline, and how MPR might be used in practice

ILLUSTRATION

The following case vignette, drawn from *PR Week* (1995), indicates how public relations can be used for marketing purposes (i.e. new product launch) and corporate public relations (i.e. issues management) and also how this may constitute 'news' in publicity terms.

'Pepsi-Co Hires Freud for 7-Up Consumer Launch' (Lexie Goddard)

Soft drinks giant Pepsi-Co International has recruited Freud Communications to handle the consumer launch of its new 7-Up Light . . . The appointment is part of a £5 million marketing push to promote the product, which will replace Diet 7-Up. The agency's budget for the four month project is thought to be around £100,000, although further consumer work on 7-Up Light and 7-Up is a possibility.

The new product launch will target a male and female youth audience. Freud managing director Matthew Freud said the new brand would fulfil a similar role for 7-Up as Pepsi Max did for Pepsi. 'It will be positioned as an edgier, more exciting drink away from the traditionally female diet market.'

Brand manager Soren Mills said the agency's brief was for an 'explosive launch' and to 'build brand credibility among 16–24 years olds'.

Corporate PR and issues management for the 7-Up brand are to be handled by

Inskip Public Relations. Pepsi-Co switched the account from Hill and Knowlton, which previously handled all its drinks brands, to Inskip in January as part of a move to favour smaller specialist agencies.

The drinks-to-restaurants giant now divides work for all its drinks brands – Pepsi Max, Diet Pepsi, Pepsi Cola and 7-Up – between agencies; Freud handles consumer project work, while Inskip deals with corporate and issues management business. Hill and Walker still handles Pepsi-Co Foods business, which includes Walkers Crisps, Smiths, and Doritos.

(*Source*: *PR Week*, 28 July 1995:2, used with permission.)

INTRODUCTION

For those involved in public relations and marketing, the relationship between the two disciplines, at least from an academic viewpoint, seems controversial. Admittedly, the 7-Up case vignette reflects that PR can be used for marketing as well as corporate purpores. What the vignette does not reflect is the earlier debate in Chapter 13 concerning the controversy which entails distinguishing between the respective roles of the two communication disciplines. Frequently PR is classified alongside advertising and promotion. This is one reason why marketing professionals and academics believe PR is or should be part of marketing and thus managed as a marketing activity. This view represents the marketing perspective of PR. On the contrary, PR professionals and academics suggest that PR activities are distinguishable from those of marketing. From a PR perspective, however, marketing and PR serve different functions and, therefore, the tendency of marketing professionals and academics to subsume PR within a dominant marketing function is erroneous.

This chapter, continues to explore the debate from the marketing and public relations literature concerning the relationship between marketing and PR. The review is important in relation to marketing PR, since examination of the relationship between the two disciplines from both perspectives provides a backdrop to the issues involved. Whether marketing PR is a new PR discipline or is likely to become a marketing management discipline may depend on reasons behind the debate as well as the controversy between the marketing and PR disciplines. The importance of exploring the above issue for both marketing and PR circles was expressed by Norman Hart (1991), who adopted a polarised position:

> It is time to put PR into proper perspective in relation to marketing. It must be realised that it cannot be treated as part of the marketing function; neither for that matter can marketing ever be part of PR.

Irrespective of Hart's viewpoint, it is necessary to present various arguments raised by marketing and PR professionals and academics concerning the relationship between marketing and PR, as a backdrop to the emergent 'marketing PR' (MPR). This discussion will delineate views identified within both sets of literature concerning the concepts on which the attempt to explore whether MPR has a legitimate claim to be a new discipline, *or* whether it is likely to become a separate marketing management discipline distinct from the broader area of corporate PR, largely depends.

A start is made by considering arguments concerning the marketing perspective of PR. Then, consideration is given to the opinions expressed by PR professionals and academics concerning the PR perspective of PR in relation to marketing. The perspective advanced by White (1991) according to which PR is a corrective and complement to marketing is explored before considering ways practitioners of the two disciplines can work together to help organisations reach corporate goals, in other words, enabling the marketing and PR disciplines to be corporate allies. Issues concerning MPR are then considered.

THE MARKETING PERSPECTIVE OF PUBLIC RELATIONS

Various authors have pointed to the use of public relations for marketing purposes, or its relevance to marketing communications. White (1991) states that Kotler, a leading American commentator on marketing practice, has a developed view that public relations is part of marketing and serves as an aid to customer relations. When marketers consider options for marketing communications, public relations is often bracketed with advertising and other forms of promotional communications. In 1988, Kotler described public relations as 'another important communication/promotion tool'. He also stated that PR has been the least-utilised tool, but it has great potential for building awareness and preference in the marketplace, repositioning products, and defending them. He compared PR with advertising indicating that as the power of advertising has weakened due to rising media costs, increasing clutter, and smaller audiences, marketing managers may be turning more to public relations. He also continued that even though PR has proved more cost-effective than advertising, it must be planned jointly with advertising because PR needs a larger budget, which may have to come from advertising (Spiro and Perreault, 1976).

From a marketing perspective, public relations is being incorporated into the marketing communications mix. According to Kotler and Mindak (1978), public relations and marketing communications are inextricably interlinked. They suggest marketers may be in a better position in planning to achieve desired responses from target publics than public relations people since very often the company's objective is to influence a public, and this is best done by considering the problem in terms of exchange theory and not simply communications theory. Extension of this argument suggests that marketers could take over the PR function. In addition, Shimp (1993) defines public relations as: 'that aspect of promotion management uniquely suited to fostering goodwill between a company and its various publics'. This definition implies that PR is mainly a form of promotion, whose task is to promote good news; or alternatively, a method of covering up or 'reprocessing' information that is likely to have an adverse effect on corporate image. Shimp's definition does not recognise public relations as an independent managerial function. The main position of PR is in relation to promotion – one of four Ps of the marketing mix, and this despite the promise of extension to fostering public(s) goodwill.

241

While PR can be used in the promotional mix, its real role may be to establish 'understanding' between a company and those bodies that have either a potential or actual interest in it. According to Lancaster and Massingham (1988), the various errors referred to have probably arisen from the fact that, even though many organisations consider and implement 'publicity' as part of their overall marketing activity, they do not usually have a separate PR department, which will co-ordinate the various promotional activities that fall under the PR label and have as well an aim to build trust and understanding by two-way communications with diverse publics who could impact on organisational performance.

In numerous publications Kotler (1982; 1986; 1988) has attempted to subsume PR activity under marketing. He suggests that PR is one part of a set of controllable variables that constitute the 'marketing mix', and as such it should be treated as part of marketing in the performance of its communication role. For example in 1982 Kotler argued that PR can be more effective if it is viewed as part of the marketing mix which is used by an organisation to pursue marketing objectives. Expressed by Grunig (1992), Kotler's perspective is that:

> PR has a minor role to play in the general activities of any organization, and if this minor role is fulfilled at all, it is one that must fit into the more inclusive and more important marketing operation.

Kotler (1982) described the relationship between PR and marketing by raising the issues presented in Figure 14.1. From this perspective, PR does not have an overarching managerial role. Also, Kotler (1986) distinctly sees the role of PR as an additional element of the marketing mix as in his article 'Megamarketing' published in the *Harvard Business Review.* Kotler defined megamarketing as:

> the strategically coordinated application of economic, psychological, political, and PR skills to gain the cooperation of a number of parties in order to enter and/or operate in a given market.

In normal marketing situations, the skilful use of marketing's traditional four Ps– product, price, place, and promotion – can create a cost-effective marketing mix

---

PR is viewed primarily as a communications tool, whereas marketing includes assessment processes, product development, price setting, and the construction of distribution arrangements alongside communication

PR in its communication role attempts to influence attitudes whereas marketing extends its efforts in influencing certain behaviours such as purchasing, voting, or joining

Marketing, unlike PR which is not involved in trying to define organisational goals, defines the organisation's mission, the target customers, and the kinds of goods and services to be produced

---

Figure 14.1 The relationship between PR and marketing.

that appeals to customers and end users. In megamarketing situations, Kotler said that executives must add two more Ps – power and PR. Megamarketing requires marketing executives to utilise the skills of corporate PR and public affairs professionals in order to influence non-consumer publics, that is government agencies, in an attempt to gain market access. However, this view is in concordance with an extended view of PR in a broader publics dimension.

Each public has an interest in a given company's corporate activity and this interest (if expressed negatively) may retard or restrain company activities. PR has the ability to influence these publics favourably. PR's role of establishing mutual understanding between a company and those publics that have an actual or potential interest in it provides for the generation and maintenance of corporate identity. However, as perceived by Grunig (1992), megamarketing is interpreted to mean that PR is again subsumed under a dominant marketing activity. It is used as a marketing tool contributing to the company's efforts to gain access into a target market, as well as a pull strategy. Its use as a pull strategy implies that it is not perceived as a distinct discipline that consists of various techniques and strategies. It is instead part of marketing strategy serving a marketing function.

Despite Grunig's interpretation Kotler's opinion concerning PR has changed notably since 'megamarketing'. His unpublished paper 'PR versus marketing: dividing the conceptual domain and operational turf' (1989) suggests that marketing and PR practitioners each manage a distinct set of activities which they can carry out relatively independently of each other. However, marketing and PR need to have some shared responsibilities in which both have strong inputs, despite the fact that one discipline may take more responsibility than the other. Kotler's present opinion is discussed at a later stage of this chapter.

Cohen (1991), another influential marketing author, classifies PR alongside advertising and promotion. To Cohen the main objective of advertising and publicity is to make the product or service known to potential buyers and to present it in the most favourable way, in comparison to competitive offerings. He further quotes PR as publicity, an opinion which reflects the US tendency to label PR loosely as 'publicity'. This view, however, does not take into consideration the fact that PR may have a different role to fulfil apart from creating awareness. For example, in considering the case of new product development, which is an area of direct relevance to marketing, the role of advertising and promotion is to appeal directly to potential customers in order to create awareness. PR may perform a distinctive supportive role alongside the one performed by advertising and promotion. PR can also communicate through press, television and radio the fact that the company has launched something new to the target market, and thus it contributes to the product launch in a tactical sense. PR also satisfies a corporate function, that of informing a wide range of interested parties that extend beyond immediate customers and suppliers. A consideration of past as well as future customers is essential because they represent potential users, and because they may influence attitudes held by the existing users towards the company (Lancaster and Massingham, 1988).

Therefore, advertising and promotion which reflect the overall promotional activity cannot be successful if different publics are not continuously informed about the firm's activities in a way that indicates a sense of responsibility and concern to its wider environment. In essence, the marketing function directs its efforts to creating exchanges between the organisation and its markets, whereas the PR function is concerned with the various publics that may have a potential or actual influence on the company. Both, however, are management functions that are concerned with organisational success or failure.

Another opinion which indirectly promotes the marketing perspective of PR is the one advanced by Harris (1993). Harris suggests that the concept of marketing public relations (MPR), which will be discussed later, is likely to cause a split-off of marketing support public relations from those other public relations activities that define the corporation's relationships with its non-customer publics. He also suggests that the corporate public relations (CPR) function should remain a corporate management function, but what is known as marketing public relations should become a marketing management function. Unquestionably, under such a scheme, the mission of CPR would be to support corporate objectives. On the other hand, MPR would support marketing objectives. Even though Harris' view recognises and accepts PR as a management function, an opinion which is obviously different from Kotler's (1988), this suggests that an emergent MPR concept is likely to move closer to marketing and potentially become part of the marketing discipline.

A wider study of the marketing management literature identifies attempts to assign public relations an inferior technical role under the stewardship of marketing (Grunig, 1992). Specifically, Shimp and Delozier (1986) saw public relations and publicity essentially as activities that 'serve to supplement media advertising, sales, and sales promotion in creating product awareness, building favourable attitudes toward the company and its products, and encouraging purchase behaviour'. Stanley (1982) saw public relations, publicity, and institutional advertising as part of a company's sales promotion effort which, in turn, is part of the marketing mix. Schwartz (1982) argued that public relations is but another form of 'consumer-oriented sales promotion' with a mission to build or shape the 'image' of a business in its support of sales promotion efforts under the control of marketing. McDaniel (1979), in turn, asserted that 'public relations, like personal selling, advertising, and sales promotion, is a vital link in a progressive company's marketing communication mix', and, further, 'public relations complements the role of advertising by building product/service credibility'.

Drobis (1991) blurred the distinction between PR strategic planning and marketing strategic planning. In his (somewhat naive) view corporate communication is a part of the marketing mix known as product promotion. This view, fits the earlier philosophy advanced by Kotler (1988), who incorporated PR into the marketing communications mix, diminishing the role of PR to one that simply supplies publicity materials to an overall promotional activity undertaken to satisfy marketing objectives. Similarly, Werner et al., (1991) equates PR with product publicity. He associates PR as publicity and ignores the strategic role of the PR function and its use and contribution in managerial planning (White, 1992). Werner et al., (1991) instead believe that, since PR and product publicity are the same, PR is associated with the company's marketing effort and hence supports sales promotion, and is one of the subfunctions of marketing communications. However, this view is not universally accepted since PR is seen as a management function used in strategic decision-making and in dispute-resolving situations (Gossen and Sharp, 1987), whereas product publicity is basically a technical activity which produces publicity materials.

A number of marketing authors concentrate their efforts in attempting to assign PR an inferior role under the superiority of marketing. However, these efforts to bring PR activity under the jurisdiction of marketing management make no reference to any empirical or conceptual base (Grunig, 1992). Generally, the marketing perspective of PR promotes a reductionistic view of PR, diminishing the PR discipline into a technical function. The diminution and potentially the absorption of the public relations function by marketing are illustrated admittedly in a simplified manner in Figure 14.2 (Kotler (1982); Shimp and Delozier (1986)).

The marketing perspective of PR suggests that public relations be incorporated as an extra element within the promotional mix in order to influence current or potential publics and markets of product or company benefits in order to achieve marketing objectives and, subsequently, corporate goals. Marketing is seen as the dominant function, whereas public relations is seen as part of promotion – a set of communication tasks and promotion techniques designed to assist the marketing function. Unwise acceptance of this type of marketing dominance ignores the volatile and hostile environment in which organisations must function. Many non-marketing problems cannot be solved by the methods and techniques as used by marketing management. Obviously, this simplistic marketing perspective of PR is

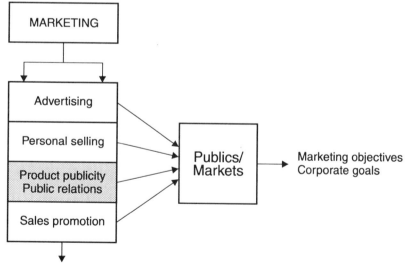

Figure 14.2 Towards a descriptive model of the marketing perspective of PR.

under intense criticism by PR professionals and academics who promote the PR perspective of public relations according to Grunig (1992). The section that follows provides insight to the public relations perspective.

THE PR VIEW OF PUBLIC RELATIONS

Ehling et al. (1992) stipulate that marketing and PR serve different functions and that PR cannot be excellent if it is subjugated to marketing. If an organisation makes PR a marketing function, practitioners are then reduced to a marketing technical support role, and the organisation loses a valuable mechanism for managing its interrelationship with strategic publics.

Ehling et al. (1992) indicate that both the PR and marketing disciplines are essential functions for a modern organisation. However, they serve different objectives as marketing is responsible for identifying markets for the products and services and for the supervision of marketing communication programmes required for creating and sustaining demand. On the other hand, PR is responsible for establishing understanding and trust in those publics that may have a potential or actual interest in the organisation. PR managers are therefore responsible for supervising those programmes needed for communicating with different publics. For this reason, if the PR function is subsumed under a dominant marketing function then the organisation may lose a competitive edge and a valuable mechanism for managing its interdependence with various publics for which the organisation has strategic interest.

Ehling et al. (1992) state that the tendency to elevate marketing activities to a dominant position has been continuously pursued by top executives and marketing managers, while marketing has been perceived as the company's most important commitment and primary activity. This view implies that all other organisational activities and functions may be resolved to subordinate or supportive roles and especially the PR function may be treated as a technical function encompassing a set of tasks designed to assist the marketing function (Ehling et al., 1992). Further, according to Ehling et al. (1992), the two functions are sometimes obfuscated by those observing small organisations, because the same person often carries out both functions. However, the greatest confusion occurs in non-profit organisations where 'non-profit marketing' or 'social marketing' is used to refer to the function of building and maintaining relationships with members and other non-consumer constituencies, a responsibility which by definition is one of the priorities of the PR function.

Confusion concerning the two disciplines often arises from the fact that the two functions are not clearly defined but are fluid in nature, job titles and nomenclature. Marketing is concerned with organisational success or failure and unlike PR the marketing function attempts to bring about exchanges between the organisation and specific types of publics (Cutlip et al., 1985). Kotler (1976) stated that 'marketing management takes place when at least one party to a potential exchange gives thought to his objectives and means to achieving desired responses from other parties'.

Ehling et al. (1992) concluded that anyone engaged in the process of achieving organisational objectives, either in the analysis, planning, implementation or control stage, is using the tactics and strategies of the marketing management function and is therefore engaged in marketing endeavours. This conclusion was based on Kotler's 1976 definition and on the following considerations:

- In any exchange, either potential or actual there are at least two parties that are willing to participate in the process in order to gain something of value.
- The term market includes a wide range of publics including potential customers, political parties and legislative bodies.
- In an organisation, there are a number of executives who are responsible of co-ordinating the activities of their departments in order to achieve organisational objectives.

Apart from the above considerations it is important to bear in mind the PR definition that has been developed by Grunig (1992) according to which, 'PR is the management of communication between an organisation and its publics'. This definition equates PR with communication management, a relationship that describes overall planning, execution, and evaluation of an organisation's communication with external and internal publics – groups that affect the ability of an organisation to meet its goals. Therefore, PR is not just a marketing communications tool, a role which equates PR solely with tactics and techniques and ignores its wider organisational communication role. Furthermore, the role of PR is to establish understanding and build up trust between a company and those bodies that have potential or actual interest in it (Lancaster and Massingham, 1988). This role indicates that the PR function covers a much broader range of relationships and goals with many publics that are not necessarily involved in any kind of direct transactions with a company.

Ehling et al. (1992) criticise the opinion expressed by Kotler (1982) concerning PR. Grunig (1992) states that under Kotler's perspective PR performs a minor role in the general activities of any organisation, which must fit into the more inclusive and more significant marketing operation. This view implies that PR is simply a marketing communications tool, and as such it aims to influence attitudes and behaviours, but in no circumstances is involved in defining and setting organisational objectives. In essence, the efforts of marketers to 'hijack' PR actually denote an attempt to absorb the PR function into marketing (Ehling et al., 1992).

When consideration is given to views and opinions identified in this section, it is important to clarify their independence as well as their interrelations. Marketing is concerned with an organisation's exchange relationships with customers in which quid pro quo transactions occur. On the other hand, PR deals with a broader range of publics involved with or affected by the organisation (Cutlip et al., 1985).

PR's basic commitment is thus to assess the environment by determining the threats and opportunities confronting the organisation (White, 1991), and then by seeking to influence publics that could potentially impact on achievement of the firm's strategic goals. Likewise, marketing has a similar basic commitment in relation to customer needs, wants and desires. Both PR and marketing thus contribute in an interactive and synergistic way to achieve overall corporate objectives.

Both marketing and PR functions are important to an organisation. Subsuming PR into marketing delimits organisational ability to function successfully in highly competitive environments. Essentially, PR is a management function, even though it should be interrelated with the marketing function; it should also be recognised by academics and practitioners as an independent and critical management function in its own right (Figure 14.3).

Figure 14.3 suggests that marketing exists to identify, serve and satisfy customer needs at a profit, through exchange processes. Public relations exists to produce understanding and goodwill in the company's various publics so that these publics do not interfere in the firm's profit-making activity. Essentially, the aim of marketing is to create exchanges that satisfy individual and organisational objectives, that is the sale of products or services in exchange for money. However, the marketing process will impact on different publics which will attempt to place requirements or constraints on the company, as well as form a view of the company's image and social responsibility. These views will impact on company success. The PR function serves as a protector and a promoter of the company's image among its various publics. Both functions are important for the organisation since they enable management to achieve corporate objectives. Subsuming public relations into marketing may result in eliminating the effectiveness of the PR function. It is crucial to any organisation that both disciplines are considered to be separate but equal functions.

The next section discusses the view advanced by Seitel (1992), Lancaster and Massingham (1988), and White (1991) that PR can be seen as both a corrective and a complement to marketing.

PR: A CORRECTIVE AND COMPLEMENT TO MARKETING

Of course, PR can play an expanded role in marketing. The reason for this trend is that there are many cases in which PR activities complement an organisation's marketing

Figure 14.3 Towards a descriptive model of the PR perspective of public relations.

objectives. For example, a number of PR techniques were used to sustain and develop Dunhill Holdings brand names in order to build brand awareness, communicate the range of the company's products, and position the Dunhill brand as one offering outstanding quality, thus contributing to the company's overall marketing effort. The PR techniques used included media relations and financial PR programmes (White, 1991). Also, in British Airways the PR function served as a complement to marketing activities by using internal communication techniques to bring about change in the organisation, improve the company's approach to customer service, and support the company's move into the private sector (White, 1991).

Seitel (1992) indicates that even though in the past marketers have treated PR as an ancillary part of the marketing mix and promoted their products and services heavily through advertising and merchandising, gradually change began to occur within these traditional notions mainly for the following reasons:

- consumer protests about both product value and safety and government scrutiny of product demands began to shake historical views of marketing
- product recalls generated negative and recurring headlines
- ingredient scares began to occur regularly
- advertisers were asked to justify their messages in terms of social needs and civic responsibilities
- rumours about particular companies could spread rapidly
- the media continuously criticised companies and industry image.

Following Seitel (1992), managers increasingly recognise that in the 1990s PR programmes and techniques can add another dimension to marketing campaigns. Ehling (1990) states:

Organisations in general and business enterprises in particular face a large class of problems which cannot be solved by the thinking, policies and procedures of marketing . . . the maximum contribution of PR may be at the CEO's 'elbow' and not as part of the marketing mix.

Thus while PR has an important role to play in relation to direct support of a firm's marketing activities a wider task, among others, is to keep publics informed about new product development. It can communicate through the press, television or radio, trade journals or press conferences the fact that something new exists, thereby fulfilling a corporate function as well as aiding the product launch in a tactical sense. In addition, PR can also 'prepare the ground for marketing activity by explaining policy changes, that is an updating in distribution strategy'. Also, PR is a method of offering a public explanation or apology.

Lancaster and Massingham (1988) stipulate that while the success or failure of PR strategy will depend on how well the marketing functions are carried out, marketing and PR are essentially complementary and working together should produce a 'synergistic' effect on total company operations. Marketing and PR must therefore work closely together to achieve corporate aims. PR has the potential to aid marketing at a tactical level, but one cannot be substituted for the other.

Furthermore, Black (1993) says that PR ideas and skills can play a valuable part in certain marketing processes, such as creating value, or sharing ideas about the value of products or services so that both parties share common perceptions. It is therefore, seldom that any marketing programme will not include supporting PR activities.

White (1991) strongly advances the opinion that PR is a complement and a corrective to the marketing approach. However, it should not be absorbed into any of the marketing activities for the reasons presented in Figure 14.4.

Specifically, PR as a complement to marketing provides information and also techniques of communication used in PR are available to marketing, and can be used in support of product and sales promotion. These communication techniques fall under the description of marketing communication when used in marketing. In fact, by building important relations and contributing to the central relationship with customers, PR can help develop a social environment in which marketing activities are more likely to be effective. Similarly, PR's contribution as a corrective to the marketing approach, is based on the fact that the perspective on which the practice is based is broader than the marketing perspective. PR can raise questions which the marketing approach, with its focus on the market, products, distribution channels and consumers, and its orientation towards growth and consumption, cannot.

Therefore, what Friend (1986a) said under this perspective may be correct:

> Working in support of marketing, PR has a primary function – to promote. It also has to protect and project. That requires PR thinking across the full spectrum of an organisation's operations, or a series of irreconcilable differences and conflicts will invariably arise.

Indeed, various authors have pointed to the use of PR for marketing purposes, that is Bernstein (1988), Kotler (1988), Gage (1981), and Kreitzman (1986), or its relevance to marketing communications (Novelli, 1988; White, 1991; Goldman,

---

1 Marketing has possessed a special place in management for a considerable number of years, because it includes and directs a number of techniques which are valuable in a highly competitive world, i.e. identifying market opportunities, contributing to the development and sale of products and building and maintaining customer satisfaction and market share. But despite its importance, the full task of management cannot be reduced to marketing as it cannot be limited to concern for the organisation's human resources and the organisation's need for financial and material resources.

2 Marketing critics refer to the fact that even though marketing is considered to be increasing organisations' sensitivity to the marketplace, and to consumer needs and expectations, it faces consumer protests concerning inferior products and questionable marketing policies.

3 Marketing is founded on beliefs in growth, production, the encouragement of consumption and the persuasion of large numbers of people to buy, to consume, to acquire and to discard. However, these beliefs are contradictory to the existing public debate about 'green' issues and environmental conservation. In other words, on whether organisations set their marketing objectives based on considerations about social and environmental issues.

Figure 14.4 Why PR should not be absorbed into marketing.

1988; Merims, 1972). Bernstein (1988), however, goes overboard when stating PR will inherit the marketing communications world having the other elements of marketing communications under its dominance. Kotler (1989) says that the part of PR function named as marketing public relations carries out activities in the domain of marketing.

Additionally, Gage (1981) believes that product publicity, a term he uses for PR, can add a new dimension to the entire marketing effort. Kreitzman (1986) indicates that PR can be used effectively in conjunction with other promotional tools to build brand images. Similarly, Novelli (1988) advances the opinion that PR should be integrated with advertising and other marketing communications tools in order to lead to integrated marketing communications. White (1991) suggests that marketing communications and PR activities can be complementary and they must be managed together in order to achieve an organisation's marketing objectives. Finally, Goldman (1988) says that PR can play a vital role in the marketing communications mix and Merims (1972) sees product publicity as marketing's stepchild and a marketing communications tool.

It would appear that while marketing and PR academics have mulled over, or continue to mull over, the parameters of their respective disciplines, many organisations are moving with alacrity towards greater synergy and interaction between the two disciplines.

MARKETING AND PR: CORPORATE ALLIES?

A number of current developments presage a closer working relation between marketing and PR in the future. Marketing practitioners are very likely to increase their appreciation of PR's potential contributions to marketing the product, because they are facing a real decline in the productivity of other promotional tools:

- Advertising costs continue to rise while advertising audiences reached continue to decline.
- Increasing clutter reduces the impact of each advertisement.
- Sales promotion expenditures continue to climb.
- Salesforce costs continue to rise.

(Kotler, 1988)

Also, according to Kitchen (1993), PR efforts may well enable the desired results in solving market-type problems. It may also be the case that PR problems can be solved through marketing's strong propensity for analysis, planning, implementation and control. For many years, each discipline and practice operated in an independent spirit and the attempt by marketing practitioners to subsume PR within a dominant marketing function resulted in a somewhat hostile attitude by PR practitioners.

Both marketing and PR can benefit from each others skills, talents and abilities. Indeed, a 'divorce' between the two communication types is a fatal mistake as this will impact directly on organisational ability to achieve objectives. This section discusses how the two disciplines are defined, the areas of overlap and the reasons for their rivalry, and proposes a potential future relationship.

251

Kotler (1989) gave the following definition of marketing:

Marketing is the business task of (1) selecting attractive target markets (2) designing customer-oriented products with the aim of producing high customer purchase and satisfaction and high company attainment of its objectives.

The aim of marketing is to satisfy individual and organisational objectives. In carrying out this task, the company interacts with numerous publics. These publics develop specific attitudes and beliefs towards the company and they form a view of the companies co-operativeness and image. The view of these publics for a given company affect behaviour toward the company and ultimately may affect organisational success. Therefore, a company's ability to attain objectives will be affected by the quality both of its marketing *and* PR.

Kotler (1989) also gave the following PR definition:

PR is the business task of (1) selecting target audiences (2) designing supportive messages for each audience and (3) developing effective distribution programs to carry these messages to the audiences with the aim of producing positive audience response and satisfaction as well as high company attainment of its objectives.

Unquestionably, PR like marketing aims to help the company achieve its objectives. This aim is achieved by building up trust and understanding through communication with various publics.

Kotler (1989) states that the objectives of a company are a) survival b) to make good financial returns and c) to deliver value and satisfaction to customers and other stakeholders. These objectives are achieved through the management of the value delivery process shown in Figure 14.5 (Kotler, 1989).

According to Figure 14.5, much of the value delivery system is marketing led. Kotler (1989) indicates that the company needs skilled marketers who can identify market opportunities, create appropriate products, and price, distribute, promote and service these products. Friend (1986) says that it is the PR professional's job to be part of the management team which develops the overall marketing strategy and positioning of a new or existing product, service or brand. The PR professional should bring to that team a combination of perspectives, an understanding of how the team sees the brand, how it wishes it to be seen, how it can be seen, and how it will be seen in the context of the overall reputation of the organisation.

The recent emergence of the term 'MPR' perhaps revitalises the debate in both the marketing and PR literatures on whether PR is, or should be, part of marketing and thus managed as a marketing activity. The main issue concerning MPR is whether it is a new PR discipline separate from corporate PR, or whether it is a new marketing management discipline. Kitchen and Moss (1995) view MPR as containing PR techniques applied in the marketing domain.

Kotler (1989) believes that PR, or at least the part called marketing public relations (MPR), manages a miscellaneous set of communication/promotion activities that marketing practitioners normally neglect or lack the skill to handle. He specifically named these activities the 'pencils' of PR:

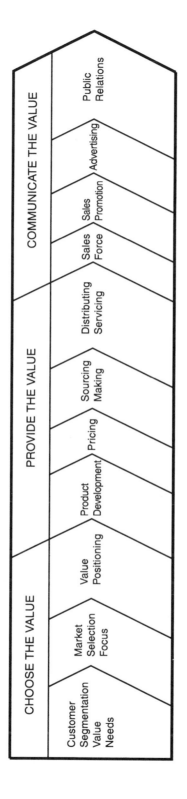

Figure 14.5 The value delivery system.

*P*ublications
*E*vents
*N*ews
*C*ommunity relations
*I*dentity media
*L*obbying
*S*ocial investments

Each of these activities create and communicate value and therefore help in the customer-creation and satisfaction process. Furthermore, in his opinion PR is performing a marketing function and thus, is serving as a marketing tool, whereas he accepts that only some PR activity performs a direct marketing function. This opinion supports one of the five possible views of the relation between marketing and PR shown in Figure 14.6 (Kotler and Mindak, 1978).

Kotler's current opinion, illustrated in Figure 14.8 further on in this chapter indicates that marketing and PR practitioners manage distinct activities, which despite the relative independence in which they are performed, do share some interrelationship.

Figure 14.6 illustrates a pattern of relationships. The suggested five models for viewing the organisational relationship between marketing and PR are outlined in Figure 14.7.

Figure 14.8 also depicts the evolution in thought taken by Kotler between 1978 and 1989 and sustains the perspective of relative independence. For example, PR is responsible for news management and despite the fact that marketing may want to advise on the news strategy PR retains the final responsibility in this area. Similarly, in matters that fall under the jurisdiction of marketing, that is price setting and distribution policies, PR practitioners may want to make suggestions. Marketing practitioners, however, have primary responsibility in these matters.

Clearly, the above division of responsibilities oversimplifies the relation between marketing and PR, judging only by the strained and sometimes hostile relations between the two disciplines in actual corporate settings. Particularly, PR practitioners have at least three complaints about marketing:

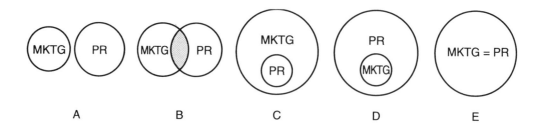

Figure 14.6 Models of possible relationships between marketing and public relations.

Model 1   *Separate but equal functions.* The traditional view that marketing and PR are different in perspectives, capacities, management, and functions

Model 2   *Equal but overlapping functions.* The view that both PR and marketing are important separate functions, but enjoy some common terrain. This position (Kotler, 1989) rules out alternative views that PR and marketing are unrelated, or that one activity is subservient to the other, or that the two are really identical activities going under different names

Model 3   *Marketing as the dominant function.* The view that PR should be placed under the control of marketing

Model 4   *PR as the dominant function.* The view that PR should control marketing

Model 5   *Marketing and PR as the same function.* The view that the two functions are converging conceptually, methodologically and in operational terms

Figure 14.7 The Kotler/Mindak models.

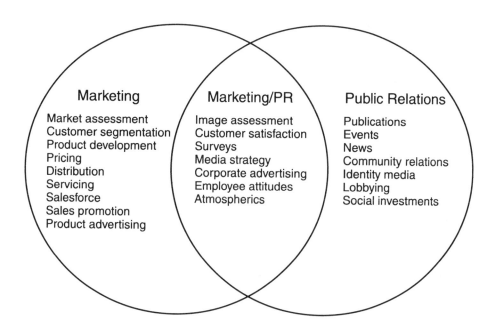

Marketing

Market assessment
Customer segmentation
Product development
Pricing
Distribution
Servicing
Salesforce
Sales promotion
Product advertising

Marketing/PR

Image assessment
Customer satisfaction
Surveys
Media strategy
Corporate advertising
Employee attitudes
Atmospherics

Public Relations

Publications
Events
News
Community relations
Identity media
Lobbying
Social investments

Figure 14.8 Spheres of responsibility for marketing and PR.

1 Marketing will undertake some short-run actions designed to sell more product, that could seriously hurt the company's image. As PR acts as the company's image watchdog, they may be resented for intruding on marketing's freedom of action.
2 Marketing neglects to use PR to its full potential.
3 Marketing disparages PR as a simple communication function lacking a strong discipline base and business-oriented framework.

Undoubtedly, marketing practitioners' attitude toward PR can only generate resentment and hostility, rather than a spirit of co-operation. Similarly, in viewing the problem from the marketer's perspective the following attitudes are found:

1 PR is seen as a hit-or-miss proposition.
2 PR's impact on sales is hard to measure except when it is unusually impactful.
3 PR people are concerned about vague things like public opinion when they ought to think more like business people trying to move the product (Kotler, 1989).

The sometimes strained relations between marketing and PR have at their source both logical and emotional reasons. Both marketing and PR practitioners may not fully understand each other but it is essential for the achievement of mutual understanding that both functions recognise the fact that they have independent, as well as interdependent, functions. Although each performs distinct activities, these activities are directed towards an identical objective: the achievement of organisational survival and success.

What Kotler (1989) describes in Figure 14.8 indicates that even though both disciplines perform distinct activities, they share some common ones, which are carried out by the MPR function. As Kotler (1989) describes it, MPR manages a miscellaneous set of communication/promotion activities that marketing practitioners lack the skills to handle. This opinion is also shared by Harris (1993), who supports that the MPR practice is separated from the general practice of corporate PR. MPR may move closer to marketing, and corporate PR (CPR) may remain a management function concerned with the company's relationships with its publics. Despite this separation, MPR and CPR will remain closely allied. An 'alliance' may bring co-operation and integration between marketing and PR disciplines. However, the opinion that MPR should be part of the CPR function could be seen to some degree as a view promoted by practitioners and PR consultancies keen to capitalise on any re-direction of marketing budgets (Kitchen and Moss, 1995).

Therefore, from both perspectives:

1 From a marketing perspective, MPR is a new approach to the practice of PR which is closely related to marketing.
2 From a PR perspective, the concept of MPR is an attempt by marketeers to 'hijack' PR, incorporating it as an extra element within the promotional mix.

It is clear that an integration of marketing and PR disciplines may never be achieved as hostility over various issues, that is MPR, between practitioners of both disciplines continues. However, many organisations have actually achieved a successful integration of the two disciplines within their management structure.

Figure 14.9 illustrates what could be considered an ideal model which could be adopted by business. This figure suggests that even though marketing and PR are independent, they are also interrelated disciplines. As Kotler (1989) suggested, each discipline encloses a distinct set of independent activities, that is marketing is responsible for market assessment and PR is responsible for community relations. At the same time, some PR activities – the 'pencils' of PR – as labelled by Kotler (1989), or as distinctly defined by, for example Harris (1993), are shared by both disciplines. These activities imply that marketing and PR are interrelated disciplines. If the on-going debate between marketing and PR practitioners does not influence negatively the viability of the MPR function and if marketing and PR practitioners and academics do not extend their debate to include the issue of MPR, then unquestionably both disciplines as well as the MPR function will facilitate achievement of organisational and marketing goals.

So far, the chapter has discussed the arguments concerning the relationship between marketing and PR disciplines. PR is viewed by many marketing practitioners and academics as part of marketing, whereas the opinion that PR is an independent management function is held by the majority of PR academics and practitioners. Furthermore, some PR academics believe that PR is a complement and a corrective to the marketing approach. These opinions have created a somewhat hostile environment between PR and marketing practitioners, but despite this conflict it is felt that both disciplines can benefit from interaction. However, the

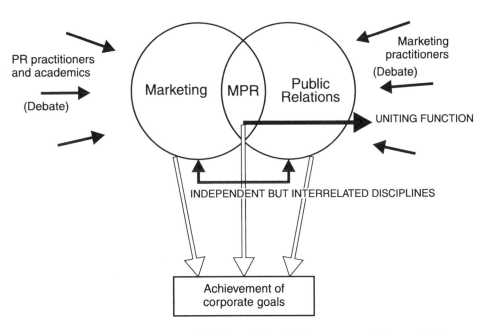

Figure 14.9 A descriptive model of the relationship between marketing and PR.

recent emergence of the concept of marketing public relations threatens to cause a new 'burst' of hostility and controversy between the two disciplines. The following section relies heavily on the work of Harris (1993) by providing an overview of MPR, and examining its emergence.

MARKETING PUBLIC RELATIONS (MPR)

MPR is an offspring of two parents: marketing and public relations whose practitioners and academics as mentioned earlier are involved in a 'war' regarding importance, independence, and their interrelations. Can MPR claim to be a distinctive new promotional discipline as proclaimed by Harris (1993)? Does it represent a significant new approach to the practice of PR? As seen already both marketing and PR practitioners have different views concerning its emergence, definition, and importance. This section explores these issues by providing information concerning the concept of MPR, discussing its benefits, and outlining reasons why MPR may have become a rapidly growing segment in the PR field. Attempts to define MPR are explored and the place of MPR in the promotional mix is analysed. The view that MPR is a distinct promotional discipline, a proposition advanced by Harris (1993), is investigated. Various uses of MPR are explored through different case vignettes. The chapter is then summarised and concluded.

As discussed earlier top executives and marketing managers have tended to elevate marketing activities to a dominant position and treated marketing as the most important commitment within an organisation. Present evidence tends to show that there is confusion concerning the distinction between PR and marketing in the literature. This is supported by an increasing number of articles in which PR and marketing communications practices are recognised as increasingly integrated and converging concepts (Goldman, 1988; Merims, 1972; Novelli, 1988). Despite the fact that these articles were initially developed to give emphasis to the emergence of the concept of PR in the marketing support context, they reflect a growing tendency for PR and marketing to be seen as converging disciplines in both professional and academic circles. This trend is supported by the emergence of the concept of marketing public relations, a term which appeared in both the marketing and PR vocabularies in the 1980s. Kotler (1982) described MPR as:

> a healthy offspring of two parents: marketing and PR. MPR represents an opportunity for companies to regain a share of voice in a message-satiated society. MPR not only delivers a strong share of voice to win share of mind and heart; it also delivers a better, more effective voice in many cases.

The growth of PR and its acceptance as a valuable or even essential marketing tool seems widespread. Companies assign PR staff specialists to their product marketing teams and engage PR firms to help them get mileage from product introductions, keep brands prominent throughout product life cycles, and defend products at risk (Harris, 1993).

Harris (1993), examining the development of MPR, argues that the 1980s has seen MPR emerge as a distinctive new promotional discipline which comprises specialised application techniques that support marketing activities. Kotler (1989),

Professor of Marketing at Northwestern University's Kellogg School of Management and author of marketing management, remarks: 'MPR in the future can only go one way: up.' He further says that: 'PR is moving into an explosive growth stage because companies realize that mass advertising is no longer the answer', and that organisations are merging PR into marketing ending a long-standing 'love/hate relationship'.

A number of surveys have been carried out in order to identify the degree of awareness of the business sector regarding MPR and general attitudes towards this concept. One of these surveys which documents the increasing awareness and use of MPR was conducted by Tom Duncan, Professor of Marketing at Ball State University, for Golin/Harris Communications. This research surveyed a sample of 286 *Advertising Age* subscribers who hold marketing and advertising positions with client organisations (Duncan, 1985). Among the key findings were the following:

1 MPR was perceived as being effective in a variety of areas that were traditionally the responsibility of advertising.
2 MPR was thought to be especially effective in building brand awareness and brand knowledge.
3 There were no areas in which the majority of clients said MPR would not be effective.
4 The importance of MPR increased in the past five years and was expected to continue to increase. The main reasons given were that marketers are becoming more sophisticated and that MPR:
   • is made cost-effective by increases in media advertising costs
   • breaks through clutter
   • complements advertising (increases the credibility of messages)
   • is proving itself (Harris, 1993).

Beyond the general uses of MPR identified in the above survey, the following MPR benefits are some of those which are accepted by organisations as ones which add value to marketing programmes. Among the ways it could be used according to Harris (1993) are the following:

• position companies as leaders and experts
• introduce new products
• cultivate new markets
• extend the reach of advertising
• break through commercial clutter
• gain exposure for products that cannot be advertised to consumers
• influence opinion leaders.

Gage (1981) said that, for whatever reasons, MPR has become one of the fastest growing segments of the PR field. Indeed, there are many signs that MPR has come of age. PR has become big and profitable business. In 1980, an article in *PR News* stated:

The proven power of PR and its cost effectiveness in contrast to advertising motivated the advertising industry to add PR departments to their operations in order to help alleviate its financial woes.

Shandwick PLC, the first worldwide publicly owned PR company, has become the largest of all PR firms, with annual fee billing of US$180m (Shandwick plc, 1989). Even though Shandwick retained its crown as a leader of the UK pack in 1991, its income dropped 18 per cent to £26.6m – a decline which indicates declining income levels in some areas of the UK PR industry, that is business-to-business marketing (UK Top 150 PR Consultancies, 1992 in *PR Week*). In 1993, the UK Top 150 PR Consultancies magazine showed Shandwick still maintaining its position at number one in the UK rankings for the sixth year in succession. Its income, however, declined somewhat. The 1994 *PR Week* Top 150 PR Consultancies had Shandwick in the first position of UK rankings. A 3 per cent fall in income at Shandwick belies the fact that the company increased its profits in every quarter of 1993 from a 12 per cent jump in the first quarter to 20 per cent by the year end. Overall, each head of staff made a profit of £9,000 during the year which was helped by a 10 per cent growth in fee income in the third quarter, resulting in a total fee income for 1993 of £22,812,000.

Secondly, MPR is the largest and fastest growing segment of a fast growing industry. A study of the world market for PR services, conducted by Shandwick (1989), estimated that 20 per cent of the fee income of PR firms throughout the world is generated by PR for consumer products. In fact, 70 per cent of the business handled by PR firms is marketing-related, with the remaining 30 per cent distributed among corporate, governmental, environmental and financial billing (Harris, 1993).

Thirdly, companies have recognised the growing importance of MPR with bigger budgets and fatter salaries. MPR now leads all PR disciplines with its rapidly increasing importance, and PR marketing skills are in greater demand than ever before, reports a recent survey conducted by Cantor Concern (1989), a leading recruiting firm in the PR field. Also, Robert Dilenschneider (1988), president and CEO of Hill and Knowlton, one of the largest worldwide public relations agencies says: 'the million-dollar worldwide program, almost unheard of ten years ago, is now experienced with increasing regularity'.

Also, PR is getting increasing interest in the marketing and business media. On 13 March 1989, *Advertising Age* ran a forum titled 'PR on the Offensive' led by Robert Dilenschneider. Additionally, *Marketing Week*'s, cover story in 1989, on 'The New Public Relations' declared that 'the new PR is used virtually everywhere', and advised its readers to 'stir some PR into their communications mix'.

Finally, the academic community is showing greater interest in PR. Universities are responding to the growing demand for business leaders trained in PR and for PR practitioners trained in business (Harris, 1993) as indicated in Chapter 16.

TOWARDS AN MPR DEFINITION

What is MPR? Definitions and interpretations vary widely. While PR experts cannot agree about what MPR is, they all agree about what it is not, that is free advertising. 'We work very hard to eliminate that misconception', stated Karen Connit, Vice President, Carl Byoir and Associates, Chicago (Gage, 1981). According to Harris (1993), the designation (MPR) arose in the 1980s because of the need to distinguish the specialised application of PR techniques that support marketing from the general practice of PR. According to Harris (1993), MPR has grown rapidly and pragmatically to meet the opportunities of a changing marketplace. In the process, it has borrowed and amalgamated thinking from traditional PR, marketing, advertising, and research. The issue of defining MPR is complicated by the fact that there are many definitions of both marketing and PR.

Variety of definitions of PR illustrate disagreements in the professional and academic PR field. Similarly, the discipline of marketing has been defined in numerous ways. Perhaps, these factors may constitute the main source of the disagreement in defining the recently emerged term of MPR in a way that is universally accepted. However, certain PR and marketing authors have attempted to precisely define the term. Harris (1993) believes that MPR can be defined more precisely than the larger concept of PR because of its relevance to marketing, especially in helping an organisation meet its marketing objectives. He suggests the following definition:

> MPR is the process of planning, executing and evaluating programs that encourage purchase and consumer satisfaction through credible communication of information and impressions that identify companies and their products with the needs, wants, concerns, and interests of consumers.

Moreover, Shimp (1993) gave the following definition:

> It is the more narrow aspect of PR which involves an organisation's interactions with consumers or with other publics (such as governments) regarding marketing matters (like safety). In short, it is the marketing-oriented aspect of PR.

Even though the old name for MPR was publicity (Black, 1952) which was seen as the task of: 'securing editorial space as divorced from paid space, in all media read, viewed, or heard by a company's customers or prospects, for the specific purpose of assisting in the meeting of sales goals,' MPR goes well beyond this. It can contribute to many tasks according to Kotler (1988). As the power of advertising weakens somewhat, due to rising media costs, increasing clutter, and smaller audiences, marketing managers may turn to MPR. In a survey of 286 *Advertising Age* subscribers who hold marketing positions in US companies, three-quarter reported that their companies were using MPR. They found it particularly effective in building awareness and brand knowledge, for both new products and established products. In several cases, it proved more cost effective than advertising (Duncan, 1985).

This section has provided evidence for the emergence of a potentially new concept. However, the existing disagreement between the marketing and PR practitioners and academics regarding a universal definition for both the marketing and PR disciplines has a negative impact in defining marketing public relations in a universally accepted way. Despite this disagreement on the MPR definition issue, it seems accepted that the contribution of this new concept may be significant. Its benefits could act, potentially, as the basis on which a single definition can be developed and, eventually, be established.

MPR IN THE MARKETING MIX

According to Harris (1993), MPR is a promotional option that rounds out the marketing mix and adds value to advertising campaigns. While it cannot substitute for advertising it can make advertising work harder. In most cases, MPR is launched in conjunction with an advertising and marketing campaign. It complements other marketing efforts, but serves a distinct and unique purpose, often giving a product, service or marketer added credibility, exposure and newsworthiness. Specifically, in some MPR efforts, one of the objects is to enhance a product's credibility and to position its marketer not only as a good business, but as a company that has a genuine concern for people – one that uses its resources and know-how to make life better for them (Gage, 1981).

In 1991, Kitchen and Proctor carried out research in fast-moving consumer goods (FMCG) firms concerning the 'Importance of PR'. The most significant finding appears to be the movement towards integration of MPR with other more common elements of the communication mix. Of four firms interviewed, all reported that the use of MPR helps achieve marketing objectives, though there was ambiguity concerning effective measurement.

Gumm (1978), in his article 'PR is primary element in Beech-Nut Food's marketing program', supports that: 'MPR can be proven to be a valuable addition to the marketing mix'. Similarly, Kitchen (1993), says:

> Latterly, advertising, sales promotion, and personal selling have undergone difficulties in relation to achievement of cost-effective communication objectives . . . the emergence and application of MPR in the communications mix may be playing a more significant complementary role in business organisations facing a more turbulent competitive environment.

Seemingly, as the power of advertising weakens as a result of cost, clutter, and audience receptivity, as criticism is levelled at sales promotions in terms of sales effects and profits, and as sales forces diminish in size due to retail concentration and key account selling, firms could practically consider MPR alongside other promotional tools (Kitchen, 1993).

According to Cushman (1988), the major rationale for MPR's development is credibility and cost effectiveness. Credibility for PR could be achieved in one way via the disinterested third party endorsement of the media vehicle and thus be responsible for consumer and trade motivation to create sales (Gage, 1981). Cost effectiveness may be achieved because of the money not spent on advertising or agencies, and various mechanisms have been put forward measuring PR's contribution in relation to what it would have cost for the same amount of space for advertising (Merims, 1972; Kotler, 1982).

Examples given elsewhere in the text illustrate that MPR can be used either alone or in conjunction with other communication mix tools to achieve marketing objectives. In fact, some firms have utilised PR in a marketing sense usually by working with and alongside highly experienced PR agencies. The key point to be derived from this is that MPR in some firms appears to be working alongside or in a complementary manner to other elements in the communications mix. It is noticeable that there is often interaction with its more important relation: corporate public relations (CPR). Throughout the literature reviewed, it seems evident that the new concept is either considered as part of CPR or as an independent approach to the broader area of PR, specifically as one which supports marketing activities. This schism of opinion suggests that it is difficult to define MPR and provide a definite answer to the issue of its legitimacy.

MPR – A DISTINCT DISCIPLINE?

Harris (1993) claims that the term MPR is used to distinguish this field from the broader one of PR. However, this opinion seems to suggest fission some time in the future, that is the split-off of marketing support PR from those other PR activities that define the corporation's relationships with its non-customer publics. The corporate public relations function may well remain a corporate management function, whereas MPR may become a marketing management function. Under this scheme, the mission of CPR would be to support corporate objectives, and the mission of MPR would be to support marketing objectives. MPR practitioners would become marketing associates, and their career paths would be directed toward marketing management. CPR practitioners will continue to report to top management (Harris, 1993).

Harris (1993) also recognises that a close working relationship needs to be maintained between the CPR and MPR disciplines not only because of the similarity of skills and experience, but also because of the need to integrate marketing objectives with corporate objectives. Relationships with government on all levels, for example, may serve to affect the environment in which the company markets its products, as do the company's public positions on a variety of existing and emerging issues that affect publics or consumers.

The need for co-operation between CPR and MPR seems vital now and may be increasingly so in the future. Inevitably, some give and take will be required from both sides. PR may have to abandon its intellectual pretensions and its disdain of the marketing function, and marketers will have to become increasingly aware of how the social, political and economic environment affects consumers and the opinion makers who influence attitudes toward companies and their products. This synergy cannot be achieved if marketing and PR are seen as rivals rather than allies (Harris, 1993). Harris (1993) states that it seems strange that many PR professionals and academics reject this view and see it as an attempt by marketers to 'hijack' an important part of the PR function and place it under marketing's control. While the evidence of the increasingly important role played by PR in support of marketing plans cannot be questioned, the logic of any attempt to dismember the PR function can be questioned.

Although there is evidence of a move towards closer integration of corporate and marketing messages, and hence the need for closer co-operation between marketing and PR practitioners, this trend alone does not support the argument for a further subdivision of the PR function in the way advocated by Harris. Such a division of responsibilities would seem to create potential for confusion and possible conflict between the messages communicated to organisations' various shareholder audiences without necessarily bringing any recognisable communications benefits. However, Cutlip et al. (1985) acknowledge that: 'in practice PR specialists are many times called upon to help in the marketing effort by writing publicity stories and arranging media coverage for new products', but they believe that because some view publicity in the same way as 'public relations', product publicity may be a source of some confusion between the marketing and PR functions.

The above view, according to Harris (1993), fails to draw a needed distinction between MPR and CPR. It specifically assigns PR a limited role of issuing new product press releases, whereas no recognition is given to the increasing role of MPR in maintaining markets for mature products and in winning consumer confidence for companies and products through sponsorship of and involvement in events and endeavours that consumers, market influencers and sellers care about.

Despite the variability of opinions concerning the legitimacy of MPR, it is evident that the concept has a wide range of uses from which many benefits may be derived, justifying the contribution of MPR to an organisation's successful implementation of promotional tools.

USING MARKETING PUBLIC RELATIONS

This section will present and discuss the different uses of marketing public relations, by referring to case vignettes in which the effective use of MPR led organisations toward achieving their corporate objectives. Initially, the discussion will refer to the use of MPR in the introduction of new products. According to Harris (1993), MPR can be used effectively throughout a product's life cycle, but its best known use has been and continues to be in the introduction of new products.

Case vignette: MPR – New product introduction: consumer electronics

MPR played a major role in the introduction of consumer electronics products in the 1980s. One worldwide success was the Sony Walkman. The product was positioned as a powerful, portable, high quality sound reproducing personal entertainment vehicle. Sony first aroused public interest by giving Walkman's to Japan's leading musicians, teen idols and magazine editors. In the USA the name 'Walkman' was timely, coinciding with the boom in walking, running and jogging for which it became standard equipment. Massive resultant publicity was heard around the world and the product became a 'runaway' success despite its price-skimming strategy (Harris, 1993).

Use of marketing-oriented PR or MPR contributed to effectively promoting a new product to a relatively familiar or unfamiliar market. The role of MPR in introducing new products is widely accepted by marketers, and MPR is almost always an integral part of the total introductory effort.

As has already been mentioned earlier in this chapter, companies have been using the MPR concept in a variety of situations thus acknowledging its benefits. Figure 14.10 presents case vignettes in summary form in relation to the multi-use role of MPR and further illustrates the benefits that organisations can obtain from its use.

Used for	Cases	Benefits from the use of MPR
Introducing new products	Sony Walkman	– received massive publicity – product's huge global success – in 10 years time, sales exceeded 50 million devices
	New Lean Cuisine range	– 90% brand awareness amongst the slimmer group – 80% brand awareness amongst customers – consistent high media visibility
Promoting mature products	USA Peanut Advisory Board (PAB)	– 6% increase in peanut butter consumption – effective repositioning of the product
Winning consumer trust	McDonald's Trust Bank (San Ysidro, California)	– the company received credit by the media – received hundreds of positive letters by the public
Celebrating special occasions	Barbie's 30th birthday Hasbro's G.I. Joe's 25th birthday Bugs Bunny's 50th birthday	– massive publicity – massive publicity – massive publicity
Sponsoring public service programmes	'We Care About New York' campaign	– 12,000 New Yorkers participated – 700 clean-up events – 12 million media impressions
Sponsoring good causes	Tang March Across America for MADD	– extensive media coverage – 13% increase of Tang consumer purchases
Sponsoring sports	Waste Management Cleans Up at Calgary	– extensive media coverage – massive publicity

Figure 14.10 Using marketing public relations.

Source: Harris (1993).

In addition to using MPR for introducing new products, Harris (1993) used the concept in various other cases, that is promotion of mature products (e.g. USA Peanut Advisory Board, PAB). These cases can be found in his milestone text.

MPR's value in growing brands, sustaining mature brands, and supporting declining brands is less universally understood than its use in introducing new products (Harris, 1993). However, while MPR may lack the ability of reminder advertising to reach the consumer with measured frequency, it can often exceed the benefits of advertising with its greater reach and it provides marketers with opportunity to extend the reach of advertising and to simultaneously capitalise on the credibility factor in building brand loyalty. As a result, its role in relaunching, revitalising, repositioning, and sustaining mature and even declining brands may be ultimately of even greater value to the company than the quick and dramatic hit that can be achieved in publicising new products. Indeed, MPR is particularly well suited in two roles: maintaining and building brand franchise, due to the variety of tools and tactics it can apply.

Among the MPR's roles which are acknowledged by companies are those of contributing in building consumer trust and positioning a company in the market as a help provider, which are interrelated.

As Kenneth Lightcap (1984), vice president of corporate communications of Reebok International says, MPR has the potential to be used as a positioning tool by companies. In Lightcap's view, it is essential that companies gradually build up impressions to publics over time, in order to gain a lasting impression that will initiate consumers to value the company's products and be more receptive to product publicity. These companies that establish themselves as 'caring' and help giving organisations, are those that eventually earn consumer loyalty and trust, and subsequently secure their 'societal' image in a highly competitive trade world.

There are many other ways in which MPR can exist in promoting products or brands as shown in Table 14.1. The unique features and the different situations identified by Harris in relation to the case vignettes in Table 14.1 show the concept of MPR as one which substantially adds credibility to companies and their products. It has the power of maintaining brand franchises by providing information and service to the consumer, by identifying the brand with causes that consumers care about, or by sponsoring high visibility events that excite consumers.

However, even if the value of MPR as a set of PR techniques and tools has been acknowledged by the business sector globally and it has been assigned to many uses, its value as a concept and its place in either the marketing or PR literature is still debated. Irrespective of the applicability and use of MPR the divergent views indicated earlier in the chapter show that a debate still exists, at least in both the

Table 14.1 MPR: The promotional variability

Type of MPR	Example
Special occasion	Mattel, Hasbro, Warner Brothers
Sponsorship of public service programmes	S.C. Johnsons Raid Big Block Clean-Up
Cause-related marketing	Tang March Across USA for MADD
Sports marketing	Waste Management Cleans Up at Calgary

Source: Harris, 1993.

marketing and PR literature. Perhaps this debate circumscribes the disagreement among the marketing and PR circles concerning the emergence of the MPR concept. Specifically, Harris (1993), although acknowledging and accepting the role of PR as a distinct discipline separate from the marketing discipline, also states that MPR and CPR should be recognised as separate, self-sufficient disciplines. However, they are closely interrelated when marketing decisions affect or are affected by corporate philosophies and actions. But the role of MPR should be focused on helping the corporation achieve its marketing objectives, while the role of CPR should be to counsel management on corporate positions and actions as they relate to the achievement of corporate goals (Harris, 1993).

But, the above opinion is contradictory to the opinion held by PR practitioners according to which the concept of MPR is seen as an attempt by marketeers to 'hijack' PR, incorporating it as an extra element within the promotional mix in order to inform, persuade, or remind existing and prospective customers of product or company benefits.

From both the PR and marketing literatures it seems that a particular application of PR publicity techniques exists. But on the basis of this evidence it is not justified whether a separate specialist area of PR or marketing practice will be established.

SUMMARY AND CONCLUSIONS

MPR is a new term which has emerged in the late 1980s and early 1990s in the marketing and PR vocabularies. Its origin and essence has been debated since marketing practitioners and academics believe that it is a separate practice from corporate public relations that may move closer to marketing, whereas the PR practitioners and academics claim that the above opinion is another attempt by marketeers to 'hijack' an important part of the PR function and place it under marketing's control.

Many authors have used their own MPR definitions since no universally accepted definition has yet been developed. Maybe, this lack of agreement is the outcome of the subsequent disagreements of both the marketing and PR academics in establishing a unique, universally accepted marketing and PR definition.

Despite the above disagreements many firms have used MPR, and in many cases its benefits have been indicated. From MPR's undoubtedly wide use in different markets and under a range of contradictory situations it is evident that a particular application of PR publicity application techniques exists. This finding was also evident in the earlier review of literature in both this chapter and the previous chapter. Despite this evidence it is not entirely justifiable to claim whether a separate specialist area of PR or marketing practice has or may be established. More empirical research is therefore required in order to provide answers to questions concerning legitimacy of the MPR and its viability.

DISCUSSION TOPICS

1 If MPR is so important, indicate why Freud Communications only received £100,000 to develop the MPR aspects of the 7-Up Light's promotion.

2 Give your opinion as to Hart's perspective of separation between marketing and PR. On what basis can Hart's position be justified?

3 Why must PR fit into the the 'more inclusive and more important marketing function'?

4 Consider Figure 14.2. Why would the authors consider this figure a 'simplification' of the issues involved?

5 Justify the view taken by PR academics that PR is not just about marketing.

6 Consider Figure 14.3. What are the strengths and weaknesses of this figure? Does it adequately conceptualise the issues involved?

7 Argue for or against the case that the 'maximum contribution of PR may be at the CEO's elbow'.

8 Explore and contrast the developing views of Philip Kotler in relation to PR and marketing. Are Grunig's criticisms still valid?

9 Explore the dynamics of Figure 14.9. Is the backdrop debate merely about semantics or does the debate have real implications for marketing and PR?

10 Using a brand of your choice illustrate how MPR has helped the brand to 'succeed'.

11 Where does MPR actually belong? To marketing or corporate communications?

CASE STUDY: TDK

Client

TDK, leading manufacturers of audio and video tapes for the consumer market; sponsorship of the Second World Athletics Championships in Rome and being arranged by the international Headquarters in Tokyo.

Objective

Maximise brand benefits, including brand sales promotion, of international sports sponsorships programme.

Audience

Audio and video tape buyers in the UK, over 16 years old, across full socio-economic spectrum throughout Britain.

Activity

– fund-raising programme linked to an on-pack offer was arranged to support British athletes through the Sports Aid Foundation.

– campaign launched with major athletics personalities in attendance.

– series of seven fun runs organised to raise further funds for young British athletes, each one in conjunction with a major regional independent radio station.

For each location:

- sponsorship forms produced and distributed to sports clubs, health centres, major employers, youth groups, local authority recreation centres, libraries, schools, and adult education centres.
- full colour poster detailing date and venue distributed and displayed as above and in TDK retail outlets.
- British athletes interviewed to promote the fun run and attendance at each run by local athletes arranged.
- branded course banners, runners stickers, balloons, display and runners certificates were produced and transported on hospitality bus roadshow.
- editorial promotion undertaken for each venue over a period of four weeks with live on-air broadcasting for each run.

The fun run programme was the core of a broader sports related public relations programme over a three-month period prior to the Rome Championships.

Results

- blanket brand publicity in each of the seven regions.
- radio and press for three weeks prior and one week after each event.
- high consumer awareness of TDK, its sponsorship of the Rome Athletics Championships, and organisation of the fun runs.
- brand endorsement by major British athletes, local sports personalities, and radio celebrities.
- trade participation in the runs through staff teams entering.
- national brand share increase throughout the three-month promotional period.

REFERENCES

Bennett, R.C., and Cooper, R.G. (1981) 'The misuse of marketing: An American tragedy', *Business Horizons*, 51–61.

Bernays, E.L. (1952) *Public Relations*, Norman, OK: University of Oklahoma Press.

Bernstein, J. (1988) 'PR in top communication role', *Advertising Age*, 59, November: 28.

Black, S. (1993) *The Essentials of Public Relations*, London: Kogan Page, pp. 40–41.

Black, G. (1952) *Planned Industrial Publicity*, Chicago: Putnam, p. 3.

Business Week (1987) 'Nothing sells like sports', 30 August.

Cohen, W.A. (1991) *The Practice of Marketing Management*, New York: Maxwell Macmillan, pp. 503–6.

Coulson-Thomas, C.J. (1990) *Marketing Communications*, London: Heinemann, p. 194.

Cushman, D.P., King, S.S. and Smith, T. (1988) 'The rules perspective on organisational communication theory', in G.M. Goldhaber and G.A. Barnett (eds) *Handbook of Organisational Communication*, Norwood: Ablex, pp. 55–94.

Cutlip, S.M., Center, A.H. and Broom, G.M. (1985) *Effective Public Relations*, Englewood Cliffs, NJ: Prentice-Hall, pp. 6–7.

Cutlip, S.M., Center, A.H. and Broom, G.M. (1993) *Effective Public Relations*, 6th edn, Englewood Cliffs, NJ: Prentice-Hall, pp. 6–8.

Dark, S., Hall, A. and Farish, S. (1993) 'Darkness before the dawn', *PR Week*: UK Top 150 PR consultancies, Haymarket Publications, 29 April, p. 31.

Dilenschneider, R. (1989) 'PR on the offensive: Bigger part of marketing mix', *Advertising Age*, 60, 13 March, p. 20.

Drobis, D.R. (1991) 'Taking corporate strategy seriously', *Public Relations Journal*, 47(8): pp. 31–2.

Drucker, P.F. (1980) *Managing in Turbulent Times*, New York: Harper and Row, pp. 219–21.

Duncan, T. (1985), *A Study of How Manufacturers and Service Companies Perceive and Use MPR*, Muncie, Ind.: Ball State University.

Ehling, W. (1990) 'How to get maximum benefit from public relations by positioning it properly in the organisation', *PR Reports and Tactics*, 10, 10 August: 1.

Ehling, W., White, J. and Grunig, J.E. (1992) 'Public relations and marketing practice', in J.E. Grunig (ed.) *Excellence in Public Relations and Communications Management*, Hillsdale, NJ: Lawrence Erlbaum.

Friend, C. (1986a), 'Public relations and marketing – the synergy and the separation', London: Institute of Public Relations, pp. 1–2.

Friend, C. (1986b), 'Public relations – not just puffering and nonsense', London: Institute of Marketing, p. 8.

Friend, C. (1994) Letter to Dr Philip J. Kitchen, Department of Management, Keele University, expressing her opinions concerning the place of public relations in the marketing mix, 7 November, p. 1.

Gage, T.J. (1981) 'PR ripens role in marketing', *Advertising Age*, 5 January: 10–11.

Goldman, T. (1988), 'Big spenders develop newspaper communications', *Marketing Communications*, 13(1): 24.

Gossen, R. and Sharp, K. (1987) 'Managing dispute resolution', *Public Relations Journal*, 43 (12): 35–8.

Grunig, J.E. (ed.) (1992) *Excellence in Public Relations and Communication Management*, Hillsdale, NJ: Lawrence Erlbaum, pp. 357–90.

Grunig, J.E. and Hunt, T. (1984) *Managing Public Relations*, New York: Holt, Rinehart and Winston.

Gumm, J. (1978) 'Public relations is a primary element in Beech-Nut food's marketing program', *Advertising Age*, 6 February: 39.

Harris, T. (1993) *The Marketer's Guide to Public Relations: How Today's Companies are Using the New Public Relations to gain a Competitive Edge*, New York: John Wiley, pp. 33–34, 46.

Hart, W. (1991) 'PRTV', *Marketing Business*, October: 7.

Hayes, R.H. and Abernathy, W.J. (1980) 'Managing our way to economic decline', *Harvard Business Review*, 58(1), July–August: 67–77.

Kitchen, P.J. and Proctor, R.A. (1991) 'The increasing importance of public relations in FMCG firms', *Journal of Marketing Management*, 7: 359–60.

Kitchen, P. (1993a), 'Towards the integration of marketing and public relations', *Marketing Intelligence and Planning*, 11(11): 15–21.

Kitchen, P. (1993b), 'PR: A rationale for its development and usage within UK fast-moving consumer goods firms', *European Journal of Marketing*, 27, 7 November: 379–84.

Kitchen, P.J. and Moss, D. (1995) 'Marketing and public relations: The relationship revisited', *Journal of Marketing Communications*, 1(2): 7–8.

Kotler, P. (1976) *Marketing Management*, 3rd edn, Englewood Cliffs, NJ: Prentice-Hall.

Kotler, P. (1982) *Marketing for Nonprofit Organisations*, 2nd edn, Englewood Cliffs, NJ: Prentice-Hall.

Kotler, P. (1986), 'Megamarketing', *Harvard Business Review*, 64(2), March/April: 29–30, 117–24.

Kotler, P. (1988) *Marketing Management*, 4th edn, Englewood Cliffs, NJ: Prentice-Hall, pp. 655–56, 661.

Kotler, P. (1989) 'Public relations versus marketing: Dividing the conceptual domain and operational turf', unpublished position paper prepared for the Public Relations Colloquium, San Diego, 24 January, pp. 1–11.

270

Kotler, P. and Mindak, W. (1978) 'Marketing and public relations', *Journal of Marketing*, 42(4), October: 13–20.

Kleiner, A. (1989) 'The public relations coup', *ADWEEK's Marketing Week*, 16 January: 17.

Kreitzman, L. (1986) 'Balancing brand building blocks', *Marketing*, 13 November, pp. 43–57.

Lancaster, G. and Massingham, L. (1988) *Marketing Primer*, London: Heinemann, pp. 125–8.

Lightcap, K. (1984) 'Marketing support', in Bill Cantor, *Experts in Action: Inside Public Relations*, New York: Longman, ch. 8.

Love, J.F. (1986) *McDonald's: Behind the Arches*, New York: Bantam Books, p. 212.

Merims, A.M. (1972) 'Marketing's stepchild: product publicity', *Harvard Business Review*, 36(5), November/December: 107–13.

McDaniel, C. (1979) *Marketing: An Integrated Approach*, New York: Harper and Row, p. 455.

Novelli, W.D. (1988) 'Stir some PR into your communications mix', *Marketing News*, 22, 5 December: 19.

Philadelphia Inquirer (1984) 'McDonald's deserves praise', editorial, July.

PR Week – UK Top 150 PR Consultancies (1992) 'Tougher all round for the top ten', Haymarket, 30 April, p. 27.

PR Week – UK Top 150 PR Consultancies (1994) 'Mixed fortunes for the top ten', Haymarket, 28 April, p. 37.

Public Relations Reporter (1989) 'Colloquium of marketing and PR spokespersons agrees organisations suffer when turf wars occur', 13 February.

Schwartz, G. (1982) 'Public relations gets short shrift from new managers', *Marketing News*, 16(6), 15 October, p. 8.

Seitel, F.P. (1992) *The Practice of Public Relations*, New York: Maxwell Macmillan, pp. 6–7, 273–91.

Sethi, P. (1979) *Promises of a Good Life: Social Consequences of Private Marketing Decisions*, Homewood, IL: Irwin.

Shandwick PLC (1989) *The Public Relations Consultancy Market Worldwide*, London: Shandwick PLC.

Shimp, T.A. (1993) *Promotion Management and Marketing Communications*, Philadelphia: Harcourt Brace, pp. 587–590, 604.

Shimp, T.A. and Delozier, M.W. (1986) *Promotion Management and Marketing Communications*, New York: Dryden, pp. 493–4.

Smith, N.C. (1990) *Morality and the Market: Consumer Pressure for Corporate Accountability*, London: Routledge.

Spiro, R.L. and Perreault W.D. Jr (1976) 'Influence use by industrial salesmen: Influence strategy mixes and situational determinants', unpublished paper, Graduate School of Business Administration, University of North Carolina.

Stanley, R.E. (1982) *Promotion: Advertising, Publicity, Personal Selling, Sales Promotion*, 2nd edn, Englewood Cliffs, NJ: Prentice-Hall.

Werner, L.R. (1991) 'Marketing strategies for the recession', *Management*, 6 August: 29–30.

White, J. (1991) *How to Understand and Manage Public Relations*, London: Business Books, pp. 95–109.

15

DEVELOPING A RESEARCH FRAMEWORK: INDUCTIVE VS DEDUCTIVE?

Philip J. Kitchen

CHAPTER AIMS

- to give an overview of different types of research available from an academic perspective
- to typify different types of research strategy/approaches
- to indicate how to develop a research method from methodology
- to discuss research objectives in the context of theoretical frameworks
- to outline research design from the context of depth interviews

ILLUSTRATION: 'TSB GROUP'

- *Client*:   TSB Group PLC – in preparation for and following its flotation.
- *Objective*: Demonstration of breadth of corporate management, style and philosophy to position a new major banking force prior to and post its flotation.
- *Audience*: The City, business, institutional and parliamentary opinion formers.
- *Activities*: – development of a chairman's platform programme
  - identification and monitoring of banking, finance and business issues
  - establishment of corporate positions on each of those issues
  - selection of speakers from the TSB management group for each issue – primarily the Chairman supported by the CEO
  - development of scripts and necessary visual aids for each opportunity
  - creation and placement of editorial material to each platform taken
- *Results*: – high awareness and understanding of TSB senior management group and the new company's philosophy
  - high visibility for TSB among the target audiences and on key banking issues
  - tactical editorial coverage and comment to reinforce the organisation's positioning as a major player in Britain's community

(*Source*: *PR Week*, 17 May 1996: 7, used with permission.)

INTRODUCTION

Whether one chooses the flotation of a major new bank, a television programme for targeted sponsorship, or the method to adopt in relation to research activity, numerous decisions are involved. Questions in relation to the TSB flotation may include: how to select the target audiences/publics; how to demonstrate breadth of corporate managerial expertise and to whom; how to identify specific issues pertinent to different publics; how to identify and position a corporation or business in relation to these issues; which medias are most appropriate for targeted PR. Or it may include the question of how to evaluate whether PR objectives have been achieved. This chapter is primarily concerned with research methodology and research method utilised to carry out empirical research.

Good research can be thought of as research that uses the scientific method. In other words, good research is systematic enquiry aimed at providing information to solve problems (Emory and Cooper, 1991). In striving to classify the principal components, controls and transformations of the scientific research process, Wallace (1971) in Bynner and Stribley (1978) compared the construction of theory with the application of theory. Theory construction, by and large, depends upon observation and understanding what is observed, primarily by inductive methods. Applying theory on the whole involves knowing what to observe, primarily by deductive methods. Deduction is a form of inference that professes to be conclusive, that is a 'conclusion reached by deduction is, in a sense, already contained in the premises' (Dewey, 1910). Induction does not enjoy the same strength of argument; to induce 'is to draw a conclusion from one or more particular facts or pieces of evidence' (Emory and Cooper, 1991). Constructing theory and applying theory indicate a series of methodological choices leading to adoption and usage of a particular research method. Such choices are not made arbitrarily on the basis of researcher whim or inclination but are dependent on the nature of the problem(s) to be addressed, mechanisms available for that address, and the theoretical background.

Postgraduate students in the public relations domain will be expected to carry out a major piece of empirical research as part of their end-of-course project or dissertation. In the vast majority of cases such research rests upon well-established theoretical foundations. Literature review usually provides those foundations. In other words, it provides a basis for exploration of research hypotheses or objectives and also the parameters for choice of method to be adopted. It also provides a basis for deriving research objectives and serves or enables the development of theoretical models.

CONTEXTUAL BACKGROUND

The various chapters in this text have indicated that although numerous articles and books have been published concerning the development of public relations in a general sense, little or nothing has been written concerning its development within a specific group of companies (i.e. an industry, for example). The beginnings of research of a fairly inductive or deductive nature has been described in some of the

273

chapters. In relation to the United Kingdom, there is a dearth of information concerning the development of public relations. These factors among those previously mentioned may serve to underpin the need for studies of an exploratory nature.

Mills (1959) typified 'exploratory studies' as 'probing new substantive or methodological areas, which may rest on still unformalised and unintegrated theoretical, hypothetical, and methodological arguments'. Crane (1972) built on Mills' assertion by suggesting that exploratory studies, and the variant of the scientific process they represent, are typical of an early stage of growth in a scientific discipline. Kuhn (1964) referred to this period as 'pre-paradigm', whereas hypothesis-testing studies are typical of a more mature ('paradigm-based') stage. These comments are pertinent in the context of student research as the possibility of 'following in someone else's footsteps', replicating previous research from a UK base, or taking advantage of a mature paradigm in the field of public relations are not viable alternatives at this time. This chapter, while necessarily concerned with these very real issues and problems, is reflective of the overall thrust of the book which can be described as an attempt to lay foundations for a paradigm upon which further 'scientific' research can be based.

Kerlinger (1986) defined scientific research as a 'systematic, controlled, empirical and critical investigation of natural phenomena guided by theory and hypotheses about the presumed relations among such phenomena'. This definition indicates the degree to which observations are controlled – implying that alternative explanations of the outcome are ruled out. When the nature of PR research in the UK is considered, however, it may not yet be possible to guide investigations by theory or hypotheses because of the paucity of research in the area. Despite the earlier chapters concerning development of public relations, such development is predicated or explained from the context of changing environmental circumstances. Those circumstances, so far as PR development is concerned, are not necessarily the same in the UK as they would be, for example, in the USA (Cutlip et al., 1985). Thus, while 'academic' debates, for example on the relationship between public relations and marketing, can be easily delineated, the issue of the relevance of such a debate needs to be tackled, ideally from the perspective of firms or businesses in the UK. Again, while the development of MPR can be indicated, the extent of that development for UK firms and its inclusion in the arsenal of marketing communication still awaits sound theoretical and empirical investigation. Likewise, PR's evolution towards a degree of maturity, as claimed by much of the USA literature, needs to be evaluated. Within each of these scenarios business organisations do (seemingly) consider public relations valuable – in a marketing communications context – and as an integrative device between corporate and marketing communications, as they exercise 'corporate citizenship' in increasingly competitive fragmented markets. A further issue concerns evaluation of the presumed dividing lines between marketing and public relations. However, in terms of corporate and business realities, there is no 'level playing field' upon which these issues can be accurately evaluated, as business organisations are likely to be in various stages of development as conditioned by historical development, organisational culture, competitive environment and target publics/audiences.

While exploration of the issues pandemic in the PR domain is evidential, and fraught with conceptual and methodological difficulties, the tasks at hand are exciting from a social science or practitioner perspective.

The theoretical literature, from what is an admittedly biased viewpoint, has all the hallmarks or characteristics of Kuhn's 'pre-paradigm period'. Even if one adopts Grunig's (1992) perspective, scenarios indicate that issues are clouded and unclear; academic opinion is divisive; the extent to which the external environment is influencing communications is uncertain; scenarios where access to quantitative information is likely have confidentiality limitations; and, perhaps most significantly – scenarios in which little research of a theoretical or empirical nature has already been carried out. This background to PR research in the UK would appear to necessitate exploratory research; in other words, it is difficult, based upon the current theoretical evidence, to develop hypotheses which can then be tested for truth or falsity. It is argued that so little is known about public relations in either a corporate or marketing sense that hypotheses become difficult to test. Thus, so far as postgraduate students are concerned there would appear to be justification for inductive as opposed to deductive research methods being developed.

DEVELOPMENT OF RESEARCH METHODS

There is a multiplicity of available techniques or methods to approach or tackle particular research problems (Emory and Cooper, 1991; McDaniel and Gates, 1991; Bynner and Stribley, 1978). Summarising their respective arguments, research methodology could be seen as the science of method. Methodology serves to provide parameters about which methods are most appropriate to achieve specific objectives. It has already been stated that an inductive as opposed to deductive process or method seems most appropriate for PR research given the nature of problems or issues to address and the paucity of previous empirical research. The required need is to 'explore' given phenomena as opposed to 'testing' specific hypotheses. Inductive research, characterised by exploratory study, seems to be desirable because of the need to probe a new substantive methodological area, for research in the PR domain rests upon still unformalised and unintegrated theoretical, hypothetical and methodological arguments (Mills, 1959). Thus, deductive research may be inappropriate at this stage. Rather than select specific hypotheses which can then be tested for agreement, which could be taken as corroboration (though not as final proof), or clear disagreement, which would be considered as refutation or falsification (Popper, 1957), what is required are inductive exploratory approaches. Such approaches have been defined by Lovelock and Weinberg (1984) as 'most often used in the problem discovery and problem-definition phases of decision making', their primary purpose being to 'outline the dimensions of a problem more clearly . . . and to learn perceptions of the users'. Churchill (1987) further argued that such approaches are justified where there is a need to gain insights and ideas. Thus exploratory approaches may be used to develop hypotheses, establish priorities for further research, and determine the viability of possible research projects. Exploratory research is used to increase familiarity with issues or problems and lay the foundations for further research.

The particular attributes of exploratory research are 'a high degree of flexibility, and reliance on secondary data, convenience or judgement samples, small scale surveys, simple experiments, case analyses, and subjective evaluation of the results' (Tull and Hawkins, 1990). Such flexibility is important, since in addition to providing a mechanism for understanding the parameters of PR problems, findings also provide the foundation for paradigm building in the field of public relations. Exploratory approaches, while serving to harvest a wealth of information, also require significant caution in interpreting findings. For example, while exploratory research is advantageous in terms of flexibility, enabling researchers to adapt and extend programmes in response to emergent findings, and in providing a mechanism for participants in the research to identify public relations issues of key concern to themselves, it is disadvantageous because of the inherent limitations associated with the research method.

For example, if the first phase of a research project adopted depth interviews and semi-structured questionnaires, this relative lack of structure entails researchers needing to avoid attributing too much importance to particular comments in isolation. In such a phase responses may be inadvertently influenced by interviewer intervention. Likewise, findings could be skewed by subjective interpretations. In the latter phases of research, which may use ordinal data gathering mechanisms, 'coding, tabulation, and analysis of responses' is invariably difficult (Churchill, 1987). When exploratory research is carried out there are inevitable risks associated with communication errors and small sample sizes, which means that research methods employed cannot guarantee clear and unambiguous interpretation of findings. For this reason findings cannot be projected across entire populations and over-generalisation needs to be avoided. Thus, conclusions relative to an inductive argument need to follow the form and reasoning associated with the exploratory research method used. For example comments like 'then it is certain that . . .', 'it cannot be denied that . . .', 'it follows inevitably that . . .', usually mark an argument as deductive or they ought to be reserved for deductive arguments. Or in the case of inductive research one could write 'it seems reasonable to suppose . . . ', 'which tends to establish . . .', 'which goes to show . . .', and the tentativeness of this type of phraseology is appropriate to an inductive argument (see Beardsley, 1956). Nevertheless, the fact that findings from different research phases may be reflected and reinforced by each other would tend to add robustness to research findings.

DEVELOPMENT OF RESEARCH OBJECTIVES/THEORETICAL MODELS

One of the problems associated with exploratory research is the development of suitable objectives, areas of exploration, or simple questions pertaining to the research domain. If work is being carried out of an exploratory or interpretative nature this would suggest meanings associated with public relations would be found via social actors (i.e. business executives) found inside specific business organisations. Thus rather than striving to test specific hypotheses, which it has been suggested are not appropriate to a pre-paradigm domain, a considered approach may be to develop objectives which could flow through different phases of research design. The rationale for such a mechanism is strengthened by the theoretical background in public relations. It is clear that development of public relations in a general sense provides interesting material for research. Still, objectives cannot be viewed in the same way as hypotheses. A hypothesis is specifically formulated for empirical testing. In this case, the pre-paradigm nature of public relations, in the view of the author at this time, precludes hypothesis testing.

The nature of a given theoretical argument may require development of a descriptive model which serves to guide and proscribe empirical findings. Such models are simply perceptions or diagramming of a complex or system. Use of analogies, constructs, verbal descriptions of systems, idealisations and graphic representations are widespread in marketing (Lazer, 1962). The term 'theoretical model' represents the fact that models and theories are often used interchangeably. According to Coombs et al. (1954): 'a model itself is not a theory; it is only an available or possible or potential theory until a segment of the real world has been mapped onto it. Then the model becomes a theory about the real world'. Such models assist in the collection, systematisation, and categorisation of data. Wiseman (1974) stipulated that development of such a model allows researchers 'to encompass the entire situation under study as though high on a mountain looking down and seeing all the action going on at once'. Development of this broad perspective enables the researcher to see the sub-parts of the action and to gear the analysis to reflect this information as closely as possible. Objectives, as part of a given theoretical model, are less than hypotheses in the sense that they are more of an opinion founded on insufficient proof, an inference, or a surmise.

RESEARCH DESIGN

The primary purpose of exploratory research is to develop insights about the nature of a situation where data needs are vague, and sources ill defined. Data collection in the first instance needed to be rather open-ended in order to generate the maximum amount of data. Interviews at this stage would serve to maximise generation of useful insights. Data collection needs suggest flexibility, typically the findings are non-quantitative. Any inferences or recommendations made at the conclusion of the research are likely to be more tentative than final (Parasuraman, 1991).

Marketing research is a complex area in its own right and specific research designs do not readily appear as the 'way forward'. A number of questions need to be answered and a number of decisions made with respect to the choice of technique or techniques to be used in order to operationalise, say, a theoretical model. Without this underlying structure it is difficult to see the interrelationships of different stages of research to the whole research design. To a very significant extent, however, research design involves a number of 'trade-offs'. Thus research design usually acknowledges that decisions made in one stage of the research process have implications for subsequent stages. An appreciation of the pervasive interactions among stages of research are often required so as to generate confidence concerning research findings. Basic research organisation could follow steps outlined in marketing research texts (Churchill, 1987; Parasuraman, 1991; Tull and Hawkins, 1990). These steps are:

1 Formulate the research problem
2 Determine the research design
3 Design the data collection method and forms
4 Design the sample and collect the data
5 Analyse and interpret the data
6 Prepare the research findings

Two types of research activity of common usage are depth interviews and survey development.

DEPTH INTERVIEWS

Depth interviews tend to be the first phase of empirical research. Often such interviews attempt to tap the experience and knowledge of those familiar with the general area being explored. In each case, given researcher unfamiliarity with the research issue or problem the persons selected for interview tend to have significant degrees of knowledge, that is they are regarded as valid commentators or experts, and are thus excellent potential sources of information. The need to save time and money usually necessitates research economy which often dictates that respondents in depth interviews should be carefully selected. Despite this careful process it may often take considerable persuasion to involve busy executives in the process of research. The all-important question needs to be tackled: 'what's in it for them'? For example, the research project may be able to provide valuable summary data to interviewees, in a macro as opposed to a micro sense. So the researcher needs to exercise both persuasion and humility. Persuasion often means persistence and pointing out the benefits of participating in the research project. Humility is always useful, as the researcher is the supplicant, the provider of information is sacrificing managerial time and, in a sense, giving expert advice. Once interviewees are accessed, however, the researcher should search for provocative ideas and useful insights, not the statistics of the business. Respondents are carefully chosen because of the likelihood that they will offer the contribution sought (Sellitz et al., 1976). Exploratory depth interviews are used to formulate the problem for more precise investigation, gather information about the practical problems of carrying out research on particular conjectural issues, increase the researcher's familiarity with the problem, and clarify any conceptual issues. This research phase should always be characterised by a degree of flexibility with respect to the methods used for gaining insight and exploring research objectives. Indeed the literature goes so far as to say that 'formal design is conspicuous by its absence in exploratory studies' (Boyd et al., 1985). It is often felt that senior executives do not respond well to formal structured interviews, a feeling corroborated by Macfarlane Smith (1972):

> The respondents are . . . usually experts holding senior management posts in business or industry. Such people do not react at all favourably to the rigidity of a formal, structured interview. It has been found from experience that most expert respondents have a story to unfold about some aspect of the subject of

the survey. This 'story' is usually very valuable and it should not be suppressed because of the limits imposed by pre-coded questions.

The interview schedule should allow the researcher freedom to create questions, add additional questions, probe responses that appeared to be relevant and develop the data in any practical way. Interviews should be recorded on cassette tape and transcribed later. Researchers should always ask permission to tape-record the interview. Where such permission has not been granted, it is useful to be able to write extremely rapidly or use shorthand.

Often in the early stages of interviews it may become evident that while firms may be willing to participate in depth interviews, they may not be willing to divulge data or information that is deemed to be quantitative or, more importantly, to fall into the realms of competitive intelligence.

Interviews can lead to problems of research access or to the need to adopt a further research strategy. 'Hollis' (1988) is a classified guide to all PR agencies in the United Kingdom and is very useful mechanism for delineating sample frames. Often such a sample may be a non-probability convenience sample. The limitations associated with non-probability samples are well recognised: sampling error cannot be computed, researchers do not know the degree to which the sample is representative of the population from which it is drawn, and the results of non-probability samples cannot be projected to the total population. Nevertheless, non-probability samples are often pertinent to research design given the inductive nature of research in public relations and the healthy endorsement of the current need to build theory rather than to test theory. Often secondary stages of research involve development of a research instrument, usually a questionnaire. This entails a) the need to design the questionnaire and b) to then administer it. Questionnaire design requires nine steps or stages (Kornhauser and Sheatsley, 1976):

1 Specify information sought
2 Determine of questionnaire type and administration method
3 Determine content of individual questions
4 Determine response format
5 Determine question wordings
6 Determine question sequencing
7 Determine physical characteristics of questionnaire
8 Re-examine steps 1–7 and revise if necessary
9 Pre-test and revise if necessary

(Source: adapted from Kornhauser and Sheatsley, 1976)

Questionnaire development basically means questions are presented with the same wording, in the same order, to all respondents. The reason for standardisation of questions and answers is to ensure that all respondents are replying to the same question. Such a design provides many advantages, notably those connected with research economy, including administration, tabulation, and analysis of responses. Widespread location of respondents usually necessitates the use of the postal questionnaire. Questionnaire content and response categories are determined by and large in terms of fixed alternatives and while every attempt should be made to include 'appropriate categories of response' in order to minimise potential bias, it is recognised that potentially this may lower response validity. Question wordings, sequencing, and physical characteristics of the questionnaire need to go through a process of revision and testing before a completed version is mailed.

The previous two sections of interview and questionnaire are interconnected. The nature of the inductive approach adopting an exploratory research design leads to the research objectives. Such an approach is contingent or dependent for its validity upon the pre-paradigm nature of the research problem as typified by the paucity of research in the area. Thus there is a necessity for a research design that unfolds gradually as greater information, knowledge and experience are developed. Thus interviews allow for significant freedom of movement. Responses from interviews are often used as the basis for questionnaire development. Note that the research objectives and derived theoretical models based upon the review of literature in Chapters 2 to 4 are, however, the fulcrum for the empirical phases of the thesis and consequently run through all phases of the research design and indeed subsequent exploration of the findings.

SUMMARY AND CONCLUSIONS

This chapter has outlined research methodology in a general sense and has focused on various techniques that could be used to explore a given research problem in public relations. The research always adopts the scientific approach – systematic enquiry in order to provide information to solve problems. The approach recommended here is primarily inductive in nature. This is based upon the literature review which to the author indicates an early stage of growth in a scientific discipline. Consequently deductive hypothesis testing approach would appear to be inappropriate at this stage. Exploratory research seems to be a way forward at this point in time. Literature > theoretical models > objectives > research design > operationalisation > analysis > discussion appears to be a very useful, even, stage model in relation to PR. Each and every research phase should be to explore set objectives or test specific hypotheses, in other words, operationalising a theoretical model.

DISCUSSION TOPICS

1 Brainstorm several potential PR research problems for different organisations. Indicate briefly how and in what way(s) such problems would be tackled from an academic perspective.

2 What is the scientific method? Why not simply base a response to an issue or problem on 'seat of the pants' thinking? How does scientific method lead to scientific research?

3 Describe the difference between a deductive and inductive research approach.

4 Why should constructing theory and applying theory lead to adoption and usage of a particular research method?

5 Hazard an opinion as to why so little empirical research on PR has been carried out in the United Kingdom.

6 In your view, is PR in a pre-paradigm state insofar as empirical work is concerned? What is the difference between pre- and post-paradigm? Where does a paradigm come from?

7 Are debates about various issues about PR merely 'academic' in nature? If they are 'academic' does this mean they are not to be taken seriously?

8 How would you differentiate between exploration of a given phenomenon versus testing specific hypotheses?

9 Why should research design involve 'trade-offs'?

10 When planning to interview senior executives would your interview schedule be highly structured, somewhat structured, or unstructured? Why?

11 Rationalise the selection of a research questionnaire OR an interview schedule for a specific problem. What factors would guide your decision?

12 Research design suggest cogently that interviewing senior executives is the best way forward in tackling a research issue, yet potential interviewees have all written very polite letters declining participation in your research. How would you deal with or get around this hurdle?

REFERENCES

Beardsley, M.C. (1956) *Practical Logic*, Englewood Cliffs, NJ: Prentice-Hall, pp. 197–223.

Boyd, H.W., Westfall, R. and Stasch, S.F. (1985) *Marketing Research: Text and Cases*, 6th edn, Homewood, IL: Irwin, p. 40.

Bynner, J. and Stribley, K.M. (1978) *Social Research: Principles and Procedures*, London: Longman in Association with the Open University Press, pp. 7–8, 9, 23–4, 227–30.

Churchill, G.A. (1987) *Marketing Research: Methodological Foundations*, Chicago: Dryden Press, p. 74.

Coombs, C.H., Raiffa, H. and Thrall, R.M. (1954) 'Some views on mathematical models and measurement theory', in R.M. Thrall, C.H. Coombs and R.L. Davis (eds) *Decision Processes*, New York: John Wiley, pp. 20–21.

Crane, D. (1972) *Invisible Colleges and Social Circles: A Sociological Interpretation of Scientific Growth*, Chicago: University of Chicago Press.

Cutlip, S.M., Center, A.H. and Broom, G.M. (1985) *Effective Public Relations*, Englewood Cliffs, NJ: Prentice-Hall.

Dewey, J. (1910) *How We Think*, Boston: D.C. Heath, p. 79.

Emory, C.W. and Cooper, D.R. (1991) *Business Research Methods*, Homewood and Boston: Irwin, pp. 14–15.

Grunig, J.E. (ed.) (1992) *Excellence in Public Relations and Communication Management*, New York: Lawrence Erlbaum.

Hollis (1988) *Press and Public Relations Manual*, 19th edn, London: Hollis Directories, pp. 457–646.

Kerlinger, F.N. (1986) *Foundations of Behavioural Research*, 3rd edn, New York: Holt, Rinehart and Winston, p. 10.

Kornhauser, A. and Sheatley, P.B. (1976) 'Questionnaire construction and interview procedure' in J.L. Sellitz et al. (eds) *Basic Methods in Social Science: The Art of Empirical Investigation*, New York: Random House, pp. 541–73.

Kuhn, T.S. (1964) *The Structure of Scientific Revolutions*, Phoenix: University of Chicago Press.

Lazer, W. (1962) 'The Role of Models in Marketing', *Journal of Marketing*, 26(2), April: pp. 9–14.

Lovelock, C.H. and Weinberg, C.B. (1984) *Marketing for Public and Non-Profit Managers*, New York: John Wiley, pp. 133–6.

Macfarlane Smith, J. (1972) *Interviewing in Marketing and Social Research*, London: Routledge and Kegan Paul, p. 142.

McDaniel, C. and Gates, M. (1991) *Contemporary Marketing Research*, New York: West Publishing Company, pp. 28–45.

Mills, C.W. (1959) *The Sociological Imagination*, New York: Oxford University Press, pp. 31–72.

Parasuraman, A. (1991) *Marketing Research*, 2nd edn, Reading, Mass.: Addison Wesley.

Popper, K.R. (1957) 'The unity of method', in *The Poverty of Historicism*, London: Routledge and Kegan Paul, pp. 130–43.

Sellitz, J.L., Wrightsman, S. and Cook, S.W. (1976) *Basic Methods in Social Science: The Art of Empirical Investigation*, New York: Random House, p. 94.

Tull, D.S. and Hawkins, D.I. (1990) *Marketing Research: Measurement and Method*, 5th edn, New York: Macmillan, pp. 392–401.

Wallace, W. (ed.) (1971) 'An overview of elements in the scientific process', in *The Logic of Science in Sociology*, Chicago: Aldine Atherton, pp. 16–25.

Wiseman, J.P. (1974) 'The research web', *Urban Life and Culture*, 3(3): 317–28.

16

MEASURING THE SUCCESS RATE: EVALUATING THE PR PROCESS AND PR PROGRAMMES

Tom Watson

CHAPTER AIMS

- to review the nature of evaluation
- to consider the practitioner culture of public relations
- to indicate barriers to and models of evaluation (existing and proposed)
- to set these factors within the context of effects-based planning which guides practitioners on the integration and planning of campaigns and programmes

ILLUSTRATION: THE NATIONAL RESCUE SERVICE

In 1990, the Association of Chief Ambulance Officers (ACAO) faced a challenge from leaders of Fire Services who were proposing a national rescue service. ACAO believed that ambulance services should stay with the NHS as a crucial initial stage in pre-hospital medical care. Using a report on the future of the ambulance service as their main campaign tool, they launched it to the media in five cities on the one day to create a truly national story. This was followed up by lobbying of MPs and other opinion leaders. ACAO and its public relations advisers used media analysis to check whether their message was being transmitted favourably by that channel of communication before pressing on with their second phase of contacts with the 'gatekeepers' to ambulance policy. A short-term evaluation strategy thus helped them judge the effectiveness of their media relations strategy ahead of implementation of their second phase. Within six months, their plans for the future of the NHS ambulance service had been endorsed by the NHS Management Executive and the Secretary of State for Health. The Fire Service leaders' proposals were dropped.

INTRODUCTION

This chapter offers an overview on the nature of public relations evaluation, the attitudes of practitioners towards evaluation and the models on which it can be based. The chapter's aim is to guide readers away from the discussion of specific methodology, which obsesses many practitioners, towards an integration of planning and evaluation in the development of public relations programmes.

The chapter begins with a discussion of evaluation and objective setting, considers the culture of public relations practice and the barriers to widespread use of evaluation techniques. Finally, the chapter reviews existing models and outlines two new approaches to evaluation.

A TOP PRIORITY?

In the Delphi study conducted by White and Blamphin among UK practitioners and academics of public relations research priorities (White and Blamphin, 1994), the topic of evaluation was ranked number 1 in the development of public relations practice and research. But what is evaluation of public relations? Is it measuring output or monitoring progress against defined objectives? Is it giving a numerical value to the results of programmes and campaigns? Is it the final step in the public relations process or a continuing activity?

When discussing this topic, there is considerable confusion as to what the term 'evaluation' means. For budget-holders, whether employers or clients, the judgements have a 'bottom-line' profit-related significance. Grunig and Hunt (1984) have written of a practitioner who justified the budgetary expenditure on public relations by the generation of a large volume of press coverage. He was perturbed by a senior executive's question of 'what's all this worth to us?' In the UK, articles in the public relations and marketing press refer to evaluation in terms of 'justifying expenditure' which is similar to Grunig and Hunt's example. White (1991) suggests that company managers have a special interest in the evaluation of public relations. 'Evaluation helps to answer the questions about the time, effort and resources to be invested in public relations activities: can the investment, and the costs involved, be justified?'

Many definitions emphasise effectiveness: Cutlip et al. (1994) – 'systematic measures of programme effectiveness'; Pavlik (1987) – 'evaluation research is used to determine effectiveness'; Blissland (1990) – 'the systematic assessment of a programme and its results'; Lindenmann – 'measure public relations effectiveness'. A development of these definitions are those which are related to programme or campaign objectives, a reflection on the management-by-objectives influence on public relations practice in the US. Cutlip et al. (1994) conclude that evaluation research (a term interchangeable with evaluation) is 'used to learn what happened and why, not to "prove" or "do" something'. Definitions of evaluation can therefore be seen to fall into three groups: the *commercial*, which is a justification of budget spend; *simple-effectiveness*, which asks whether the programme has worked in terms of output; and *objectives-effectiveness*, which judges programmes in terms of meeting objectives and creation of desired effects.

For effective evaluation to be undertaken, starting points have to be set out, a basis of comparison researched and specific objectives established. Dozier (1984a) says that 'measurement of programmes without goals is form without substance; true evaluation is impossible'. Weiss (1977) says the 'purpose [of evaluation] should be clearly stated and measurable goals must be formulated before questions can be devised and the evaluation design chosen'. The start point and the objective must be set as part of the public relations programme design. If it is, interim measurement of objectives can take place and thus effectiveness and impact can be assessed both as the PR programme unfolds, and at the end. Indeed, White (1990) argues that 'setting precise and measurable objectives at the outset of a programme is a prerequisite for later evaluation'.

Simplistic media measurement or reader response analysis only considers output – volume of mentions – and not effects. 'Objectives' of, say, more mentions in the *Financial Times* which may be sought by a quoted company are little more than a stick with which to beat the public relations (more correctly, press relations) practitioner. Dozier (1985) refers to this approach as 'pseudo-planning' and 'pseudo-evaluation'. Pseudo-planning is the allocation of resources to communications activities, where the goal is communication itself and pseudo-evaluation is 'simply counting news release placements, and other communications'.

Historically, the measurement of column inches of press cuttings or 'mentions' on electronic media were seen as adequate evaluation techniques. These were supplemented by *ad hoc* personal observation measures, such as those promoted by Jefkins (1987) based on experience and observation. Experiential methods, he says, are 'what changes have affected the situation which was assessed before planning the campaign' while observation is seeing that 'some changes will be physically apparent or visible'. Jefkins also points to 'scientific' methods of evaluation such as media coverage rating charts and judgements on the perceived value. While all these types of assessment are widely practised, they are not valid and reliable methods of evaluation undertaken with any consistency or objectivity.

They fail as objective measures because they cannot demonstrate the requirements for validity and reliability. They can be skewed by the subjectivity of different personalities undertaking the judgement and cannot be replicated. Some are little more than sales leads measures and others that consider the 'tone' of articles (cf. rigorous content analysis), opportunities to see or media ratings, are judgements which are made to suit the client/employer rather than to measure the effectiveness of reaching target markets. Too often, the evaluation is determined after the campaign has been set in motion.

Another method of judgement is advertising value equivalents (AVE, also called advertising cost equivalent) where an advertising space value is given to media coverage. This is a measure often claimed from media coverage. For example, a public relations consultancy stated in the *Marketing* magazine (23 April 1992) that a brand of rum, which it was promoting, had 'received the equivalent of £75,000 in advertising, nearly three times the [public relations] budget. A further £9,000 of free advertising was achieved.' There was no indication in the report as to the impact of this publicity, which was sponsorship of activities at the Notting Hill Carnival organised by the Afro-Caribbean community in London each year. No measures were given of any effect on the carnival participants or visitors.

McKeone (1993) says, 'the whole concept of AVEs is based on false assumptions and any conclusions based on them are misleading and dangerous'. Wilcox et al. (1992) describe this methodology as 'a bit like comparing apples and oranges', because advertising copy is controlled by the space purchaser while news mentions are determined by media gatekeepers and can be negative, neutral or favourable. It is also inherently absurd to claim a value for something which was never going to be purchased in the first place.

PRACTITIONER CULTURE

Evaluation is a subject widely written about at academic and practitioner level. Pavlik (1987) commented that measuring the effectiveness of public relations has proved almost as elusive as finding the Holy Grail. Cline (1984) reviewed around 300 articles and reports in the mid-1980s and found no consensus of effective methodology. She comments that 'there was a pervasive desire to reinvent the wheel' rather than apply proven social science methodology.

The culture of public relations practitioners is a fundamental issue when considering attitudes towards evaluation and the methodology used. In textbooks and articles about public relations, writers and academics are almost unanimous in their advice that programmes must be researched during preparation and evaluated during and after implementation. However, researchers have found that scientific evaluation methods are used by a minority of practitioners only.

Grunig (1984) has a celebrated *cri de coeur* on the subject:

I have begun to feel more and more like a fundamentalist preacher railing against sin; the difference being that I have railed for evaluation in public relations practice; just as everyone is against sin, so most public relations people I talk to are for evaluation. People keep on sinning, however, and PR people continue not to do evaluation research.

David Dozier's research and writing on evaluation over the past 15 years has encompassed local (San Diego), national (PRSA) and international (IABC) samples (Dozier 1981; 1984a; 1984b; 1985; 1988). One consistent finding of his studies has been that evaluation of programmes increases as the practitioner's management function develops whereas it either plateaus or falls away if he or she has a technician role (writing, media relations, production of communication tools). Dozier says:

Some practitioners do not engage in any programme research, others conduct extensive research. Practitioners vary in the kinds of research methods they use from intuitive, informal 'seat-of-the-pants' research to rigorous scientific studies. Although little longitudinal scholarly research is available, the best evidence is that – over time – more practitioners are doing research more frequently.

Although there have been many small sample studies, the main extensive national and international studies have been conducted by Dozier among PRSA and IABC members (referred to above), by Lindenmann among a selected group of US practitioners (Lindenmann, 1990) and by Watson among IPR members on the UK (Watson, 1993; 1994).

In 1988, Lindenmann undertook a nationwide survey amongst major corporations, large trade and professional associations, large non-profit organisations, the 20 largest public relations consultancies and academics. The key findings were:

- 57.4 per cent believed that outcomes of public relations programmes can be measured; 41.8 per cent disagreed

- 75.9 per cent agreed that research is widely accepted by most public relations professionals as a necessary part of planning programmes
- 94.3 per cent agreed that research is still more talked about than done (54.2 per cent strongly agreed with this)
- research was undertaken for the purposes of planning (74.7 per cent), monitoring or tracking activities (58.1 per cent), evaluating outcomes (55.7 per cent), publicity polls (41.1 per cent) and tracking of crisis issues (36.4 per cent) (multiple responses were sought for this question).

The expenditure on research and evaluation showed wide variations. Many respondents, principally in large corporations, utilities, trade associations and non-profit bodies claimed that it was included in budgets, but they were almost equally balanced by those who claimed not to have budgets for this activity. Lindenmann found that the 89 respondents who did allocate funds for research indicated that the sums were small: 22.5 per cent said it was less than 1 per cent of the total PR budget; 31.5 per cent said it was between 1 and 3 per cent; 21.3 per cent between 4 and 6 per cent and 12.3 per cent said it was 7 per cent or above.

The issues which Lindenmann considered negative were:

the acknowledgment by better than 9 out of every 10 PR professionals that research is still more talked about in PR than is actually being done. Also of concern was the finding that, in the view of 7 out of every 10 respondents, most PR research that is done today is still casual and informal, rather than scientific or precise.

Watson's survey (1993; 1994) among IPR members found that evaluation was viewed very narrowly and that they lacked confidence to promote evaluation methods to employers and clients. Practitioners claimed they lacked time, budget and knowledge of methods to undertake evaluation. They also feared evaluation because it could challenge the logic of their advice and activities. Yet they said public relations suffered as a communication discipline because of the inability to predict and measure results. It was also not easy to isolate its effects from other variables such as advertising and other promotional activity. They believed future public relations performance would be aided by applied measures, probably based on software.

The most widely used techniques relied on some form of output measurement of media coverage. There was a reluctance to pre-test or research when preparing public relations activities. Most often, practitioners relied on experience, knowledge of markets and the media and client/employer imperatives. The picture which emerged was of the practitioner as a 'doer' rather than as an adviser or consultant.

There were some evaluation strategies occasionally undertaken such as 'attending relevant meetings and hearings', 'monitoring of relevant meetings and hearings' and 'interviews of the public to check impact'. The bulk of responses indicated that output measurement was considered more relevant than either gauging impact or the gaining of intelligence to further improve programmes.

The lack of knowledge or, possibly, disinclination to learn about evaluation techniques also showed up as the most commonly offered reason why programmes were not formally evaluated. This was followed by 'costs' and 'lack of time' and 'lack of budget'. When the results for 'cost' and 'lack of budget' were added together as a global financial excuse, they became the dominant reason.

Motives for undertaking evaluation were also sought. By almost double any other category, PR practitioners nominated 'prove value of campaign/budget' followed by 'help campaign targeting and planning' and 'need to judge campaign effects' and a distant fourth, 'help get more resources/higher fees'.

The use of evaluation techniques to improve programmes or to judge the effects of current activities was considered to be half as important as 'proving value' which implied that practitioners were defensive about their activities. They aimed to present data on which they would be judged, rather than acting proactively to improve or fine tune campaigns.

An indicator that attitudes may be slowly changing was the snapshot study undertaken by Blissland (1990) of entries in the Public Relations Society of America's (PRSA) annual Silver Anvil case study competition. Blissland compared entries from 1988/89 with those at the beginning of the decade in 1980/81 to see if there were changes in attitude to evaluation methods over the period. A cosmetic change was that in the early 1980s only one entrant used the term 'evaluation' but 88 per cent used 'results'. By 1988–9, 83 per cent were using 'evaluation' as the term to describe their outcomes section. They also used more evaluation methods, too. This rose from a mean of 3.6 methods/winner to 4.57 methods/winner.

The statistically significant changes were the use of behavioural science measures, and two measures of organisational goal achievement – inferred achievement and substantiated achievement. Blissland concluded that by the end of the decade there was marginally greater reliance on the output measure of media coverage which rose from 70.0 per cent to 79.2 per cent. However, as inferred (that is, unsubstantiated) achievement claims rose from 53.3 per cent to 87.5 per cent, it is hard to agree with Blissland's conclusion that, 'Clearly, progress has been made.'

European research on evaluation which is comparable with the study on UK practitioners' attitudes has been undertaken in Germany. Baerns (1993) studied attitudes among German in-house public relations managers in 1989 and 1992 and found that the majority of respondents (55 per cent) regarded long-term public relations planning as 'indispensable' while 39 per cent referred to the priority of day-to-day events. A small number (7 per cent) regarded planning in public relations as 'impossible'. Baerns then explored the ways in which planning took place and found a considerable gap between the reported attitudes towards planning and the reality of what took place.

Baerns (1993) found that 63 per cent of respondents believed that 'scientific findings' play only a minor part in public relations practice. This corresponds with the 'seat of the pants' attitudes identified in the US and the UK by Dozier (1984a: 1984b; 1985 and 1988) and Watson (1993 and 1994), respectively. Her conclusion was that when evaluation or monitoring took place '[it was] mostly as press analyses'.

Among the US studies are contributions from Chapman (1982), Finn (1982), Judd (1990) and Hiebert and Devine (1985). Chapman found that practitioners in Chicago relied less on the media for evaluation purposes but there was a seat-of-the-pants category called 'general feedback' used by 83 per cent of respondents. Finn

(1982) found that 38 per cent of senior communications executives in major companies were studying impact of programmes.

Judd (1990) found 67 per cent of a sample of practitioners used formal research or evaluation. He also cross-checked his results by analysing whether those who say they evaluate actually do so and is satisfied that there is a clear correlation between saying and doing. His results, however, are at variance with most US and overseas practitioner studies.

Hiebert and Devine (1985), however, found the reverse in an earlier study of government information officers in the US of whom 85 per cent thought evaluation 'was either an important or very important activity', but who conducted almost no research. Research in Australia by MacNamara (1992) also detected a gap between saying and doing, but, more significantly, a reliance on measurement of media indicators and the absence of objective research methods. He found that only three of 50 senior public relations consultancies surveyed could nominate an objective methodology used to evaluate media coverage, despite 70 per cent of respondents claiming that they undertook qualitative judgement of media coverage.

BARRIERS TO EVALUATION

The barriers to the more widespread evaluation of public relations activity are many, as has been demonstrated above. Dozier (1984a) indicated several reasons: previous working experience of practitioners, lack of knowledge of research techniques, the manager/technician dichotomy, the practitioners' participation in decision-making. Lindenmann (1990) believes that practitioners were 'not thoroughly aware' of research techniques. He also found that respondents to his survey complained of a lack of money with 54 per cent spending 3 per cent or less (often much less) on evaluation. Watson (1993; 1994) has indicated that time, knowledge, budgets and costs were the principal difficulties for UK public relations people. Baerns (1993) found similar barriers in Germany with time, lack of personnel, inadequate budgets and doubts about the process all being important. MacNamara's research found practitioners lacked knowledge of methodology, but did not explore other explanations. In the UK, one strong reason advanced by Bell (1992) was money and client reluctance to spend it:

> And the problem I fear lies with money – too many clients are still not prepared to allocate realistic budgets to pay for the process. But I concede that it's a Catch 22; until clients have become accustomed to what's possible on evaluation, they won't begin to demand it. That's the basic problem that our industry as a whole must aim to solve.

These barriers follow a circular argument – most practitioners' education does not include social science research techniques; therefore they do not use them, but concentrate on technician skills, which means they do not rise into the manager roles and participate in decision-making. This would give access to budgets for planning and evaluation, thus creating programmes and campaigns that can enhance their personal standing and meet the objectives of their client or employer.

MODELS OF EVALUATION

When practitioners undertake evaluation, there is a tendency to take a narrow view of the methods used and to concentrate on simplistic methodologies. However, there are at least four models which are familiar to the more widely read practitioners. In this chapter, two more models are proposed, based on recent research. In the United States, one of the best-known models is that of Cutlip et al., (1985) which has been included in many of the seven editions of their standard text, *Effective Public Relations*, widely used in undergraduate education.

Cutlip et al.'s evaluation model is widely taught to students in the US. Known as PII (preparation, implementation and impact), it is a step model which offers levels of evaluation for differing demands. It does not prescribe methodology, but accepts that 'Evaluation means different things to different practitioners'. They make the key point that 'the most common error in programme evaluation is substituting measures from one level for another'. For example, an implementation measure such as the number of press releases disseminated is used to claim impact. This 'substitution game' is frequently seen when reading articles in the trade press or when reviewing award entries.

Each step in the PII model, say Cutlip et al., contributes to increased understanding and adds information for assessing effectiveness. The bottom rung of *preparation evaluation* assesses the information and strategic planning; *implementa-*

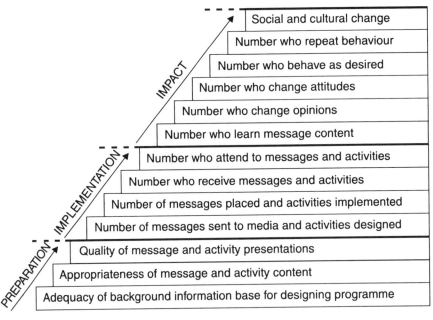

Figure 16.1 Cutlip et al.'s (1985) planning implementation impact model.

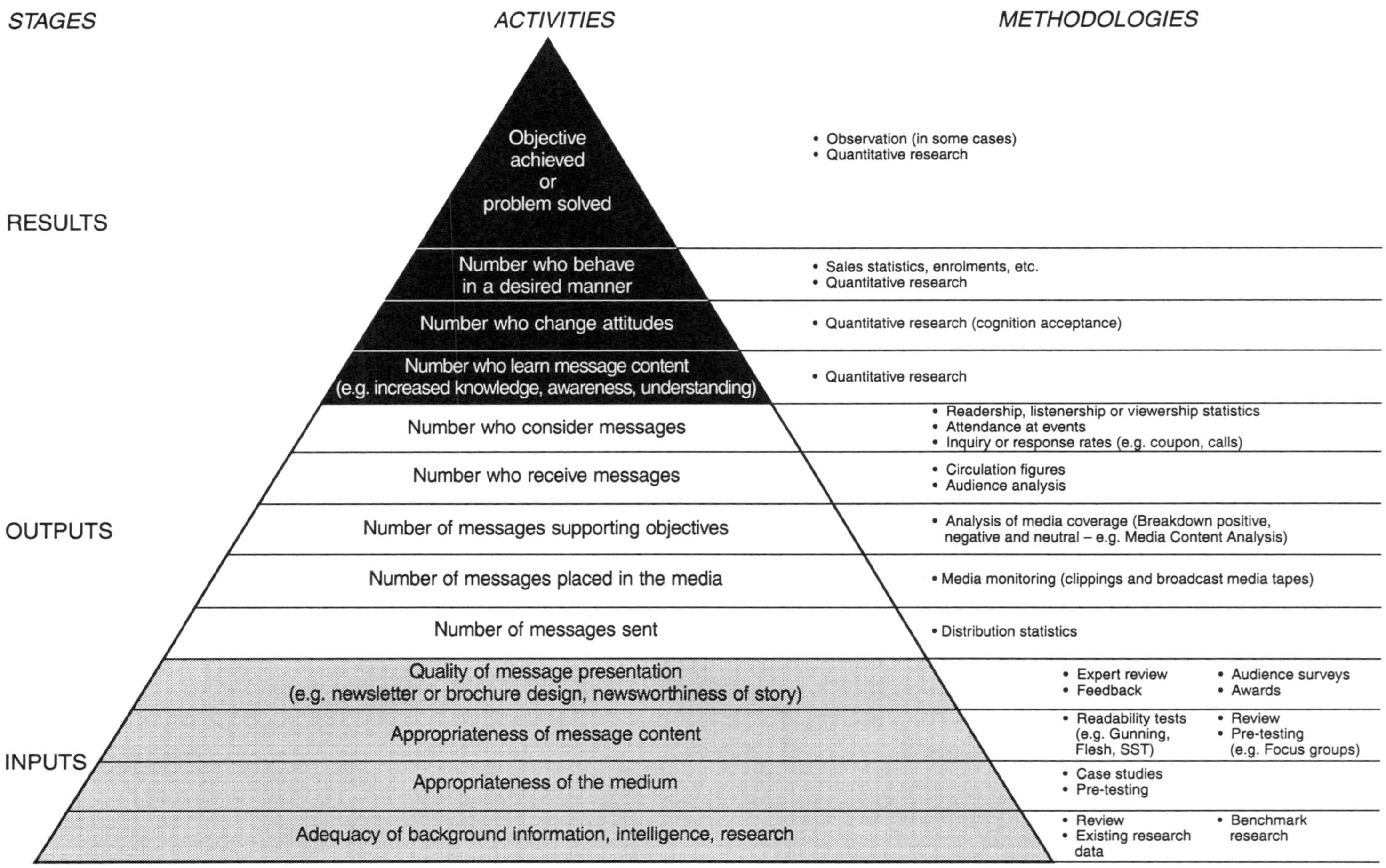

Figure 16.2 MacNamara's macro model.

tion evaluation considers tactics and effort; while *impact evaluation* gives feedback on the outcome.

The PII model is valuable for its separation of output and impact and for counselling against the confusion of these two very different judgements. It acts as a checklist and a reminder when planning evaluation. However, like many academic models, it assumes that programmes and campaigns will be measured by social science methodologies that will be properly funded by clients/employers. As a model it puts short- and long-term public relations activity together without allowing for their often very different methodologies and goals.

The importance of PII, through its widespread teaching, is highlighted by the next two models which are discussed: MacNamara's (1992a) Macro model (see Figure 16.2) and Nobel's (1994) Dimensional Model of Media Evaluation.

MacNamara's model, which he calls 'macro communication', is similar to PII and represents public relations programmes and campaigns in a pyramidal form which rise from a broad base of inputs, through outputs to results with the pinnacle being 'objectives achieved'. The base inputs are analogous to PII and include background information, appropriateness of media and the quality of message. In the middle of the pyramid is a message sequence starting at distribution and ending with the 'number who consider messages'. The results section is concerned with stages of research and ends with the judgement on whether or not objectives have been reached or problems solved.

The model separates outputs and results. For example, a news release can be evaluated as an output in terms of quality, readability and timeliness but not as to whether a communication effect has been achieved. The macro communication model lists evaluation methodologies which can be applied to each of the steps in an attempt at developing a completed measurable process. Macnamara says it 'presents a practical model for planning and managing evaluation of public relations' and recognises communication as a multi-step process.

Noble has proposed a dimensional model of evaluation concentrating on media relations (Noble, 1994), which he argues is an important component in the mainstream of public relations practice.

> It is crucial to understand that media evaluation has a role to play in public relations evaluation generally, but equally important to understand the limitations that media evaluation has in fulfilling this role.
>
> Media evaluation is concerned with outputs – not the results – of a public relations programme so it can be used as feedback to improve the quality of those results and – if we accept a link between outputs and results – can be used to make cautious, limited references about results where direct measurement is impossible or impractical.

Noble's model differs from the progressively staged models of Cutlip et al. and MacNamara in two ways. It has four axes and it concentrates on media relations. The axes are quantitative, qualitative, focus and time.

With four sets of variables, this four-dimensional model theoretically gives 256 separate analyses. Practical usage, says Noble, finds that not all combinations are meaningful. For each evaluation exercise a small number of meaningful analyses are selected by first choosing from time and focus dimensions and then, for each of these dimensions, selecting from the quantitative and qualitative analyses. In this way, he argues, a customised evaluation approach can be developed for the brand, company or situation.

Lindenmann's Public Relations Yardstick model (Lindenmann, 1993) differs from the other models because its staging does not progress from planning to objectives. It encapsulates Lindenmann's experience in advising an international public relations consultancy and aims to make evaluation more accessible. He argues that it is possible to measure public relations effectiveness and that there is growing pressure from clients and employers to be more accountable and adds:

> Measuring public relations effectiveness does not have to be either unbelievably expensive or laboriously time consuming. PR measurement studies *can* be done at relatively modest cost and in a matter of only a few weeks.

The yardstick consists of a two-step process. First, setting public relations objectives and, second, determining at what levels (of expenditure and depth) public relations effectiveness is to be measured. The extent of measurement is gauged by the three levels. Level 1 is the basic level which measures PR 'outputs' – the ways in which the programme or campaign is presented through, typically, media relations. It is measured in terms of media placements and the likelihood of reaching the target groups.

Level 2 is termed by Lindenmann as the intermediate level which uses 'outgrowth' measures. These judge whether or not the target audience actually received the messages and so evaluates retention, comprehension and awareness. Practitioners will use a mix of qualitative and quantitative data collection techniques such as focus groups, interviews with opinion leaders and polling of target groups.

'Outcomes' are measured in level 3. These include opinion, attitudes and behavioural changes. Lindenmann says that this is where the role of pre- and post-testing comes into its own with the use of before and after polling, observational methods, psychographic analysis and other social science techniques.

Lindenmann concludes his article with a statement which emphasises his practical approach in developing the yardstick:

> it is important to recognize that *there is no one simplistic method* for measuring PR effectiveness. Depending upon which level of effectiveness is required, an array of different tools and techniques is needed to properly assess PR impact.

UNIVERSALITY OF THE MODELS

The four models discussed above have varying provenances. Cutlip et al.'s PII is well known, the macro and dimensional models are much less so. Lindenmann's yardstick has been publicised in the US and the UK. As Noble's dimensional model was first proposed in 1994, it is difficult to establish workability.

Research among practitioners (Watson, 1995) has found, however, that existing evaluation models are too complex, do not have an integral relationship with the

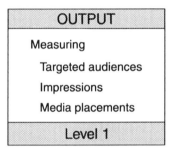

Figure 16.3 Lindenmann's public relations yardstick.

creation of effects and lack a dynamic element of feedback. These models all fit that hypothesis. They are essentially static, step-by-step processes which, to quote Cutlip et al. (1985; 1994), are 'the final stage in the [public relations] process'. Yet public relations activity is not a 'start/stop' communications process where, for instance, a company stops all interactions with its many publics while it measures the results of a media relations programme.

To develop a more complete approach to planning (and subsequent evaluation), the 'effects-based planning' theories put forward by VanLeuven (1988) are valuable. These are closely associated with management-by-objectives techniques used widely in industry and government. Underlying VanLeuven's approach is the premise that a programme's intended communication and behavioural effects serve as the basis from which all other planning decisions can be made. The process involves setting separate objectives and sub-objectives for each public. He argues that the planning becomes more consistent by having to justify programme and creative decisions on the basis of their intended communication and behavioural effects. It also acts as a continuing evaluation process because the search for consistency means that monitoring is continuous and the process of discussion needs evidence on which to reach decisions. Effects-based planning, says VanLeuven, means that programmes can be compared without the need for isolated case studies.

TWO NEW EVALUATION APPROACHES

Taking into account the need for accessible, dynamic models of evaluation, two models have been proposed by Watson (1995): the short-term model for short time-span, largely media relations-based campaigns and activities which seek a rapid result, and the continuing model for long-term activities where the consistent promotion of messages is a central strategy and the outcome may occur after a long period (a year or more) of continuous activity.

These models link with Grunig's four summations of public relations activity (Grunig and Hunt 1984). The short-term model is similar to the press agentry and public information one-way summations as it does not seek a dialogue or feedback. The continuing model fits with the two-way asymmetric and two-way symmetric models which cover a broader band of communication methods and rely on feedback for campaign monitoring and modification of messages. These models can be expressed graphically (see Figures 16.4 and 16.5).

The short-term model has a single track, linear process with an outcome. It does not set out to measure effects and because it does not have a continuing existence, there is no feedback mechanism. Typically, a public relations campaign has a simple awareness objective with one or two strategies. A common example of public relations practice in the public information summation is the distribution of news releases about products or services to the media. This is a technician skill of assembling information and photographs or drawings in the manner most acceptable to the media. Measuring achievement of the objectives can be by media analysis, sales responses or phone research among the target audience.

Figure 16.4 Short-term model of evaluation.

Source: Adaped from Watson (1995).

Using the short-term model, the objectives could be set on the basis of obtaining coverage in specific media (chosen for its relevance to target audiences), the number of sales responses (realistically set according to the appropriateness of the media and the attractions of product or service) or quantitative techniques such as telephone research or mail surveys. The judgement of success or failure is thus made on whether or not the targets are reached. If the client or employer sets unrealistic objectives, this simple model will be as irrelevant as a step-by-step model or informal 'seat of the pants' judgement. The quality of the model's results depends on the professionalism of the practitioner in designing the campaign.

The continuing model has been designed for use in long-term public relations activity. In reviewing the case studies, the need for a dynamic model to cope with ever-changing circumstances was identified. A programme such as that for the new settlement, with multiple long-term corporate and planning objectives, or for the industrial redevelopment, with a medium term objective of planning permission and a long-term objective of improved relations with the local community, needed a flexible evaluation model.

The continuing model offers elements that have not been included in step-by-step models. It has an iterative loop and takes into account the effects that are being created by the programme. An additional element is that it offers an opportunity to make a judgement on 'Staying alive' – the important stage in a long-term, issues-centred programme when keeping the issue in the decision frame is important. The continuing model epitomises VanLeuven's effects-based planning approach. By adopting these principles within the continuing model, a dynamic and continuing evaluation process is created because the search for consistency means that monitoring is continuous.

Consistency is one of the most difficult practical issues facing public relations practitioners. The continuing model, using effects-based planning, offers a more disciplined approach that allows the parameters of the programme to be more closely defined and enables continuous monitoring to replace after-the-event evaluation. The consistency of effects-based planning also aids validity and reliability of data.

The elements of the continuing model are: an initial stage of research; the setting of objectives and choice of programme effects; from these follow the strategy selection and tactical choices. As the programme continues, there are multiple levels

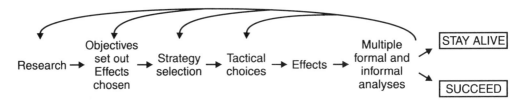

Figure 16.5 Continuing model of evaluation.

Source: Adapted from Watson (1995).

of formal and informal analysis from which judgements can be made on progress in terms of success or 'staying alive'. The judgements are fed back to each of the programme elements. These iterative loops assist the practitioners in validating the initial research and adding new data, adjusting the objectives and strategy, monitoring the progress to create the desired attitudinal or behavioural effects and helping with the adjustment or variation of tactics. This model is a continuing process which can be applied to a specific programme or to the overall public relations activities of an organisation.

SUMMARY AND CONCLUSIONS

The search for consistency is one of the most difficult practical issues faced by the public relations professional. A more disciplined approach will allow the parameters of the programme to be more closely defined and for continuous monitoring to replace a single post-intervention evaluation. It will also bolster the objectivity of the evaluation process.

Unless evaluation becomes less of a mystery and a more accessible process, it would appear that a generation of better-educated practitioners is needed to break the technician mould. Technicians will always be needed to carry out the operational aspects and tactical implementation of programmes and campaigns, especially those which are based on media relations and publications.

If the evaluation models are simpler to operate, then technicians can participate in them. As they are producing many of the materials for the strategy, it makes sense for them to aid the evaluation process. Money and time will always be in short supply, but simpler models to enable evaluation to take place more frequently would prove a more convincing case when budgets are set.

DISCUSSION TOPICS

1 Most public relations practitioners claim to evaluate activities, but almost all judge their own work, without independent criteria. Why do you think this is so?
2 In this chapter, four barriers to evaluation were identified: lack of knowledge, cost of evaluation, lack of time, and lack of budget. How can practitioners overcome these barriers?
3 Typically, between nil and 3 per cent of public relations budgets are spent on evaluation. How much would you allocate to this activity? Consider also the methodology that you would use.
4 Are one model or two models needed for public relations evaluation? Is there an advantage in separating short-term and long-term activities?
5 There is much talk about media analysis as the main methodology for evaluation of public relations programmes. What other strategies would you use and why? Is there too much emphasis on media analysis?
6 In a qualitative, social sciences-based activity such as public relations, are numerical judgements of effectiveness to be regarded as valid and reliable?
7 Can a three-line, single-column 'filler' article have the same importance in a media relations campaign as a page lead article 10 times longer?

8 How would you define 'success' in public relations? Is it the same as 'effectiveness'?

CASE STUDY: 'COMMUNITY RELATIONS AND BAT'

When BAT decided to apply for planning permission for its main UK manufacturing unit in Southampton, the community relations programme was a major strategy in its bid to gain council approval. An innovative approach was chosen using all day 'information fairs' and these were attended by several hundred local residents. Although the company gained the council's approval, the impact of the community relations programme was not immediately apparent. BAT's local public relations advisers undertook a postal survey of 1,000 local households to evaluate the impact.

The results were very supportive, but with some conclusions that favoured a simpler approach in future. The community relations programme has been modified and subsequently two more planning applications have been approved. Public interest and involvement in discussions over the company's plans has remained high and constructive.

REFERENCES

Baerns, B. (1993) 'Understanding and development of public relations in Germany, East and West', *Proceedings of the 2nd European Seminar for Teachers, Practitioners and Researchers*. Prague, pp. 63–74.

Bell, Q. (1992) 'Evaluating PR', *IPR Handbook*, London: Kogan Page, pp. 21–22.

Blissland, J. (1990) 'Accountability gap: evaluation practices show improvement', *Public Relations Review*, 16(2), Summer: 25–32.

Chapman, R. (1982) 'Measurement: it is alive and well in Chicago', *Public Relations Journal*, 38, May: 28–9.

Cline, C. (1984) *Evaluation and Measurement in Public Relations and Organizational Communications: A Literature Review*, San Francisco, CA: IABC Foundation.

Cutlip, S.M., Center, A.H. and Broom, G.M. (1985 and 1994) *Effective Public Relations*, 6th and 7th edns., Englewood Cliffs, NJ: Prentice-Hall.

Dozier, D.M. (1981) 'The diffusion of evaluation methods among public relations practitioners'. Paper presented to the Association for Educators in Journalism Conference, East Lancing, MI, August.

Dozier, D.M. (1984a) 'The evolution of evaluation methods among public relations practitioners', paper presented to the Educators Academy, International Association of Business Communicators, Montreal, June 1984.

Dozier, D.M. (1984b) 'Program evaluation and roles of practitioners', *Public Relations Review*, 10(2): 13–21.

Dozier, D.M. (1985) 'Planning and evaluation in PR practice', *Public Relations Review*, 11, Summer: 17–24.

Dozier, D.M. (1988) 'Organic structure and managerial environment sensitivity as predictors of practitioner membership of the dominant coalition', paper presented to the Public Relations Division, Association for Educators in Journalism and Mass Communications Conference, Portland, Oregon, July 1988.

Finn, P. (1982) 'Demystifying public relations', *Public Relations Review*, 38, May: 18–20.

Grunig, J.E. (1984) 'Organisations, environments and models of public relations', *Public Relations Research and Education*, 1: 6–29.

Grunig, J.E. and Hunt, T. (1984) *Managing Public Relations,* New York: Holt, Rinehart and Winston, p. 179.

Hiebert, R.E. and Devine, C.M. (1985) 'Government's research and evaluation gap', *Public Relations Review,* 11, Fall: 47–57.

Judd, L.R. (1990) 'Importance and use of formal research and evaluation', *Public Relations Review,* XVI(4), Winter: 17–28.

Jefkins, F.R. (1987) *Public Relations For Your Business,* London: Mercury, p. 43.

Lindenmann, W.K. (1990) 'Research, evaluation and measurement: a national perspective', *Public Relations Review,* XVI(2), Summer, pp. 3–16.

Lindenmann, W.K. (1993) 'An "effectiveness yardstick" to measure public relations success', *Public Relations Quarterly,* Spring, pp. 7–9.

MacNamara, J. (1992a) 'Evaluation of public relations: the Achilles' heel of the PR profession', *International Public Relations Review,* 15(2): 19.

MacNamara, J. (1922b) 'Macro communication: a model for integrated, strategic marketing and corporate communication', a paper presented to Marcom Asia '92, Singapore, 22 May.

McKeone, D. (1993) 'Paying a price for false comparisons', *PR Week* 24 July: 10.

Noble, P. (1994) 'A proper role for media evaluation', paper presented to the International Public Relations Research Symposium, Bled, Slovenia, July 1994.

Pavlik, J.V. (1987) *Public Relations: What Research Tells Us,* Newbury Park, CA: Sage, p. 66.

Valleaven, J.K et al. (1988) 'Effects-based planning for public relations campaigns', paper presented to PR Division, Association for Education in Journalism and Mass Communications, Portland, Oregon, July.

Watson, T. (1993) 'Output measures rule in evaluation debate', *IPR Journal,* 12(15): 13–14.

Watson, T. (1994) 'Public relations evaluation: nationwide survey of practice in the United Kingdom', paper presented to the International Public Relations Research Symposium, Bled, Slovenia, July.

Watson, T. (1995) 'Evaluating public relation: models of measurement for public relations practice', paper presented to the International Public Relations Research Symposium, Bled, Slovenia, July.

Weiss, C.H. (1977) *Evaluation Research – Methods of Assessing Program Effectiveness,* Englewood Cliffs, NJ: Prentice-Hall.

White, J. (1990) 'Evaluation in public relations practice', unpublished paper, Cranfield Institute of Management/PRCA.

White, J. (1991) *How To Understand And Manage Public Relations,* London: Business Books p. 141.

White, J. and Blamphin, J. (1994) *Priorities for Research into Public Relations Practice in the United Kingdom,* London: City University Business School/Rapier Marketing.

Wilcox, D.L, Ault, P.H. and Agee, W.K. (1992) *Public Relations: Strategies and Tactics,* 3rd edn, New York: Harper-Collins, pp. 210–28.

ROLE AND FUNCTION: PRINCIPLES AND PRACTICE REVISITED

Philip J. Kitchen

CHAPTER AIMS

- to provide a summary of and conclusion to the text

ILLUSTRATION: 'CULTIVATING PR'S NEXT GENERATION'

As MP's savour the possibility of a 30 per cent pay rise, the pundits rehearse the usual arguments for and against. As ever, those in favour will stress the need to pay a 'market rate' to attract sufficiently talented candidates.

In this respect, politics has something in common with PR. But while Westminster lures budding politicians away from a host of better-paid industries, PR firms are, for the most part, scrabbling to retain talent from other parts of the same business.

Post-recession, there is a distinct shortage of experienced PR people. The pressure to compete with other consultancies for tantalising slabs of new business is therefore driving pay deals to exorbitant heights. It is difficult to escape the conclusion that the PR industry is in the grip of a damaging round of salary inflation which will put further pressure on profit margins at a time when wary clients are screwing them down.

Yet, money is not always the answer. Experience shows that a consultancy's ability to retain staff in the face of determined poaching frequently depends on other factors such as the reputation and culture of the company, future prospects, and the potential for owning a stake in the business. The consultancies with the best record of retaining talent are also those who invest in their staff – not with exaggerated basic pay, but with performance bonuses, share options and training.

Big salaries may form a short-term recruitment problem but it is likely to store up trouble for the future. It won't improve the quality of the candidates, or increase the overall talent pool available. Nor will it necessarily secure loyalty. Paying over the odds for new staff may just encourage your existing staff to seek the same, either with you, or elsewhere.

It may also lead to something even more damaging for the fragile reputation of PR – job title inflation. As during the 1980s boom, relatively inexperienced executives find themselves catapulted into senior positions before they are ready. Some will rise to the challenge, but many will not, and overall standards will fall accordingly.

There is no easy answer. The long-term solution is training and recruitment at the junior end of the business. In other words, grow your own talent. In the short-term, the challenge for agencies will be to retain their existing talent in the face of some tempting offers, without breaking the bank on salaries. And to take on new business without overstretching their resources. For some this will be a difficult balancing act!

(*Source*: *PR Week*, 21 June 1996:9, used with permission.)

INTRODUCTION

A start to this final chapter is deliberately focused on a major issue surrounding the public relations industry. Currently, the industry is facing a problem of where to recruit new progressive managerially adept future PR practitioners. Shortage, as stated in the article, implies a need to pay higher salaries to existing staff, who, as with all young people, seek opportunities to climb hierarchical ladders and so further career progression. Yet, with the many institutions offering public relations courses or modules or its close relations, public affairs or corporate communications, this must be music to their ears. For many graduates the future is not very bright, as the prospect is one of potential short-term unemployment, further studies, or perhaps a job not necessarily related to the first degree subject. For qualified, presumed able, graduates in PR, job opportunities seem to be expanding at this time.

We started this textbook by stating that PR was undergoing rapid and diverse change with regard to what the subject constituted, how it works, and its relevance and meaning to modern business organisations. It is now evident that public relations is an exciting contemporary managerial discipline with many skills, techniques, and strategies to offer to business organisations in both a corporate and marketing communications domain. The following points, derived from previous chapters, are pertinent.

PUBLIC RELATIONS AND THE MANAGERIAL COALITION

Moss and Warnaby (Chapter 2) suggested powerfully that PR practitioners need to learn to operate in the expert prescriber or problem-solving facilitation role as opposed to communications technicians. They concluded that there was little evidence of in-company PR practitioners helping to develop managerial policy; rather they seemed to be more focused on policies which were already developed. Clearly, PR managers and the PR industry as a whole need to find ways in which to gain access to the dominant management coalitions in major organisations. Such access will not just be on the basis of managerial skill, talent and ability, but also on the perceived ability of PR to contribute effectively to business growth, identity, and image. In other words, the door for PR people seems to be just as 'open' as it is for accountants, marketeers and so forth. The view of the Editor is that opportunities for a 'seat at the table' in terms of board level access appear to be multiplying at this time (see regular issues of *PR Week* for new appointments), ostensibly providing such access.

THE EVOLUTION OF PR – A COMING OF AGE

Supporting the development of public relations, Chapter 3 indicated that PR has a well-developed theoretical framework which is, however, not firmly grounded in empirical evidence. Certainly in terms of subject matter, academic course developments (in the UK), environmental circumstances, and developments of in-house PR departments, and the burgeoning growth of the PR industry, public relations does appear to 'coming of age'. PR is soundly defined, and has numerous elements, parts or activities, each of which are crucial to modern business development, growth, and even survivability. Marketing PR, again in the Editor's view, is far from being yet another example of 'marketing imperialism' but is reflective of the depth, variety and applicability of PR tools and techniques. Marketing PR by no means describes the full range of PR relevance to businesses toward the next millennium. Public relations, having undergone a century of development, is of crucial significance and relevance to businesses today.

THE STRATEGIC MANAGEMENT OF PUBLIC RELATIONS

Moss and Warnaby further develop their argument of public relations relevance in Chapter 4. Strategy and strategy development indicate the need for PR to take on board new ideas, techniques and principles, in order to ensure further progression of the subject. Admittedly, strategy can be seen as expressing a linear planning view of the strategic management process. Such a view is shortsighted and myopic, as more recent conceptualisations of strategy – that is adaptive, interpretive and systemic models – appear to be focused in a more dynamic flexible mode of how businesses approach strategy development. Such a mode points to a role which PR could play, given their unique pivotal role in relation to impactual publics. At its most basic level, strategy could be regarded as 'the art of the general' in other words steering the organisation amidst increasingly competitive markets, with ever-vigilant (sometimes erstwhile) publics.

INTERNAL COMMUNICATIONS STRATEGY

Following on from Chapters 2 to 4, Chapters 5 to 7 then explore the internal and external organisational context and activities. Puchan et al. picks up the internal organisational context in Chapter 5. Given organisations that are governed by unifying and centrifugal forces creating and sustaining complex organisational environments there is a firm need to develop soundly-based internal communications strategies, led by PR. Such strategies are structured around three communication dimensions: flexibility, multi-dimensionality, and co-ordination. In this context, public relations can be seen as the co-ordinator of multi-departmental effort to create and sustain relationships with a diversity of publics who could impact on organisational success or contribute to impoverishing organisational image. Supportive of the previous chapter, Puchan et al. argue for the need for PR to adopt a strategic approach based upon a clear informational base.

AN EXTERNAL COMMUNICATIONS CONTEXT FOR PUBLIC RELATIONS

Again, related to the strategy dimension, public relations concerns harmonising organisational interests with those of external publics, who could impact on organisational success or contribute to failure. Richard Varey (Chapter 6) indicates the need to assemble an inclusive database of its stakeholders and key publics, and recognises that the importance of each of these groups may change, and may need to be addressed differently, as the key focus of public relations effort. Such 'focus' reflects the dynamics of the organisational environment. Such understanding or 'reading' of the contextual environment is decisive for public relations planning and objective setting. Public(s) demand for satisfaction would appear to fulfil the performance standards for public relations work.

EXTERNAL COMMUNICATIONS ACTIVITIES

As witnessed in the BNFL Sellafield visitors centre case there are many and diverse external public relations activities (see Chapter 7). Richard Varey argues strongly that these activities must again be co-ordinated and evaluated (see Chapter 7) to meet organisational and key publics needs – planning is of course part of the basic managerial paradigm for PR managers. Public relations management suggests the need to confront problems or issues openly and honestly and then acting to develop solutions, thus revealing an active social conscience or displaying social responsibility (see Chapter 8). While external public relations activities are many and varied, as they are of an internal nature, they must be unified into a single function when seen from a PR managerial perspective.

BEHAVIOUR, REPUTATION AND THE PRELUDE OF SOCIAL RESPONSIBILITY

Geraldine Hanrahan (Chapter 8) draws upon numerous examples (e.g. Yorkshire Electricity, Boots the Chemist, W.H. Smith, Tesco, Barclays Bank, Severn Trent Water, IBM, Dixons, B&Q and Proctor & Gamble) to illustrate how well-defined community involvement programmes can serve to illustrate social responsibility in action (i.e. behaviour) and thus underpin corporate reputation. The role of business extends well beyond sales, profits, market share, and return on investment toward becoming social actors in the environments in which they operate. In order to balance such a wide role, business firms need to balance a number of mutual reinforcing interests and thus arrange social responsibility programmes with corporate objectives. In today's environmentally conscious and competitively straitened world, it is argued that social responsibility plays a significant and substantive strategic role. Moving beyond the glitz of promotional outlay, social responsibility suggests a scenario where initiatives really work in supporting and underpinning corporate behaviour not just because 'good business is good business' but because real altruism and open ethical activity is an essential characteristic of modern organisations in the wealth creating sector.

FINANCIAL AND INVESTOR PUBLIC RELATIONS

In an excellent turn of phrase, Oxley quoted by Geraldine Hanrahan (Chapter 9) states that 'new publics emerge and combine with existing ones the way atoms combine to form molecules'. This is very much the case in the financial sector where deregulation, globalisation, technology and service innovation have resulted in mass re-alignments of corporate financial holdings and dealings. For the financial public relations specialist or manager there is a need to promote a consistent image or reputation. Financial sector intensity of competition has created the need for market organisers to distinguish, observe and commune specifically with highly segmented target publics or audiences. Four strategies for such communication were outlined by Hanrahan: creative, expansive, adaptive, and defensive. These are not intended to be all-inclusive but so suggest alternative mechanisms by which effective messages can be deployed. A major problem in this area is the need for a more substantive body of behavioural and audience research; the difficulty of course is accessibility and confidentiality in this highly specialised area.

GOVERNMENT AND LOBBYING ACTIVITIES

A further highly specialised subdivision of public relations is addressed by Kevin Moloney in Chapter 10 defined as 'monitoring public policy-making for a group interest, building a case in favour of that interest, and putting it privately with varying degrees of pressure to public decision makers for their acceptance and support through favourable political intervention'. That such intervention can be successful is seen in the recent recommendation that Japan lower the very high rates of tax on imported spirits – a case in point which has recognisable benefits for manufacturers in the UK spirits industry seeking to build market share in what will soon be a 'level playing field'. That such lobbying is or can be effective is related clearly to the pluralistic nature of Western-style liberal democracies. That lobbying can be effective is answered positively and affirmatively.

SUPPORTING THE GENERIC IMAGE – CORPORATE ADVERTISING

Ralph Tench (Chapter 11) addressed the issue of corporate advertising as a major plank in developing and sustaining a generic or core image or reputation. First pointing to the various types of corporate advertising that can be differentiated (public relations, issue, and image) Tench argues that such advertising can be used for a variety of purposes and through diverse media. Corporate advertising appears to 'work' in much the same way(s) as product/brand advertising – seeking to affect opinions, cognitions and emotions. Notably, the future of this public relations activity is being affected by the rapidly advancing communications technologies, globalisation of markets and environmentalism. Further, the role of politics and politicians will also impact on future developments in this area.

ISSUE AND CRISIS MANAGEMENT – FAIL-SAFE PROCEDURES

Two practitioners in the issue and crisis management domain (Regester and Larkin) provide an overview of potential issues and crises which could impinge on sale, profits, ROI, and market share. The corporate image or reputation (see Chapter 12) can be damaged markedly by poor, or unrefined, planning procedures and scenarios. Far from being an 'academic' exercise, such plans and procedures, once in place, are closely aligned to overall corporate strategy and need to be 'skill-trained' at regular and timely intervals. Regester and Larkin suggest the need for a 'managerial response mode' that is comprehensible in which a designated span of control is clearly communicated and understood.

PUBLIC RELATIONS AND MARKETING – INTERACTION

Without doubt, the two primary vehicles for organisational communication are public relations and marketing. Moreover, these two disciplines are interactive and mutually reinforcing (Chapter 13). Creating functional specialisms which are then hierarchically positioned in a neat organisational chart does little to portray the complex and needful interactions required. Drawing upon recent research evidence by Kitchen and Moss (1995), it is argued that currently marketing would appear to be the pre-eminent communications weapon. However, it is also argued that the two functions need to work increasingly together in order to produce the messages that will contribute to organisational and product/brand success.

One aspect of this point is that of the proclaimed emergence of MPR as taken up in Chapter 14 by Kitchen and Papasolomou.

MARKETING PUBLIC RELATIONS (MPR) – EMERGENCE

MPR is a relatively new term which is now used in marketing and PR lexicons. However, its meaning and 'ownership' has been hotly debated since the mid-1980s. Questions such as: Where does MPR belong – to marketing or PR? seem to be ongoing. However, while academics from both sides of the divide continue the debate, there is little doubt that companies are moving ahead to utilise the skills, techniques and benefits of MPR in a variety of seemingly contradictory situations and in many different marketing scenarios. A point to note is that further empirical research is needed to justify whether a new promotional discipline is emergent – the evidence provided indicates MPR may be being rapidly overtaken by integrated marketing communications (IMC).

A PROPOSAL FOR FUTURE RESEARCH

Chapter 15 concerns itself with various techniques or methodologies that could be applied in relation to empirical research for there are (still) many research issues to be tackled. Kitchen proposed that whichever research method is applied the researcher should keep in mind the 'scientific approach' which is predicated on systematic structured enquiry to provide solutions to research problems, or, explore particular issues. The approach Kitchen recommends, that of induction, is based upon the pre-paradigm nature of the PR field indicative of growth in an academic discipline that is still emergent and in which many issues have yet to be tackled.

EVALUATING THE PR PROCESS AND PR PROGRAMMES

The penultimate Chapter 16 draws upon original practitioner research by Tom Watson in relation to just how success rates for the PR process and PR programmes can be evaluated, a topic likely to prove of marketable interest to other practitioners. The main issue is that of providing consistent measurability and greater objectivity. Underpinning such factors is the need for well-qualified, better educated practitioners, an issue already being addressed by education providers. Watson reviews several models of the evaluation process before proposing two new models to move the discipline in its practical aspects forward.

SUMMARY AND CONCLUSIONS

This textbook has sought to tackle numerous issues and questions relating to public relations as we approach the twenty-first century. It has tried to deliver the knowledge base, skills, and to develop ability in the public relations discipline. This has been done by means of the information provided in the text, the readings, end-of-chapter questions for discussion and case studies. However, the field of PR is expanding almost exponentially. Students and practitioners should see this text as a *starting point* for their continued study of the discipline. Remember, in Chapter 1, readers were urged to become contemporary, dynamic and knowledgeable about the domain of public relations. The latest information has been derived from the academic and practitioner literature to underpin development of this text.

It is hoped that studying the book has been enjoyable, interesting, and that it will serve to provoke further learning. As you now come to the end of the first phase of a learning/experience curve in public relations, it is hoped that your further studies and/or PR practices will be reflected in future editions of this text.

REFERENCES

PR Week, 21 June 1996:9, used with permission.

BIBLIOGRAPHY

Adams, H.C. (1902) 'What is publicity?', *North American Review*, 175 (57), December.

Alderman, G. (1984) *Pressure Groups and Government in Great Britain*, London: Longman.

Aldrich, H. and Herker, D. (1977) 'Boundary spanning roles and organisational structures', *Academy of Management Review*, 2.

Allaire, Y. and Firsirotu, M. (1984) 'Theories of organizational culture', *Organization Studies*, 5 (3).

Allen, F. and Kraft, C. (1982) *The Organizational Unconscious: How to Create the Corporate Culture You Want and Need*, Englewood Cliffs, NJ: Prentice-Hall.

Andrews, K.R. (1987) *The Concept of Corporate Strategy*, Burr Ridge, Ill.: Richard D. Irwin.

Andrews, P.N. (1985) 'The sticky wicket of evaluating public affairs: thoughts about a framework', *Public Affairs Review*, 6.

Ansoff, H.I. (1987) *Corporate Strategy – rev'd edn*, Harmondsworth: Penguin.

Ansoff, H.I. (1992) 'Critique of Henry Mintzberg's *The Design School*: reconsidering the basic premises of strategic management', *Strategic Management Journal*, 12.

Argyyris, C. (1985) *Strategy Change and Defensive Routines*, Marshfield, MA: Pitman Publishing.

Axelrod, R. (1976) *Structure of Decision: The Cognitive Maps of Political Elites*, Princeton: Princeton University Press.

Baerns B. (1993) 'Understanding and development of public relations in Germany, East and West', *Proceedings of the 2nd European Seminar for Teachers, Practitioners and Researchers*. Prague.

Beardsley, M.C. (1956) *Practical Logic*, Englewood Cliffs, NJ: Prentice-Hall.

Bell, Q. (1992) 'Evaluating PR', *IPR Handbook*, London: Kogan Page.

Bell, S.H. and Bell, E.C. (1976) Public relations: functional or functionary?', *Public Relations Review*, 2.

Bem, D.J. (1972) 'Self perception theory', in L. Berkowitz (ed.) *Advances in Experimental Social Psychology*, Vol 6, New York: Academic Press.

Bennett, R.C. and Cooper, R.G. (1981) 'The misuse of marketing: An American tragedy', *Business Horizons*.

Bernays, E.L. (1931) 'A public relations counsel states his views', *Advertising and Selling*, January: 31.

Bernays, E.L. (1952) *Public Relations*, Norman, OK: University of Oklahoma Press.

Black, G. (1952) *Planned Industrial Publicity*, Chicago: Putnam.

Black, S. (1993) *The Essentials of Public Relations*, London: Kogan Page.

Black, S. (1995) *The Practice of Public Relations*, 4th edn, Butterworth-Heinemann.

Blau, P.M. and Schoenherr, R.A. (1971) *The Structure of Organisations*, New York: Basic Books.

Blissland, J. (1990) 'Accountability gap: evaluation practices show improvement', *Public Relations Review*, 16 (2), Summer: 25–32.

Boskin, A.J. and Aronoff, T.S. (1988) *Public Relations: The Profession and the Practice*, Dubuque: William Brown.

Boyd, H.W., Westfall, R. and Stasch, S.F. (1985) *Marketing Research: Text and Cases*, 6th edn, Homewood, IL: Irwin.

Briggs, W. and Tucson, M. (1993) *PR vs. Marketing, Communication World*, San Francisco: IABC.

Bromley, D.B. (1993) *Reputation, Image and Impression Management*, London: Wiley.

Broom, G.M. and Smith G.D. (1979) 'Testing the practitioner's impact on clients', *Public Relations Review*, 5 (3).

Broom, G.M. (1982) 'A comparison of sex roles in public relations', *Public Relations Review*, 8 (3).

Broom, G.M. (1986) 'Public relations roles and systems theory: functional and historicist causal models', Paper presented at the meeting of the Public Relations Interest group, International Communications Association, Chicago.

Broom, G.M. and Dozier, D.M. (1990) *Using Research in Public Relations: Applications in Programme Management*, NJ. Prentice-Hall,:

Brownlie, D. (1991) 'Environmental scanning', in M.J. Baker (ed.) *The Marketing Book* (2nd edn), London: Butterworth-Heinemann.

Brownlie, D. (1994) 'Environmental scanning', in M.J. Baker (ed.) *The Marketing Book* (3rd edn), London: Butterworth-Heinemann.

Bryman, A. (ed.) (1994) *Doing Research in Organizations*, London: Routledge.

Burdus, A. (1980) 'Communicating confidence: will the big corporation please speak up?, *Advertising*, Summer 1980; reprinted in *Corporate Advertising: A Selection of Articles and a Bibliography of Recent Developments*, London: Institute of Practitioners in Advertising.

Business Week (1979a) 'The corporate image: PR to the rescue', Special Report, 22 January: 47–61.

Business Week (1979b) 'Perils of not minding the store', Editorial, 15 January: 56.

Business Week (1987), 'Nothing sells like sports', 30 August.

Bynner, J. and Stribley, K.M. (1978) *Social Research: Principles and Procedures*, London: Longman in Association with the Open University Press.

Cadbury, Sir A. (1995) Letter to the author, 17 October.

Carroll, A.B. (1993) *Business and Society: Ethics and Stakeholder Management*, South-Western Publishing.

Cates, P. (1988) 'Realities of lobbying and government affairs', in R. Heath et al. *Strategic Issues Management*, San Francisco, Cal: Jossey Bass.

Chaffee, E.E. (1985) 'Three models of strategy', *Academy of Management Review*, 19 (1).

Chandler, A.D. (1962) *Strategy and Structure: Chapters in the History of American Industrial Enterprise*, Cambridge, MA: The MIT Press.

Chapman, R. (1982) 'Measurement – it is alive and well in Chicago', *Public Relations Journal*, 38, May: 28-9.

Chase, H. (1977) 'Public management: the new science', *Public Relations Journal*, 33 (10), October.

Chase, W.H. (1975) 'How companies are using corporate advertising', *Public Relations Journal*, 31 (11).

Child, J. and Mansfield, R. (1972) 'Technology, size and organisation structure', *Sociology*, 6.

Christensen, C.R., Andrews, K.R., Bower, J.L., Hamermesh, R.G. and Porter, M.E. (1982) *Business Policy: Text and Cases*, Burr Ridge, Ill.: Richard D. Irwin.

Churchill, G.A. (1987) *Marketing Research; Methodological Foundations*, Chicago: Dryden Press.

Churchill, G.A. (1991) *Marketing Research: Methodological Foundations*, 5th edn, Chicago: The Dryden Press.

Clarke, G. (1996) 'Investment companies: the content of the chairman's letter', in G. Comstock, S. Chaffee, N. Katzman, M. McCombs and D. Roberts (1978) *Television and Human Behaviour*, Columbia University Press.

Clancy-Kelly, S. (1995) 'Hooked into a whole new world', *People Management,* 31 (5).

Clegg, S. (1990) *Modern Organisation – Organisation Studies in the Post Modern World,* London: Sage.

Cline, C. (1984) *Evaluation and Measurement in Public Relations and Organizational Communications: A Literature Review,* San Francisco, CA: IABC Foundation.

Clutterbuck, D., Dearlove, D. and Snow, D. (1992) *Actions Speak Louder,* London: Kogan Page.

Cohen, W. (1991) *The Practice of Marketing Management,* 2nd edn, New York: Collier Macmillan.

Cohen, W.A. (1991) *The Practice of Marketing Management,* New York: Maxwell Macmillan.

Collins, M. (1993) 'The challenge of corporate social responsibility', *The Business Studies Magazine,* 6 (2).

Coombs, C.H., Raiffa, H. and Thrall, R.M. (1954) 'Some views on mathematical models and measurement theory', in R.N. Thrall, C.G. Voombs and R.L. Davis (eds) *Decisions Processes,* New York: John Wiley.

Coulson-Thomas, C.J. (1990) *Marketing Communications,* London: Heinemann.

Crable, R. and Vibbert, S. (1986) *Public Relations as Communication Management,* Edina: Bellwether.

Cushman, D.P., King, S.S. and Smith, T. (1988) 'The rules perspective on organisational communication theory', in G.M. Goldhaber and C.A. Barnett (eds) *Handbook of Organisational Communication,* Norwood: Ablex.

Crane, D. (1972) *Invisible Colleges and Social Circles: A Sociological Interpretation of Scientific Growth,* Chicago: University of Chicago Press.

Cutlip, S.M. (1957) *A Public Relations Biography,* Madison: University of Wisconsin.

Cutlip, S., Center, A.H. and Broom, G.M. (1985) *Effective Public Relations,* London: Prentice-Hall.

Cutlip, S., Center, A.H. and Broom, G.M. (1993) *Effective Public Relations,* 6th edn, Englewood Cliffs, NJ: Prentice-Hall.

Cutlip, S., Center, A.H. and Broom, G.M. (1994) *Effective Public Relations* (7th edn), Englewood Cliffs, NJ: Prentice-Hall.

Cutlip, S.C., Center, A.H. and Broom, G.M. (1985 and 1994) *Effective Public Relations,* 6th and 7th edns., Englewood Cliffs, NJ: Prentice-Hall.

Cyert, R.M. and March, J.G. (1963) *A Behavioural Theory of the Firm,* Englewood Cliffs, NJ: Prentice-Hall.

Dahl, R. (1961) *Who Governs?,* New Haven, Conn.: Yale University Press.

Daily Mail (1989) 23 February.

Dark, S., Hall, A. and Farish, S. (1993) 'Darkness before the dawn', *PR Week*: UK Top 150 PR consultancies, Haymarket Publications, 29 April.

Davis, K. (1967) 'Understanding the social responsibility puzzle', *Business Horizons,* 10, Winter.

Davis K. and Blomstrom, R. (1966) *Business and its Environment,* New York: McGraw-Hill.

Dawson, Sandra (1992) *Analysing Organisations,* 2nd edn, Basingstoke and London: Macmillan.

Deal, T. and Kennedy, A. (1982/1988) *Corporate Cultures: The Rites and Rituals of Corporate Life,* Harmondsworth: Penguin; first published in Reading, MA: Addison-Wesley, 1982.

Denbow, C.H. and Culbertson, H.M. (1985) 'Linkage beliefs and diagnosing an image', *Public Relations Review,* 11 (1).

Dewey, J. (1910) *How We Think,* Boston: D.C. Heath, p. 79.

Dilenschneider, R. (1989) 'PR on the offensive: Bigger part of marketing mix', *Advertising Age,* 60, 13 March.

Dixon, P. (1993) *Making a Difference: Women and Men in the Workplace,* London: Heinemann.

Donohue, D.M., Olien, C.N. and Tichoner, P.J. (1985) 'Leader and editor views of role of press in community development', *Journalism Quarterly,* 62 (3).

Dowling, G.R. (1986) *Corporate Reputations: Strategies for Developing the Corporate Brand*, London: Kogan Page.

Dozier, D.M. (1981) 'The diffusion of evaluation methods among public relations practitioners. Paper presented to the association for educators in Journalism Conference, East Lancing MI, August.

Dozier, D.M. (1984a) 'The evolution of evaluation methods among public relations practitioners', paper presented to the Educators Academy, International Association of Business Communicators, Montreal, June 1984.

Dozier, D.M. (1984b) 'Program evaluation and roles of practitioners', *Public Relations Review*, 10 (2).

Dozier, D.M. (1988) 'Organic structure and managerial environment sensitivity as predictors of practitioner membership of the dominant coalition; paper presented to the Public Relations Division, Association for Educators in Journalism and Mass Communications Conference, Portland, Oregon, July 1988.

Dozier, D.M. (1990) 'The innovation of research in public relations practice: review of a programme of studies', in L.A. Grunig and J.E. Grunig (eds) *Public Relations Research Annual, Vol. 2*, Hillsdale, NJ: Lawrence Erlbaum.

Drake, P., Penny, J. and Sammuels, J. (1981) *Britain at its Best: Researching the Effectiveness of a Major Corporate Image Advertising Campaign*, Amsterdam: ESOMAR Congress.

Drobis, D.R. (1991) 'Taking corporate strategy seriously', *Public Relations Journal*, 47 (8).

Drucker, P.F. (1980) *Managing in Turbulent Times*, New York: Harper and Row.

Dubs, A. (1989) *An Insider's Guide to the Parliamentary Process*, London: Pluto Press.

Duncan, C. (1995) Speech given at the Launch of the BNFL Corporate Communications Unit, University of Salford, 27 November.

Duncan, R.B. (1972) 'Characteristics of organisational environment and perceived environmental uncertainty', *Administrative Science Quarterly*.

Duncan, T. (1985), *A Study of How Manufacturers and Service Companies Perceive and Use MPR*, Muncie, Ind.: Ball State University.

Economist, The (1989) 'Corporate eyes, ears and mouth', 18 March.

Ehling, W. (1990) 'How to get maximum benefit from public relations by positioning it properly in the organisation', *PR Reports and Tactics* 10, 10 August.

Ehling, W., White, J. and Frunig, J.E. (1992) 'Public relations and marketing practice', in J.E. Grunig (ed.) *Excellence in Public Relations and Communications Management*, Hillsdale, NJ: Lawrence Erlbaum.

Emory, C.W. and Cooper, D.R. (1991) *Business Research Methods*, Homewood and Boston: Irwin.

Eisenhardt, K.M. and Zbaracki, M.J. (1992) 'Strategic decision-making', *Strategic Management Journal*.

Embley, L.L. (1983) *Doing Well While Doing Good*, NJ: Prentice-Hall.

Evans, J.R. and Berman, B. (1990) *Marketing* 4th edn, Collier Macmillan.

Farish, S. (1994) 'DTI report endorses the use of PR', *PR Week*, 9 December.

Festinger, L. (1957) 'A theory of cognitive dissonance' 'Stanford SU Press.

Fill, C. (1995) *Marketing Communications: Frameworks Theories and Applications*, Hemel Hempstead: Prentice-Hall.

Fineman, S. and Gabriel, Y. (1996) *Experiencing Organizations*, London: Sage.

Finer, S.E. (1958, 1966) *Anonymous Empire: A Study of the Lobby in Great Britain*, London: Pall Mall.

Finn, P. (1982) 'Demystifying public relations', *Public Relations Review*, 38, May.

Fishbein, M. and Ajzen, I. (1975) *Belief, Attitude, Intention and Behaviour*, Reading, MA: Addison-Wesley.

Foweather, R. and Stillwell, S. (1994) *SCIP News*, 37, Warwick: University of Warwick.

Frazier Moore, H. and Kalupa, F.B. (1985), *Public Relations: Principles, Cases and Problems*, 9th edn, Homewood, Boston: Richard D. Irwin.

Frederick, W., Post, J. and Davis. K. (1992) *Business and Society*, 7th edn, New York: McGraw-Hill.

Freeman, R.E. (1984) *Strategic Management: A Stakeholder Approach*, Pitman, Chicago.

Friedman, M. (1962) *Capitalism and Freedom*, Chicago: University of Chicago Press.

Friend, C. (1986a) 'Public relations and marketing – the synergy and the separation', London: Institute of Public Relations.

Friend, C. (1986b) 'Public relations and marketing – not just puffering and nonsense', London: Institute of Marketing.

Friend, C. (1993) 'Public relations and marketing – the synergy and the separation'. A position paper developed for the IPR, Managing Director, Pielle Public Relations, (unpublished 2pp report).

Friend, C. (1994) Letter to Dr Philip J. Kitchen, Department of Management, Keele University, expressing her opinions concerning the place of public relations in the marketing mix, 7 November.

Futrell, J. (1993) 'Leader of the Pack', *The Times*, 16 October.

Gage, T.J. (1981) 'PR ripens role in marketing', *Advertising Age*, 52, January.

Gandy, O. (1982) *Beyond Agenda Setting: Information Subsidies and Public Policy*, Norwood: Ablex.

Gandy, O. (1992) 'Public relations and public policy: the structuration of dominance in information age', in E. Togh and R. Heath, *Rhetorical and Critical Approaches to Public Relations*, Hove: Lawrence Erlbaum.

Garbett, E. (1981) *Corporate Advertising the What, Why and How*, Maidenhead, Berks: McGraw-Hill.

Garbett, T.F. (1988) *How to Build a Corporation's Identity and Project its Image*, Lexington, MA., D.C. Heath & Co.

Gart, A. (1994) *Regulation, Deregulation and Reregulation – The Future of the Banking, Insurance and Securities Industries*, New York: John Wiley.

Gatewood, E. and Carroll, A.B. (1981) 'The anatomy of corporate social response: the Rely, Firestone 500, and Pinto cases', *Business Horizons*, 24 (5), September/October.

Giacalone, R.A. and Rosenfeld, P. (eds) (1991) *Applied Impression Management: How Image-Making Affects Managerial Decisions*, Sage.

Godwin, R. (1988) *One Billion Dollars of Influence*, Chatham, NJ: Chatham House.

Goldberg, H. (1983) *Sponsorship and the Performing Arts*, London: Goldberg.

Goldman, J. (1984) *Public Relations in the Marketing Mix*, Henley-on-Thames: NTC Business Books.

Goldman, T. (1988) 'Big spenders develop newspaper communications', *Marketing Communications*, 13 (1).

Good, T. (1980) 'The death of the old ivory tower image', *Campaign*, 22 August.

Gossen, R. and Sharp, K. (1987) 'Managing dispute resolution', *Public Relations Journal*, 43 (12).

Gouldner, A.W. (1954) *Patterns of Industrial Bureaucracy*, New York: Free Press.

Grant, W. (1995) *Pressure Groups. Politics and Democracy in Britain*, Hemel Hempstead: Harvester Wheatsheaf.

Grantham, C. and Seymour-Ure, C. (1990) 'Political consultants', in *Parliament and Pressure Politics*, Oxford: Clarendon Press.

Gregory, J.R. (1991) *Marketing Corporate Image: The Company as Your Number One Product*, Lincolnwood, IL: NTC Business Books.

Greyser. S. (1981) *Public Relations Journal*, 37 (1).

Grunig, J.E. (1976) 'Organisations and public relations: testing a communications theory', *Journalism Monographs*, No. 46.

Grunig, J.E. (1979) 'Time budgets, level of involvement and use of mass media', *Journalism Quarterly*, 55 (1).

Grunig, J.E. (1982) 'Developing economic education programmes for the Press', *Public Relations Review*, 8 (3).

Grunig, J.E. (1983) 'Communication Behaviours and Attitudes of Environmental Publics: Two Cases', *Journalism Monographs*, No. 81.

Grunig, J.E. (1983) 'Washington reporter publics of corporate public affairs programmes, *Journalism Quarterly*, 39 (4).

Grunig, J.E. and Ipes, D.A. (1983) 'The anatomy of a campaign against drunken driving', *Public Relations Review*, 9 (2).

Grunig, J.E. (1984), 'Organisations and public relations: testing a communications theory', *Public Relations Research and Education*, 1 (1).

Grunig, J.E. and Hunt T. (1984) *Managing Public Relations*, London: Holt, Rinehart and Winston.

Grunig, J.E. and Grunig, L.S. (1986), 'Applications of open systems theory to public relations; Review of a program of research'. Paper presented to the meeting of International Communication Association, Chicago.

Grunig, J. (1989) 'Symmetrical presuppositions as a framework for public relations', in C. Botan and V. Hazelton, Jr (eds) *Public Relations Theory*, Hove: Lawrence Erlbaum.

Grunig, J.E. (ed.) (1992) *Excellence in Public Relations and Communications Management*, Hillsdale, NJ: Lawrence Erlbaum.

Grunig, J.E. and Grunig, L.A. (1992) 'Models of public relations and communications', in J.E. Grunig (ed.) *Excellence in Public Relations and Communications Management*, Hillsdale, NJ: Lawrence Erlbaum.

Grunig, J.E., Grunig, L.A. and Ehling, W.P. (1992) 'What is an effective organisation?', in J.E. Grunig (ed.) *Excellence in Public Relations and Communications Management*, Hillsdale, NJ: Lawrence Erlbaum.

Grunig, J.E. and Repper, F.C. (1992) 'Strategic management, publics and issues', in J.E. Grunig (ed.) *Excellence in Public Relations and Communications Management*, Hillsdale, NJ: Lawrence Erlbaum.

Gumm, J. (1978) 'Public relations is a primary element in Beech-Nut food's marketing program', *Advertising Age*, 6 February.

Hainsworth, B.E. (1990) 'The process of issue development: the distribution of advantages and disadvantages', Working Paper, Brigham Young University.

Hambrick, D.C. (1983) 'Some tests of the effectiveness and functional attributes of Miles and Snow's strategic types', *Academy of Management Journal*, 26.

Harlow, R.F. (1976) 'Building a public relations definition', *Public Relations Review*, 2 (4).

Harris, T. (1991) *The Marketers Guide to Public Relations: How Today's Companies are Using the New PR to Gain a Competitive Edge*, New York: John Wiley.

Harris, T. (1993) *The Marketer's Guide to Public Relations: How Today's Companies are Using the New Public Relations to gain a Competitive Edge*, New York: John Wiley.

Harrison, S. (1995) *Public Relations: An Introduction*, London: Routledge.

Hart, N. (1995) *Strategic Public Relations*, London: Macmillan.

Hart, W. (1991) 'PRTV', *Marketing Business*, October: 7.

Hayes, R.H. and Abernathy, W.J. (1980) 'Managing our way to economic decline', *Harvard Business Review*, 58 (1), July–August, 67–77.

Haywood, R. (1994) *Managing Your Reputation: How to Plan and Run Communications Programmes that Win Friends and Build Business*, London: McGraw-Hill.

Hax, A.C. and Majluf, N.S. (1988) 'The concept of strategy and the strategy formulation process', *Interfaces*, May–June.

Hax, A.C. and Majluf, N.S. (1991) *The Strategy Concept and Process: A Pragmatic Approach*, Englewood Cliffs, NJ: Prentice-Hall.

Heath, R.L. and Nelson, R.A. (1986) *Issues Management: Corporate Policymaking in an Information Society*, Beverley Hills: Sage.

Heath, R.L. (1994) *Management of Corporate Communication: From Interpersonal Contacts to External Affairs*, Hillsdale, NJ: Lawrence Erlbaum.

Hiebert, R.E. and Devine, C.M. (1985) 'Government's research and evaluation gap', *Public Relations Review*, 11, Fall.

Heilbroner, R. Chapter 1 in Cutlip, S.M., Center, A.H. and Broom, G.M. (1985) *Effective Public Relations*, 6th edn, Englewood Cliffs, NJ: Prentice-Hall.

Heinz, J., Laumann, E., Nelson, R. and Salisbury, R. (1993) *The Hollow Core*, Cambridge, MA: Harvard University Press.

Hesse, M.B. (1981) 'Strategies of the political communication process', *Public Relations Review*, 7 (1).

Hofer, C.W. (1973) 'Some preliminary research on patterns of strategic behaviour', *Academy of Management Proceedings*.

Hofstede, G. (1990) *Cultures and Organisations: Software of the Mind*, London: McGraw-Hill.

Hofstetter, C.R., Zirkin, C. and Bass, T.F. (1978) 'Political information and imagery in an age of television', *Journalism Quarterly*, 55 (3).

Hollis (1988) *Press and Public Relations Manual*, London: Hollis Directories.

Horsfall, J. (1990) 'Corporate advertising: a city view', *Admap*, 26 (6).

Hovland, C.I., Janis, I.L. and Kelley, H.H. (1953) *Communication and Persuasion*, New Haven, CT: Yale University Press.

House of Commons (1987–88) *Select Committee on Members' Interests. Parliamentary Lobbying*, HC 518.

Howard, H., Hellweg, H. and Flacione, R. (1988) 'Organizational Communication: An Overview 1950–81', in G. Goldhaber and G. Barnell *A Handbook of Organisational Communication*, New York: Ablex.

Hutchins, H. (1994) 'Annual reports: earning surprising respect from institutional investors', *Public Relations Review*, 20 (4).

'Identity Crisis', *PR Week*, 26 April 1996: 5, used with permission. (Readers are strongly encouraged to read the entire article.)

Interbrand (1990) *Brands*, London: Mercury Business.

IPR (Institute of Public Relations) (1991) 'Public Relations as a Career', pamphlet, London.

Jack, A. (1995) 'A question of trust', *Financial Times*, 29/12/95.

Jeffres, L. (1975), 'Functions of media behaviours', *Communication Research*, 2.

Jefkins, F. (1980, 1983, 1988, 1992) *Public Relations*, London: M&E Handbooks.

Jefkins, F. (1987) *Public Relations For Your Business*, London: Mercury, 43.

Jefkins, F. (1991) *Modern Marketing Communications*, London: Blackie.

Jefkins, F. (1994) *Public Relations Techniques*, 2nd edn, London: Butterworth-Heinemann.

Jemison, D.B. (1981) 'The importance of boundary spanning roles in strategic decision making', *Journal of Management Studies*, 21.

Johnson, G. and Scholes, K. (1993) *Exploring Corporate Strategy* (3rd edn), London: Prentice-Hall International.

Jones, B.L. and Chase, H.W. (1979) 'Managing public policy issues', *Public Relations Review*, 5 (4).

Jones, B. (ed.) (1991) *Politics UK*, Hemel Hempstead: Philip Allan.

Jones, J.F. (1975) 'Audit: a new tool for public relations', *Public Relations Journal*, 31 (7).

Jordan, A.G. and Richardson, J.J. (1982) 'The British policy style or the logic of negotiation?' in J.J. Richardson (ed.) *Policy Styles in Western Europe*, London: George Allen and Unwin.

Jordan A.G. and Richardson, J.J. (1987) *Government and Pressure Groups in Britain*, Oxford: Clarendon.

Jordan, A.G. (ed.) (1991) *The Commercial Lobbyists Politics for Profit in Britain*, Aberdeen: Aberdeen University Press.

Jordan, A.G. and Moloney, K. (1993) 'Why are lobbyists successsful: God, background or training?' For a symposia at London School of Economics held 24 March, organised by Politics Department, Newcastle University and Hansard Society. Paper available from authors.

Judd, L.R. (1990) 'Importance and use of formal research and evaluation', *Public Relations Review*, XVI (4), Winter.

Kay, J. (1993) *Foundations of Corporate Success*, Oxford: Oxford University Press.

Kerin, R.A., Mahajan, V. and Varadarajan, P.R. (1990) *Contemporary Perspectives on Strategic Market Planning*, Needham Heights, MA: Ally and Bacon.

Kerlinger, F.N. (1986) *Foundations of Behavioural Research*, 3rd edn, New York: Holt, Rinehart and Winston.

King, S. (1978) 'Public response: the key to corporate advertising', *Advertising*, Winter; reprinted in *Corporate Advertising: A Selection of Articles and a Bibliography of Recent Developments*, London: Institute of Practitioners in Advertising.

Kitchen, P.J. (1990) 'Let's hear it for brand X', *The Times Higher Education Supplement*, 16 February.

Kitchen, P.J. (1991) 'Developing use of PR in a fragmented demassified market', *Market Intelligence and Planning*, 9 (2).

Kitchen, P.J. and Proctor, R.A. (1991) 'The increasing importance of public relations in FMCG firms', *Journal of Marketing Management*, 7.

Kitchen, P.J. (1993) 'Public relations: a rationale for its development and usage within UK FMCG firms', *European Journal of Marketing*, 27 (7).

Kitchen, P.J. (1993a) 'Towards the integration of marketing and public relations', *Marketing Intelligence and Planning*, 11 (11).

Kitchen, P.J. (1993b) 'PR: A rationale for its its development and usage within UK fast-moving consumer goods firms', *European Journal of Marketing*, 27, 7 November.

Kitchen, P.J. and Moss, D. (1995) 'Marketing and public relations: the relationship revisited', *Journal of Marketing Communications*, 1 (2).

Kleiner, A. (1989) 'The public relations coup', *ADWEEK's Marketing Week*, 16 January.

Kornhauser, A. and Sheatley, P.B. (1976) 'Questionnaire construction and interview procedure' in J.L. Sellitz et al. (eds) *Basic Methods in Social Science: The Art of Empirical Investigation*, New York: Random House.

Kotler, P. (1976) *Marketing Management*, 3rd edn, Englewood Cliffs, NJ: Prentice-Hall.

Kotler, P. and Mindak, W. (1978) 'Marketing and public relations', *Journal of Marketing*, 42 (4).

Kotler, P. (1982) *Marketing for Non-profit Organisations*, 2nd edn, Englewood Cliffs, NJ: Prentice-Hall.

Kotler, P. (1986) 'Megamarketing', *Harvard Business Review*, 64 (2), March/April.

Kotler, P. (1988) *Marketing Management*, 4th edn, Englewood Cliffs, NJ: Prentice-Hall.

Kotler, P. (1989) 'Public relations versus marketing: dividing the conceptual domain and operational turf', a position paper prepared for the Public Relations Colloquium, San Diego, 24 January.

Kotler, P. (1991) *Marketing Management*, 9th edn, Englewood Cliffs, NJ: Prentice-Hall.

Kreitzman, L. (1986) 'Projecting an image', *Marketing*, 25 September.

Kreitzman, L. (1986) 'Balancing brand building blocks', *Marketing*, 13 November.

Kuhn, T.S. (1964) *The Structure of Scientific Revolutions*, Pheonix: University of Chicago Press.

Lancaster, G. and Massingham, L. (1988) *Marketing Primer*, London: Heinemann.

Lang, G.E. and Lang, K. (193) *The Battle for Public Opinion*, New York: Columbia University Press.

Lasswell, H.D. (1972) 'The structure of communication in society', in W. Schramm and D.F. Roberts (eds) *The Process and Effects of Mass Communication*, Urbana, IL: University of Illinois Press.

Lawrence, P.R. and Lorsch, J.W. (1967) *Organisation and Environment*, Boston, Mass.: Graduate School of Business Administration, Harvard University.

Lazer, W. (1962) 'The roles of models in marketing', *Journal of Marketing*, 26 (2), April.

Leifer, R.P. and Delbecq, A. (1978) 'Organisational/environmental interchange: a model of boundary spanning activity', *Academy of Management Review*, 3.

Leiss, W., Kline, S. and Jhaly, S. (1990) *Social Communication in Advertising*, 2nd edn, London: Routledge.

Lenz, R.T. and Engledow, J.L. (1986) 'Environmental analysis: the applicability of current theory', *Strategic Management Journal*, 7.

Lesly, P. (ed.) (1991) *The Handbook of Public Relations and Communications*, London: McGraw-Hill.

Lesly, P. (ed.) (1950) *Public Relations Handbook*, New York: Prentice-Hall.

Lesly, P. (ed.) (1983) *Lesly's Public Relations Handbook*, Englewood Cliffs, NJ: Prentice-Hall.

Levy, L. (1990) 'Brand aid for Britain', *Management Today*, September.

Lightcap, K. (1984) 'Marketing support', in Bill Cantor, *Experts in Action: Inside Public Relations*, New York: Longman.

Lindblom, C.E. (1959) 'The science of muddling through', *Public Administration Review*, 19.

Lindblom, C.E. (1977) *Politics and Markets*, New York: Basic Books.

Lindenmann, W.K. (1990) 'Research, evaluation and measurement: a national perspective', *Public Relations Review*, XVI (2), Summer.

Lindenmann, W.K. (1993) 'An "effectiveness yardstick" to measure public relations success', *Public Relations Quarterly*, Spring.

Linstead, S. and Turner, K. (1986) 'Business sponsorship of the arts: corporate image and business policy', *Management Research News*, 9 (3).

Lippmann, W. (1921) *Public Opinion*, New York: Macmillan.

Long, J.C. (1924) *Public Relations: A Handbook of Publicity*, New York: McGraw-Hill.

Love, J.F. (1986) *McDonald's: Behind the Arches*, New York: Bantam Books.

Lovelock, C.H. and Weinberg, C.B. (1984) *Marketing for Public and Non-Profit Managers*, New York: John Wiley.

Maccoby, N., Farquhar, J.W., Wood, P.D. and Alexander, J. (1977) 'Reducing the effect of cardiovascular disease: effects of a community based campaign on knowledge and behaviour', *Journal of Community Health*, 3.

Macfarlane Smith, J. (1972) *Interviewing in Marketing and Social Research*, London: Routledge and Kegan Paul.

Maitland, A. (1984) 'Corporate advertising', in N. Hart (ed.) *Effective Public Relations*, Maidenhead: McGraw-Hill.

Marcus, A.A. and Kaufman, A.M. (1988) 'The continued expansion of the corporate public affairs function', *Business Horizons*, 31 (2), March/April.

Marketing Pocketbook 1994, Top 100 advertisers derived from Register Meal Data.

Marston, J. (1979) *Modern Public Relations*, McGraw-Hill.

Mayer, M. (1961) *Madison Avenue, USA*, Harmondsworth: Penguin.

McCauley, H.S. (1922) *Getting Your Name in Print*, New York: Funk and Wagnalls.

McDaniel, C. (1979) *Marketing; An Integrated Approach*, New York: Harper and Row.

McDaniel, C. and Gates M. (1991) *Contemporary Marketing Research*, New York: West Publishing Company.

MacDonald, A. (1991) 'Financial public relations in a global context', in M. Nally (ed.) *International Public Relations in Practise*, London: Kogan Page.

McDonald, M.H.B. (1992) 'Strategic marketing planning: a state of the art review', *Marketing Intelligence and Planning*, 10 (4).

McGuire, W.J. (1981) 'Theoretical foundations of campaigns', in R.E. Rice and W.J. Paisley (eds) *Public Communications Campaigns*, Newbury Park, CA: Sage.

McKeone, D. (1993) 'Paying a price for false comparisons', *PR Week* 24 July.

MacNamara, J. (1992a) 'Evaluation of public relations: the Achilles' heel of the PR profession, *International Public Relations Review*, 15 (2).

MacNamara, J. (1924) 'Macro communication: a model for integrated, strategic marketing and corporate communication', a paper presented to Marcom Asia '92, Singapore, 22 May.

Meikle, J. (1995) 'Take a gamble for charity', *The Guardian*, 8 November.

Mendelsohn, H. (1973) 'Some reasons why information campaigns succeed', *Public Opinion Quarterly*, 37 (1).

315

Merims, A.M. (1972) 'Marketing's stepchild: product publicity', *Harvard Business Review*, 36 (5), November/December.

Merton, R.K. (1940) 'Bureaucratic structure and personality', *Social Forces*, 18.

Merton, R.K. (1957) *Social Theory and Social Structure*, rev. edn. Chicago: Free Press.

Miller, C. (1987) *Lobbying Government*, Oxford: Blackwell.

Mills, C.W. (1959) *The Sociological Imagination*, New York: Oxford University Press.

Mintzberg, H. (1979) *The Structuring of Organisations*, Englewood Cliffs, NJ: Prentice-Hall.

Mintzberg, H. (1987) 'Crafting strategy', *Harvard Business Review*, July/August.

Mintzberg, H. (1991) 'Five P's for strategy', in H. Mintzberg and J.B. Quinn *The Strategy Process: Concepts, Contexts, Cases*, 2nd edn, Englewood Cliffs, NJ: Prentice-Hall.

Mintzberg, H. (1989) 'Strategy formation: schools of thought', in J. Frederickson (ed.) *Perspectives on Strategic Management*, San Francisco: Ballinger.

Mintzberg, H. (1994) 'The fall and rise of strategic planning', *Harvard Business Reviews*, January/February.

Mitchell, A. 'In good company', *Marketing*, 3 March.

Moloney, K. (1996) *Lobbyists for Hire*, Aldershot: Dartmouth.

Montgomery, C.A. and Porter, M.E. (1991) *Strategy – Seeking and Securing Competitive Advantage*, Boston: Harvard Business School Press.

Morgan, G. (1986) *Images of Organization*, Newbury Park, London: Sage.

Morgan, G. (1992) *Imaginization*, Newbury Park, London: Sage.

Moss D. (ed.) *Public Relations in Practice*, London: Routledge.

Mullins, L.J. (1994) *Management and Organisational Behaviour*, London, Pitman.

Nally, M. (ed.) (1991) *International Public Relations in Practise*, London: Kogan Page.

Newman, K. (1983) 'Financial communications and the contested takeover bid, 1958–1982', *International Journal of Advertising*, 2 (1).

Newman, W. (1995) 'Community relations', in N. Hart (ed.) *Strategic Public Relations*, Basingstoke: Macmillan.

Newsom, D., Scott, A. and Vanslyke, T.J. (1993) *This is PR: The Realities of Public Relations*, 5th edn, New York: Wadsworth Publishing Company.

Noble, P. (1994) 'A proper role for media evaluation', paper presented to the International Public Relations Research Symposium, Bled, Slovanis, July.

Nolan Committee (1995) First Report of the Committee on Standards in Public Life HMSO, Cm2850-1, Vol. 1: Report.

Norton, P. and Grantham, C. (1986) 'The hyphen in British politics? Parliament and professional lobbying', in *British Politics Group Newsletter*, No. 45.

Novelli, W.D. (1988) 'Stir some PR into your communications mix', *Marketing News*, 22 December: 19.

Nutt, P.C. (1984) 'Types of organisational decision processes', *Administrative Science Quarterly*, 29 (4).

O'Hare, F.J. (1954) 'A reference guide to the study of public opinion', unpublished doctoral thesis, Columbia University.

Olasky, M. (1987) *Corporate Public Relations: A New Historical Perspective*, Hove: Lawrence Erlbaum.

OLR (1993) *Business and Community: A New Partnership for Mutual Benefit*, London: Opinion Leader Research.

O'Shaughnessy, J. (1988) *Competitive Marketing: A Strategic Approach*, Boston, MA: Unwin Hyman.

Ostrom, T.M. (1969) 'The relationship between the affective, behavioural and cognitive components of attitude', *Journal of Experimental Social Psychology*, 5.

Ouchi, W. (1981) *Theory Z: How American Business Can Meet the Japanese Challenge*, Reading, MA: Addison-Wesley.

Oxley, H. (1989) *The Principles of Public Relations*, London: Kogan Page.

PR Week (1994) UK Top 150 PR Consultancies 'Mixed fortunes for the top ten', Haymarket, 28 April.

PR Week (1995) 'What the papers say; can anyone be sure of Shell any more?', *PR Week*, 24 November.

PR Week (1996) 'Desperate bid to build confidence for Wickes', Haymarket Publications, 6: 5 July, used with permission. (Students are strongly encouraged to read *PR Week* as part of their public relations course).

PR Week (1996) 'We come not to bury Chernobyl, but to explain it', by Roger Hayes, Director-General, British Nuclear Industry Forum, Haymarket Publications, 17 May, used with permission.

PR Week, 21 June 1996, used with permission.

Panigyrakis, G.G. (1994) 'The public relations managers' role in four European countries', Proceedings of the 23rd European Marketing Academy Conference, Maastricht, The Netherlands.

Parasuraman, A. (1991), *Marketing Research*, 2nd edn, Reading, Mass.: Addison Wesley.

Park, R.E. (1923) 'The natural history of the newspaper', *American Journal of Sociology*, 29.

Pavlik, J.V. (1987) *Public Relations: What Research Tells Us*, Newbury Park, CA: Sage.

Parkinson, C.N. and Rowe, N. (1977) *Communicate: Parkinson's Formula for Business Survival*, Prentice-Hall.

Peach, L. (1987) 'Corporate responsibility', in N. Hart (ed.) *Effective Corporate Relations*, Maidenhead: McGraw-Hill.

Pearson, R. (1992) 'Perspectives on public relations history', in E. Toth and R. Heath (eds) *Rhetorical and Critical Approaches to Public Relations*, Hove: Lawrence Erlbaum.

Peters, T. and Waterman, R. (1992) *In Search of Excellence: Lessons from America's Best-run Companies*, New York: Harper Collins; first published in 1982.

Pettigrew, A.M. (1992) 'The character and significance of strategy process research', *Strategic Management Journal*, 13.

Philadelphia Inquirer (1984) 'McDonald's deserves praise', editorial, July.

Popper, K.R. (1957) 'The unit of method', in *The Poverty of Historicism*, London: Routledge and Kegan Paul.

Porter, M.E. (1980) *Competitive Strategy: Techniques for Analysing Industries and Competitors*, New York: The Free Press.

Porter, M.E. (1985) *Competitive Advantage: Creating and Sustaining Superior Performance*, New York: The Free Press.

Portway, S. (1995) 'Corporate social responsibility: the case for active stakeholder management', in N. Hart (ed.) *Strategic Public Relations*, Basingstoke: Macmillan.

Post, J.E., Murray, E.A., Dickie, R.B. and Mahon, J.F. (1982) 'The public affairs function in American corporations: development and relations with corporate planning', *Long Range Planning*, 15 (2).

Price, B. (1992) 'Corporate advertising makes BP's mission possible', *Media International*, June 1992.

Priestley, J.B. (1984) *The Image Men*, London: Allison.

Public Policy Consultants (1987) *The Government Report*, London: PPC.

Public Relations Reporter (1989) 'Colloquium of marketing and PR spokespersons agrees organisations suffer when turf wars occur', 13 February.

Pugh, D.S. and Hickson, D.J. (1976) *Organizational Structure in its Context*, The Aston Programme, Vol. 1, Farnborough: Saxon.

Pugh, D.S. and Hinings, C.R. (1976) *Organization structure: Extensions and Replication*, The Aston Programme, Vol. 2, Farnborough: Saxon.

Pugh, D.S., Hickson, D.J. and Hinings, C.R. (1969a) 'The context of organization structures', *Administrative Science Quarterly*, 14.

Pugh, D.S., Hickson, D.J. and Hinings, C.R. (1969b) 'An empirical taxonomy of structures of work organisations', *Administrative Science Quarterly*, 28.

Purvis, S. (1995) 'From an address at the CAM/TAS lecture at Trinity and All Saint's College, Horsforth, West Yorkshire.

Quinn, J.B. (1980) *Strategies for Change: Logical Incrementalism*, Burr Ridge, Ill., Richard D. Irwin.

Raucher, A. (1990) 'Public Relations in Business: A Business of Public Relations', *Public Relations Review*, 16 (1).

Ray, M.L. (1973) 'Marketing communication and the hierarchy of effects', in P. Clarke (ed.) *New Models for Mass Communication Research*, Newbury Park, CA: Sage.

Reagan, J. and Ducey, R.V. (1983) 'Effect of news measures' on selection of state government', *Journalism Quarterly*, 60 (12).

Reed, D. (1992) 'How the green sell has failed', Campaign, 4 (9).

Revell, J. (ed.) (1994) *The Changing Face of European Banks and Securities Markets*, Basingstoke: Macmillan.

Rice, M. (1980) 'Press agents that became part of a management team', *Campaign*, August.

Richardson, J. (ed.) (1993) *Pressure Groups*, Oxford: Oxford University Press.

Robinson, C. (1931) 'The new science of public opinion management', *Harvard Business School Alumni Association Bulletin*, July.

Rowell, A. (1995) 'Trouble flares in the delta of death', *The Guardian*, 8 November.

Rush, M. (1990) *Parliament and Pressure Politics*, Oxford: Clarendon Press.

Rybczynski, T. (1994) 'The development of European capital markets: the main trends and their implications', in J. Revell (ed.) *The Changing Face of European Banks and Securities Markets*, Basingstoke: Macmillan.

Schultz, D.E., Tannenbaum, S.I. and Lautternorn, R.F. (1992, *Integrated Marketing Communications*, Chicago: NTC Business Books.

Schumann, D.W., Hathcote, J.M. and West, S. (1991) 'Corporate advertising in America', a review of published studies on use, measurement and effectiveness', *Journal of Advertising*, 20 (3).

Schwartz, G. (1982) 'Public relations get short shift from new managers', *Marketing News*, 16 (4).

Schwartz, P. (1991) *The Art of the Long View*, London: Century.

Seitel, F. (1992) *The Practice of Public Relations*, (5th edn), Columbus, OH: Macmillan.

Seitel, F.P. (1995) *The Practice of Public Relations*, 6th edn, Englewood Cliffs, NJ: Prentice-Hall.

Sellitz, J.L., Wrightsman, S. and Cook, S.W. (1976) *Basic Methods in Social Science: The Art of Empirical Investigation*, New York: Random House.

Selznik, P. (1949) *TVA and the Grass Roots*, Berkley: University of California Press.

Sethi, P. (1979) *Promises of a Good Life: Social Consequences of Private Marketing Decisions*, Homewood, IL: Irwin.

Shandwick PLC (1989) *The Public Relations Consultancy Market Worldwide*, London: Shandwick PLC

Shannon, C. (1983) Corporate advertising: A Selection of articles and a Bibliography of Recent developments, London: Institute of Practitioners in Advertising.

Sheth, J.N., Gardner, D.M. and Garrett, D.E. (1988) *Marketing Theory: Evolution and Evaluation*, New York: John Wiley.

Shimp, T.A. and Delozier, M.W. (1986) *Promotion Management and Marketing Communications*, New York: Dryden Press.

Shimp, T.A. (1993) *Promotion Management and Marketing Communications*, Philadelphia: Harcourt Brace.

Simon, R. (1980) *Public Relations – Concept and Practices*, London: Grid.

Smircich, L. (1983) 'Concepts of culture and organisational analysis', *Administrative Science Quarterly*.

Smith, H. (1915) *Publicity and Progress*, New York: George H. Doran.

Smith, I.J. (1993) *Pressure, Power and Policy*, Hemel Hempstead: Harvester Wheatsheaf.

Smith, M. (1992) *Lobbying*, London: Government Policy Consultants.

Smith, N.C. (1990) *Morality and the Market: Consumer Pressure for Corporate Accountability*, London: Routledge.

Smythe, D. (1981) *Dependency Road: Communications, Capitalism, Consciousness and Canada*, Norwood: Ablex.

Smythe, J., Dorward, C. and Lambert, A. (1992) *Corporate Reputation: Managing the New Strategic Asset*, London: Random Century.

Speed, R. (1989) 'Oh Mr Porter! A reappraisal of competitive strategy', *Marketing Intelligence and Planning*, 7(2).

Spicer, C.H. (1991) 'Communications functions performed by public relations and marketing practitioners', *Public Relations Review*.

Spiro, R.L. and Perreault, W.D. Jr (1976) 'Influence used by industrial salesmen: Influence strategy mixes and situational determinants', unpublished paper, Graduate School of Business Administration, University of North Carolina.

Stanley, R.E. (1982) *Promotion: Advertising, Publicity, Personal Selling, Sales Promotion*, 2nd edn, Englewood Cliffs, NJ: Prentice-Hall.

Starbuck, W.H. (1976) 'Organisations in their environments', in M.D. Dunnette (ed.) *Handbook of Organisational Psychology*, Chicago: Rand McNally.

Steiner, G.A. and Miner, J.B. (1977) *Management Policy and Strategy*, New York: Macmillan.

Tedeschi, J.T. and Rosenfeld, P. (1982) 'Impression management and the forced compliance situation' in J.T. Tedeschi. *Impression Management Theory and Social Psychological Research*, New York: Academic Press.

Tench, R. and Yeomans, L. (1995) 'Corporate Advertising a UK Perspective', unpublished MS.

Toth, E.L. and Heath, R.L. (1992) *Rhetorical and Critical Approaches*, Hillsdale, NJ: Lawrence Erlbaum.

Truman, D. (1951) *The Governmental Process*, New York: Alfred A. Knopf.

Tull, D.A. and Hawkins, D.I. (1990) *Marketing Research: Measurement and Method*, 5th edn, New York: Macmillan.

Turner, B. (ed.) (1990) *Organisational Symbolism*, Berlin: de Gruyter.

Valleaven, J.K. et al. (1988) 'Effects-based planning for public relations campaigns', paper presented to PR Division, Association for Education in Journalism and Mass Communications, Portland, Oregon, July.

Van Riel, C.B.M. (1995) *Principles of Corporate Communication*, Hemel Hempstead, Prentice-Hall.

Walker, A. (1988) 'The public relations literature: a narrative of what's been published by and about the profession, 1922–1988', *Public Relations Quarterly*, Summer.

Walker, A. (1978) 'Public relations bibliography: sixth edition, 1976–1977', *Public Relations Review*, Winter: 1.

Walker, R.L. (1974 and 1976) *Public Relations: A Comprehensive Bibliography*, Ann Arbor: The University of Michigan Press.

Wallace, W. (ed.) (1971) 'An overview of elements in the scientific process', in *The Logic of Science in Sociology*, Chicago: Aldine Atherton.

Watson, T. (1993) 'Output measures rule in evaluation debate', *IPR Journal*.

Watson, T. (1994) 'Public relations evaluation: nationwide survey of practice in the United Kingdom', paper presented to the International Public Relations Research symposium, Bled, Slovania, July.

Watson, T. (1995) 'Evaluating public relation: models of measurement for public relations practice', paper presented to the International Public Relations Research symposium, Bled, Slovania, July.

Wedgewood, D. (1987) 'Dialogue with Whitehall and Westminster', for Conference on

Corporate Communications, London International Press Centre, 15 October, organised by Tolloy Conferences.

Weick, K.E. (1969) *The Social Psychology of Organising*, Reading, Mass.: Addison-Wesley.

Weick, K.E. (1979) 'Cognitive processes in organisations', *Research in Organisational Behavior*, 1.

Weick, K.E. (1987) 'Substitutes for corporate strategy', in D.J. Teece (ed.) *The Competitive Challenge; Strategies for Industrial Innovation and Renewal*, Cambridge, MA: Ballinger.

Weiss, C.H. (1977) *Evaluation Research – Methods of Assessing Program Effectiveness*, Englewood Cliffs, NJ: Prentice-Hall.

Werner, L.R. (1991) 'Marketing strategies for the recession', *Management*, 6 August.

White, J. (1990) 'Evaluation in public relations practice', unpublished paper, Cranfield Institute of Management/PRCA.

White, J. (1991) *How to Understand and Manage Public Relations*, London: Business Books.

White, J. and Dozier, D.M. (1992) 'Public relations and management decision-making', in J.E. Grunig (ed.) *Excellence in Public Relations and Communications Management*, Hillsdale, NJ: Lawrence Erlbaum.

White, J. and Bramphin, J. (1994) *Priorities for Research into Public Relations Practice in the United Kingdom*, London: City University Business School/Rapier Marketing.

White, J. and Lazur, L. (1995) *Strategic Communications Management*, Wokingham: Addison-Wesley.

White, R. (1988) *Advertising: What is it and How to do it*, London: McGraw-Hill.

Whittington, R. (1993) *What is Strategy – and Does it Matter?*, London: Routledge.

Wilcox, D.L., Ault, P.H. and Agee, W.E. (1986) *Public Relations: Strategies and Tactics*, New York: Harper and Row.

Wilcox, D.L., Ault, P.H. and Agee, W.K. (1992) *Public Relations: Strategies and Tactics*, 3rd edn, New York: Harper-Collins.

Wilson, C.E. and Howard, D.M. (1978) 'Public perception of media accuracy', *Journalism Quarterly*, 55 (1).

Wilson, D. and Rosenfeld, R. (1990) *Managing Organisations*, Maidenhead: McGraw-Hill.

Wiseman, J.P. (1974) 'The research web', *Urban Life and Culture*, 3 (3).

Wolfe, A. (1978) 'How to adapt research techniques to design and assess corporate image advertising' (ESOMAR seminar, Barcelona); reprinted in *Corporate Advertising: A Selection of Articles and a Bibliography of Recent Developments*, London: Institute of Practitioners in Advertising.

Wolfe, A. (1983) Preface to *Corporate Advertising: A Selection of Articles and a Bibliography of Recent Developments*, London: Institute of Practitioners in Advertising.

Wood, D. (1982) 'Types of media', in W. Howard (ed.) *The Practice of Public Relations*, Oxford: Heinemann Professional Publishing.

Worcester, R. (1986) 'Why corporate advertising is the key to public goodwill', *Campaign*, 16 May.

Wright, J.H. and Christian, B.H. (1949) *Public Relations in Management*, New York: McGraw-Hill.

Yankelovich, P. and Partners (1979) Corporate advertising phase II an expanded study of corporate advertising effectiveness conducted for Time magazine, Time Inc.

Yankelovich, P. (1993) 'Leveraging corporate equity: a pilot investigation', *Fortune* magazine.

Zikmund, W.T. and D'Amico, B. (1988) *Marketing*, 2nd edn, New York: John Wiley.

INDEX